HISTORY OF CHINESE LITERATURE

B.R. Deepak

Translated from Chinese by

Wang Hanbing

PENTAGON PRESS LLP

First published in 2025 by
PENTAGON PRESS LLP
206, Peacock Lane, Shahpur Jat
New Delhi-110049, India
Contact: 011-26490600

Typeset in Times New Roman, 10.5 Point
Printed at Aegean Offset Printers, Greater Noida

ISBN 978-81-993527-5-9

www.pentagonpress.in

Contents

Introduction

Chinese literature boasts one of the longest and richest continuous traditions in the world, spanning thousands of years. Its development mirrors the evolution of Chinese civilisation, reflecting the country's philosophical, cultural, political, and social changes. From its primitive oral roots to the flourishing literary traditions of the Ming and Qing dynasties, Chinese literature encompasses a diverse array of genres and styles, making it a cornerstone of global literary heritage.

The origins of Chinese literature can be traced to primitive times, when oral traditions served as the primary means of storytelling and knowledge transmission. Myths, legends, and folk songs formed the earliest expressions of literary creativity. Tales like *Pangu and the Creation of the World* and *Nvwa Mending the Sky* not only explain the universe's origins but also reflect the values and worldviews of early Chinese society. These oral traditions laid the foundation for written literature, which began to emerge with the advent of Chinese characters. Following the general trend of the classification of Chinese history, the book has largely arranged the history of Chinese literature into the following periods:

- Primitive and Pre Qin Literature (From remote antiquity to – 221 BCE)
- Qin-Han Literature (221 BCE – 220 CE)
- Wei-Jin and Northern and Southern Dynasties Literature (220 – 581 CE)
- Tang-Song Literature (581 – 1271 CE)
- Yuan-Ming-Qing Literature (1271 – 1911 CE)

During the pre-Qin period, Chinese literature saw significant development with the establishment of written texts. This era produced the *Classic of Poetry* (*Shijing*), the oldest known anthology of Chinese poetry, comprising 305 poems that reflect various aspects of life, from courtly rituals to rustic love songs. Another major work is the *Book of Documents* (*Shujing*), a collection of speeches and historical accounts that provide insight into early Chinese governance and moral philosophy.

Philosophical writings flourished during the Warring States period, with seminal texts such as Confucius' *Analects* (*Lunyu*), Laozi's *Tao De Jing*, and the works of Zhuangzi, Mozi and Han Feizi. These texts shaped Chinese thought and became cornerstones of Confucianism, Daoism, and other schools of philosophy.

The *Spring and Autumn Annals* (*Chunqiu*) and the *Zuo Commentary* (*Zuo Zhuan*) also reflect the era's historical and intellectual rigor.

The unification of China under Qin Shihuang of Qin dynasty and the subsequent Han dynasty brought significant changes to literature. The standardisation of the script and the promotion of Confucianism during the Han dynasty led to the compilation of classical texts. *Records of the Grand Historian* (*Shiji*) by Sima Qian is a monumental historical work, blending narrative history with biography and political analysis.

The Han dynasty also saw the development of *fu* (*rhapsody*), a prose-poetry hybrid that combined descriptive richness with lyrical expression. Authors like Sima Xiangru and Ban Gu excelled in this genre. The *Songs of the South* (*Chuci*), attributed to Qu Yuan and others, introduced a distinct lyrical and mythological style that contrasted with the more formal *Classic of Poetry*.

Wei-Jin and Northern and Southern Dynasties period was marked by political fragmentation and cultural diversification, which deeply influenced literary expression. The *Seven Sages of the Bamboo Grove*, including figures like Ji Kang and Ruan Ji, embodied a spirit of intellectual freedom and individualism, often reflected in their poetry and essays.

During this period, the *yuefu* (Music Bureau poetry) gained prominence. These poems, often derived from folk songs, conveyed vivid and emotional narratives. Additionally, the emergence of landscape poetry, exemplified by poets like Xie Lingyun, highlighted a growing appreciation for nature and its spiritual resonance.

Wei-Jin and Northern and Southern Dynasties represent a period of political fragmentation and cultural integration in Chinese history. This era saw significant developments in literature, influenced by various philosophical and religious movements, particularly Buddhism. Buddhism, introduced to China during the Han dynasty, gained substantial traction during this period. It provided a new spiritual framework and worldview, inspiring many writers to explore existential questions, metaphysical concepts, and the nature of human suffering. This influence is evident in both poetry and prose, as writers blended Buddhist themes with native Confucian and Daoist ideas. One of the most significant literary contributions of this era was the translation of Buddhist scriptures. Scholars such as Kumārajīva and Dao'an translated key texts like the *Lotus Sutra* and the *Vimalakīrti Sutra* into Chinese, making Buddhist philosophy accessible to a wider audience. These translations introduced new vocabulary, metaphors, and narrative techniques, enriching Chinese literary traditions. Works like *Luoyang Qielanji* or *Record of Buddhist Monasteries in Luoyang*, is a significant work by Yang Xuanzhi that provides a rich historical and cultural account of the Buddhist monasteries in Luoyang, the capital of the Northern Wei, while also highlighting the profound connections between Chinese Buddhism and its Indian roots. Excerpts from the text have been cited in chapter 3 of the book

The reunification of China under the Sui and Tang dynasties heralded a golden age of Chinese literature. Tang poetry (*Tang shi*) represents the pinnacle of classical Chinese poetry, with renowned poets such as Li Bai, Du Fu, and Wang Wei. Their works explored themes ranging from romantic escapism and philosophical introspection to social criticism and historical reflection. Prose also flourished during the Tang dynasty. Writers like Han Yu and Liu Zongyuan revitalized prose with their advocacy of the guwen (*ancient prose*) movement, emphasizing clarity and moral purpose. The Tang dynasty also saw the emergence of short stories and tales, often featuring supernatural or romantic themes with definite Indian import.

The Song dynasty witnessed the rise of *ci* poetry, a lyrical form set to musical tunes. Poets such as Su Shi (Su Dongpo) and Li Qingzhao excelled in this genre, using it to express deep personal emotions and reflections. Prose continued to evolve, with the development of detailed essays and historical commentaries. Song scholars like Sima Guang, author of the *Comprehensive Mirror to Aid in Governance* (*Zizhi Tongjian*), contributed significantly to historiography. The period also saw advancements in drama and storytelling, which would later influence Yuan and Ming theatre.

Under Mongol rule, Chinese literature experienced a shift, with drama and vernacular fiction emerging as dominant forms. The *zaju* (variety play) genre flourished, characterized by its structured acts and lyrical arias. Playwrights such as Guan Hanqing and Wang Shifu created enduring works like *The Injustice to Dou E* or the *Midsummer Snow* and *Romance of the Western Bower*. This era also saw the beginnings of vernacular fiction, with stories written in everyday language gaining popularity among a broader audience.

The Ming and Qing periods were marked by the flourishing of novels and popular literature. The Ming dynasty produced four great classical novels: *Romance of the Three Kingdoms* (*Sanguo Yanyi*), *Outlaws of the Marshes* (*Shuihu Zhuan*), *Journey to the West* (*Xiyou Ji*), and *Jin Ping Mei* (*The Plum in the Golden Vase*). These works combined history, folklore, and imagination, creating richly layered narratives.

In the Qing dynasty, *Dream of the Red Chamber* (*Honglou Meng*) by Cao Xueqin emerged as a masterpiece of Chinese literature, offering a profound exploration of family, society, and human emotions. The era also saw the growth of *chuanqi* (marvel tales) and *gong'an* (court case fiction), reflecting popular tastes.

The history of Chinese literature, therefore, is a testament to the enduring power of words to capture the human experience. From ancient oral traditions to sophisticated novels, Chinese writers have continually expanded the boundaries of expression, leaving a legacy that resonates across cultures and epochs. Each period brought new genres, styles, and themes, creating a rich tapestry that continues to inspire and enlighten. However, due to the lack of a formal Chinese literary history textbook in India and the difficulty of obtaining works on this subject during the 1990s, I decided to compile *A History of Chinese Literature in Chinese* based on my lecture notes. This book is designed as a Chinese literary history textbook for graduate students specializing in Chinese language and literature at the Centre for Chinese and Southeast Asian Studies, Jawaharlal Nehru University (JNU), India.

The greatest innovation of the Chinese edition published in 2001 and the second edition in 2013 is its integration of Chinese history and literary history with introductions to writers, excerpts from original texts, representative works, and accompanying annotations. Most of the annotations in the English edition have been removed as the texts are in English.

From the perspective of the development of literary history, ancient Chinese literature should be introduced before modern and contemporary literature. However, considering the difficulty of classical Chinese, we have introduced it at the graduate level of JNU's Chinese language curriculum. In other words, students are introduced to this textbook only after completing four years of Chinese language learning. Practicality is a key feature of this textbook. *A History of Chinese Literature* consists of eight chapters in the chronological order as mentioned above. The course is taught over one academic year, with two classes per week, each lasting two hours. The language of the book is concise, clear, and easy to understand, making it highly readable and suitable for self-study. The analyses of literary works are vivid and engaging, further enhancing the book's accessibility.

Since the first edition of this textbook, the book has undergone further revisions, becoming an even more polished and distinctive resource for graduate students studying Chinese language and literature in India. Given the richness of Chinese historical texts concerning India, I have also include some historical materials such as *Accounts of the Southwestern Barbarians* (*Xinan Yilie Zhuan*) and *Accounts of Dayuan* (*Dayuan Lie Zhuan*) from *Records of the Grand Historian* (*Shiji*), as well as references to India from the *Treatise on Geography* (*Dili Zhi*) in the *Book of Han* (*Han Shu*) and *Record of Buddhist Monasteries in Luoyang* in the second and current English edition of the book.

As regards the English edition, this is a translation of the 2014 Chinese edition published by the Pegion Books, New Delhi. The book has been translated by Ms. Wang Hanbing of the Institute of Indian Studies, Lanzhou University, People's Republic of China. Ms. Wang was introduced to me by an old friend and eminent Indologist, Professor Mao Shichang, of the same University who is also an alumnus of Jawaharlal Nehru University. I wish to record my gratitude to professor Mao, as well as to Ms. Wang who not only completed the translation in time but also cited desired sources while incorporating translated texts.

At the end of the book, I have included a brief write-up in the appendix about the translation of classical, modern, and contemporary Chinese literary works by Indian Sinologists. This serves to highlight how little work has been done in India to engage with the vast repository of Chinese literature. I hope this will inspire more Indian scholars specializing in Chinese studies to undertake research and translation projects focused on Chinese literary works.

Finally, I extend my heartfelt gratitude to my wife, Wang Yao, and Ms. Yang Jinghong from the Graduate School at Nanjing University for their invaluable support during the preparation of the first Chinese edition, which laid the foundation for the English translation.

B.R. Deepak
Jawaharlal Nehru University
New Delhi
January 3, 2025

Chapter One

The Primitive and Pre-Qin Literature

As early as over a million years ago, there have already appeared the ancient human in China. Yuanmou county of Yunnan province, Lantian county of Shanxi province, Zhoukoudian near Beijing, etc. are all places for the Chinese ancestors to have settled down. Then emerged the earliest matriarchal clan commune in China, i.e., the blood was determined by the maternal line. The Yangshao culture and the Majiayao culture the representatives of this commune. About 5,000 years ago, the patriarchal clan commune came into being in China, in which the blood relations began to be determined by the paternal line, the typical culture lying in the Longshan culture, the Qijia culture and the Qingliangang culture.

1. THE PRIMITIVE LITERATURE

During the primitive period, the ancient people made significant achievements on conquering nature, especially on flood control. The well-known examples about nature conquering include legends of Suiren's invention of fire (*The Han Feizi: Five Worms*), Shennong's invention of plough and teaching people how to farm (*Bai Hu Tong*), the flood control of Yu the Great, who "followed the method of Gonggong (God of water), the method of river dredging", etc.

The literature in the primitive period can be mainly classified into two categories.

1.1. The Primitive Poetry

The primitive poetry is an oral creation appearing before written words were employed, handed down by the word of mouth. Primitive poetry in China has its roots in the earliest human activities and is deeply intertwined with labour, ritual, and collective expression. It reflects the initial stages of human attempts to make sense of the world, articulate desires, and communicate emotions through rhythmic and melodic language. The key features and examples of primitive poetry in China are: one, labour and rhythm; two, magical and religious functions; three, integration with music and dance; and four, reflection of daily life and aspirations.

Primitive poetry often emerged from the rhythm of collective labour. The calls and chants used to coordinate efforts, reduce fatigue, and enhance efficiency became the earliest forms of poetic rhythm. These rhythmic calls were simple, repetitive, and functional, serving as tools to unify group actions. It won't be wrong to say that literature was created during the course of the collective labour, for language came into being during the same course. As interpreted in *The Huainanzi: Responses of Dao*, "When people lift large logs, those at the front call out 'Xie Xu,' and those at the back respond in turn. This is a song to encourage strength in lifting."

Second, primitive poetry was often used as incantations or prayers, reflecting the belief that language could influence nature or divine forces. These poetic forms were employed in rituals to express desires or commands directed at the natural world or deities. For example, The *Lac Speech* (蜡辞) attributed to Yi Qi in the *Book of Rites* has the following:

> Let the earth return to its home,
> Let the waters flow back to their valleys,
> Let no insects arise,
> Let the grasses and trees return to their marshes.

Third, primitive poetry was not an isolated art form but part of an integrated performance involving song, dance, and music. This holistic expression of emotion and ritual was central to early human communities. For example, descriptions in *Lüshi Chunqiu* of three people holding ox tails, stamping their feet, and singing eight songs about nature, agriculture, and divine reverence.

Finally, primitive poetry often depicted the realities of life, including labour, agriculture, and communal desires. It idealised human capabilities and expressed collective hopes for prosperity and harmony. *Song of Shots*, recorded in *The Spring and Autumn Annals of Wu and Yue* is an example. According to Volume Five of this book, Fan Li recommended a good shooter Chen Yin to King Goujian of Yue. When asked about the use of "slings and shots", Chen Yin mentioned *Song of Shots*:

> Cut bamboo,
> Join bamboo,
> Scatter soil,
> Chase prey

The poem reveals human began to use slings and shots as early as in the primitive period. Primitive poetry in China thus represents the foundation of Chinese literary tradition, embodying the earliest expressions of human creativity and cultural identity.

1.2. Mythology

The other oral literature popular in the primitive period is mythology. There originated a great number of myths in ancient China, reflecting the conflict between man and nature. However, the existing myths today have already lost their original flavour. Myths appeared at the humble beginning of the wild primal era, and the Shennong Era in Chinese legends is equivalent to this period. The existing Chinese myths are fragmentary, without any systematic and integrated anthology, only scattering in *Shanhaii Jing*, *Chu Ci*, *The Tale of King Mu* and other few works from the Pre-Qin and Han masters such as *The Zhuangzi* and *The Huainanzi*. The one with relatively focused materials should go to *Shanhai Jing* or the *Classic of Mountains and Seas*

Jingwei Fills the Sea[1]

The Classic of Mountains and Seas:
The Classic of the Northern Mountains

200 li further north is a mountain called Fajiu where there are plenty of three-bristle cudrania trees. There is a bird called jingwei which looks like a crow and has white markings on its head, a white beak and red claws. It is named after its call -*jingwei*. The bird was originally Nü Wa, the youngest daughter of Emperor Yandi. She was drowned when swimming in the East Sea and was unable to return. Thus, she transformed herself into the bird jingwei and often carried broken woods and pebbles in the mouth to fill the East Sea.

Kuafu Races with the Sun[2]

The Classic of Mountains and Seas:
The Classic of Areas Overseas: the North

Kuafu races with the sun and finally approaches the scorching sun. Feeling thirsty, he drinks up all the water in the Yellow River and the Wei River, but he still cannot quench his thirst. He then goes to the north, desiring for the water in a big marsh there. Unfortunately, he dies of thirst half the way. On the verge of death, he throws away his walking stick, which immediately transforms into a forest called Denglin.

Nvwa Mends the Sky[3]

The Huainanzi: Lanmingxun

In ancient times, the four corners of the sky collapsed and the world with its nine regions split open. The sky could not cover all the things under it, nor could the Earth carry all the things on it. A great fire that could not be extinguished and an unyielding flood raged; savage beasts devoured innocent people and vicious birds preyed on the weak and elderly.

Then Nv Wa melted down the five-coloured stones to mend the tear in the sky. She supported the four corners of the sky with the legs she had cut off from a giant turtle. She killed the black dragon to save the people of Jizhou, and blocked the flood with the ashes of reeds.

Thus the sky was mended, its four corners lifted, the flood tamed, Jizhou pacified, and harmful birds and beasts killed, and the innocent people were able to live on the square Earth under the dome of the sky.

Houyi Shoots down the Suns[4]

The Huainanzi: Benjingxun

In the remote past, it is said, there were ten suns in the sky, veritable burning fires which scorched the plants, the grass and the woods. Nothing could grow and there was great famine. On top of this, snakes and beasts roamed everywhere, endangering the people

In view of this, King Yao ordered Houyi, the master of archery to shoot down the suns and kill the beasts to rescue the people from their misery. Houyi defied all difficulties to carry out this order, and succeeded in shooting down all the surplus suns and finishing off the ferocious animals. After shooting the suns he killed Yayu. He slew Zaochi at Chouhua and put Jiuying in the troubled waters, and shot Dafeng to death in Qingqiu Swamp. The Xiu snake was cut into pieces in the Dongtinghu Lake and Fengxi among mulberry trees.

Since then, there has been only one sun shining in the sky, making for a temperate climate, lush vegetation, fine harvests and consequently general well-being. His immortal feats for the people and for posterity won Houyi universal admiration and support. The land under heaven was in peace and harmony. The cheerful people gave cries of triumph everywhere and celebrated his feats.

Pan Gu Splits the Heaven from the Earth

(From The Classic of Mountains and Seas)

Once upon a time, the world was in such chaos that it was like an egg, and Pan Gu lived in it, who was 18,000 years old. He separated the heaven from the earth, hence the clear one became the heaven, and the dark one the earth, while he lived in the area between the heaven and the earth. With nine changes in a day, the heaven became godly and the earth holy. Each day, the heaven would be ten feet higher than it was in the previous day, while the earth ten feet thicker. Meanwhile, Pan Gu would also be ten feet taller each day. 18,000 years later, the heaven was extremely high, the earth extremely deep, and Pan Gu extremely tall, therefore it was 90,000 li from the heaven to the earth. Later, there emerged the Three August Ones.[5]

Nv Wa Created Human Beings

(From Volume 78 of Taiping Yulan)

It is said that there was no man when the heaven was separated from the earth. The goddess Nv Wa created human beings by clay. The work was so hard that she soon became exhausted, so she dipped a rope in clay and flicked it and each blob of clay became a man. Therefore, the figures handcrafted by Nv Wa became the significant while the flicked blobs the poor and the low.

Primitive mythological stories in China are deeply rooted in the country's early history, reflecting the worldview, spiritual beliefs, and cultural values of ancient Chinese societies. These myths served as explanations for natural phenomena, origins of the world (as in Pan Gu and Nv Wa myths), human existence, and the establishment of order (Nv Wa fills the sky and Hou Yi Shooting the suns). They were transmitted orally before being recorded in early texts, and their themes often combined cosmology, morality, and heroism. The myths reflect the experiences of early Chinese people with their surroundings, such as rivers, mountains, and celestial bodies, as well as their struggles with natural disasters like floods and droughts. Myths often emphasise the relationship between humans and nature, portraying natural forces as divine or sentient beings.

Chinese myths provide insights into the values, beliefs, and aspirations of early Chinese societies. They also laid the foundation for later Chinese literature, art, and philosophy, influencing Daoism, Confucianism, and popular culture. Through these stories, ancient Chinese people sought to understand their world and their place within it, leaving a rich legacy of mythological tradition.

2. THE PRE-QIN LITERATURE

The Pre-Qin literature includes the entire Age of Slavery before Qin conquered the other six kingdoms, and the period from the slave society to the beginning of the feudal society. The slave society covers four periods in history: Xia Dynasty (ca. 2100-1600 BCE), Shang Dynasty (ca. 1600-1050 BCE), the Western Zhou Dynasty (1046-256 BCE) and the Spring and Autumn Period (770-ca 475 BCE). The most reliable evidence of Shang Dynasty is "Ruins of Yin", with "oracle bone script" unearthed. The Spring and Autumn Period is an age of the gradual decline of the slavery and the initial formation of the feudal society, during which time the royalty was losing its power, leaving the feudal princes fighting for power. As a consequence, six great kingdoms rose to power: Qi, Chu, Qin, Jin, Wu and Yue. During the Warring States Period, there were seven kingdoms, Qi, Chu, Yan, Han, Zhao, Wei, and Qin, fighting fiercely against each other for annexation. Eventually, First Emperor of Qin united China and established the first highly centralised feudal state of absolutism in Chinese history. During the Pre-Qin period, a large quantity of literary works came out in the Spring and Autumn Period and the Warring States Period. The Pre-Qin literature mainly comprises *The Classic of Poetry,* historical prose, the various schools of thoughts during the axial age and the works of Qu Yuan.

2.1. The Classic of Poetry

The Classic of Poetry is the earliest collection of poetry in Chinese literature, including 305 poems in about 500 years dating from the early Western Zhou Period (ca. 1046-771 BCE) to the mid Spring and Autumn Period, the overwhelming majority of writers being anonymous. Initially, the book was named as *The Songs*, or *Three Hundred Songs*, ranking among "Six Classics of Confucianism" *(Book of Poetry*, *Book of Documents*, *Book of Rites*, *The Classic of Music*, *Book of Change*, and the *Spring and Autumn Annals*) during the Warring States Period (ca. 475-221 BCE), with the authorised name *The Classic of Poetry* appearing formally in times of Emperor Wu of Han. During Han Dynasty (206 BCE-220 CE), four different versions of *The Classic of Poetry* emerged to make it popularised, with annotations and interpretations, namely, the Lu Tradition (by Shen Peigong), the Qi Tradition (by Yuan Gusheng), the Han Tradition (by Han Ying) and the Mao Tradition (originally *The Songs* edited and annotated by Mao Heng of Lu and Mao Chang of Zhao in Western Han Period (206 BCE-9CE), which was developed into the present *The Classic of Poetry*.) Nevertheless, the former three all became oblivious, leaving the Mao Tradition preserved and popularised.

The Classic of Poetry is the earliest collection of Chinese songs as well. According to *The Mozi: Chapter Gong Meng*, "(people) recite 300 poems, play 300 poems, sing 300 poems, and dance to 300 poems," from which it can be traced that the poems collected in *The Classic of Poetry* are all lyrics in songs. It is believed that there existed the poetry collecting system in ancient China, that is, to help the emperor to know more about the local customs and policy implementation, or merely on the purpose of entertainment, the royal musicians would dedicate the poems they had collected to the emperor after editing and revising them, with musical setting attached. As is recorded in *History of Han Dynasty: Treatise on Literature*, "In ancient times, there were officials serving as poetry-collector, so that the prince was able to know about the customs, hence discerning the gains and losses of his ruling by self-examination."

The Classic of Poetry can be divided into three sections according to the lyrical qualities, that is, regional folk lyrics (feng), court odes (ya) and sacrificial hymns (song). The later Confucian scholars all adopt the theory of "Six Principles" (*liuyi*) of the *Book of Poetry* to interpret this great work, namely, regional folk songs, court odes, and sacrificial hymns, straightforward narrative (fu), explicit comparison (bi), and implied comparison (xing), among which the first three are in terms of the categories of the songs, while the other three the literary styles and techniques used to convey ideas, emotions, or artistic intent in the songs.

'Feng' are regional folk lyrics collected from 15 different regions, altogether there being 160 poems. Zheng Qiao from Song Dynasty called them "songs showing the local customs". Some of the ppems belong to folk songs, whereas some have an aristocratic tint. 'Ya' are "court lyrics", songs from the regions directly under the rule of the court of Zhou. There are 105 such songs, divided into "Major Court Odes" (Da Ya) and Lesser Court Odes (Xiao Ya) according to different lyrical qualities, the majority of which are songs for court feasts. 'Song' are "religious lyrics" or sacrificial odes, performed on occasions of sacrificial offerings. There are 40 such odes, comprising Eulogies of Zhou, Eulogies of Lu and Eulogies of Shang. Fu, Bi and Xing are literary techniques employed in the songs. Fu is the direct narrative to the target objects, while Bi is explicit comparisons and Xing implied comparisons serving as the beginning of a song.

The Classic of Poetry manifests from various perspectives the panorama of the social life in Zhou Dynasty, reflecting in a relatively truthful way the vicissitude of the slavery society in China. In terms of its contents, there exist the following categories:

1. Expose the merciless exploitation and oppression the slave-owners on the slaves, showing the slaves' fury and rebellion.
2. Include the songs on the theme of war and corvee.
3. Depicting the situations concerning hunting, ranching and farming in the ancient times.
4. Include the songs on the theme of love and marriage.
5. Some songs eulogize the achievements made by the forebears of Zhou Dynasty.

Woodcutter's Song[6]

(Wei Feng)

Cut the sandalwood trees with the sound ding-dong, and we pile the wood on the bank of the river. The water of the river is so clear that the ripples twinkle.
You never reap nor sow. Why have you moved three hundred sheaves of corns to your home?
You never hunt nor chase. Why is your courtyard full of so many badgers?
You are the noble so that you eat without labour!

Cut the sandalwood to make the wheel-spokes with the sound ding-dong, and we pile the wood on the bank of the river. The water of the river is clear with ripples.
You are easy and free while the others reap and sow. Why have you moved three thousand sheaves of corns to your home?

You are careless there while the others hunt and chase. Why is your courtyard full of so many wild animals?
You are the noble so that you eat without labour!

Cut the sandalwood trees to make the wheels with the sound ding-dong, and we pile the wood on the side of the river. The water of the river is clear with the waves as stars to twinkle.
You do nothing while the others reap and sow. Why have you moved three hundred thousand sheaves of corns to your home?
You never labour while the others hunt. Why is your courtyard full of so many quails? You are the lords so that you eat without labour!

Large Rat[7]

(Wei Feng)

Large rat, large rat,
Eat no more millet we grow!
Three years you have grown fat;
No care for us you show.
We'll leave you now, I swear,
For a happier land,
A happier land where
We may have a free hand.

Large rat, large rat,
Eat no more wheat we grow!
Three years you have grown fat;
No kindness to us you show.
We'll leave you now, I swear,
For a happier state,
A happier state where
We can decide our fate.

Large rat, large rat,
Eat no more rice we grow!
Three years you have grown fat;
No rewards to our labour go.
We'll leave you now, I swear,
For a happier plain,
A happier plain where
None will groan or complain.

Without Dress[8]

(Qin Feng)

Who says I live without dress? There is a robe for you and I to share.
The king is ready to make war. We must go to make the lance shine and fight against the enemy together.

Who says I live without dress? There is a vest for you and I to share.
The king is ready to make war. We must go to make the halberds shine and fight against the enemy together.

Who says I live without dress? There is a dress for you and I to share.
The king is ready to make war. We must go to make both swords and amours shine and march on the battle field together.

Cooing and Wooing[9]

(South of Zhou)

By riverside a pair
Of turtledoves are cooing;
There is a maiden fair
Whom a young man is wooing.

Water flows left and right
Of cresses here and there;
The youth yearns day and night
For the maiden so fair.

His yearning grows so strong,
He cannot fall asleep,
But tosses all night long,
So deep in love, so deep!

Now gather left and right
Cress long or short and tender!
O lute, play music light
For the fiancée so slender!
Feast friends at left and right
On cresses cooked tender!
O bells and drums, delight
The bride so sweet and slender!

The Creeping Grass[10]

(Zheng Feng)

Afield the creeping grass
With crystal dew o'erspread,
There's a beautiful lass
With clear eyes and fine forehead.
When I meet the clear-eyed,
My desire's satisfied.

Afield the creeping grass
With round dewdrops o'erspread,
There's a beautiful lass
With clear eyes and fine forehead.
When I meet the clear-eyed,
Amid the grass let's hide!

A Deer Killer and a Jadelike Maiden[11]

(Zhao Nan)

An antelope is killed
And wrapped in white afield.
A maid for love does long,
Tempted by a hunter strong.

He cuts down trees amain
And kills a deer again.
He sees the white-drest maid
As beautiful as jade.

"O soft and slow, sweetheart,
Don't tear my sash apart!"
The jadelike maid says, "Hark!
Do not let the dog bark!"

An Old Maid[12]

(Zhao Nan)

The fruits from mume-tree fall,
One-third of them away.
If you love me at all,
Woo me a lucky day!

The fruits from mume-tree fall,
Two-thirds of them away.
If you love me at all,
Woo me this very day!

The fruits from mume-tree fall,
Now all of them away.
If you love me at all,
You need not woo but say!

King Wen's Temple [13]

(Zhou Song)

King Wen's Temple
Solemn's the temple still;
Princes their duties fulfil.
Numerous officers,
Virtuous King Wen's followers,
Worship his soul on high,
Whom they hurry to glorify.
There are none but revere
Tirelessly their ancestor dear.

3. THE PRE-QIN PROSE

The Pre-Qin prose can be divided into two categories. One is historical prose, or chronicle prose, including works that record political, military and diplomatic affairs as well as views of rulers and their strategists, with the representative works *Spring and Autumn Annals*, *The Commentary of Zuo*, *Discourses of States*, and *Strategies of the Warring States*, etc. The other is the writings from the Hundred Schools of Thought, or philosophical prose, covering argumentative treatises from various schools intended to illustrate their viewpoints and opinions, with the representative works *The Analects of Confucius*, *Dao De Jing*, *The Mozi*, *The Mencius*, *The Zhuangzi*, *The Xunzi*, and *The Han Feizi*, etc.

3.1. Historical Prose

3.1.1. The Book of Documents (Shangshu)

The *Book of Documents* is the first collection of prose works in ancient China, meaning "ancient books". One of the Five Classics of Confucianism in ancient China, it was named *Book* in the Spring and Autumn and Warring States Period, only changed to *Book of Documents* during Han Dynasty. It is said to have included 100 chapters originally, only leaving 28 chapters after the "Book

Burning Incident" in Qin Dynasty. During the reign of Emperor Wu of Han, an old version, known as *The Old Text Version of Documents*, was discovered in the wall of Confucius' family estate, with 16 more chapters than The New Text. However, most of these 16 chapters have already been lost. During Jin Dynasty, 25 chapters in The Old Text were counterfeited. Anyway, the present version comprises of 58 chapters.

The *Book of Documents* include four sections: Yu, Xia, Shang and Zhou Books. The sections of Yu and Xia were not composed during the reign of Yu, the Great and Xia Dynasty, on the contrary, they are the counterfeits compiled by the later Confucian scholars on the basis of ancient tradition they had traced. The contents in the *Book of Documents* consists of speeches, decrees, admonitions, and proclamations etc., among which Speech of King Tang should be the earliest work in terms of the era, while the three parts of Pan Geng are all archaic and abstruse, most of which have the original flavour. The chapter record the speeches made by King Pan Geng of the Shang Dynasty during the relocation of the capital. The section of Zhou includes the documents from the beginning of Zhou to the early time of the Spring and Autumn and Warring States Period.

3.1.2. The Spring and Autumn Annals (Chunqiu)

The Spring and Autumn Annals used to be the general term of the official chronicles for different states during the Pre-Qin period. Nevertheless, the only surviving one is *The Spring and Autumn Annals of Lu*, hence it has become the specific term for the official chronicle of the State of Lu, which was included as one of "the Five Classics" of Confucianism. It is the first chronicle in Chinese history, compiled by Confucius according to the historical records of the State of Lu, covering all the historical events of Zhou Dynasty, as well as those of the state of Lu and the other states, from King Lu Yin's first year (722 BC) to King Lu Ai's 14th year (481 BC).

The *Spring and Autumn Annals* reflect Confucius's political ideology of respecting the royal authority and restoring the 'Great Unity' of the early Zhou dynasty. The events in the text are generally recorded in chronological order, specifying the year, month, day, location, persons involved, events, and outcomes. The Confucian school believes that every word and sentence in the *Spring and Autumn Annals* carries implicit judgments on people and events, employing the distinctive evaluative style known as the "Spring and Autumn writing method.

3.1.3. The Commentary of Zuo (Zuozhuan)

According to the *Records of the Grand Historian* (*Shiji*), the *Zuo Zhuan* was originally titled *Zuo's Spring and Autumn Annals*. Since the Western Han Dynasty, it has been named *The Commentary of Zuo*, namely, *Spring and Autumn Annals of Master Zuo's*. There has been much debate about the authorship, the time of composition, and its relationship with the *Spring and Autumn Annals*. As to its author, according to Sima Qian's *Records of the Grand Historian* and Ban Gu's *The Book of Han: Treatise on Literature*, author was said to be Zuo Qiuming, a prefect of the state of Lu. Nevertheless, many scholars since Tang Dynasty disapprove of this statement. The modern scholar Kang Youwei claimed that the work might have been counterfeited by Liu Xin of Han Dynasty. While others suggest that, judging from the historical details of the Spring and Autumn period recorded in the text, it was compiled by someone in the Warring States period based on historical materials from the Spring and Autumn period.

The Commentary of Zuo records events from King Lu Yin's first year (722 BC) to King Lu Ai's 27th year (468 BC), covering 13 more years than the *Spring and Autumn Annals*. However, in some parts of this book, there is only "Jing"[14] without "Zhuan"[15], while in some other parts, there is only "Zhuan" without "Jing". Nonetheless, there do exist some parts that have both "Jing" and "Zhuan", which is in accordance with *Spring and Autumn Annals*. Hence the canon can be regarded as a book closely related to *Spring and Autumn Annals*, and in the meantime, it is also greatly influenced by the latter.

The Commentary of Zuo is is the first detailed and comprehensive chronological history in Chinese history. It covers the political, military, diplomatic, cultural and other activities of various states in the Spring and Autumn Period, reflecting relatively truthfully the history at that time. Additionally, it contains many accounts of celestial phenomena, spirits, omens, divination, and dream interpretation. In terms of the relationship between the heaven and human, it emphasises human will and action. In terms of the relationship between the ruler and his subjects, it values the power of the people, embodying a "people-centered" ideology.

It exposes the atrocities, ugliness, and internal contradictions of the ruling class while praising capable politicians and patriots. For example, in the essay *Cao Gui's Discussion on War,* before the war between the two states Qi and Lu was started, Cao Gui clearly pointed out to Duke Zhuang of Lu that the key to victory in war lies in gaining the people's trust politically, while divine blessings and aristocratic support are secondary.

The Commentary of Zuo excels in its depiction of warfare, recording over 480 military engagements of various scales. The author clearly explains the causes, processes, and outcomes of wars. Notable battles include the wars between Lu, Qin, Jin, and Han; the Battle of Chengpu between Jin and Chu; the Battle of Xiao between Qin and Jin; and the Battle of An between Qi and Jin.

3.1.4. Discourses of States (Guoyu)

The Discourses of States consisting of 21 volumes, is a historical work focused primarily on speeches, categorised by individual states. It records historical fragments of eight states: Zhou, Lu, Qi, Jin, Zheng,

Chu, Wu and Yue. Because it primarily documents speeches, it is called *Guoyu* ("Discourses of the States"). The *Guoyu* covers approximately 500 years of history, from King Mu of Zhou to Duke Dao of Lu (circa 1000 BCE to 440 BCE). According to Sima Qian, the author of *Guoyu* was Zuo Qiuming, a historian of the State of Lu. However, this claim is widely debated, and there is no consensus. Many believe it was likely compiled during the Warring States period based on historical records from various states.

Discourses of States is not a comprehensive and systematic historical record of various states at that time. Instead, it focuses more on the discourses of some important figures, reflecting the fierce and complicated class conflict and political strife during the Spring and Autumn Period. For instance, in *Discourses of the State of Jin*, extensively documents Duke Wen of Jin's efforts to dominate the feudal lords and the conflicts among the major aristocratic families of Jin.

The *Guoyu* shares a similar "people-centered" ideology with the *Zuo Zhuan*. This is evident in chapters such as *The Speech of Duke Zhao on Suppressing Slander* and *Jing Jiang's Discussion on Labour and Leisure*. However, the *Guoyu* also contains many conservative and backward ideas, promoting beliefs in divine will, spirits, and loyalty to the ruler. Liu Zongyuan, the eminent writer in Tang Dynasty, composed a work entitled *An Antithesis of the Discourses of States*, criticising many absurdities found in the *Guoyu*.

3.1.5. Strategies of the Warring States (Zhanguoce)

Strategies of the Warring States is another notable historical work following the *Discourses of States*, comprising 33 chapters. Initially it was entitled *National Strategies*, *National Affairs*, *Short and Long* etc. Later, Liu Xiang from Han Dynasty reorganised it and endowed it with the present title. Basically, the book was written in the same style as that of *Discourses of States*, mainly in the form of discourses. Altogether it includes 12 strategies: Strategies of Eastern Zhou, Western Zhou, Qin, Qi, Chu, Zhao, Wei, Han, Yan, Song, Wey, and Zhongshan.

The basic content of *Strategies of the Warring States* is a record of the speeches and activities of strategists and advisors during the Warring States period. During this time, the seven powerful states coexisted, and the warfare of the Spring and Autumn period was particularly intense. Some strategists and advisors took advantage of the political situation to propose political views or strategies for warfare. The progressiveness of *Strategies of the Warring States* lies in its prominent "people-oriented" philosophy.

The section *Feng Xuan as a Guest of Mengchang Jun* in *Strategies of the Warring States* consists of two parts. The first one depicted how Feng Xuan requested the permission of Meng Changjun, an influential aristocrat of Qi, to be one of his patronised hangers-on, while the second focuses on his capacity and achievements. Similarly, *Su Qin Begins to Advocate the Strategy of Horizontal Alliance* is also divided into two parts. The first part describes Su Qin's failure in advocating the "horizontal alliance strategy" with Qin, and the second part describes his success in promoting the "vertical alliance strategy" with the six states.

Figures like Su Qin and Zhang Yi did not adhere to the Confucian virtues of loyalty, trust, and propriety. In order to achieve certain goals, they often resorted to unscrupulous means, reversing their stance and lacking consistency. Su Qin originally advocated for the horizontal alliance, but after his failure with Qin, he switched to promoting the vertical alliance with the Eastern six states. He was criticised as someone who "could not be trusted by the world." Zhang Yi, who was sent by Qin to negotiate with Chu, used the offer of 600 *li*[16] of land as a lure to persuade Chu to sever ties with Qi. When the King of Chu sent envoys to Qin, Zhang Yi reneged and offered only six *li* of land. This was a clear example of using political deception to gain benefits.

King Pan Geng

(The Book of Documents)

The king said: "Come, all of you, I will tell you and guide you. You must control your selfish desires and not seek comfort through arrogance. In the past, our ancestors, the former kings, only sought to employ trusted officials to manage state affairs together. They followed the teachings of the former kings and did not conceal the essence of their instructions. The former kings respected them for this. They did not utter erroneous words, and as a result, the people underwent great changes. Now, you reject my advice, act arrogantly, and rise to speak of dangerous and empty words. I do not understand the purpose of your dispute.

"It is not that I have abandoned the virtue of employing the old and trusted officials, but rather that you harbour good intentions that you cannot offer to me. I see the current situation as clearly as watching a fire. If I am not good at planning and acting, then that is my fault. It is like tying a net to a string—only then can it be orderly and not chaotic; it is like a farmer working the fields—only by diligently ploughing can there be a good harvest. If you can control your selfish desires and bring real benefits to the people, even to your relatives and friends, then you can boldly claim that you have accumulated virtue. If you do not fear the disasters that may come from near and far, and if you are like lazy farmers seeking comfort without working hard, then you will have no crops.

You do not proclaim my good words to the people. This is your own self-inflicted disaster, leading to evil and calamity, and you will harm yourselves. If you have already led the people to do wrong, and now you must endure the consequences, how can you regret it when it is too late? Look, even they still heed the warnings and reflect on their wrong words. How much more should I, who control your lives, be concerned? Why do you not come directly to me, but instead stir up false and dangerous rumours, inciting the people? It is like a great fire burning on the plain, which cannot be approached, cannot be faced, and can it be extinguished? It is you, the people, who have caused this bad situation, not me."

Cao Gui's Strategies on War

The Tenth Year of Duke Zhuang's Time [684 BC][17]
(The Commentary of Zuo)

In spring of the tenth year, the army of Qi made its attack on the state of Lu. As the duke of Lu was ready to meet the army of Qi, Cao Gui, a man in Lu, asked to see the duke. One who lived in his same village said to him: "These nobles have their own plan, what would you do?" Cao Gui answered: "They are all shallow and ignorant, and cannot make far-reaching plans." Then he entered the palace to see the duke, and he asked the duke what method he will use to fight with the enemy. The duke said: "I cannot dare to enjoy all good clothes and food alone, which should be distributed to others." Cao Gui said: "This is but a little favor that cannot reach all people, and they will not follow you." The duke said again: "Oxen, sheep, gems and silks used in sacrifice, I cannot dare to go beyond our regulations. The prayer I make must be carried out very exactly." Cao Gui remarked: "An insignificant sincerity cannot cause the people to believe, and the gods and spirits will not give you blessings." The duke said again: "Though I cannot investigate all legal cases, small or great, thoroughly, yet I may do it in accordance with the real circumstance." Then Cao Gui nodded, saying: "This is called the the sincerity of the people and the spirits. You may fight on that. I beg to be allowed to attend you for fight."

When they set out, Duke Zhuang had Cao Gui with him to take the same chariot. The armies of Lu and Qi clashed at Changshao. The duke was about to command to beat the battle drums for the advance. Cao Gui said: "Not yet now." After the Qi's drums to be beaten the advance three times, Cao Gui said to the duke: "It's time for us now to beat drums." It followed his suggestion and the army of Qi was defeated crushingly. When the duke was about to pursue the enemy while they were routed, Cao Gui advised again: "Not yet now." Then he got down from the chariot and examined the tracks left by the wheels of the enemy chariots in a careful way. On return to the chariot he gazed into far for a while, then said to the duke: "It's time for us now to chase the enemy!" With that, the chase of the enemy started.

After the winning of the troops of Qi, the duke inquired of Cao Gui why he had done that. Cao Gui said: "The most important in battle depends on courage. The first beating of drums will excite the soldier's spirits; the second beating will drop it and the third, the spirit will be exhausted. When the enemy's spirits were exhausted, ours were at the highest, so we defeated them. It is hard to fathom the scheming of a big state as Qi so I was afraid there might be an ambush and I looked for their wheel's tracks. I found them all in confusion and their banners drooped. In this case, I held it was the time to pursue."

Duke Zhao Remonstrated with King Li on Silencing People's Criticism

(Discourses of States)

King Li of Zhou was tyrannical and the people of the country criticised him. Duke Zhao spoke to him, "The people cannot stand it any longer!" The king was angry and employed a wizard from the state of Wei to monitor his people. Anyone reported by the wizard would be put to death. The people were afraid to speak out and would only use their eves to communicate when coming across each other on the road.

The king was pleased with this and said to Duke Zhao, "I have silenced all criticism and now no one dares to speak out against me." Duke Zhao replied, "This is a block. Blocking people's mouth is worse than blocking a river. If you dam a river, it will eventually flood its banks and bring great harm. The same is true for the people. Therefore, to prevent a river from flooding, you need to dredge it, and to prevent people from revolting, you need to let them speak out. This is why the king holds the court, he will ask his officials, from the highest to the lowest ranks, to collect the satirical poems from the common people, the music officials to collect the folk compositions, the historians to collect the classical canons, the scholars give advice, the blinds give warnings, all the officials can voice their opinions, and the commons' opinions can also reach the ruler. The courtiers around the ruler can remonstrate, and the relatives can remind the ruler and remedy the wrong. The music officials and historians can admonish by the compositions and classical canons, and the senior and aged officials give further admonishment. The ruler listens to them all and weighed before making a decision. This is why his rule is successful without going against the people's will. If the people can voice their opinions, as there are mountains and rivers on the earth, then it will be the source of wealth and necessities. It is also like there are fertile fields both on the highlands and lowlands, and it will be the source of clothes and food. If the speech is encouraged, the advantages and disadvantages of the policies can be showed. The advantages can be advanced, while the disadvantages can be remedied, and this is the right way to win wealth and clothes and food. If the people have dissatisfaction, it will be the spontaneous overflow of their feelings to voice their opinions, then how can their speech be restricted? If they are forbidden to air their opinions, then how many people will support the ruler?

However, the king did not follow the advice, and the people were afraid to speak out. Three years later, the king was deposed and exiled to the county of Zhi.

Zou Ji Was More Than Eight Chi Tall[18]

(Strategies of the Warring States)

Zou Ji was more than eight chi tall. He was very handsome and glowed with health. One morning, he got dressed and looked at himself in the mirror. He asked his wife, "Who do you think is more handsome, Mr. Xu living in the northern part of the capital or I?" His wife said, "You are very handsome. Mr. Xu cannot match you!" Mr. Xu who lived in the northern part of the capital was the most handsome man in the state of Qi. Zou Ji was not so confident about his ownlooks, so he asked his concubine the same question: "Who do you think is more handsome, Mr. Xu or I?" The concubine replied, "How can Mr. Xu match you!" The next day, a guest came to visit Zou Ji. They sit down and talked. Zou Ji asked him, "Who do you think is more handsome, Mr. Xu or I?" The guest said, "Mr Xu is not as handsome as you!"

Mr. Xu himself came the next day. Zou Ji observed him thoroughly and thought that he himself was not as handsome as Mr. Xu. He then looked in the mirror and found that he was much less handsome than Mr. Xu. He thought it over and over from morning till night and said, "My wife considered me more handsome than Mr. Xu because of her favouritism towards me. My concubine considered me more handsome, because she was afraid of me and therefore wanted to please me. My guest considered me more handsome, because he was going to ask me for help."

Then Zou Ji went to the court to see King Wei of Qi and said, "I know for sure that I am not as handsome as Mr. Xu. However, my wife loves me, my concubine is afraid of me and my guest is going to ask me for help, so they all said that I am more handsome than Mr. Xu. Now Qi has one thousand li of land and owns one hundred and twenty cities and towns. All the women and beloved ones in the palace love you. All the court officials are afraid of you. And all the people living within our borders on all four sides are going to seek your help. From this point of view, you must have been cheated very badly, Your Majesty." King Wei said, "You are right." Then he issued an order as follows: "Among all the high- ranking court officials, officers and ordinary people, those who can point out my errors frankly will be rewarded with top awards. Those who write to me to remonstrate with me will be rewarded with medium awards. Those who can openly discuss my mistakes will be rewarded with third-class awards."

After this order was issued, all the high-ranking court officials and officers vied with each other to remonstrate with the king. The front of the court was as crowded as the market. A few months later, someone would come to argue with the king between times. After a year, there was nothing to remonstrate with the king. When the states of Yan, Zhao, Han and Wei heard this story, they all went to say congratulations and show their respect to the king of Qi. This is regarded as defeating the enemy states without stepping out of the court hall.

A Man from Qi Named Feng Xuan[19]

(Strategies of the Warring States)

Once in the state of Qi, there was a man named Feng Xuan. He was too poor to support his family. So he asked someone to tell Lord Mengchang that he wanted to become one of the lord's hangers-on to make a living. Lord Mengchang asked Feng Xuan, "What's your hobby?" Feng Xuan replied, "I have no hobby." Lord Mengchang asked, "What talent do you have?" Feng Xuan said, "I have no talent at all." "I see. You can stay here." Lord Mengchang smiled and accepted him. The people around Lord Mengchang thought that the lord looked down upon Feng Xuan, so they only gave him simple food.

After some time, Feng Xuan leaned on a post, played his sword and sang, "My long sword, let's go. I am not served with fish." Other people there told Lord Mengchang about it. Lord Mengchang said, "Serve him with fish. Give him the same food as that of other hangers-on." After some time, Feng Xuan played his sword again and sang, "My long sword, let's go. When I go out, I don't have a carriage." All the people there laughed at him and they told the lord about it. Lord Mengchang said, "Prepare a carriage for him. Treat him the way we treat those who have carriages." Then Feng Xuan took his sword to visit his friend in his carriage and told him, "Look, Lord Mengchang has accepted me as one of his hangers-on." Some time later, he played his sword and sang again, "My long sword, let's go. I don't feel settled here." All the other people then disdained him and considered him too greedy to be satisfied. Lord Mengchang asked Feng, "Do you have a family, Mr Feng?" He replied, "I have a mother who is very old." Lord Mengchang then sent some people to support his mother with enough food, cover all her expenses and make sure that she was short of nothing. Feng Xuan didn't sing again.

After that, Lord Mengchang put up a notice looking for an accountant. And he asked his hangers-on, "Who is familiar with accounting and able to collect money from my debtors in Xue for me?" Feng Xuan wrote his name on the notification and said, "I can do that." Lord Mengchang wondered about this and asked, "Who is this man?" The people around him said, "That's the one who used to sing 'let's go, my long sword'." Lord Mengchang smiled and said, "As expected, he is talented. I am sorry that I have not visited him." He then invited Feng to his home and apologised to him, "I am very tired of everyday trifles and often disturbed by some problems. Moreover, I am not born wise and am also very busy with government affairs. Thus I have offended you[20]. Yet you are not angry with me and still want to ask the debtors in Xue to settle their debts to me?" "Feng Xuan said, "Yes, I want to do that for you." Then he prepared his carriage, took his luggage and all the bills and said good bye to the lord. He asked, "After I collect the debts, shall I buy anything for you before I come back?" Lord Mengchang said, "You can buy something I don't have at home."

Feng Xuan drove to Xue and asked the officers in charge of Xue to summon all the debtors owing money to the lord to come to him to check their bills. After all the bills were checked, Feng Xuan stood up and issued a false order to exempt all the debts on behalf of the lord. Subsequently, he burnt all the bills. All the people there jubilantly and loudly expressed their gratitude to the lord.

Then Feng Xuan drove directly back to Qi and went to see the lord in the morning. Lord Mengchang wondered why he came back that quickly, so he got dressed to meet him and asked, "Have you collected all the debts? Why did you come back so quickly?" Feng Xuan said, "Yes, I have finished the task." "What did you buy for me then?" asked the lord. Feng Xuan replied, "You told me to buy something you don't have at home. I think your buildings are full of treasures, all the stalls are crowded with dogs and horses, and you also have many beautiful women in the harem. So I believe that the thing you don't have here is 'righteousness'. So I bought righteousness for you without asking for your permission." Lord Mengchang said, "How could you buy righteousness?" Feng Xuan replied, "Now you own Xue. However, you don't treat the people there as if they were your own children. On the contrary, you take advantage of them to make huge profit for yourself. I issued a false order in your name to exempt all their debts. Then I burnt all the bills, and the people celebrated and applauded you. That's how I bought righteousness for you." Lord Mengchang was not happy with him and said, "Hold your tongue!"

After a year, the king of Qi told Lord Mengchang, "I dare not employ the high-ranking court officials of our deceased king at my court." Lord Mengchang then resigned and went back to his fief-Xue. When he was still one hundred li from Xue, all the people, young and old, came to welcome him on the road. Lord Mengchang turned around and told Feng Xuan, "Now I witness first-hand the righteousness you bought for me." Feng Xuan said, "A sly hare digs three burrows for itself. Then it can merely survive. Now you only have one 'burrow', therefore, you are still not safe. Please allow me to dig two more 'burrows' for you." Lord Mengchang then gave him fifty carriages, five hundred jin of gold and sent him to travel to the west to consult with the king of Wei. Feng Xuan told the king, "Qi has dismissed its high-ranking court official Lord Mengchang – from office and thus provided him the chance to serve other states. The sovereign who employs him first will enrich his state and strengthen his military forces." Hence, Wei's king emptied out the highest position[21], appointed the former prime minister to be Commander-in-Chief and sent emissaries with one thousand jin of gold and one hundred chariots to invite Lord Mengchang to work for him. Feng Xuan drove back to the lord first and warned him, "One thousand jin of gold is a very generous gift. One hundred chariots show the prime importance of this diplomatic mission. The king of Qi should have heard about it." The emissaries of Wei came three times, but Lord Mengchang flatly refused them. When the king of Qi heard that, both he and his court officials were terrified. Then the king sent the Grand Tutor with one thousand jin of gold, two well decorated carriages, a sword and a letter to apologise to the lord. The letter said, "I am a person of no good. I have suffered from disasters caused by the deceased sovereigns at the ancestral temple and been cheated by devilish and toady court officials. As a result, I offended you. I know that I am not worthy to ask you to work for me again. But would you please come back to govern the people for the sake of our deceased sovereigns?" Feng Xuan cautioned Lord Mengchang, "Please ask for the utensils used in rituals to worship our deceased sovereigns and build an ancestral temple in Xue." After the ancestral temple was finished, Feng Xuan returned to report to Lord Mengchang and said, "Now all the three 'burrows' are ready. You can lay back and enjoy yourself." Lord Mengchang served as prime minister for dozens of years and was not involved in any problems because of Feng Xuan's strategies.

Notes:

During the Warring States Period, it was a fashion for the lords to keep advisors (Shi), and the Shi became a specific group in the society. The most famous Shi-keepers include Lord Mengchang of Qi, Lord Pingyuan of Zhao, Lord Xinling of Wei, Lord Chunshen of Chu (the lords above are called "the Four Lords in the Warring States Period"), Lord Lu Buwei of Qin, etc., all of whom kept thousands of retainers[22] to extend their political influence. This story is an account of Lord Mengchang's treating the hanger-on Feng Xuan with respect and Feng's rewarding him out of gratitude with offering advice and running service for him, winning Lord Mengchang a great reputation and benefits. Besides, Feng Xuan issued a false order to exempt all the debts of the people on behalf of the lord and burn all the bills, which has a great progressive meaning under the contemporary historical circumstance, though his original intention was to buy the hearts of the people for his lord. However, the story recorded in *Strategies of the Warring States* is a little different from that in *Records of the Grand Historian.*

3.2. Prose Works of the Hundred Schools of Thought

The prose of the *Zhuzi* (Philosophical Masters) refers to the writings of various schools of thought during the Spring and Autumn and Warring States periods, which articulated their respective doctrines. These works were a product of the "Hundred Schools of Thought" era. During this period, a rich and diverse body of prose emerged, representing the ideas of the "Nine Schools and Ten Traditions."

Sima Tan, in his *Discussion on the Essentials of the Six Schools* (*Lun Liu Jia Yao Zhi*), categorised the "literature of the Hundred Schools" into six major schools: Yin-Yang, Confucianism, Mohism, Logicians, Legalism, and Daoism. Later, Ban Gu, in the *Treatise on Literature* (*Yiwen Zhi*) in the *Book of Han* (*Han Shu*), further divided the various factions of *Zhuzi* prose into ten schools:

Confucianism, Daoism, Yin-Yang, Legalism, Logicians, Mohism, Diplomacy, Agrarianism, Miscellaneous, and Fiction.

The development of the prose classics of Hundred Schools of Philosophy can be divided into three phases:

1. *The Analects of Confucius* and *The Mozi* in the transition between the Spring and Autumn Period and the Warring States Period.
2. *The Mencius* and *The Zhuangzi* in the mid-Warring States Period.
3. *The Xunzi* and *The Han Feizi* in the late Warring States Period.

3.2.1. Confucius and The Analects

Confucius (551 BCE – 479 BCE), whose given name was Qiu and courtesy name was Zhongni, is widely known as Confucius. A native of the State of Lu, he was the founder of the Confucian school of thought and a renowned philosopher and educator of ancient China during the Warring States period.

In his youth, Confucius worked as a minor official, overseeing the management of warehouses and herding livestock. Later, he travelled to various states, including Song, Wei, Chen, and Cai, but was not appointed to any significant position. In his later years, he returned to the State of Lu, where he dedicated himself to writing and teaching. It is traditionally said that he edited and organised ancient classics such as the *Book of Poetry* (*Shi*), the *Book of Documents* (*Shu*), and the *Spring and Autumn Annals* (*Chunqiu*) etc.

As to *The Analects of Confucius*, *The Book of Han: Treatise on Literature* mentions that, "At that time, each of the disciples of Confucius had their version of the teaching of their master. After the death of Confucius, the disciples collected all these records and compiled into a book, hence the title *The Analects of Confucius*." The *Analects* specifically documents the words and actions of Confucius, serving as an important resource for studying his life and thoughts. The text consists of 20 chapters and was likely completed during the Spring and Autumn or Warring States period. It primarily records the dialogues and interactions between Confucius and his disciples, making it a classic work of the Confucian school.

3.2.1.1. Confucius' Thought

Confucius proposed the concept of *ren* (benevolence), which is the core of his entire philosophy. *Ren* represents the fundamental essence of *li* (rites/ritual), serves as the basic foundation of ethical and moral principles, encapsulates the essential truths of being human, and represents the highest ideal that people should strive to achieve. Confucius's introduction of the concept of *ren* was not accidental; it reflected, to a certain extent, the social developments of the Spring and Autumn period.

During this time, "thirty-six rulers were assassinated, fifty-two states were destroyed, and the number of feudal lords fleeing without being able to protect their ancestral lands was countless." In this context, Confucius, in response to the demands of society and to restore the "ritual and music system," proposed that people should regard others as "human." When his disciples asked him what *ren* meant, Confucius replied: "To love others." For people from the working class, "loving others" meant that rulers should also treat this class as "human" and care for them. Regarding the adjustment of relationships among rulers, it required them to "restrain oneself and return to *li*." Since the Western Zhou dynasty, rulers had adhered to governance through "ritual and music." By the time of Confucius, however, this system had "collapsed." According to Confucius, the reason for this collapse was that *li* had lost its internal spirit. Thus, Confucius said: "If a person lacks benevolence, what use is *li* to them? If a person lacks benevolence, what value does music have for them?"

Confucius further explained: "*Ren* means restraining oneself and returning to *li*. Once you achieve this, the world will recognise your benevolence. *Ren* depends on oneself; how could it depend on others?" Restraining personal desires and ensuring that one's words and actions align with the requirements of *li* constitutes *ren*. Once achieved, people across the world will recognise you as a virtuous person. There are two key aspects in Benevolence that should be paid close attention to: one is to "restrain oneself" (*keji*) that is, setting standards for oneself, extending one's consideration to others, and following the principle of "Do not impose on others what you do not desire for yourself." The other one is "Return to *li*" (*fuli*), that is to promote *ren*, there must be a standard, and this standard is provided by *li*, which regulates human behaviour. Thus, Confucius said: "Do not look at what is contrary to *li*, do not listen to what is contrary to *li*, do not speak what is contrary to *li*, and do not act in ways contrary to *li*." These teachings undoubtedly supported the rulers' governance.

In addition, Confucius pioneered private authorship and private education. His goal in education was to cultivate individuals who were "steadfast in their faith, eager to learn, and willing to sacrifice their lives for the right path." He advocated for "education without discrimination," emphasising open-mindedness, a love for learning, repeated study and reflection, and rejecting the pretense of knowledge. He said, "Learn without growing weary, teach without tiring," "Among three people, there is always something I can learn," and "To know what you know and admit what you do not know is true knowledge."

Clearly, Confucius placed great importance on learning. He proposed that the content of learning should encompass two main aspects: 1) Historical knowledge acquired through the study of ancient texts and institutional traditions, including classics such as the *Book of Songs* (*Shi*), *Book of Documents* (*Shu*), and *Music* (*Yue*); and 2) Practical knowledge gained from real-life experiences, which can be described as knowledge relevant to contemporary society.

On Learning

(From The Analects)

The Master said, To learn and at due times to repeat what one has learnt, is that not after all a pleasure? That friends should come to one from afar, is this not after all delightful? To remain unsoured even though one's merits are unrecognised by others, is that not after all what is expected of a gentleman?[23]

The Master said, He who by reanimating the Old can gain knowledge of the New is fit to be a teacher.[24]

The Master said, "He who learns but does not think, is lost." He who thinks but does not learn is in great danger.[25]

The Master said, I have listened in silence and noted what was said, I have never grown tired of learning nor wearied of teaching others what I have learnt. These at least are merits which I can confidently claim.[26]

The Master said, Only one who bursts with eagerness do I instruct; only one who bubbles with excitement, do I enlighten. If I hold up one corner and a man cannot come back to me with the other three, I do not continue the lesson.[27]

The Master said, The wise man delights in water, the Good man delights in mountains. For the wise move; but the Good stay still. The wise are happy; but the Good, secure.[28]

The Master said, Only when the year grows cold do we see that the pine and cypress are the last to fade.[29]

Zilu, Zeng Xi, Ran You, and Gongxi Hua in Attendance with Confucius[30]

(The Analects)

Zilu, Zeng Xi, Ran You, and Gongxi Hua were sitting with Confucius. The Master said, "Because I am older than you by a single day, do not think too highly of me. When you are at leisure, you often say, 'No one understands me.' But if someone were to understand you, what would you do?"

Zilu responded impetuously, "If I were in charge of a state with a thousand chariots, situated between powerful neighbouring states, suffering from military invasions and famine, within three years, I could make its people courageous and guide them to understand proper conduct."

Confucius smiled at him.

"Qiu (Ran You), what about you?"

Ran You replied, "If it were a state with a territory of sixty or seventy *li*, or fifty or sixty *li*, within three years, I could ensure the people were well provided for. As for rituals and music, I would leave that to the guidance of a superior man."

"Chi (Gongxi Hua), what about you?"

Gongxi Hua replied, "I do not claim to have the ability, but I would like to learn. In matters concerning ancestral temples or diplomatic gatherings, I would wear my ceremonial cap and gown and serve as a minor assistant."

"Dian (Zeng Xi), what about you?"

Zeng Xi was playing the zither softly, producing a few harmonious notes. He set the zither aside, stood up, and replied, "My aspirations differ from those of the other three."

Confucius said, "What harm is there in that? Each of you is merely expressing your own aspirations!"

Zeng Xi said, "In the late spring, when the spring clothes have been made, I would like to go out with five or six young men and six or seven boys. We would bathe in the Yi River, enjoy the breeze at the Altar of the Spirits of the Land, and return home singing."

Confucius sighed deeply and said, "I am with Dian!"

When the other three disciples had left, Zeng Xi remained behind. He asked, "What do you think of the aspirations of the other three?"

Confucius replied, "Each of them simply expressed their own ambitions, that is all."

Zeng Xi asked, "Why did you smile at Zilu?"

Confucius replied, "He spoke about governing a state with rituals, but his words lacked humility. That is why I smiled."

Zeng Xi asked, "Do you think Qiu's aspiration was not about governing a state?"

Confucius replied, "How can you say that a state of sixty or seventy *li*, or fifty or sixty *li*, is not a state?"

Zeng Xi asked, "Do you think Chi's aspiration was not about governing a state?"

Confucius replied, "Matters of ancestral temples and diplomatic gatherings —if these are not the responsibilities of a ruler, then whose, are they? If Chi cannot handle the minor tasks, who else can take on the major ones?"

3.2.2. Laozi and Dao De Jing

Laozi (c. 571–471 BCE), courtesy name Boyang, posthumously titled Dan, and also known as Li Er (as "Lao" and "Li" were homophones in ancient Chinese, and "Dan" and "Er" were synonyms), was a native of Qurenli in Lixiang, Ku County, Chu State. He served as the "Keeper of the Archives" during the Zhou dynasty, a position responsible for managing the royal library. Laozi is one of China's greatest philosophers and thinkers and is venerated as the founder of Daoism.

The *Dao De Jing*, also known as *Laozi*, is traditionally believed to have been written by Laozi at the request of Yin Xi, the commander of the Hangu Pass, when Laozi was leaving to escape political turmoil. The text, consisting of approximately 5,000 characters, is regarded as one of the three most influential works in Chinese thought, alongside the *Yi Jing* and *The Analects*.

The *Dao De Jing* primarily expounds the philosophy of naturalness and non-action (*wu wei*), incorporating simple dialectical ideas of transformation and opposition. Written in a terse, aphoristic style, the text uses rhythmic prose with parallelism and antithesis. Its concise and resonant rhetoric has inspired generations of writers. While its philosophy is profound and abstract, its literary form is vivid and expressive, making extensive use of metaphor and analogy. Despite its brevity, the *Dao De Jing* is a profound and expansive work, often regarded as the foremost text of Chinese philosophy. It centres on the principle of "Dao follows nature" and discusses how individuals can cultivate themselves to achieve contentment, simplicity, and humility. It also explores how people can navigate life through flexibility and harmony, how rulers can govern effectively through non-intervention and moral authority, and how societies can sustain themselves by aligning with the natural order of all things.

3.2.2.1 Laozi's Thought

Laozi's philosophy is centered on the concept of Dao (the Way), which serves as the foundation for understanding the universe, human behaviour, and governance. His ideas emphasise harmony with nature, simplicity, and the balance of opposites. Key aspects of his thought include:

1. The Concept of Dao as the Basis of Nature: Dao is the core of Laozi's philosophy. He stated, "Dao gives birth to One, One gives birth to Two, Two gives birth to Three, and Three gives birth to all things" (*Dao De Jing*, Chapter 42), asserting that all things originate from Dao. Laozi described Dao in several ways:

(a) **The Indefinable Nature of Dao:** "The shape of the shapeless, the image of the imageless" (*Dao De Jing*, Chapter 21). "It is elusive and intangible, yet within it is form" (*Dao De Jing*, Chapter 14).

(b) **Dao as the Origin of All Things:** "There was something undifferentiated and complete, born before heaven and earth, silent and empty, standing alone and unchanging, pervading everywhere and inexhaustible. It can be regarded as the mother of all things" (*Dao De Jing*, Chapter 25).

(c) **Dao as Non-Being:** "All things under heaven are born of being, and being is born of non-being" (*Dao De Jing*, Chapter 40). Here, "non-being" equates to Dao, which is the ultimate source of existence.

2. Dialectical Philosophy: "Reversal is the Movement of Dao": Laozi observed that both nature and human society are in constant flux, with opposing forces such as existence and non-existence, hardness and softness, strength and weakness, fortune and misfortune, and so on. He argued that these opposites are interdependent and interconnected:

(a) "Being and non-being produce each other; difficult and easy complete each other; long and short contrast with each other" (*Dao De Jing*, Chapter 2).

(b) "Misfortune is what fortune depends upon; fortune is what misfortune lurks beneath" (*Dao De Jing*, Chapter 58).

Laozi recognised that opposites transform into each other: "Straightness comes from bending, fullness comes from emptiness, renewal comes from wear" (*Dao De Jing*, Chapter 22). He emphasised achieving harmony through non-contention: "The sage does not contend, and no one in the world can contend with him" (*Dao De Jing*, Chapter 22).

His dialectical thinking also influenced military strategy, advocating for "using the unexpected in warfare" and emphasising flexibility, such as "to weaken something, first strengthen it; to take something, first give it" (*Dao De Jing*, Chapter 36). He highlighted the strength of softness: "Nothing in the world is softer than water, yet nothing is better at overcoming the hard and strong" (*Dao De Jing*, Chapter 78).

3. Epistemology of "Emptiness" and "Mystical Insight": Laozi denied that knowledge comes solely from sensory experience: "Without leaving the house, one can know the world; without looking out the window, one can see the Dao of heaven. The farther one goes, the less one knows" (*Dao De Jing*, Chapter 47). He advocated for intuitive understanding, urging people to "cleanse the mind and reflect inwardly" (*Dao De Jing*, Chapter 10).

From a ruler's perspective, he opposed enlightening the populace, promoting instead "abandoning wisdom and knowledge" to maintain social stability: "The ancient masters of Dao did not seek to enlighten the people but to keep them simple" (*Dao De Jing*, Chapter 65).

4. The Vision of a "Small State with Few People": Laozi idealised a primitive society: "A small country with few people, where the people have tools but do not use them, value life and do not migrate far. Though they have boats and carriages, they do not ride them; though they have armour and weapons, they do not display them. They return to tying knots for record-keeping" (*Dao De Jing*, Chapter 80). He envisioned a society where people "enjoy their food, take pleasure in their clothing, are content in their homes, and delight in their customs," reflecting a nostalgic and conservative outlook.

Dao Dejing

(Chapter 1)

"Tao that can be spoken of,
Is not the Everlasting (*ch'ang*) Tao.
Name that can be named,
Is not the Everlasting (*ch'ang*) name.

Nameless (*wu-ming*), the origin (*shih*) of heaven and earth;
Named (*yu-ming*), the mother (*mu*) of ten thousand things.
Alternate,
Non-being (*wu*) to name (*ming*) the origin (*shih*)
of heaven and earth;
Being (*yu*), to name (*ming*) the mother of ten thousand things.

Therefore, always (*ch'ang*) without desire (*wu-yü*),
In order to observe (*kuan*) the hidden mystery (*miao*);
Always (*ch'ang*) with desire (*yu-yü*),
In order to observe the manifestations (*chiao*).
Alternate,

Therefore, by the Everlasting (*ch'ang*) Non-Being (*wu*),
We desire (*yü*) to observe (*kuan*) its hidden mystery (*miao*).
By the Everlasting (*ch'ang*) Being (*yu*),
We desire (*yü*) to observe the manifestations (*chiao*).

These to issue from the same origin,
Though named differently,
Both are called the dark (*hsüan*).
Dark and even darker,
The door to all hidden mysteries (*miao*)."

3.2.3. Mo Di and *The Mozi*

Mozi (c. 468–376 BCE), whose given name was Di, was a native of the State of Lu (or possibly the State of Song) during the early Warring States period. He was a renowned Chinese thinker and the founder of the Mohist school of thought. Originally a court official in the State of Song, Mozi studied Confucianism in his youth but became disillusioned with its elaborate rituals and music. He then gathered disciples and established a philosophy that stood in opposition to Confucianism. Coming from a commoner background, Mozi worked as an artisan and was closely connected to ordinary people. His teachings reflected the interests of small-scale producers and private individuals, embodying the aspirations and demands of the general labouring class of his time.

The Mozi is a foundational text of the Mohist school, compiled by Mozi's disciples and their successors. In the Han dynasty, the book comprised 71 chapters, of which 53 remain today. The text mainly consists of records of Mozi's teachings but also includes contributions from later followers. Although primarily a philosophical work and an essential resource for studying Mozi and Mohist thought, many chapters are written in a literary style. These writings combine narrative, reasoning, and emotional expression, evolving into a more structured form of argumentative prose. The text employs various rhetorical techniques such as analogies, metaphors, and deductive reasoning, making its arguments clear, logically rigorous, and emotionally resonant, with simple and evocative language.

3.2.3.1. The Philosophy of Mozi

Mozi's philosophy centres on practical and ethical principles aimed at creating a harmonious and equitable society.

His core ideas include: 1) Universal Love and Mutual Benefit (*Jian Ai, Jiao Xiang Li*). Mozi proposed the concept of "universal love," advocating that individuals should care for and benefit one another without bias or discrimination. He believed that social harmony could be achieved if people treated others with the same regard they have for themselves and their families. This principle opposed the Confucian emphasis on hierarchical relationships and familial loyalty, promoting instead an egalitarian ethic of care and mutual support. 2) Opposition to Warfare (*Fei Gong*). Mozi strongly condemned aggressive wars, arguing that they bring immense suffering to the people and drain societal resources. He advocated for defensive strategies and peaceful coexistence among states, urging rulers to prioritise the welfare of their subjects over territorial expansion or personal glory. 3) Government by the Worthy (*Shang Xian*). Mozi emphasised the importance of meritocracy in governance. He believed that leaders should be chosen based on their virtue and ability rather than their social status or lineage. This "rule of the virtuous" aimed to ensure that governance served the interests of the people and maintained social order. 4) Frugality and Simplicity. Mozi criticised the extravagance of the ruling elite and proposed policies of frugality, such as "economising on resources" (*Jie Yong*) and "simplifying funerals" (*Jie Zang*). He argued that excessive spending on rituals, luxury, and lavish ceremonies diverted resources away from addressing the needs of the common people. 5) Practical Ethics and Action. Mozi's philosophy was deeply practical. He sought to apply his ideas to real-world problems, often traveling extensively to mediate disputes, prevent wars, and offer counsel to rulers. His teachings emphasised that ethical principles must be implemented through concrete actions to improve society.

Through these principles, Mozi envisioned a society where resources were distributed equitably, conflicts were minimised, and the well-being of all individuals was prioritised. His ideas provided a counterbalance to the dominant Confucian ideology of his time and remain influential in discussions of ethics, governance, and social justice.

In order to fulfil his political dream, Mozi spared no pains to travel across the states of Song, Wei, Chu and Qi, covering thousands of miles even with the risk of his own life. The following is the excerpt of *Gongshu* from *The Mozi*, fully embodying his thought of "Opposition to Warfare" and his efforts to carry it out.

Gongshu[31]

(The Mozi)

Gongshu Pan had completed for the State of Chu the construction of scaling ladders that were to be used to attack the State of Song. Hearing the news, Master Mozi decided to go to see Gongshu Pan in person. He left the State of Qi and walked for ten days and nights on foot before he finally arrived at Ying, the capital of Chu.

Seeing Master Mozi, Gongshu Pan asked: "What can I do for you?" Master Mozi replied: "Someone in the north insults me. I hope that you can lend me a hand and kill him." Gongshu Pan was displeased. Master Mozi said: "If you help me, I will give you fourteen pounds of gold." Gongshu Pan said: "I am a man of righteousness. I will never kill people." Master Mozi bowed again, saying: "Please listen to me. While I was in the north, I heard that you were making scaling ladders to be used to attack the State of Song. On what ground have you made such a plan? The State of Chu is a country with vast land and small population. It cannot be called wise to sacrifice what is sparse and strive for what is plenty. It cannot be called magnanimous to attack an innocent state like Song without any reason. It cannot be called loyal knowing that it is neither wise nor magnanimous to attack Song but at the same time unwilling to fight against it with rational arguments. It cannot be called effective to have fought against the war but failed to stop it. And you cannot be called insightful if you hold a principle that forbids the killing of few but allows the killing of many." Gongshu Pan was convinced of what Master Mozi said. Then Master Mozi asked: "Why don't you stop the war?" Gongshu Pan said:"I can't. I have promised the Lord of Chu." Master Mozi said: "Can you introduce me to the Lord of Chu?" Gongshu Pan agreed. Master Mozi saw the Lord of Chu and said: "If we see a man repeatedly doing the following things such as abandoning his elegant carriage and stealing his neighbour's broken cart, discarding his embroidery and finery and stealing his neighbour's coarse jacket, giving up his rice plus meat and stealing his neighbour's husks, what kind of a man would this be?" The Lord of Chu said: "A man like this must be addicted to kleptomania. Master Mozi continued: "The land of Chu amounts to one thou- sand square miles while the land of Song is only one hundred square miles. This is like the contrast between the elegant carriage and the bro ken cart. In the State of Chu, there is a big lake called Yun Meng in which abound rhinoceroses and deer. The fish, tortoises and crocodiles in the Yangtze and the Han Rivers are the richest in the world. In the State of Song there aren't even pheasants, hares, or small carps. This is like the contrast between rice plus meat and husks. In the State of Chu there are many tall trees such as pines, catalpas, nanmu and camphor trees while in the State of Song there isn't even a single tall tree. This is like the contrast between the embroidery and finery and the coarse jacket. Judging by what I said above, if the lord is to attack Song, you will degrade yourself into those who are addicted to kleptomania. And I think you will surely damage righteousness and gain nothing." The Lord of Chu said: "I see your point. But with the help of the scaling ladders Gongshu Pan has made for me, I can certainly capture Song."

Then Master Mozi went to see Gongshu Pan again. First, he unfastened his belt and took it as the city wall. Then he used some wood chips as weapons of defence. Gongshu Pan set up nine different weapons to attack the city. Master Mozi repulsed him nine times. When Gongshu Pan was at his wit's end in launching the attack, Master Mozi was still able to think out of the ways to ward off the enemy. Gongshu Pan had to acknowledge the defeat in the end, but he said: "I know how I can get the upper hand of you, but I won't say it to you." Master Mozi replied: "I know how you can get the upper hand of me, I won't say it to you either." The Lord of Chu was a little puzzled and asked what it was about. Master Mozi said: "Gongshu Pan intends to kill me. He thinks that once I am killed, the State of Song will become powerless in defence. But the truth is that more than three hundred of my disciples such as Qin Hua Li and others are already armed with weapons of defence I just used and are waiting on the city wall of Song for the invading army from Chu. You may kill me, but you couldn't win the battle." The Lord of Chu said: "Well, I will not attack Song anymore."

3.2.4 Meng Ke and *The Mencius*

Mencius (approximately 370 BCE – approximately 289 BCE), whose personal name was Ke and courtesy name was Ziyu, was a renowned thinker, politician, and educator during the Warring States period. He studied under Kong Ji, the grandson of Confucius, and was the most important representative of the Confucian school during the mid-Warring States period, following Confucius. Mencius travelled to various feudal states, including Liang (Wei), Qi, Song, and Teng, to advocate his ideas. However, his teachings were not adopted, and he did not gain political recognition. He then retired to write and teach his disciples.

The Mencius is a book that records the thoughts and actions of Mencius, compiled by his disciples and their successors. It is one of the most important classical works of Confucianism. After the Song Dynasty, *Mencius* was placed alongside *The Analects of Confucius* as one of the Four Books, along with *The Great Learning* and *The Doctrine of the Mean*. The book consists of fourteen chapters, each named after the first two or three characters in the opening sentence. Each chapter contains several sections, recording Mencius's political activities as well as his views on politics, philosophy, and education, making the content very rich.

Mencius is primarily a collection of sayings in a dialogue format, but compared to *The Analects of Confucius*, it shows a clear development, forming a style of argumentative writing. The text is strong in logical reasoning, lively in tone, and full of humour. Mencius was skilled in using metaphors and parables to vividly explain principles and distinguish right from wrong. The language is clear and straightforward, with a sharp and convincing tone, full of persuasive power. *Mencius* is not only an important academic work but also a collection of Chinese classical prose with distinctive literary features, which has had a profound influence on the development of literary prose in later generations.

3.2.4.1. Mencius's Philosophy

Mencius directly inherited Confucius's teachings and further developed them. The core of Mencius's philosophy is "benevolence and righteousness," "benevolent governance," "the way of kingship," and the idea of the people as the foundation of political power. While these ideas were initially aimed at maintaining the feudal system, they objectively contributed to the development of social economy, alleviating the people's burdens, and reducing the suffering caused by warfare at the time. Mencius's thoughts were relatively conservative. Politically, he advocated for the ways of the ancient rulers Yao and Shun. Although he also believed that "the people are most important, the state second, and the ruler is least important," he nevertheless looked down upon labour and manual workers. He said, "Without noble, there would be no way to govern the common people; without common people, there would be no way to support nobles." He also said, "Those who labour with their minds govern others, while those who labour with their bodies are governed by others; those who are governed by others feed on others, while those who govern others feed on others," and so on. These views served to justify the exploitation of the people by the feudal ruling class. His theories of "innate goodness," "conscience," and "natural ability" (the so-called "good conscience is knowing without thinking," and "natural ability is being able without learning") are also idealistic. The theory of innate goodness is the theoretical foundation of Mencius's benevolent governance. He believed that human emotions such as compassion, shame, dislike of evil, and the sense of right and wrong were the beginnings of the four virtues: benevolence, righteousness, propriety, and wisdom.

About the domination of Princes by Duke Huan of Qi and Duke Wen of Jin[32]

(The Mencius)

King Xuan of Qi asked Meng Ke: "Could you tell me about the domination of princes by Duke Huan of Qi and Duke Wen of Jin?"

Answered Meng Ke: "Disciples of Kong Qiu did not talk about the accomplishments of Duke Huan of Qi and Duke Wen of Jin, which have not been passed down, and have not heard of them. If you insist I would like to tell you. I'll tell you of the kingy way to unify the lands under heaven with virtuous force."

King Xuan of Qi asked: "With what kind of virtue can the lands under heaven be unified?" Answered Meng Ke: "Nobody can stop the unifying of lands under heaven only he does it by making the lives of the people stable."

King Xuan asked Meng Ke: "Can I, as a ruler, protect the people?" Answered Meng Ke: "Sure."

King Xuan asked: "How do you know that I can?"

Meng Ke said: "I was told by Hu He that one day you were sitting in the hall, when someone was leading an ox to pass by it. You asked him where the ox was going. He answered that he was going to consecrate a treat bell. Then you said to him: 'Let it go. I cannot bear its trembling. It was such an ox innocent going to the execution ground.' The man asked: 'Shall we omit the consecration of the bell?' And you answered: 'How it be omitted? Change it for a sheep.' I wonder whether it was true."

"It was sure," King Xuan said.

Meng Ke said: "You can unify all the lands under heaven by your kind heart. The ordinary people think you grudged an ox, but I know it was that you could not bear the sight."

Replied King Xuan: "Right. It is certain some people think like that. How should I grudge an ox though Qi is a small state? Actually, I could not bear to see its trembling, going to the execution with innocence, so I changed it for a sheep."

Meng Ke said: "It is not strange that the people consider that you are grudging. How should they understand the reason why you changed a large ox for a small sheep? what was the difference between the killing of an ox and a sheep if you felt sorry for the trembling ox led to death with innocence?"

The king said with laugh: "I don't know my psychology then. I did not grudge the expense to change an ox for a sheep. On hearing what you said, that my people thought I grudged the expense should be natural."

Meng Ke said: "It does not matter in their saying so you're not bearing your sight was out of your benevolent mind. You felt sorry for an ox's trembling, but not for a sheep's. A junzi is happy to find birds and animals alive, but never bears to see them die; and he cannot bear to eat their hearts while hearing their dying cries. So, he places his kitchen far from him."

After that King Xuan said in a pleasant way: "It was said in Shijng: 'I can guess what other's thought. What you said is right.' I just did it. I asked myself why I did it, but I couldn't answer. Your words made me suddenly see the light. But I don't understand the relation between my emotion and the way of unifying the lands."

Meng Ke replied: "Suppose someone said to you: 'I can lift three catties with my strength, but I can't lift one feather; I can see clearly the tiny hair of the autumnal birds with my sight, but I can't see a cartload of fagots in front of me.' Would you believe what he said?" King Xuan answered: "No, I don't believe him."

Meng Ke continued: "Now your good intention is kind to animals, but what is the reason why you cannot profit the common people? In this way, we say that one's failure to lift a feather is his not using strength, and one's failure to see a cartload of fagots in front of him is his not using eyesight. And the common people cannot live in a stable way is you're not extending your good intention. Therefore, your failure to rule by benevolent government is you're not doing it, and not that you're not being able to do it."

The king asked: "May you tell me the difference in appearance between not being willing to do and not being able to do?"

Meng Ke said: "You want someone to hold Taishan Mountain under his arms to leap over the North Sea, and he said that he could not; you want someone to break a branch from a tree for an old man, and he said that he could not. The former is that he is unable to do it; the latter, he will not do it. You're not practicing a benevolent government is different from not holding Taishan Mountain under the arms to leap over the North Sea, but the same as not breaking a branch from a tree for an old one. It is not that you are unable to do it, but you will not do it. Respect your aged parents, then respect all the aged; love your own children, then love all the children. The use of such principles makes the ruler unify the lands under heaven as easy as turning his palm over. It is said in Shijing: 'Treat your wife due respect, then extend it to your brothers, and to your family and your state, the above means that you should extend your kind mind to other things. You extend your favor from the near to the distant, then you can keep the lands under heaven in stable. Otherwise you cannot keep your wife and children. There is no secret of success for the ancient sages to overstep the ordinary people, but they were good at extending their fine deeds. Now your favor causes the animals happy, but the common people are still in bad condition. I don't know the reason. Weigh it in the balance, and you know its weight; measure it and you know its length. All things follow their laws and the human mind is no exception.

You may have a consideration. It is that you collect your forces, make your generals and soldiers risk their lives and excite resentment of the other states, then feel pleasure, don't you?" The king answered: "No. How should I get pleasure from that? What I did is to seek the satisfaction of my great desire."

Meng Ke asked the king: "May I know what your great desire is?" On hearing that, the king smiled without words. Meng Ke said: "Does the rich and delicate food not satisfy your taste? Does the light and warm clothing not satisfy your body? Or does the beautiful colour not satisfy your eyes? Or the touching sound does not satisfy your ears? Or your favourites do not follow your orders? All these may be supplied by your officials and how can you seek such a desire about them?"

The king said that his desire was not for them.

Meng Ke said: "I am now to know what your desire is. You want to enlarge the territory of your state and make the big states of Qin and Chu be respectful and faithful to your court. In this way you may lead the prince-states in the plains to reassure and pacify the minority nationalities around. That you take such a way to seek your desire is like to climb a tall tree to catch fish."

The king said: "Is it so bad as what you say?"

Meng Ke said: "It may be worse than that. If you climb a tree to catch fish, you will not invite calamity though you catch nothing. But you try your utmost to seek your desire with your whole heart, and the result will bring calamity to you."

The king wished to know the reasons.

Meng Ke asked him: "If the states of Zou and Chu fight, which of the two will win?" King Xuan said that the people of Chu would conquer.

Meng Ke said: "That is to say the small state cannot win the big one, and few soldiers cannot win many, and the weak cannot win the strong. The land within the four seas has 9 divisions and each has a thousand li square. All together of the state Qi is but one-ninth. If you take one part to conquer the eight parts, what is the difference between the battle of Zou and Chu? Now let's return to your desire. If you may practice benevolent government now, you can make the officials under heaven willing to serve the state of Qi, the farmers in the world willing to plough in the land of Qi, the merchants willing to do business in Qi's markets, and the people willing to travel through the roads of Qi. If the people who hate their sovereigns come to you and complain to you, who will be able to resist you?"

The king answered: "I am too muddle-headed to reach the state you said. I hope you may assist me to fulfil my ideal and teach me how to do in clear. I want to have a try though I am not alert and resourceful."

Meng Ke said: "Only the learned can walk the way with morality and ideals though without a certain livelihood. But the common people cannot keep the way with morality and ideals if they have not a certain livelihood. They will do whatever they like, violate the law and at last be punished. This is to use a trap to entice the people to go into. Where to find a benevolent sovereign who lets the common people walk right into trap? Therefore, the intelligent sovereign will help the people to make their livelihood, cause them to serve their parents above and support their wives and children below. In a good year, they may have enough food to eat and enough clothing to keep warm; in a bad year, they may not be hungry or cold to death. After this it is easy for the sovereign to lead the people to walk the way to benevolence and righteousness.

"Now, the people's livelihood regulated by sovereign is not sufficient to serve their parents above and support their wives and children below. In a good year, they labour hard all the year long, and in a bad year they could not escape death of hunger and cold. In this way, the people could not escape death. How could they have time to cultivate both propriety and righteousness? You, the great king, want to practice benevolent government. Why not begin with the root? To plant mulberry trees in a homestead with 5 mu of land, the people over fifty years may wear silk dress. To keep domestic fowls and animals in seasons, the people over seventy may eat flesh. To plough on the fields with hundred mu according to the right season, a family with eight members may not suffer hunger. To run schools in earnest and tell them the filial and fraternal duties, the men with grey hair will not walk on the way with burdens on their heads or backs. If the old men have silk clothing to wear and flesh to eat and the common people suffer neither from hunger nor cold, the king cannot be without being supported by the people."

Mencius: Gongsun Chou I

(Excerpt)

Gongsun Chou asked, "May I ask, what is meant by the 'vast and unyielding energy'?"

Mencius replied:"It is difficult to explain. This energy is supremely great and supremely strong. When nourished with uprightness and free from harm, it fills the space between heaven and earth. This energy aligns with righteousness and the Way; without these, it weakens. It is generated by the accumulation of righteousness, not something that can be acquired through sudden effort. If one's actions do not satisfy the heart, it will weaken.

"This is why I say Gaozi never truly understood righteousness, for he treated it as something external. One must actively cultivate it but not force it. Do not forget it in your heart, but do not artificially hasten its growth. Do not be like the man of Song:

"In Song, there was a man who was troubled that his crops were not growing, so he pulled them up to help them grow. Exhausted, he returned home and said to his family, 'I am worn out today; I have helped the crops grow.' His son rushed out to see and found that the crops had withered.

"Few in the world refrain from 'helping the crops grow.' Those who think it is useless and abandon them are those who do not weed their crops. Those who 'help them grow' are those who pull them up. Not only does this not help, but it also harms them."

Gongsun Chou asked, "What is meant by understanding words?"

Mencius replied: "To discern deceitful words, one must understand their distortions. To discern excessive words, one must understand their traps. To discern wicked words, one must understand their deviations. To discern evasive words, one must understand their limitations.

"When such words arise in the heart, they harm governance. When they manifest in governance, they harm affairs. If a sage were to rise again, he would certainly agree with my words."

3.2.5. Zhuangzi and the *Zhuangzi*

Zhuangzi (approximately 369 BCE – approximately 286 BCE), whose personal name was Zhou, was a native of the State of Song. He once served as a minor official in Qiyuan, Meng. From his philosophical system and political views, Zhuangzi can be seen as a philosopher representing the declining social classes. Deeply dissatisfied with the turbulent and transformative social realities of the late Warring States period, Zhuangzi lacked the power to change them and instead chose a path of passive withdrawal from the world.

Zhuangzi despised the powerful and wealthy throughout his life, was indifferent to fame and fortune, and advocated for "governing by non-action," leaving everything to fate and abandoning all struggles in life. He adopted a nihilistic attitude toward all things in the world. In his philosophy, Zhuangzi excessively emphasised the relativity of things, denying the essential differences between them. He pursued a life free from notions of right and wrong, gain and loss, honour and disgrace, aiming for carefree detachment. His attitude toward life was extremely unserious, cynical, and dismissive. He believed that distinctions such as right and wrong, good and evil, big and small, or longevity and early death were all the same.

Zhuangzi's ideas of "non-action," "nihilism," and pessimism had a significant negative influence on later disillusioned and destitute scholars. He sought ways for individuals to achieve self-liberation and self-preservation in a heavy and dark society. For Zhuangzi, the ideal society was the chaotic state of ancient times, where all artificial systems and cultural measures were seen as violations of human nature. To pursue the "Dao," one must abandon all worldly knowledge, fame, and status. However, his disdain for the powerful and refusal to cooperate with the ruling class also had some positive impact during specific historical periods.

The Zhuangzi is another masterpiece of Taoism, consisting of 33 chapters, among which the 7 chapters in *Inner Chapters* are believed to be written by Zhuang Zhou himself, while the 15 chapters in *Outer Chapters* and the 11 chapters in *Miscellaneous Chapters* are believed to be written by his disciples and the later followers. While the prose canon Zhuangzi belongs to the category of philosophical works, rich literary colour and romantic elements pervade the entire book, having a unique style in the Pre-Qing literature. Instead of abstract moralisation, the writer used a great many fables as the origin of his reasoning to illustrate his philosophical and political viewpoints. The language is poignant, humorous, visualisable, vivid and appealing.

A Butcher was Carving a Bullock[33]

(The Zhuangzi)

A butcher was carving a bullock for Lord Wenhui. At every touch of his hand, every move of his shoulder, every stamp of his foot and every nudge of his knee, there came the sound of slicing the flesh and wielding the knife - a perfect rhythm to the Dance of Mulberry Trees and a perfect tune of the music in King Yao's time.

Lord Wenhui remarked, "Oh, splendid! That you have such a masterful skill!"

The butcher put down his knife and responded, "What I love is Tao, which is much more splendid than my skill. When I first began to carve a bullock, I saw nothing but the whole bullock. Three years later, I no longer saw the bullock as a whole but in parts. Now I work on it by intuition and do not look at it with my eyes. My visual organs stop functioning while my intuition goes its own way. In accordance with the natural grain', I cleave along the main seams and thrust the knife into the big cavities. Following the natural structure of the bullock, I never touch veins or tendons, much less the big bones! A good butcher changes his knife once a year because he cuts the flesh; an ordinary butcher changes his knife once a month because he hacks the bones. Using this knife for nineteen years, I have carved thousands of bullocks, but the edge of my knife is still as sharp as if it had just come from the whetstone. There are crevices between the joints, but the edge of my knife is very thin. When I insert the thin edge of my knife into these crevices, there is plenty of room for it to pass through That is why, after nineteen years, the edge of my knife is still as sharp as if it had just come from the whetstone. Nevertheless, whenever I come to a complicated spot and see that there are difficulties here, I proceed with great caution. I keep my eyes on what I am doing and wield the knife slowly. With a very slight movement of the knife, I cut off the flesh - it falls to the ground like a clod of earth. Holding the knife in my hand, I stand there, looking proudly around. Then I clean the knife and put it carefully away."

Lord Wenhui said, "Splendid! From what you just said, I've learned how to keep good health."

3.2.6. Xunzi and *The Xunzi*

Xunzi (birth and death years unknown), whose given name was Kuang, was respectfully referred to as "Xun Qing"[34] by his contemporaries. During the Han dynasty, to avoid the taboo of Emperor Xuan's name (Liu Xun), he was renamed "Sun Qing." He was a native of the State of Zhao and a prominent thinker and writer during the Warring States period. Xunzi lectured in the State of Qi, and the renowned Legalist figures Han Fei and Li Si were among his students. He later travelled to the states of Qin and Chu, where the prime minister of Chu, Chunshen Jun, appointed him as the magistrate of Lanling (modern-day Shandong Province). After being dismissed from office, Xunzi settled in Lanling and devoted himself to writing.

The book *Xunzi* comprises 32 chapters, most of which were authored by Xun Kuang during the late Warring States period. The last six chapters are generally considered to be compilations by his disciples. This work is a significant academic text among the pre-Qin philosophical classics. *Xunzi* moves beyond the aphoristic style of earlier writings, evolving into thematic essays. These essays are longer, meticulously organised, logically rigorous, precise in judgment, and highly persuasive. The text is notable for its eloquence, abundant use of metaphors, and frequent employment of parallelism. Its rhythmic language makes it particularly engaging to read.

3.2.6.1. Xunzi's Thought

Xunzi's philosophy inherits the tradition of Confucianism but includes critical evaluation and development. It also incorporates certain elements of Legalist thought to establish his unique ideological system. His most valuable contribution lies in his materialistic worldview. Xunzi denied the existence of divine mandates and spirits, asserting that "the nature of heaven is constant; it does not persist for Yao nor perish for Jie" He proposed the idea that "man can conquer nature."

On the issue of human nature, Xunzi opposed Mencius' ideas of "innate knowledge," "innate ability," and the "inherent goodness of human nature." Instead, he put forward the concept of "human nature is evil." By "human nature is evil," Xunzi meant that humans are naturally driven by various desires, which, if left unchecked, would inevitably lead to chaos and conflict. In contrast to Mencius' a priori view of "born with knowledge," Xunzi emphasised the importance of postnatal learning. He believed that through continuous learning, later generations could surpass their predecessors and achieve progress. He stated, "Indigo is extracted from the blue plant but is bluer than the plant itself; ice is formed from water but is colder than water." Xunzi also recognised the significance of practice in gaining understanding. He remarked, "If one does not climb a high mountain, one cannot know how high the heavens are; if one does not approach a deep stream, one cannot know how thick the earth is."

In addition to his theoretical writings, Xunzi also composed rhapsodies and poems. His works include five pieces: *Rituals* (*Li*), *Knowledge* (*Zhi*), *Clouds* (*Yun*), *Silkworms* (*Can*), and *Admonitions* (*Zhen*). These are written in a question-and-answer format, where riddles are posed in the first half and solved in the second half. Structurally, his *Rhapsody Chapters* are considered a precursor to the Han rhapsodies (*fu*). Moreover, his *Cheng Xiang Chapter* uses folk songs to express his political ideas.

An Exhortation to Learning[35]

(Excerpt)

The gentleman says: "Learning must never be concluded."

Though blue dye comes from the indigo plant, it is bluer than indigo Ice is made from water, but it is colder than water. A piece of wood straight as a plumb line can, by steaming, be made pliable enough to bend into the shape of a wheel rim, so its curvature will conform to the com pass. Yet, even though it is then allowed to dry out completely in the sun, it will not return to its former straightness because the process of steaming has effected this change in it.

So, too, wood that has been marked with the plumb line will be straight and metal that has been put to the whetstone will be sharp. In broadening his learning, the gentleman each day examines himself so that his aware- ness will be discerning and his actions without excess.

I once spent a whole day in thought, but it was not so valuable as a moment in study. I once stood on my tiptoes to look out into the distance, but it was not so effective as climbing up to a high place for a broader vista. Climbing to a height and waving your arm does not cause the arm's length to increase, but your wave can be seen farther away. Shouting downwind does not increase the tenseness of the sound, but it is heard more distinctly. A man who borrows a horse and carriage does not improve his feet, but he can extend his travels 1,000 li. A man who borrows a boat and paddles does not gain any new ability in water, but he can cut across rivers and seas. The gentleman by birth is not different from other men; he is just good at "borrowing" the use of external things.

If you accumulate enough earth to build up a high hill, rain and wind will flourish because of it. If you accumulate enough water to fill a chasm, dragons and scaly dragons will be born within it. If you accumulate enough good to make whole your inner power, a divine clarity of intelligence will be naturally acquired and a sage like mind will be fully realised. Accordingly, if you do not accumulate paces and double paces, you will lack the means to reach 1,000 li, and if you do not accumulate small streams, you will have no way to fill a river or sea. Even a famous thoroughbred like Qiji cannot cover ten paces in a single stride. But in ten yokings even a worn-out nag can. Its achievement consists in its not giving up.

If you start carving but give up, you cannot cut even a rotting piece of wood in two. Yet if you carve away and never give up, even metal and stone can be engraved. Though the earthworm has neither the advantage of claws and teeth nor the strength of muscles and bones, it can eat dust and dirt above ground and drink from the waters of the Yellow Springs below, because its mind is fixed on a constant end. The crab has eight legs and two claws; still if there is no hole made by an eel or snake, it will have no safe place to live, because its mind moves in every direction at once.

3.2.7. Han Fei and *The HanFeizi*

Han Fei (circa 280–233 BCE) was a native of the state of Han and a student of Xunzi. Living during the late Warring States period, he was a major synthesiser of Legalist thought. Han Fei repeatedly submitted proposals to the King of Han advocating for reforms, but his advice was not heeded. Later, he entered the state of Qin, where the First Emperor of Qin initially admired his writings greatly. However, Han Fei's classmate, Li Si, fearing that Han Fei might be favoured and jeopardise his own position, framed him, leading to Han Fei's death in prison.

The work *Han Feizi*, comprising 55 chapters, was written by Han Fei during the late Warring States period and is a representative text of the Legalist school. The essays in *Han Feizi* are characterised by clear viewpoints, incisive arguments, and sharp prose. Many of the chapters use concise and humorous fables to illustrate principles. Longer pieces, such as *The Five Vermin* (*Wu Du*), which is nearly 7,000 characters long, mark the maturation of pre-Qin political prose.

3.2.7.1. Han Feizi's Philosophy

Han Fei summarised and further developed the Legalist theories of earlier thinkers such as Li Kui, Wu Qi, and Shang Yang. He proposed the integration of *fa* (law), *shu* (methods), and *shi* (power) to establish a unified, centralised autocratic state for the emerging landlord class. This provided a strong theoretical foundation and ideological tool for consolidating and advancing the policies of the landlord class.

> **Law (*fa*)**: Refers to the rules and regulations that uphold the orders of the ruling class. Han Fei advocated "teaching by law" and "taking officials as teachers," emphasising generous rewards and severe punishments.

Methods (*shu*): Denotes the techniques and strategies for identifying deceit, eliminating flattery, and effectively selecting and managing capable officials.

Power (*shi*): Represents the authority and influence of the ruler.

3.2.7.2. Historical Perspective

Han Fei believed that history is continuously evolving and that times are always advancing. Therefore, societal life, political systems, and laws should change accordingly. He opposed the Confucian reverence for the ancient kings and their retrogressive ideals, instead proposing the theory of "different times, different affairs" and "changing measures with changing circumstances." This reflects the progressive spirit of the emerging landlord class in reforming outdated systems.

He also proposed policies to "enrich the state through agriculture and defend it with soldiers," encouraging farming and warfare. These policies played a positive role in consolidating the rule of the emerging landlord class and promoting economic development. However, Han Fei was undoubtedly a politician representing the interests of the landlord class, and his theories, as part of the ideology of an exploitative class, also had their class-based and historical limitations.

The Han Feizi

(Excerpt)

The Man Who Pretended He Could Play Reed Pipes[36]

When Prince Xuan of Qi called for reed pipe music, he would have three hundred men playing at the same time. Then a scholar named Nanguo asked for a place in the orchestra, and the prince, taking a fancy to him, gave him a salary large enough to feed several hundred men. After Prince Xuan's death, however, Prince Min came to the throne, and he liked solo performances. There upon the scholar fled.

Buying Shoes[37]

A man of the state of Zheng wanted to buy a pair of shoes. He measured his foot and put the measurement on a chair. When he set out for the market, he forgot to bring it along. It was after he had found the pair he wanted that this occurred to him.

"I forgot the measurement," said he.

He went home to get it, but when he returned, the market had broken up and he did not get his shoes after all.

"Why didn't you try on the shoes with your feet?" He was asked.

"I'd rather trust the measurement than trust myself."

The Man Who Sold Spears and Shields[38]

In the state of Chu lived a man who sold shields and spears.
"My shields are strong," he boasted, "that nothing can pierce them. My spears are so sharp that there is nothing they cannot pierce."
"What if one of your spears strikes one of your shields?" someone asked him.
The man had no answer to that.

IV. QU YUAN AND *THE CHU CI*

4.1. Qu Yuan and *The Chu Ci*

Qu Yuan (approximately 340 BCE – approximately 287 BCE), whose given name was Ping and courtesy name was Yuan, was a great Romantic poet in Chinese literary history. He lived during the late Warring States period and was a native of the State of Chu. At that time, Chinese society was on the verge of abolishing feudal fragmentation and establishing a unified, centralised state. Qu Yuan's greatness lies in his ability to reflect these historical changes through his uniquely created artistic forms.

Qu Yuan was born into an aristocratic family. In his youth, he demonstrated exceptional talent and earned the trust and favor of King Huai of Chu. Qu Yuan's life spanned the reigns of three monarchs: King Wei, King Huai, and King Qingxiang. His political activities were primarily concentrated during the 30-year reign of King Huai.

In politics, Qu Yuan advocated for "benevolent governance," which involved improving domestic policies, caring for the people, valuing their welfare, promoting capable individuals, and implementing reforms to strengthen the state. In diplomacy, he supported forming alliances with the State of Qi to resist the State of Qin. However, these proposals faced opposition from conservative and corrupt forces within Chu, led by the aristocratic group under Shangguan Dafu Jin Shang. These factions marginalised, attacked, and slandered Qu Yuan, leading King Huai to distance himself from him and eventually exile him to the upper reaches of the Han River.

During King Huai's later years, after Chu suffered military and diplomatic failures, Qu Yuan was briefly recalled. However, after King Huai's death in 299 BCE while in Qin, King Qingxiang ascended the throne. Qu Yuan once again fell victim to aristocratic machinations and was exiled to the regions around the Yuan and Xiang Rivers in southern China. In 278 BCE, when Qin forces captured Chu's capital, Ying, Qu Yuan, devastated by the worsening state of his country, committed suicide by drowning himself in the Miluo River.

Qu Yuan's Works

According to *The Book of Han: Treatise on Literature*, Qu Yuan's works comprised 25 pieces: *Li Sao*, *Nine Songs*, *The Great Unity, God of the Eastern Sky*, *The Lord of the East*, *The Lord within the Clouds*, *The God of the Xiang*, *The Lady of the Xiang*, *The Greater Master of Fate*, *The Lesser Master of Fate*, *The River Earl*, *The Mountain Spirit*, *Hymn to the Fallen*, *Honouring the Dead*, *Nine Pieces: Grieving I Make My Plaint*, *Crossing the River*, *A Lament for Ying*, *The Outpouring of Sad Thoughts*, *Embracing Sand*, *Thinking of a Fair One*, *Alas for the Days Gone By*, *In Praise of the Orange-Tree*, *Grieving at the Eddying Wind*, *Questions to Heaven*, *Summons of the Souls*, *Divination*, *The Fisherman*, etc.

Among these, some works' authenticity remains debated in academic circles. However, *Nine Chapters* (eleven pieces), *Nine Songs* (nine pieces), *Li Sao*, *Heavenly Questions*, and *Summoning the Soul* are widely recognised as Qu Yuan's genuine works. On the other hand, *Divination Dwelling* and *The Fisherman* are generally not considered his creations. These works reflect the conflicts and tensions between the old and new societal forces of the time. Qu Yuan stood on the side of progress, fighting against the conservative and corrupt powers of society.

Li Sao

Qu Yuan's most representative work is *Li Sao*, and as a result, later generations often use the word "Sao" to represent all of Qu Yuan's works. In what circumstances did Qu Yuan write *Li Sao*? At that time, he had held important positions in the Chu Kingdom and had earned the trust of King Huai of Chu. However, due to slander and accusations from the old noble factions, he was eventually alienated by King Huai. After repeated struggles, Qu Yuan became increasingly isolated. To express his progressive ideals, his loyalty to the state, and his noble character, and to vent his anger, he wrote *Li Sao*. The term "Li Sao" means encountering adversity. From the poem, it is also clear that when he wrote this great work, he had not yet left the political centre of Chu, Yingdu (roughly present-day Jiangling in Hubei).

Why was Qu Yuan attacked by the old noble factions of Chu? It was because Qu Yuan wanted to implement "benevolent governance" in Chu to strengthen the state. This required political reform, which, in simple terms, mainly involved the rule of law and the promotion of virtuous and capable individuals. However, these two reforms would prevent the old nobility from breaking the law and acting as they pleased, and would also challenge their hereditary privileges. As a result, they naturally saw Qu Yuan as a thorn in their side. *Li Sao* is the longest lyrical poem in Chinese classical literature and a brilliant, timeless masterpiece of romanticism.

The Chu Ci

Chuci (The Songs of Chu) is a form of poetry created by the people of the Chu state during the Warring States period, with Qu Yuan as its representative. It is a new poetic form that followed the *Book of Songs* (*Shijing*). The name *Chuci* is of uncertain origin. In the Western Han dynasty, Liu Xiang compiled the works of Qu Yuan and other writers who imitated him, and named the collection *Chuci*. In the *Book of Han: Treatise on Literature* by Ban Gu of the Eastern Han dynasty, Qu Yuan's works were referred to as "fu" (rhapsodies), so *Chuci* came to be known as "fu" as well. Later generations often use Qu Yuan's *Li Sao* to represent *Chuci*, which is why *Chuci* is also called "Chuci" or "Sao" (Sao-style poetry).

Compared to the *Book of Songs*, *Chuci* is longer in length, with lines of varying lengths, and displays a strong sense of romanticism and regional characteristics. After Qu Yuan, other notable writers include Song Yu, Tang Le, and Jing Cha. According to the *Book of Han: Treatise on Literature*, Song Yu wrote sixteen "fu" works. The titles of these works are no longer precisely known, but *Jiu Bian* (Nine Discourses) is generally accepted as one of Song Yu's works. As for the works of Tang Le and Jing Cha, they are even more difficult to verify. Throughout history, there have been many studies on Qu Yuan and *Chuci*, with some important commentaries including Wang Yi's *Chuci Zhangju* from the Eastern Han, Song Hongxingzu's *Chuci Buzhu*, and Zhu Xi's *Chuci Jizhu* from the Southern Song dynasty.

Sorrow after Departure[39]

Descendant of High Sunny King, oh!
My father's name shed sunny ray.
The Wooden Star appeared in spring, oh!
When I was born on Tiger's Day.

My father saw my birthday bright, oh!
He gave me an auspicious name.
My formal name was Divine Right, oh!
I was also called Divine Flame.

I have so much beauty inside, oh!
And add to it a style ornate.
I weave sweet grass by riverside, oh!
Into a belt with orchids late.

Like running water years will pass, oh!
I fear time and tide wait for none.
At dawn I gather mountain grass, oh!
At dusk I pick secluded one.

The sun and the moon will not stay, oh!
Spring will give place to autumn cold.
Grass will wither and trees decay, oh!
I fear that beauty will grow old.

Give up the foul while young and strong, oh!
Why won't you my lord, change your style and way?
Ride your fine steed, gallop along, oh!
I'll go before you lest you stray.

Three ancient kings were pure and true, oh!
Around them flocked all fragrant things
Pepper and cassia also grew, oh!
Sweet orchids were formed into rings.

The first two monarchs were so bright, oh!
That they followed and gained the way.
The two last kings were in sad plight, oh!
They sought bypaths and came to bay

Your partisans love stolen pleasure, oh!
Their way is dark, with perils sown.
Do I dread my personal woe? oh!
I fear the royal cab o'erthrown.

I run before it and behind, oh!
I wish you would follow your sire.
To my loyalty you're unkind, oh!
You heed slander and burst in fire.

With frank advice you won't comply, oh!
I endure and cannot have done.
Be my witness, Ninth Heaven high, oh!
I've done all for you Sacred One.

The word you've given still remains, oh!
But you go back on it and stray.
Departure causes me no pains, oh!
Of your fickleness what to say?

I grow spring orchids in fields nine, oh!
And a hundred acres of clover.
I plant peonies line by line, oh!
Mixed with fragrant grass all over.

I'd see their leaves green and blooms red, oh!
And reap the fruit in season due.
I am not grieved they're withered, oh!
But they decay 'mid weeds in view.

All vie in avarice and greed, oh!
Their lust is never gratified.
Judging others by their own deed, oh!
They're jealous-minded and green-eyed.

I am not so eager as they, oh!
To run after wealth here and there.
Old age draws near from day to day, oh!
Have I a name lasting and fair?

From magnolia I drink the dew, oh!
And feed on aster petals frail.
My spirit being pure and true, oh!
Do I care to grow lank and pale?

I string clover with gathered vine, oh!
And fallen stamens thereamong.
I plait cassia tendrils and twine, oh!
Some strands ofivy green and long.

I'll imitate the ancient sage, oh!
Not the vulgar world of today.
Though I displease the modern age, oh!
I will follow the ancient way.

I sigh and wipe away my tears, oh!
I'm grieved at a life full of woes.
Good and just, I hear only jeers, oh!
Morning and night I suffer blows.

I make a belt of grasses' sweet, oh!
And add to it clovers and thymes.
My heart tells me it's good and meet, oh!
I won't regret to die nine times.

The Sacred One neglects his duty, oh!
He will not look into my heart.
The slanderers envy my beauty, oh!
They say I play licentious part.

The vulgar praise what is unfair, oh!
They reject common rules with pleasure
They like the crooked and not the square, oh!
Accommodation is their measure.

Downcast, depressed and sad am I, oh!
Alone I bear sufferings long.
I would rather in exile die, oh!
Than mingle with the vulgar throng.

The eagle cleaves alone the air, oh!
Since olden days it has been fleet.
The round cannot fit with the square, oh!
Who go different ways ne'er meet.

I curb my will and check my heart, oh!
Endure reproach as well as blame.
I'd die to play a righteous part, oh!
The ancient sages would bear no shame.

Regretting I've gone a wrong way, oh!
I hesitate and will go back.
Before I go too far astray, oh!
I wheel my cab to former track.

I loose my horse by waterside, oh!
At Pepper Hill I take a rest.
I won't advance to turn the tide, oh!
I will retire to mend my vest.

I'll make a coat with lotus leaves, oh!
And patch my skirt with lilies white.
Unknown, I care not if it grieves, oh!
My heart will shed fragrance and light.

I raise my headdress towering high, oh!
And lengthen pendants sparkling long.
My fragrance 'mid the dirt won't die, oh!
My brilliancy ne'er wanes thereamong.

I look around and feast my sight, oh!
On scenes north and south, east and west.
My pendants seem all the more bright, oh!
My fragrance outshines all the rest.

All men delight in what they please, oh!
Alone I always love the beauty.
My body rent, my heart at ease, oh!
Can I change and neglect my duty?

The Goddess of the Mountain[40]

(Nine Songs 9)

In mountains deep, oh! looms a fair lass,
In ivy leaves, oh! girt with sweet grass.
Amorous looks, oh! and smiling eyes,
For such a beauty, oh! there's none but sighs.

Laurel flags spread, oh! over fragrant cars
Drawn by leopards, oh! dotted with stars.
Orchids as belt, oh! and crown above,
She plucks sweet blooms, oh! for her dear love.

The bamboo grove, oh! obscures the day;
I come too late, oh! hard is the way.
Standing alone, oh! on mountain proud,
I see below, oh! a sea of cloud.

The day is dark, oh! as dark as night;
The east wind blows, oh! rain blurs the sight.
Waiting for you, oh! I forget hours.
Late in the year, oh! who'd give me flowers?

Amid the mountains, oh! I seek herbs divine,
Here rock on rock, oh! there vine on vine.
Longing for you, oh! I forget to return.
Are you too busy, oh! for me to yearn?

Amid the mountains, oh! I feel not at ease;
I drink from springs, oh! beneath pine trees.
From missing you, oh! I am not free;
I doubt if you, oh! are missing me.
Thunder rumbles, oh! rain blurs the eye;
At night apes wail, oh! and monkeys cry.
Winds sigh and sough, oh! leaves fall in showers.
Longing for you, oh! how to pass lonely hours!

NOTES

1 《精卫填海》, Jingwei Fills the Sea,《山海经（北山经）》, *The Classic of Mountains and Seas: The Classic of the Northern Mountains*, translated into modern Chinese by Chen, Chengjin and into English by Wang, Hong and Zhao, Zheng, Hunan People's Publishing House (2010, 97).

2 Ibid., p. 233.

3 《女娲炼石补天》, from 《淮南子故事》Stories from Huananzi, compiled by Jin, Yu and translated by Han, Jianghong and Hu, Zuoyou, Anhui People's Publishing House (2008, 257).

4 Ibid., p. 258-259.

5 The Three August Ones refer to the legendary Three Rulers in ancient China, namely, Sui Ren, Fu Xi and Shen Nong, "三皇" in Chinese.

6 Luo, Zhiye.《伐檀》, Woodcutter's Song, in 《〈诗经〉,〈论语〉,〈孟子〉英译》, English Translation of the *Book of Poetry*, *The Analects*, and *The Mencius*. A compilation of Confucius and Mencius, and translated by Luo, Zhiye. Southeast University Press (2017, 31).

7 Xu, Yuanchong.《硕鼠》, Large Rat 《画说诗经》 *The Book of Poetry in Pictures*. Translated by Xu, Yuanchong, China Publishing Group, China Translation Publishing House (2021, 144).

8 Luo, Zhiye. (2017, 37-38).

9 Xu, Yuanchong. (2021, 4).

10 Xu, Yuanchong. (Transl.) 《诗经》*Book of Poetry*. Beijing: China Foreign Translation Publishing House (2009, 93-94).

11 Ibid., p. 21.

12 Ibid., p. 18.

13 Ibid., p.392

14 "Jing" (经) is the original texts recorded in *Spring and Autumn Annals.*

15 "Zhuan" (传) is the annotation or supplement made by Zuo Qiuming.

16 ½ kilometres.

17 Luo, Zhiye 罗志野. (Transl.)《曹刿论战》, "Cao Gui's Strategies on War" in 《左传英译》, *The Commentary of Zuo* Originally compiled by Zuo, Qiuming . Jinan: Shandong University Press (2017, 43-44).

18 Zhai, Jiangyue. 翟江月 (Transl.)《邹忌讽齐王纳谏》, "Zou Ji Persuades the King of Qi to Accept Criticism" in《战国策 I》*Strategies of the Warring States,* vol. 8, Guangxi Normal University Press. (2008, 351-355).

19 Ibid., (2008, 431-439).

20 It refers to his having not visited him in person.

21 It refers to an opening for prime minister.

22 These were guests (门客, 食客) employed by noblemen, or a powerful landlords to provide varied services ranging from offering advise, doing clerical work, acting as bodyguards, mercenaries and even spies.

23 Waley, Arthur. (Transl.). 《论语》*The Analects,* Foreign Language Teaching and Research Press, (1998, 3).

24 Ibid., p. 17.

25 Ibid., p. 19.

26 Ibid., p. 79.

27 Ibid., p. 81.

28 Ibid., p. 75.

29 Ibid., p. 115.

30 Ibid., p. 139-143. Translation varies with that of Waley's in terms of pinyin and a few other aspects.

31 Wang Rongpei 汪榕培 and Wang Hong 王宏 (Transl.)《公输》 "Gongshu" in 《墨子》 *Mozi* . Changsha: Hunan People's Publishing House. (2006, 485-489).

32 Luo, Zhiye. (Transl.)《齐桓晋文之事》 "About the domination of Princes by Duke Huan of Qi and Duke Wen of Jin" in 《〈诗经〉、〈论语〉、〈孟子〉英译》*English rendition of The Book of Poetry, The Analects, and The Mencius.* Dongnan University Press (2017, 170-173).

33 Wang, Rongpei 汪榕培. (Transl)《庖丁解牛》 "A Butcher was Carving a Bullock" in 《庄子（上）》, *Zhuangzi* volume 1, Shanghai: Shanghai Translation Publishing House (2021, 67-71).

34 卿：Qing, a minister or a high official in the ancient times.

35 Knoblock, John. (Transl.) 《劝学》 "An Exhortation to Learning" in 选自《荀子》 *Xunzi.* Changsha: Hunan People's Publishing House (1999, 3-11).

36 "滥竽充数" "Masquerading" in《韩非子•内储说上》*Han Feizi: Inner Reserve*, Part I. Translation available at https://m.kekenet.com/kouyi/202002/604595.shtml

37 "郑人买履" "A person from Zheng buying shoes" in 《韩非子•外储说左上》*Han Feizi: Inner Reserve*, Part I. Translation available at https://zhidao.baidu.com/question/1795694177233993867.html

38" 自相矛盾" "Self Contradiction" 《韩非子• 难一》 in Han Feizi: Translation available at http://www.kekenet.com/kouyi/202002/604596.shtml

39 Xu, Yuanchong (Transl.)《离骚》 "Sorrow after Departure" in 《许渊冲译楚辞》 *Translation of Chuci by Xu Yuanchong*, Beijing: China Translation Publishing House (2021, 3-17).

40 Ibid., (2021, 65-67).

Chapter Two

Literature in Qin and Han Dynasty

In 221 BCE, Emperor Qin Shi Huang unified the six states, achieving China's great unification and establishing the first powerful, centralized, feudal autocratic dynasty in Chinese history. He instituted many policies and took numerous effective measures, such as abolishing the feudal system, implementing the prefecture-county system, establishing a new administrative structure, unifying the written script, and standardizing weights and measures. Along with the unification of the written script, he ordered ideological control. Historical records from various states, except for the *Records of Qin*, were all burned, and privately owned copies of *The Book of Songs* and *The Book of Documents* were confiscated and destroyed. Anyone daring to discuss *The Book of Songs* or *The Book of Documents* faced the death penalty. The infamous "burning of books and burying of scholars" originated from his actions.

In 210 BCE, Emperor Qin Shi Huang died, and his son Hu Hai ascended the throne, ruling with even greater cruelty. This led to the outbreak of a peasant uprising in July 209 BCE, led by Chen Sheng and Wu Guang. Although this uprising was suppressed, it was followed by the efforts of Liu Bang and Xiang Yu, who overthrew the Qin Dynasty in 206 BCE. Subsequently, in 203 BCE, Liu Bang defeated Xiang Yu and established the Han Dynasty.

1. LITERATURE IN QIN DYNASTY

The literature of the Qin Dynasty is relatively sparse due to the political and cultural climate of the time. The era was marked by significant efforts to centralize power and control thought, including the infamous "burning of books and burying of scholars" under Emperor Qin Shi Huang. These actions led to the destruction of many literary works and a suppression of intellectual diversity. However, some forms of literature and writing persisted, primarily in the realms of political essays and inscriptions.

1.1. Political Essays

Political writings from this period reflect the centralized authority and ideological control of the Qin Dynasty. These works were often used to justify policies or to provide guidance on governance. The representative writer of this period was the Qin Chancellor Li Si. Li Si (died 208 BCE), a native of Chu, was a student of Xunzi. He entered the state of Qin in 247 BCE and successively served as the Minister of Justice and Chancellor. He assisted Emperor Qin Shi Huang in unifying China and formulating various systems. After Qin Shi Huang's death, Li Si was executed by Hu Hai. According to *Records of the Grand Historian* (*Shiji*), Li Si's surviving works include *Memorial on the Expulsion of Guests* (*Jian Zhu Ke Shu*), a political essay advocating for the expulsion of foreign scholars and officials to strengthen the Qin state's internal governance, and *On Supervising Officials* (*Lun Du Ze*), a discourse on the importance of strict oversight of government officials to maintain order and efficiency.

1.2 Inscriptions

Inscriptions were often engraved on monuments, steles, and other structures to commemorate achievements, promote the emperor's authority, or propagate state ideology. These inscriptions served as both political propaganda and historical records. Some of the key features include:

(a) **Imperial Authority and Achievements**
Many inscriptions celebrated Emperor Qin Shi Huang's accomplishments, such as the unification of China, the standardization of weights and measures, the construction of roads and canals, and military victories. They often highlighted his role as the "First Emperor" (Shi Huangdi) and emphasized the permanence of his rule.

(b) **Standardized Script**
The Qin Dynasty is known for unifying the written script into a standardized form called Small Seal Script (Xiaozhuan). This script was used in inscriptions, ensuring uniformity across the empire and reinforcing centralized control.

(c) **Commemorative Nature**
Some inscriptions were created to commemorate specific events, such as imperial tours, construction projects, or territorial expansions. These texts often included lofty language to glorify the emperor and his achievements.

(d) **Legal and Administrative Records**
Inscriptions also included legal decrees, administrative orders, and announcements. These were often carved on stone or bronze to signify their authority and permanence.

Qin Shi Huang's **Mount Tai inscriptions** are among the most famous commemorative texts of the Qin Dynasty. These inscriptions were created during the emperor's imperial tours, particularly at Mount Tai, a sacred mountain in Chinese tradition associated with the legitimacy of rulers and the mandate of heaven. The inscriptions proclaimed his achievements, expressed his divine authority, and symbolized his unification of China. One inscription praised the emperor for bringing order to the world, unifying the writing system, and promoting harmony under heaven.

Memorial on the Expulsion of Guests (Jian Zhu Ke Shu)

Your Majesty,

I have heard that officials have proposed expelling foreign guests. I humbly believe this is a mistake.

In the past, Duke Mu of Qin sought talented individuals. He brought You Yu from the Rong tribes in the west, Bai Li Xi from Wan in the east, Jian Shu from Song, and Pi Bao and Gongsun Zhi from Jin. These five individuals were not native to Qin, yet Duke Mu employed them. As a result, he annexed twenty states and became the hegemon of the western Rong.

King Xiao used the reforms of Shang Yang to transform customs and habits, leading to a thriving population and a wealthy, strong state. The people were content, and the feudal lords respected and obeyed Qin. Qin defeated the armies of Chu and Wei, expanded its territory by a thousand li, and remains strong to this day.

King Hui adopted the strategies of Zhang Yi, seizing the land of Sanchuan, annexing Ba and Shu in the west, reclaiming Shangjun in the north, and capturing Hanzhong in the south. He subdued the Nine Yi tribes, controlled Yan and Ying, occupied the strategic pass of Chenggao in the east, and divided the fertile lands of his enemies. He dissolved the alliance of the six states, forcing them to bow to Qin. His achievements endure to this day.

King Zhao employed Fan Ju, dismissed Marquis Rang, exiled Huayang, strengthened the royal court, and eliminated private power factions. He gradually annexed the feudal lords' territories, establishing Qin's imperial foundation.

These four rulers achieved their successes through the contributions of foreign talents. From this, it is clear that foreign guests have not harmed Qin. If these rulers had rejected foreign guests and dismissed capable individuals, Qin would have lacked material prosperity and the reputation of being a great power.

Today, Your Majesty possesses treasures like jade from Kunshan, the He Shi Bi, pearls as radiant as the moon, the Tai'e sword, the agile Xianli horses, banners adorned with emerald phoenixes, and drums made of sacred alligator skins. None of these treasures originated in Qin, yet Your Majesty cherishes them. Why? If only items produced in Qin were acceptable, then luminous jade would not adorn the court, rhinoceros and elephant artifacts would not be admired, women from Zheng and Wei would not grace the palace, and fine horses would not fill the royal stables. Gold and tin from the south of the Yangtze River would be unusable, and pigments from Shu would remain unutilized.

If ornaments for the court, pleasures for the mind, and delights for the senses must all originate in Qin, then pearl hairpins from Wan, jade earrings from Fu, delicate robes of fine silk, and embroidered garments would not be offered at court. Nor would refined customs and elegant ladies from Zhao stand by your side.

The music of banging jars and drums, plucking zithers, clapping thighs, and singing joyfully is truly Qin's native sound. Yet the music of Zheng and Wei, as well as the refined melodies of Shao and Wu, come from other lands. Now you abandon Qin's native music for that of Zheng and Wei, and set aside native instruments for the refined melodies of Shao and Wu. Why? It is simply because they bring immediate pleasure and delight.

However, when it comes to people, this is not the case. Without considering their abilities or merits, you dismiss those who are not native to Qin and expel those who are foreign guests. This means that you value treasures and pleasures above people. Such a policy is not the way to dominate the world and subdue the feudal lords.

I have heard that vast lands yield abundant grain, great states have numerous people, and strong armies produce brave soldiers. Therefore, Mount Tai does not reject soil, which is why it becomes so majestic. Rivers and seas do not refuse small streams, which is why they grow so vast. Kings do not reject the common people, which is why they can illuminate their virtue.

Thus, when there are no boundaries in the land, no distinctions among the people, the seasons bring abundance, and the spirits bestow blessings. This is why the Five Emperors and Three Kings were invincible.

But now, you abandon your subjects, strengthening enemy states. You reject foreign guests, benefiting rival lords. This causes the talented individuals of the world to retreat, unwilling to turn westward, and avoid entering Qin. This is akin to arming robbers with weapons and supplying thieves with provisions.

There are many treasures not produced in Qin that are still valuable, and many individuals not born in Qin who are still loyal. Expelling foreign guests strengthens enemy states, weakens your people, and sows resentment among the feudal lords. If you seek to ensure Qin's safety while pursuing such a policy, it will be impossible.

2. LITERATURE IN HAN DYNASTY

The Han Dynasty (206 BCE–220 CE) was a golden age for Chinese literature, marked by the development of diverse genres and the refinement of earlier literary traditions. Literature during this period reflected the political stability, cultural sophistication, and intellectual vibrancy of the era. The popular literary forms during the Han Dynasty included political essays, *fu*,[1] rhapsodies, prose, and *yuefu*[2] poetry. Among these, the most powerful works were first political essays, followed by *fu* rhapsodies. Representative writers of this period include Jia Yi, Chao Cuo, Mei Cheng, and Zou Yang.

2.1. Political Texts

The political texts and essays of the Han Dynasty provided a foundation for Chinese political thought for centuries. They blended practical administrative concerns with philosophical ideals, creating a framework that emphasized the moral and ethical responsibilities of rulers and officials. Jia Yi (200–168 BCE) was an early Han scholar who wrote essays critiquing the Qin Dynasty's harsh Legalism and offering advice for sustainable governance. His key themes included:The importance of moral leadership, balancing central authority with regional autonomy, and promoting agriculture and reducing economic inequality.

Lu Xun gave high praise to the works of Jia Yi and Chao Cuo, considering their writings to be "masterpieces of the Western Han, benefiting future generations and having a far-reaching impact." Jia Yi's *"On the Faults of Qin"* (*Guo Qin Lun*), *"Strategies for Maintaining Stability"* (*Zhi An Ce*), and *"On the Accumulation of Reserves"* (*Lun Ji Zhu Shu*), along with Chao Cuo's *"On the Value of Grain"* (*Lun Gui Su Shu*) and *"On Defending the Borders and Encouraging Agriculture"* (*Shou Bian Quan Nong Shu*), represent the stylistic features of prose during this period.

"On the Faults of Qin" *(Guo Qin Lun)*

(Part I)

King Xiaogong of Qin took advantage of the stronghold of the Xian and Hangu Passes, controlled the land of Yongzhou, and with his ministers firmly holding onto their positions, he observed the Zhou Dynasty from a distance, with ambitions to sweep across the world, to encompass the entire realm, and to unite the four seas. At this time, Shang Yang assisted him, establishing internal laws, focusing on farming and weaving, and preparing the necessary military equipment; externally, he allied with others and fought the vassal states. As a result, the Qin people easily took the land beyond the Western River.

After King Xiaogong passed away, King Huiwen, King Wuwang, and King Zhaoxiang inherited his legacy, continuing his strategies. They conquered the southern region of Hanzhong, advanced westward into Bashu, took the fertile eastern lands, and secured the crucial northern territories. The vassal states were filled with fear, and they held a conference to weaken Qin, not cherishing valuable treasures or fertile lands, but rather uniting all the scholars of the world to form alliances. At that time, the rulers of Qi, Zhao, Chu, and Wei were wise and loyal, kind and loving, respecting the virtuous and valuing the learned, and they formed alliances with other states such as Han, Wei, Yan, Chu, Qi, Zhao, Song, Wei, and Zhongshan. The scholars and strategists of the six states, including Ning Yue, Xu Shang, Su Qin, Du He, and others, worked together to advise them. The military strategists, such as Qi Ming, Zhou Zui, Chen Zhen, Zhao Hua, Lou Huan, Zhai Jing, Su Li, and Le Yi, communicated their intentions, while generals like Wu Qi, Sun Bin, Dai Tuo, Ni Liang, Wang Liao, Tian Ji, Lian Po, and Zhao She formulated their military strategies. With ten times the land and a million-strong army, they marched towards Qin, but Qin opened the gates and invited the enemy in. The nine-state army hesitated and dared not advance. Qin did not waste arrows or other resources, and soon the entire world was exhausted. The vassal states then broke their alliances, fighting for land to offer as tribute to Qin. Qin, with its remaining strength, took advantage of the situation, pursued the fleeing armies, and conquered the north. The battlefield was littered with millions of corpses, and blood flowed freely. Seizing the opportunity, Qin divided the world and its territories, with strong states submitting and weaker states entering into tribute. This continued through the reigns of King Xiaowen and King Zhuangxiang, whose time on the throne was short, and the state faced no significant trouble.

When Emperor Shi Huang ascended to the throne, he exerted the achievements of his ancestors, taking bold measures to unite the world. He conquered the two Zhou dynasties, destroyed the vassal states, established supreme power, and controlled the six directions. His power spread across the four seas. He took the land of the Baiyue in the south, establishing the counties of Guilin and Xiang, with the local rulers bowing their heads and submitting to his authority. He sent Meng Tian to build the Great Wall in the north, pushing the Xiongnu back by over 700 miles. The barbarians dared not move south or graze their horses, and the soldiers did not dare to draw their bows in retaliation. He abolished the laws of the former kings, burned the writings of the Hundred Schools, and dumbed down the common people. He destroyed famous cities, executed heroes, gathered all the armies of the world in Xianyang, and destroyed weapons, melting them down to create twelve golden statues, weakening the people of the world. Then, he built the city of Hua as a fortress, using the river as a moat, and constructed a massive city with walls stretching for miles. He stationed strong generals and skilled archers to defend key points. With his ministers and elite soldiers, he strengthened his control. The world was pacified, and Emperor Shi Huang believed his control over the land was secure, with the Qin's stronghold in the heart of the country and an empire that would last for generations.

After Emperor Shi Huang passed away, his influence still spread across foreign lands. However, Chen She, the son of a common man, who had been a laborer and a migrant, though not as talented as the middle-class people or as wise as Confucius or Mozi, nor as rich as Tao Zhu or Yi Dun, rose from humble beginnings, leading a small group of exhausted soldiers. He rallied several hundred followers, attacked Qin, cut trees to make weapons, raised a banner, and called for the people to rise up. Soon, the world responded, and the army gathered supplies to follow him. The heroes of Shandong then rose up and overthrew the Qin dynasty.

Furthermore, the world was not weak. The land of Yongzhou and the stronghold of the Xian and Hangu Passes were formidable. Chen She's position was not superior to that of the rulers of Qi, Chu, Yan, Zhao, Han, Wei, Song, Wei, or Zhongshan. His weapons were not as powerful as the hooks and halberds of the Qin army. His exiled soldiers were not as strong as the armies of the nine states. His strategies and tactics were not as advanced as those of the generals of the time. Yet, success and failure can be unpredictable, and the results can be opposite. Why? If we compare the power of the states in Shandong with that of Chen She, it is clear that they were not comparable. Yet, Qin, with its small land, achieved the power of a great empire, united the eight states, and ruled for over a hundred years. Then, it made the entire world its home, and the Hangu Pass its palace. A single rebellion caused the collapse of the empire, and the world laughed at it. Why? Because benevolence and righteousness were not applied, and the strategies of attack and defense were reversed!

2.2. Poetry

The *fu* style of poetry flourished during the Han Dynasty. Combining prose and verse, *fu* were often long, elaborate descriptions of objects, events, or places. Notable poets include Sima Xiangru, who composed intricate *fu* pieces celebrating imperial grandeur and natural beauty. There are five categories in Han Fu:

(a) Fu on palaces: mainly describing the urban life in the palaces.
(b) Fu on hunting: mainly describing the hunting scenes of the emperors and aristocrats.
(c) Fu on traveling: mainly describing the experience during the journeys.
(d) Fu on determination: mainly describing feelings and emotions when failing to be recognized.
(e) Fu on other things: mainly describing other things such as flowers, grass, insects, fish, wind, clouds, mountains and rivers, etc.

Among these categories, the first two are the most brilliant.

Besides *fu* style, there is *yuefu* or the folk songs collected by the Han court's Music Bureau (yuefu), these folk songs reflect the lives and emotions of ordinary people. *Yuefu* songs later influenced classical Chinese poetry. During the reign of Emperor Wu of Han, the Music Bureau (*Yuefu*) was established. Originally, the

Yuefu was a governmental institution responsible for music. Later generations referred to the folk songs collected and preserved by the *Yuefu* as *Yuefu poetry* or simply *Yuefu*. Thus, the term *Yuefu* evolved from being the name of an institution to becoming the name of a poetic genre. Although the number of Han *Yuefu* folk songs preserved today is relatively small, they reflect a wide range of social aspects. To a certain extent, they portray the lives, thoughts, and emotions of the people, addressing social realities with a strong spirit of realism. Among these, *The Peacock Flies Southeast* stands out as a masterpiece of realism and is regarded as an artistic model of ancient Chinese long narrative poetry.

In the history of Chinese literature, the most comprehensive collection of *Yuefu* poetry is the *Collection of Yuefu Poems* compiled by Guo Maoqian during the Song dynasty. Han *Yuefu* poetry is generally divided into two main categories: hymns for sacrificial ceremonies and *Yuefu* folk songs. Broadly speaking, *Yuefu* reflects the following themes:

(a) **Exposing the Cruelty of the Ruling Class:** Many poems reveal the brutality and oppression of bureaucrats and aristocrats while depicting the suffering lives of the oppressed people. For example, "The rich own fields that stretch for miles, while the poor have no land to stand a needle on," or "The poor wear the clothes of oxen and horses, eat the food of dogs and pigs," and "They sell their land and houses, even their children, to pay off debts." These works highlight the immense pain caused by war and forced labor.

(b) **Reflecting the Suffering of Women:** Many poems expose the oppression women faced under reactionary political regimes, religious authority, clan power, and patriarchal dominance.

In the late Eastern Han period, the creation of five-character poetry (*wuyan shi*) by literati emerged, building on the foundation of *Yuefu* folk songs. Among these works, the anonymous *Nineteen Old Poems* stand out. Their content often revolves around the laments of women separated from loved ones, the homesickness of travelers, or reflections on the impermanence of life. While their ideological tone is not particularly lofty, they indirectly reflect the dark and chaotic social realities of the late Eastern Han. Despite this, their artistic achievements are remarkable. These poems excel in expressing emotions, skillfully employing metaphor and allusion, and conveying profound meaning through subtle language. They mark the maturity of five-character poetry.

Song of the East Gate[3]

Out of East Gate,
He won't come back.
Now back again,
He finds the lack

Of rice in the pot,
And coat on the peg.
With pain
He grieves,
Sword in hand, he starts out; his wife
Clutches at his sleeves
And weeps to beg
Him not
To risk his life.
"Others for wealth may care;
Your gruel I would share.
For Heaven above,
For our unweaned baby we love,
Please do not go!"
"Bah! It's already late.
Shall we drag on till white hairs grow?"

Homecoming After War[4]

At fifteen I left home to fight the foe
And cannot come back till I am fourscore.
On the way I meet a countryman I know;
I ask him who remains within my door.
"Seen from afar, your house is over there,"
"Mid graves where pine and cypress stand aloof"
Arrived, I see in dog hole run a hare
And pheasants fly from the beam of my roof.
In middle courtyard grows only wild grain
And by the well grows mallow I can eat.
I pluck the grain and boil it as food plain
And put the mallow in the soup I heat.
When I have cooked the simple, homely fare,
Who will eat it with me? No one appears.
I go outdoors and eastwards fix my stare,
My furrowed face and clothes wet with tears.

Nineteen Old Poems I[5]

You travel on and on,
Leaving me all alone.
Long miles between us lie
As earth apart from sky.
The road is steep and far;
I can't go where you are.

Northern steeds love cold breeze,
And southern birds warm trees.
The farther you're away;
The thinner I'm each day.
The cloud has veiled the sun;
You won't come back, dear one.
Missing you makes me old;
Soon comes the winter cold.
Alas! Of me you're quit;
I wish you will keep fit.

The Roadside Mulberry[6]

The rising sun from southeast nooks
Shines on the house of Qin, who
Has a daughter of lovely looks;
The daughter calls herself Luo-fu.

She picks mulberry leaves still new
To feed silkworms in southern nook,
Her basket's bound with silk thread blue,
Of laurel bough is made a hook.

Her hair is dressed in pretty braid,
Like moonbeams her pearl earrings shine,
Of yellow silk her apron's made,
Her cloak of purple damask fine.

When she is seen by passers-by,
They stroke their beards and there take root;
When she appears in young men's eye,
They doff their caps and make salute.

The ploughman thinks not of his plough,
The hoer leaves in field his hoe.
Back, they find fault with their wives now,
For they have seen Luo-fu aglow.

From the south comes the governor,
Whose carriage and five stop and stay.
He sends men to inquire of her.
"Who are you, pretty maid?"ask they.

"I call my humble self Luo-fu."
"Pretty Luo-fu, how old are you?"
"My age is still less than a score,
But much more than fifteen, much more."

"Our lord bids us to ask Luo-fu,
Will you ride with our lord, will you?"

Luo-fu steps forth and makes reply:
"What nonsense you are talking! Why,
Your Excellency has his wife;
I have my husband dear for life.
There are more than a thousand steeds
In the east that my husband leads. "

"But how can I your husband know?"
"Ah, by his horse as white as snow,
Whose tail is tied with a blue thread,
With golden halters round its head;
By the sword with its hilt of jade,
For which its weight in gold he paid.

"At fifteen he was a junior clerk;
At twenty he did a courtier's work;
At thirty he wore chamberlain's gown;
At forty he was lord of a town.

"His face and skin are white and fair,
A rather long beard he does wear.
In the Court he walks to and fro,
And goes to the palace with steps slow.
Among the thousands in the hall,
He's deemed the most distinguished of all. "

2.3. Historical Writings

The highest literary achievement of the Han Dynasty was in prose, with the most outstanding prose writer of the Western Han being Sima Qian. A monumental work of historiography, *Shiji* spans from the mythical Yellow Emperor to the early Han Dynasty. Sima Qian's narrative style, critical analysis, and biographical approach set a standard for Chinese historical writing. Although primarily a historical work, the *Shiji* contains essays and commentaries on political ethics, the behavior of rulers, and the causes of dynastic decline. Sima Qian critiques the moral failings of leaders and highlights the importance of virtue in maintaining political stability.

In the same vein, the *Hanshu*, the History of Han Dynasty by Ban Gu also includes political analysis and reflections on governance. Ban Gu emphasized the successes and failures of Han rulers as lessons for future governance.

2.3.1. Sima Qian and Records of the Grand Historian

His *Records of the Grand Historian* (*Shiji*) stands as the pinnacle of prose literature. Sima Qian, a native of Zuofengyi Xiayang (modern-day southern Hancheng in Shaanxi Province), was born in the fifth year of Emperor Jing's Zhongyuan reign (145 BCE). The exact year of his death is uncertain, but after the third year of Emperor Wu's Zhenghe reign (90 BCE), he ceased all public activities, suggesting that he may have died in that year. His life spanned the entirety of Emperor Wu's rule.

Sima Qian was not only a great historian but also the greatest prose writer. His *Records of the Grand Historian* summarizes three thousand years of history and culture prior to Emperor Wu. His father, Sima Tan, served as the Grand Historian for over thirty years. Sima Tan wrote an academically and politically significant essay, *On the Essentials of the Six Schools*, from a Daoist perspective. In it, he criticized the Confucian, Mohist, Logician, Legalist, and Yin-Yang schools, while fully affirming Daoism. This Daoist philosophy left a profound influence on Sima Qian.

The *Records of the Grand Historian* was written based on extensive field research and real-life experiences. In 99 BCE, Li Ling resisted the Xiongnu but was forced to surrender after being defeated. Upon learning of this, Emperor Wu was enraged, and the court officials joined in condemning Li Ling. Sima Qian, in his indignation, argued that Li Ling's surrender was out of necessity and that he would eventually find an opportunity to repay the Han Dynasty. This statement angered Emperor Wu, who sentenced Sima Qian to "castration." Sima Qian spent four years in prison and completed the *Records of the Grand Historian* in 93 BCE.

The *Records of the Grand Historian* (*Shiji*) is China's first general history written in the biographical style, covering approximately 3,000 years of history from the time of the Yellow Emperor to the Taichu era of Emperor Wu of Han. The *Shiji* is divided into 130 chapters across five sections: 12 *Basic Annals* (*Benji*), 10 *Tables* (*Biao*), 8 *Treatises* (*Shu*), 30 *Hereditary Houses* (*Shijia*), and 70 *Biographies* (*Liezhuan*).

(a) **Basic Annals (*Benji*)**:
The *Basic Annals* record major political, military, and other significant events of the empire, arranged chronologically according to the reigns of emperors.

(b) **Tables (*Biao*)**:
The *Tables* present a comparative and parallel arrangement of major political and military events involving successive dynasties and feudal states.

(c) **Treatises (*Shu*)**:
The *Treatises* are specialized essays discussing topics such as economics, culture, astronomy, and the calendar.

(d) **Hereditary Houses (*Shijia*)**:
The *Hereditary Houses* detail the histories of the feudal states of the pre-Qin period and the noble families and meritorious officials granted fiefs during the Han Dynasty.

(e) **Biographies (*Liezhuan*)**:
The *Biographies* provide accounts of notable figures in society.

2.3.2 The Outstanding Achievements of Records of the Grand Historian (Shiji)

2.3.2.1 Creation of the Biographical Style in Chinese Historiography

Records of the Grand Historian established the "biographical style" (*jizhuanti*) in Chinese historiography. This style is characterized by centering historical narratives around monarchs. Specifically, it organizes significant events during the reigns of successive rulers into sections called "Basic Annals" (*Benji*), such as *Annals of Gaozu* and *Annals of Emperor Wen*. These *Benji* serve as the backbone of the entire work. Around this framework, other sections—*Hereditary Houses* (*Shijia*), *Ranked Biographies* (*Liezhuan*), *Tables* (*Biao*), and *Monographs* (*Shu*)—provide detailed records of specific aspects, including the roles and impacts of kings, nobles, ministers, and others, as well as the development of national institutions and policies. While earlier works had some rudimentary elements of this style, Sima Qian fully developed it by building on the achievements of his predecessors.

From a political perspective, this style emphasizes the supreme authority of the monarch, aligning with the needs of a unified state. From a historiographical perspective, it highlights major national events through the *Benji* while capturing political, military, economic, and cultural details through other sections. This approach achieves clarity and coherence while encompassing diverse and extensive content without becoming overly cumbersome. This balance is a key reason why subsequent official histories over the next two millennia adopted the biographical style.

2.3.1.2 Compiling a Comprehensive 3,000-Year History of China, Including Minority Regions

Records of the Grand Historian is the first Chinese historiographical work to cover a 3,000-year history of China on a national scale, including many minority regions—an unprecedented accomplishment. It is important to emphasize that during Sima Qian's time, due to the underdeveloped economy and culture and the weak transportation links, ancient historical records were scarce, fragmented, and often contradictory. Materials related to minority groups were even rarer. Writing a comprehensive 3,000-year history that covered politics, military affairs, economy, and culture was an enormous undertaking, unimaginable for most scholars of the time. However, Sima Qian boldly took on this challenge and ultimately succeeded. Through extensive collection and brilliant analysis and verification of historical materials, he created a work of remarkable richness.

2.3.1.3 Reflecting Historical Truth with Integrity

While Sima Qian aimed to praise the Han dynasty, he also inherited the pre-Qin tradition of historical objectivity: "neither embellishing virtues nor concealing faults." This means he avoided blind praise and did not hide flaws, adhering to a factual approach that reflected historical reality, earning the work the reputation of being a "true record" (*shilu*).

For instance, while *Records of the Grand Historian* acknowledges and affirms Emperor Wu of Han's significant accomplishments in governance and military achievements, it also unflinchingly exposes his vanity, extravagance, harsh punishments, and exploitation of the people. Similarly, while the harsh rule of Qin Shi Huang was widely regarded in Western Han society as the primary cause of the Qin dynasty's rapid downfall, Sima Qian did not deny this but also objectively recorded the Qin state's significant contributions to unifying China. He praised Qin's "great success" and advocated learning from its positive experiences—an example of his commitment to truth.

Particularly noteworthy is his treatment of Xiang Yu, Liu Bang's main rival in the struggle for supremacy. On the one hand, influenced by Confucian thought, Sima Qian attributed Xiang Yu's failure to his "tyranny," documenting his atrocities such as burning, looting, and alienating the people. On the other hand, he vividly depicted Xiang Yu's virtues, such as sharing hardships with his soldiers, his unmatched bravery, and his pivotal role in defeating Qin forces. Remarkably, Sima Qian used the highest-ranking format, the *Benji*, to recount Xiang Yu's deeds—a rare honor.

Of course, it is worth noting that the political pressure to "neither embellish virtues nor conceal faults" was less intense during the Western Han than in later periods. Nonetheless, Sima Qian's commitment to objectivity deserves high praise.

2.3.1.4 Exceptional Literary Achievement

Records of the Grand Historian holds an esteemed place in the history of Chinese prose. Its vivid writing, concise language, and lifelike character portrayals greatly enhance its historiographical value.

In summary, *Records of the Grand Historian* is the first Chinese work to adopt the biographical style to document a 3,000-year history of China, reflecting a multi-ethnic nation centered on the Han people. Its content is rich and detailed, its prose elegant and dynamic, and it aligns with contemporary trends by praising the Han dynasty and promoting Confucian ideals to strengthen the unified empire. Yet it also adheres to the principle of truthfulness, avoiding falsification or concealment, thus setting a model for subsequent historiographical works.

The Feast at Hong Gate

(Records of the Grand Historian)

Duke Pei's (Liu Bang's) army was stationed at Ba Shang but had not yet met Xiang Yu. Liu Bang's Left Sima, Cao Wushang, secretly sent a message to Xiang Yu, saying:

> "Duke Pei intends to declare himself king of Guanzhong. He plans to appoint Ziying as his chancellor and take all the treasures for himself."

Xiang Yu was furious and said, "Tomorrow morning, I will host a feast for the troops, and then we will crush Duke Pei's army!"

At that time, Xiang Yu had 400,000 troops at Hong Gate in Xinfeng, while Duke Pei had 100,000 soldiers at Ba Shang. Fan Zeng advised Xiang Yu, saying:

> "When Duke Pei was in Shandong, he was greedy for wealth and loved beautiful women. Now that he has entered Guanzhong, he has taken neither riches nor women. This shows that his ambition is not small. I sent someone to observe his aura, and it appeared as dragons and tigers, shimmering in five colors—this is the aura of an emperor. Strike quickly and do not miss this chance!"

Xiang Bo, a Left Minister of Chu and Xiang Yu's uncle, had a longstanding friendship with Zhang Liang, who was then serving Duke Pei. That night, Xiang Bo rode to Duke Pei's camp and secretly met Zhang Liang, informing him of the situation. He urged Zhang Liang to flee with him, saying, "Do not stay and die with them!"

Zhang Liang replied, "I was sent by the King of Han to assist Duke Pei. Now that Duke Pei is in danger, it would be unjust for me to abandon him. I must inform him."

Zhang Liang entered the camp and relayed the news to Liu Bang, who was greatly alarmed and asked, "What should we do?"

Zhang Liang asked, "Who suggested this plan to you?"

Liu Bang replied, "A petty officer advised me, saying, 'Block the passes and prevent the other lords from entering. Then you can take all of Qin's land as your own.' I followed his advice."

Zhang Liang said, "Do you think your troops can match Xiang Yu's forces?"

Liu Bang fell silent and admitted, "Certainly not. What should we do now?"

Zhang Liang said, "Allow me to speak with Xiang Bo and assure him that Duke Pei has no intention of opposing Xiang Yu."

Liu Bang asked, "How do you know Xiang Bo?"

Zhang Liang explained, "During the Qin dynasty, he and I were friends. When Xiang Bo killed someone, I saved him. Now that the situation is urgent, he has come to inform me."

Liu Bang asked, "Is he older or younger than you?"

Zhang Liang replied, "He is older."

Liu Bang said, "Invite him in so I can treat him as an elder brother."

Zhang Liang went out and invited Xiang Bo in. Liu Bang offered him wine and pledged to form a familial alliance through marriage. He said:

> "When I entered Guanzhong, I did not dare to take even a hair's breadth of anything. I recorded the names of officials and civilians, sealed the treasuries, and waited for the general's arrival. The reason I stationed guards at the passes was to prevent thefts and unexpected events. I have been eagerly awaiting the general's arrival and would never dare to rebel. Please convey my sincerity to the general."

Xiang Bo agreed and advised Liu Bang, "Tomorrow morning, you must go early to apologize to Xiang Yu."

Liu Bang promised to do so. Xiang Bo returned to Xiang Yu's camp and reported Liu Bang's words. He also said, "If Duke Pei had not first taken Guanzhong, would you have been able to enter? Attacking someone who has achieved great merit is unjust. It would be better to treat him kindly." Xiang Yu agreed.

The next morning, Liu Bang, accompanied by over a hundred horsemen, went to meet Xiang Yu at Hong Gate. He apologized, saying:

> "I joined forces with the general to attack Qin. While the general fought north of the Yellow River, I fought to the south. I never

> expected to be the first to enter Guanzhong and defeat Qin, allowing me to meet the general here. However, certain petty individuals have caused a rift between us."

Xiang Yu said, "It was your Left Sima, Cao Wushang, who said these things. Otherwise, how could I have been so angry?"

Xiang Yu invited Liu Bang to stay and drink with him. At the feast, Xiang Yu and Xiang Bo sat facing east, Fan Zeng faced south, Liu Bang faced north, and Zhang Liang stood to the west, serving.

Fan Zeng repeatedly signaled Xiang Yu with his eyes and raised his jade pendant three times, but Xiang Yu remained unmoved. Frustrated, Fan Zeng left the tent and summoned Xiang Zhuang, instructing him:

> "The king is too soft-hearted. When you go in to offer a toast, request to perform a sword dance. Take the opportunity to kill Liu Bang. If you do not, we will all be captured by him someday!"

Xiang Zhuang entered the tent, toasted, and said, "Let me perform a sword dance for the king and Duke Pei to entertain the troops."

Xiang Yu agreed. Xiang Zhuang drew his sword and began to dance. Xiang Bo also drew his sword and danced, positioning himself to shield Liu Bang. Xiang Zhuang was unable to strike.

Outside the camp, Zhang Liang met Fan Kuai, who asked, "What is the situation?"

Zhang Liang replied, "It is critical. Just now, Xiang Zhuang danced with his sword, but his true intent was to kill Duke Pei."

Fan Kuai said, "This is urgent! Allow me to enter and face them."

Fan Kuai armed himself with a sword and shield and barged into the tent. The guards tried to stop him, but he shoved them aside, knocking one to the ground. He entered the tent, stood with his shield, and glared at Xiang Yu. His hair stood on end, and his eyes bulged with rage.

Xiang Yu, startled, placed his hand on his sword and asked, "Who is this?"

Zhang Liang introduced him, saying, "This is Fan Kuai, Duke Pei's charioteer."

Xiang Yu said, "A brave man! Give him a cup of wine."

Fan Kuai drank it all in one gulp. Xiang Yu then ordered a roasted pig's shoulder to be given to him. Fan Kuai placed it on his shield, cut it with his sword, and ate it.

Xiang Yu asked, "Can you drink more?"

Fan Kuai replied, "I would face death without hesitation; why would I refuse a cup of wine? The King of Qin had the heart of a tiger and a wolf, killing indiscriminately and oppressing the people. Thus, all under heaven rebelled against him. King Huai promised that whoever first entered Xianyang would be made king. Now, Duke Pei has entered, sealed the treasuries, and returned to Ba Shang to await you. Despite his great merit, he has not been rewarded, yet you listen to slander and plan to kill him. This is no different from Qin's downfall. I fear it will not end well for you."

Xiang Yu had no response and said, "Sit down." Fan Kuai sat with Zhang Liang.

After a short while, Liu Bang excused himself to use the latrine and summoned Fan Kuai outside.

Once outside, Xiang Yu sent his officer, Chen Ping, to call Liu Bang back. Liu Bang said, "I left without formally taking my leave. What should I do?"

Fan Kuai said, "In great matters, do not bother with minor courtesies. Right now, they are the butcher, and we are the fish. Why waste time?"

Thus, Liu Bang left immediately, instructing Zhang Liang to stay and apologize on his behalf.

Zhang Liang asked, "What gifts should I present?"

Liu Bang replied, "I have two pairs of fine jade discs to offer Xiang Yu and two jade cups for Fan Zeng. I was too afraid to present them myself, so please do so for me."

Zhang Liang agreed. At that time, Xiang Yu's camp was at Hong Gate, while Liu Bang's was at Ba Shang, forty li apart. Liu Bang abandoned his carriage and horses, taking only Fan Kuai, Xiahou Ying, Jin Jiang, Ji Xin, and a few others. They carried swords and shields, traveling on foot through the wilderness, avoiding the main roads, and reached their camp safely.

Meanwhile, Zhang Liang presented the gifts, saying, "Duke Pei was too intoxicated to bid farewell properly. He sends these jade discs to the king and these jade cups to the general."

Xiang Yu accepted the jade discs and placed them on his seat. Fan Zeng, however, smashed the jade cups with his sword and said angrily, "This petty man is unworthy of our plans. The one who will take the world from Xiang Yu is surely Duke Pei. We will all be his captives!"

Upon returning to his camp, Liu Bang immediately executed Cao Wushang.

Chen She[7]

(Records of the Grand Historian)

Chen Sheng, whose other name was She, was a native of Yangcheng. Wu Guang, or Wu Shu, was a native of Yangxia. Chen She was a farm hand when young. One day when resting from his labours he climbed up a mound and brooded morosely for some time. "If I become rich and noble, I will not forget the rest of you," he said. The other farm hands laughed. "How can a farm labourer become rich and noble?" they asked. "Ah!" said Chen She with a deep sigh. "Can a sparrow know a wild swan's ambition?"

In the seventh month of the first year of the Second Emperor of Qin, nine hundred men from the poor end of their village were conscripted for garrison service at Yuyang. On the way they stopped at Dazexiang. Chen She and Wu Guang, who were among the conscripts, were camp leaders. There was heavy rain, the roads were impassable, and they saw that they could not arrive on time. The penalty for delay was decapitation. Chen She and Wu Guang took stock of the situation. "Desertion means death and so does revolt," they argued. "Since the risk is the same, why not die for our counrty?" "The people have groaned long enough under Qin," said Chen She. "I have heard that the Second Emperor is a younger son, and not the rightful heir. Prince Fusu was the rightful heir, but because he often disagreed with his father, he was given a frontier command. Now they say the Second Emperor has killed him, although he had done no wrong. Many of the common folk have heard well of him, but do not know of his death. Then there is Koneral Xiang Yan of Chu, who is popular there for his many deeds of daring and the good care he takes of his men. Some say he is dead and some that he may have gone into hiding. If we pretended to be Prince Fusu and Xiang Yan and called on the people to rise, many would respond." Wu Guang agreed with him and they consulted a diviner, who, knowing what they had in mind, declared, "You will succeed in all you undertake and achieve great deeds. But why not ask aid from the spirits?" Chen She and Wu Guang, pleased with this suggestion, said, "He means us to awe men first." So they worte "Chen She will be king!" in vermilion on silk and placed it in the belly of a fish someone had caught. When the conscripts bought the fish and cooked it, they were amazed to find this writing in its belly. Chen She secretly sent Wu Guang at night with a lantern to the forest shrine near their camp, to cry like a fox, "Great Chu will rise again! Chen She will be king!" The conscripts were terrified at hearing this cry at night. The next day they kept talking among themselves with many a side long glance at Chen She.

Wu Guang was good to his men, all of whom obeyed him. One day when the commanding officers were drunk, he persuaded the conscripts to run away and goaded the officers to punish him nad thus enrage the men. Sure enough, the officers had Wu Guang flogged. But when one of them drew his sword, Wu Guang snatced it away and killed him. Chen She came to his aid and killed the other officer too. Then they called their men together and said, "This rain has already made all of us late, and the penalty for this is decapitation. Even if we do not lose our heads, seven out of ten will die at the frontier. If a stout fellow must die, let it be for some great cause. How can our birth pervent us from becoming princes and barons, generals and ministers?" "We will do whatever you say," responded the men. To win popular support, they gave not that their leaders were Prince Fusu and General Xiang Yan. Baring their right arms, they called themselves the army of Great Chu. They built an altar and made an oath, using the officer's heads as sacrifice. Chen She made himself general with Wu Guang as his chief commander. After storming Dazexiang they took the county of Ji and sent Ge Ying of Fuli with troops to take the districts east of Ji. Zhi, Cuo, Ku, Zhe and Jiao all fell to them. As they advanced, their ranks swelled. By the time they reached Chen they had about seven hundred chariots, more than a thousand cavalrymen and several tens of thousands of infantry. When they attacked the county seat of Chen the magistrate was away and the deputy magistrate held the city gate against them. But they defeated the defenders, killed the deputy magistrate and occupied the city. A few days later they summoned the elders and chief citizens to a conference. "My lord," said these men, "you have come wearing armour and carrying sharp weapons to attack an unjust government, to punish the Qin tyranny and reestablish the kingdom of Chu. Your achievements fit you to be our king." So Chen She made himself king, calling himself the Magnifien of Chu. Thereupon, all in the provinces and counties who hated the rule of Qin rose against their governors and magistrates and killed them in order to follow Chen She's lead.

The Account of the Southwestern Barbarians[8]

(Records of the Grand Historian 'Shih chi 116')

In the first year of yüan-shou [122 B.C.] Chang Ch'ien, the Po-wang marquis, returned from his mission to the land of Ta-hsia [Bactria] and reported that while he was there he had seen cloth produced in Shu and bamboo canes from Ch'iung. On inquiring how they had gotten to Ta-hsia, he was told, "They come from the land of Shen-tu [India], which lies some several thousand *li* southeast of here. We buy them in the shops of the Shu merchants there." He was also told that Shen-tu was situated some two thousand *li* west of Ch'iung. "Ta-hsia, which is situated southwest of our country," Chang Ch'ien reported to the emperor with enthusiasm, "is eager to open relations with China and is much distressed that the Hsiung-nu are blocking the road in between. If we could find a new route from Shu via the land of Shen-tu, however, we would have a short and convenient way to reach Ta-hsia which would avoid the danger of the northern route!"

The emperor therefore ordered Wang Jan-yü, Po Shih-ch'ang, Lü Yüch-jen, and others to go on a secret expedition through the region of the southwestern barbarians and on to the west to search for the land of Shen-tu. When they got as far as Tien, Ch'ang-ch'iang, the king of Tien, detained them and sent a party of ten or twelve men to the west to find out the way to Shen-tu for them. The Chinese party waited over a year, but all the roads to the west had been closed off by the inhabitants of K'un-ming, so that none of the men who had been sent ahead were able to reach Shen-tu.

The Account of Ta-yüan[9] (Excerpt)

(Records of the Grand Historian 'Shih chi 123')

"When I was in Ta-hsia," Chang Ch'ien reported, "I saw bamboo canes from Ch'iung and cloth made in the province of Shu. When I asked the people how they had gotten such articles, they replied 'Our merchants go to buy them in the markets of Shen-tu.' Shen-tu, they told me, lies several thousand *li* southeast of Ta-hsia. The people cultivate the land and live much like the people of Ta-hsia.The region is said to be hot and damp. The inhabitants ride elephants when they go into battle. The kingdom is situated on a great river.

"We know that Ta-hsia is located twelve thousand *li* southwest of China. Now if the kingdom of Shen-tu is situated several thousand *li* southeast of Ta-hsia and obtains goods which are produced in Shu, it seems to me that it must not be very far away from Shu. At present, if we try to send envoys to Ta-hsia by way of the mountain trails that lead through the territory of the Ch'iang people, they will be molested by the Ch'iang, while if we send them a little farther north, they will be captured by the Hsiung-nu. It would seem that the most direct route, as well as the safest, would be that out of Shu."

Thus the emperor learned of Ta-yüan, Ta-hsia, An-hsi, and the others, all great states rich in unusual products whose people cultivated the land and made their living in much the same way as the Chinese. All these states, he was told, were militarily weak and prized Han goods and wealth. He also learned that to the north of them lived the Yüeh-chih and K'ang-chü people who were strong in arms but who could be persuaded by gifts and the prospect of gain to acknowledge allegiance to the Han court. If it were only possible to win over these states by peaceful means, the emperor thought, he could then extend his domain ten thousand *li*, attract to his court men of strange customs who would come translating and retranslating their languages, and his might would become known to all the lands within the four seas.

The emperor was therefore delighted, and approved Chang Ch'ien's suggestion. He ordered Chang Ch'ien to start out from Chien-wei in Shu on a secret mission to search for Ta-hsia. The party broke up into four groups proceeding out of the regions of Mang, Jan, His and Ch'iung and P'o. All the groups managed to advance one or two thousand *li*, but they were blocked on the north by the Ti and Tso tribes and on the south by the Sui and K'un-ming tribes.

The K'un-ming tribes have no rulers but devote themselves to plunder and robbery, and as soon as they seized any of the Han envoys they immediately murdered them. Thus none of the parties were ever able to get through to their destination. They did learn, however, that some one thousand or more *li* to the west there was a state called Tien-yüch whose people rode elephants and that the merchants from Shu sometimes went there with their goods on unoffcial trading missions. In this way the Han, while searching for a route to Ta-hsia, first came into contact with the kingdom of Tien.

Earlier the Han had tried to establish relations with the barbarians of the southwest, but the expense proved too great and no road could be found through the region and so the project was abandoned. After Chang Ch'ien reported that it was possible to reach Ta-hsia by traveling through the region of the southwestern barbarians, the Han once more began efforts to establish relations with the tribes in the area.

Notes:

The Account of Ta-yüan is a truthful historical account of the countries in the Western Regions, with the detailed description of the eight countries among them: Ta-yüan, Wu-sun, K'ang-chü, the Great and Lesser Yen-ts'ai, Yüeh-chih, An-hsi, T'iao-chih and Ta-hsia. Besides, the other nine countries are also mentioned: Yü-mo, Yü-t'ien, Lou-lan, Ku-shih, Li-hsüan, Shen-tu, Huan-ch'ien, Ta-i and Su-hsieh, as well as the ten countries in the Southwestern Barbarians: Mang, Jan, His, Ch'iung, P'o, Ti, Tso, K'un-ming, Tien and Yüch. Anyway, the account mainly focuses on Ta-yüan and Wu-sun, starting with Ta-yüan and ending with it as well, hence the title *The Account of Ta-yüan.* The account describes the local conditions and customs in the countries of the Western Regions, and highlights the two journeys of Chang Ch'ien to the Western Regions as an envoy, revealing the subtleties of the relationship between the Kingdom of Han and the countries of the Western Regions, showing the historical illustration of the long time political, economic and cultural intercourses between the two parts. Besides, the writer implies implicitly his ridicule and lament on Emperor Wu of Han's policy of the military expedition year after year, and his overambitious focus on grandiose things. Nevertheless, by dispatching Chang Ch'ien the envoy to establish relations with the Western Regions and ruling the Hexi Corridor in a wise way, Emperor Wu of Han made a great contribution to strengthening the economic and cultural intercourses between the Kingdom of Han and the courtries in Central Asia, maintaining the unity of China and making it a powerful and influential country, all of which have a positive historic significance.

2.3.2. Ban Gu and The Book of Han

Ban Gu (32–92), courtesy name Mengjian, was a native of Fufeng Anling (modern-day eastern Xianyang, Shaanxi) and a renowned historian and writer of rhapsodies during the Eastern Han dynasty. His father, Ban Biao, was well-versed in historiography and literary composition, greatly influencing Ban Gu. Ban Biao once continued Sima Qian's *Records of the Grand Historian* by writing the *Later Biographies of the Records of the Grand Historian*. After Ban Biao's death, Ban Gu collected historical materials and continued the work. During the reign of Emperor Ming of Han, Ban Gu was appointed as a Lantai official (responsible for managing documents and archives) and was tasked with compiling the *Book of Han* based on the previous groundwork. During Emperor He's reign, Ban Gu accompanied General-in-Chief Dou Xian on a campaign against the Xiongnu and served as the Central Protector of the Army. Later, Dou Xian abused his power and was executed for his crimes, implicating Ban Gu, who was imprisoned and died in custody. The unfinished portions of the *Book of Han* were completed by his sister Ban Zhao and her student Ma Xu.

The *Book of Han* (*Han Shu*) is the first dynastic history written in a biographical format (jizhuanti) in China. In terms of content and structure, it largely followed the *Records of the Grand Historian*. The work comprises 100 volumes, divided into 12 imperial annals, 8 chronological tables, 10 treatises, and 70 biographies. It records 229 years of history, from the first year of Emperor Gaozu (206 BCE) to the fourth year of Emperor Wang Mang's Di Huang era (23 CE).

Ban Gu upheld Confucian ideals and lived in an era where theology and classical studies were highly prevalent. Consequently, the *Book of Han* reflects a certain orthodoxy and conservatism, lacking the sharp insights and critical edge found in the *Records of the Grand Historian*. For instance, when writing about the Western Han emperors in the imperial annals, Ban Gu often used words that downplayed their faults, obscuring their shortcomings. He also showed disdain for lower-class individuals, such as merchants and wandering knights. While Sima Qian praised figures like Zhu Jia and Guo Jie, Ban Gu deemed them "deserving of severe punishment." Furthermore, the *Book of Han* frequently discusses celestial phenomena and records strange occurrences, making it less engaging to read and diminishing its literary appeal. Nevertheless, the *Book of Han* remains a significant historical work. Apart from the *Records of the Grand Historian*, it is considered the finest among the official histories.

The Geographic Records of the Han Dynasty (Excerpt)

From the barriers of Rinan, Xuwen, and Hepu, it takes about five months by sea to reach the Duyuan Kingdom. Further, it takes about four months by boat to reach the Yilumei Kingdom, and about twenty days of sailing will get one to the Shenli Kingdom. Then, it takes one about ten days on foot to reach the Fugandoulu Kingdom, from where it takes over two months by sea to reach the Huangzhi Kingdom, whose customs are similar to those of Zhuya. The region is vast, and its population is large, with many rare and exotic goods. Since the reign of Emperor Wu of Han, these goods have been presented as tributes. There are interpreters who belong to the Imperial Yellow Gate, who venture into the sea alongside the enlistees to trade pearls, jades, glazes, precious stones and rare items with gold and various silk. Upon arrival at a foreign kingdom, the authorities offer feasts to the company and their merchant ships even escort when departing. This mutually beneficial trade also involves risks, such as being robbed or even killed, some drowned due to storms, the survivors coming back several years later. The largest pearl measures around two inches. During the year of Yuanshi of Emperor Ping, Wang Mang became the regent, who sought to display his power and virtue by sending envoys to the king of Huangzhi with lavish gifts as live rhinos. From Huangzhi, it takes about eight months by boat to reach Pizong, and about two months by sea to reach the border between Rinan and Xianglin. To the south of Huangzhi lies the Yichengbu Kingdom. The Chinese envoys and interpreters returned from there.

Besides, the Han Dynasty saw the development of encyclopedic works and scientific treatises. Notable works are *Huainanzi (The Master of Huainan)* compiled by Liu An, and *Chunqiu Fanlu* (Luxuriant Dew of the Spring and Autumn Annals) by Zhang Heng.

The *Huainanzi*, is an influential Chinese text from the Western Han Dynasty. Compiled under the patronage of Liu An, the King of Huainan and a grandson of Emperor Gaozu, it is a comprehensive work blending philosophy, cosmology, political theory, and practical knowledge. The *Huainanzi* consists of 21 chapters, each focusing on a specific theme. A preface introduces the text's purpose and methodology. The chapters cover topics such as the Dao (the Way), governance, military strategy, natural phenomena, and ethical behavior. Some of the key concepts of Daoism such as Wu Wei (Non-Action), Unity of Heaven, Earth, and Humanity, and The Dao as the Ultimate Guide have been highlighted.

Dong Zhongshu (179–104 BCE) was a prominent scholar and politician during the Western Han Dynasty. He is credited with advocating for the adoption of Confucianism as the official state philosophy during the reign of Emperor Wu (r. 141–87 BCE). He argued that Confucian principles of morality and governance were essential for maintaining social order and harmony in the empire. He played a pivotal role in the establishment of Confucianism as the foundation of Han political philosophy, influencing the imperial examination system and governance for centuries to come. Dong Zhongshu integrated Confucian teachings with cosmological theories, particularly those of Yin-Yang and the Five Elements (Wu Xing). He believed that the natural world was governed by a harmonious balance, and that human society should reflect this cosmic order. Dong Zhongshu's ideas had a lasting impact on Chinese philosophy, particularly through his synthesis of Confucianism with elements of cosmology, Daoism, and

Legalism. His works helped to establish Confucianism as a central pillar of the Han state's political and cultural life.

The *Chunqiu Fanlu* is a commentary on the *Spring and Autumn Annals* (a historical text attributed to Confucius), in which Dong Zhongshu elaborates on the Confucian classics, interpreting them through the lens of cosmology and moral philosophy.

The *Chunqiu Fanlu* is a commentary on the *Spring and Autumn Annals* (a historical text attributed to Confucius), in which Dong Zhongshu elaborates on the Confucian classics, interpreting them through the lens of cosmology and moral philosophy. The work integrates Confucian moral teachings with Daoist cosmology, advocating for the emperor's moral responsibility to maintain harmony between Heaven, Earth, and humanity. It emphasizes the importance of virtues such as benevolence (*ren*), righteousness (*yi*), and propriety (*li*), as well as the ruler's duty to embody these virtues for the stability of the state. Dong Zhongshu also introduces the idea that the emperor is the "Son of Heaven", a concept that reinforces the emperor's divine mandate to rule in accordance with the cosmic order.

NOTES

1. "辞赋", a literary form in the ancient China that originated from the Warring States Period, sentimental or descriptive composition, often rhymed.
2. Yuefu:"乐府", ancient Chinese poems composed in a folk song style.
3. Xu, Yuanchong. (Transl.) 《汉魏六朝诗选》*Selected Poems from Han, Wei and Sixteen Kingdoms.* Beijing: Wuzhou Communication Press and Zhonghua Book Company (2012, 28).
4. Ibid., (2012, 66).
5. Ibid., (2012, 50).
6. Xu, Yuanchong. 《中诗英韵探胜》*On Chinese Verse in English Rhyme*. Beijing: Peking University Press (1992, 103-104)
7. Yang, Xuanyi and Dai, Naixuan 杨宪益、戴乃迭. (Transl.).《史记：陈涉世家》Selection from *Records of the Historian*. Beijing: Foreign Language Press (2008, 89-95)
8. From *Records of the Grand Historian of China, translated from the Shih-chi of Ssu-ma Ch'ien by Burton Watson*, volume ii: The age of Emperor Wu 140 to circa 100 B.C., Columbia University Press, New York and London (1961, 293-294).
9. Ibid., (269-270).

Chapter Three

Literature in Wei-Jin and the Northern and Southern Dynasties

From the Yellow Turban Peasant Uprising in AD 184 to Emperor Yang of Sui unifying the Northern and Southern Dynasties in 589, this 400-year period in Chinese history was marked by political turmoil and fragmentation. During the chaos, three major feudal political and military groups emerged, represented by Cao Cao, Sun Quan, and Liu Bei. Although each sought to unify the country, none succeeded.

In 220, Cao Cao died, and his son Cao Pi usurped the Han throne to become Emperor Wen of Wei. Shortly afterward, Sun Quan and Liu Bei established the states of Wu and Shu, respectively. In 264, Wei conquered Shu, and the following year, Sima Yan replaced the Wei dynasty and founded the Western Jin. By 280, the Western Jin had defeated Wu, achieving national unification. However, in 317, Sima Rui established the Eastern Jin. In 420, Liu Yu supplanted the Jin dynasty and became Emperor Wu of Song. Over the next century, the region witnessed the emergence of three additional dynasties: Qi, Liang, and Chen.

In northern China, long-term conflicts occurred among feudal noble groups of various ethnicities. Over a hundred years, they established sixteen different feudal regimes. By 440, Northern Wei had unified the north, though it later split into Eastern Wei and Western Wei, eventually evolving into Northern Qi and Northern Zhou. In 581, Yang Jian replaced the Northern Zhou, declared himself emperor, and established the Sui dynasty. By defeating the Chen dynasty, he ended the division between the Northern and Southern Dynasties, creating a unified empire.

The Wei-Jin, and the Northern and Southern Dynasties period is characterized as an "Era of Literary Awakening," reflected in the following developments:

(a) **The maturation and development of poetry**: Represented by the Cao family and scholars from humble backgrounds, their poetry set a significant literary trend. For the first time, there was a surge in poetry creation, marked by profound content and a fully matured form.

(b) **The proliferation of anecdotal novels**: Notable works include supernatural tales such as *In Search of the Supernatural* (*Sou Shen Ji*) and anecdotal collections like *A New Account of Tales of the World* (*Shi Shuo Xin Yu*). These marked a pivotal stage in the development of Chinese novels.

(c) **Significant advancements in literary theory**: Monumental works such as The Literary Mind and the Carving of Dragons (Wenxin Diaolong), Discourse on Literature (Dianlun Lunwen), Gradations of Poetry (Shipin), and Rhyme-Prose on Literature (Wen Fu) represented the pinnacle of ancient Chinese literary criticism.

(d) **Innovative insights into "prose versus verse"**: Scholars of the time gained a deeper understanding of literary characteristics, explicitly distinguishing between *wen* (prose) and *bi* (plain writing).

(e) **The flourishing of ornate prose**: Large-scale descriptive rhymed prose evolved into lyrical and concise prose. In terms of structure, parallelism was emphasized; in prosody, tonal patterns were refined; in language, rhetorical embellishment was prized; and in content, the use of classical allusions became prominent. This marked the maturity and peak of *pianwen* (parallel prose).

1. POETRY

The primary literary achievement during the Wei, Jin, and Northern and Southern Dynasties was poetry. This period saw the development of five-character ancient-style poetry, spanning from Cao Cao and Cao Zhi to Ruan Ji, Zuo Si, and finally Tao Yuanming, who is considered the highest literary figure of this era. Subsequently, the evolution of poetry experienced a complex trajectory. The major poetic schools of this time include:

(a) Pastoral Poetry School: Poets who depicted rural scenery and countryside life.

(b) Landscape Poetry School: Poets who described the natural beauty of mountains and rivers.

(c) Historical Allusion Poetry School: Poets who emphasized the extensive use of historical allusions in their works.

(d) Palace-style Poetry School: Poets who viewed literature as a tool for feudal aristocratic indulgence, focusing on elaborate and sensual depictions.

(e) New-style Poetry School: Poets who explored the transition from ancient-style poetry to regulated verse, laying the groundwork for the flourishing of Tang dynasty regulated poetry.

1.1. Jian'an Poetry

Jian'an poetry represents the most brilliant chapter in the literary history of this period. "Jian'an" was the reign title of Emperor Xian of the Eastern Han dynasty, lasting from AD 196 to 220. This period also includes the early years of the Cao Wei dynasty, specifically the Huangchu and Taihe eras (220–232).

The characteristics of Jian'an poetry are as follows:

- **In content**, it inherited and developed the realistic spirit of Han dynasty folk ballads, truthfully reflecting social realities and expressing the poets' desires for national unification and aspirations for achievements.
- **In form**, it often utilized ancient folk song themes (*yuefu*) to depict contemporary events.
- **In style**, it was characterized by a somber and heroic tone, marked by strength and vigour.

Cao Cao

Cao Cao (155–220) was a renowned literary figure in Chinese history and a pioneer in the Jian'an poetic tradition of learning from Han dynasty *yuefu* folk ballads. More than twenty of his poems survive, all in the *yuefu* style. These works either depict the chaos of the late Han period and the suffering of the people or express his ambition to unify the country and his political ideals. Cao Cao excelled in both four-character and five-character verse, with a simple yet vigorous style, often described as "the old general of You and Yan, with profound and heroic spirit." Representative works include *Short Song Ballad* (*Duange Xing*) and *Walking Out of Summer Gate* (*Bu Chu Xia Men Xing*).

A Short Song[1]

We should sing before wine.
For how long can life last?
Like dew on morning fine,
So many days have passed.
How can we be unbound
By grief which weighed us down?
Grief can only be drowned
In wine of good renown.
Talents with collars blue,
For you I pine away;
So much I long for you,
My heart aches night and day.
How gaily call the deer
While grazing in the shade!
When I have talents here,

Let lute and lyre be played!
Bright as the moon on high,
How can I bring it down?
Grief from within comes nigh;
Ceaselessly it flows on.
Across the fields and lanes,
You are kind to come here.
Talking of far-off plains,
You cherish friendship dear.
The moon's bright and stars nice,
The crows in southward flight
They circle the trees thrice;
There's no branch to alight.
With crags high mountains rise;
With water the sea's deep.
With the help of the wise,
An ordered world we'll keep.

The Sea[2]

I come to view the boundless ocean
From Stony Hill on eastern shore.
Its water rolls in rhythmic motion
And islands stand amid its roar.
Tree on tree grows from peak to peak;
Grass on grass looks lush far and nigh.
The autumn wind blows drear and bleak
The monstrous billows surge up high.
The sun by day, the moon by night
Appear to rise up from the deep.
The Milky Way with stars so bright
Sinks down into the sea in sleep.
How happy I feel at this sight!
I croon this poem in delight.

Graveyard Song[3]

East of the Pass there're heroes brave and bright,
They rose in arms against the worst man of all.
They formed alliance first on River's right
And joined their force to take the capital.
But they were not united with might and main,
So like wild geese they straggled all about.

They fought each other for power or gain,
And tried to kill each other and fell out.
The self-styled monarch rules the southern shore;
The royal seal is carved on northern land.
Men long in arms grow lousy more and more;
Countless people die when they cannot stand.
Afield lie bones of those who lost their lives;
For miles and miles no cock is heard to crow.
Among a hundred people one survives;
My heart would break on thinking of the woe.

Cao Pi

Cao Pi (187–226) was the second son of Cao Cao. After Cao Cao's death, Cao Pi usurped the Han throne and declared himself emperor, ruling for seven years. Politically, he achieved little of significance.

A total of 40 of his poems have been preserved, primarily focusing on themes of romantic love and the homesickness of travelers. While his subject matter is relatively narrow, and his style tends to be delicate, his *Yan Song Xing* (Song of a lonely wife, first version) stands out. Its language is elegant, its lyrical expression and depiction of scenery are vivid and detailed, and it is considered an artistic success. Moreover, it holds historical importance as the earliest surviving complete seven-character poem in Chinese literary history.

Song of a Lonely Wife[4]

The weather turns cold when bleak blows the autumn breeze;
The leaves shiver and fall into frost dew-drops freeze;
Swallows in group fly south together with wild geese.
I miss you far apart till broken is my heart.
A traveler may roam but he'll yearn for his home.
Why so long should you stay in a land far away?
I remain sad and lonely in empty chamber only.
Though grieved, I dare not my dear lord to forget, yet
I do not know my gown wet with tears streaming down.
I take my lute and ring its melancholy string.
I sing low a short song. Oh how can it be long?
The bright moon overhead sheds its light on my bed.
The River of Stars peep westward when night is deep.
The Cowherd from afar gazes on Weaving Star,
What is wrong on their part to be kept far apart!

Cao Zhi

Cao Zhi (192–231) was the fourth son of Cao Cao. Favored by his father, Cao Cao once considered making him the crown prince, but Cao Zhi ultimately lost to his brother Cao Pi. His poetry can be divided into two periods, separated by the year 220, when Cao Pi ascended the throne. In the earlier period, his works primarily expressed his ideals and ambitions of "working tirelessly for the state and benefiting the people." In the later period, his poems mainly conveyed feelings of frustration and sorrow over being unrecognized for his talents and being unable to fulfill his aspirations.

Cao Zhi was the first poet to extensively compose five-character poems. His poetic style was described as possessing "extraordinarily lofty spirit and brilliant diction." This is evident in the following ways:

(a) His works were rich in pursuit and resistance, filled with momentum and strength. He shifted the focus of Han dynasty *yuefu* poetry from narrative to lyrical themes, marking a significant development in *yuefu* poetry.
(b) He transformed the simplicity and rustic beauty of Han yuefu into a more ornate and refined aesthetic.
(c) He excelled in using literary techniques such as metaphor, parallelism, and precise wordsmithing. Additionally, he was skilled at crafting striking opening lines and creating memorable epigrams.

When comparing the poetry of the "Three Caos," Cao Cao's works are characterized by their tragic grandeur, Cao Pi's by their melancholy, and Cao Zhi's by their poignant sorrow.

Song of the White Horse[5]

A white horse gallops in its golden gear
As if in flight to north western frontier.
Who is the cavalier in hurry great?
A gallant hero of the northern state.
While he was young, he left his native land;
His name was known as far as border sand.
Since then he's learned to draw the strongest bow
And shoot arrows of hard wood high and low.
He bends the string and hits the target at left,
And at destroying that at right he's deft.
Looking up, he shoots a bird fast in speed;
Bowing down, he breaks the hoof of a steed.
To be more swift than gibbons is not hard,
Nor to be strong and daring like a pard.

The border towns along northwest frontiers
Are oft invaded by Hunnish cavaliers.
When urgent messages come from northern side,
At once to the high fortress he would ride.
Straightforward he would drive against the Huns;
Turning back, he would beat Tartarian sons.
At the point of the sword in the hard strife,
How could he care for individual life?
He'd take no heed of his father and mother,
Let alone wife, children or any other.
Of heroes brave his name is on the roll;
He would not care when his death knell would toll.
The state at stake, he would give his last breath.
Would a homegoing soul fear to face death?

An Oriole in the Field[6]

The grievous wind raves through tall trees
And raises billows on the seas.
Without a sharpened sword in hand,
In vain have I friends in the land.
Have you not seen an oriole fall
In trap on hearing a hawk's call?
The fowler's glad to trap the bird.
Could I stand by without a word?
I cut the net to set it free
So that from the trap it may flee.
It flies up to the azure sky
And down to thank the stander-by.

Seven Masters of Jian'an

The major writers of the Jian'an period, apart from the "Three Caos," are collectively referred to as the "Seven Masters of Jian'an." These writers include Kong Rong, Chen Lin, Wang Can, Xu Gan, Ruan Yu, Ying Chang, and Liu Zhen, who were prominent literary figures at the end of the Han dynasty. Among them, Kong Rong belonged to an earlier generation, and the works of the other six writers have been largely lost.

Some notable examples include Chen Lin's (?-217) *"Yin Ma Changcheng Ku Xing"* (*Drinking Horses at the Long Wall Cave*) and Ruan Yu's (?-212) *"Jia Chu Beiguo Men Xing"* (*Setting Out from the Northern City Gate*), both of which reflect, to a certain extent, the social realities of the time. Their styles are also akin to the folk songs of the Han dynasty's *Yuefu* tradition.

Among the "Seven Masters," Wang Can achieved the greatest literary success and was honoured as the "foremost of the Seven Masters." His representative work, the *"Seven Laments"* (*Qi Ai Shi*), profoundly reveals the suffering inflicted on the people by the internecine wars among warlords. Another notable piece, *"Fu on Climbing the Tower"* (*Deng Lou Fu*), portrays feelings of unfulfilled ambition and the desire to achieve great deeds, making it a representative work of Jian'an lyrical *fu*.

Drinking Horses at the Long Wall Cave

Chen Lin

By the green grass along the riverbank,
I linger in endless thoughts of the distant road.
That distant road is beyond reach,
Yet in dreams, I see it vividly.
In my dreams, you are by my side,
But waking, you are in another land.
Another land, a far-off county,
Wandering apart, we do not meet.
The withered mulberry knows the heavenly winds,
The sea's waters know the heavenly cold.
Upon entering the house, all flatter themselves;
Who is willing to speak for another?
A guest arrives from a distant place,
Bringing me a pair of carp.
I call my son to cook the fish,
Inside I find a letter of silk.
Kneeling long, I read the silk letter;
What does it say within?
"Above, it says: Take care of your meals;
Below, it says: I miss you always."

Seven Sorrows I[7]

Wang Can

The Western Capital in woe:
Nowhere but wolves and tigers go.
I leave the central land again,
And go off to southern plain.
Facing me, kin and parents grieve;
Following me, friends will not leave.
What do I see out city gate?

White bones strew the plain desolate,
A starving woman cannot feed
Her child and lays it in the weed.
She looks back at its wailing sound,
And goes in tears, not turning round.
"I know not how long I'll survive.
Can I keep both of us alive?"
I whip my horse and leave them there;
To hear such words I cannot bear.
I go south on Royal Tomb's crest,
And gaze back on Capital West.
How could a patriot from it part?
I heave a sigh with broken heart.

Cai Yan (Wenji)

Cai Yan (also known as Cai Wenji) is recognized as the first distinguished female writer in Chinese literary history. It is said that she authored three works: the five-character *"Poem of Sorrow and Resentment"* (*Beifen Shi*), the *Sao*-style *"Poem of Sorrow and Resentment"*, and *"Eighteen Songs of a Nomad Flute"* (*Hujia Shiba Pai*). However, only the first can be definitively attributed to her. Cai Yan's five-character *"Poem of Sorrow and Resentment"* is a masterpiece of the Jian'an poetic tradition.

Its achievements lie in the following aspects:

(a) Grand structure: It is an extended narrative poem of 540 characters, an unprecedented length among earlier literary works.
(b) Profound thought: Through the recounting of the author's own unfortunate experiences, the poem exposes the evils of the warlord conflicts, reflects the humiliation and suffering of the people, and vividly portrays the chaotic and dark social conditions of the late Han dynasty. It embodies a strong spirit of the era.
(c) Exquisite technique: The poem excels in realistic and detailed depictions, vividly portraying various scenes of life and the psychological states of characters in different situations. This creates a sense of immediacy and realism, making readers feel as though they are witnessing the events first-hand.

Poem of Sorrow and Resentment

In the late Han, authority was lost,
Dong Zhuo defied Heaven's laws.
His ambition sought to usurp and murder,
First he harmed all virtuous scholars.

He forced the court to abandon the old capital,
Seizing the emperor to strengthen himself.
Across the land, righteous armies rose,
United in resolve to punish the wicked.

Dong Zhuo's forces marched eastward,
Golden armor gleamed in the sunlight.
The people were weak and defenseless,
The invading troops were all Hu and Qiang.

They hunted fields and besieged cities,
Wherever they went, destruction followed.
None were spared, all were slaughtered,
Corpses piled upon one another.

By the horses hung severed heads of men,
Behind them, they dragged captive women.
Driving west, they entered the passes,
The roads were long, treacherous, and rough.

Looking back, the world faded into shadow,
Our hearts and minds rotted like decaying flesh.
The captives numbered in the tens of thousands,
Scattered, without shelter or protection.

Some families were taken together,
But dared not speak a single word.
If despair overcame someone briefly,
They were struck down or forced to surrender.

"If you must die, meet the blade of the pavilion!
We won't let you live on!" they cried.
Who could still care for their lives,
When insult and abuse were unbearable?

Some were beaten with sticks,
Enduring torment upon torment.
By day, they wept as they marched,
At night, they sorrowfully sang while seated.

They longed for death but could not find it,
Yet found no reason to live.
What crime had Heaven committed,
To inflict such calamity and suffering?

On the frontier, alien to China's ways,
The people lacked morality and justice.

Frost and snow were ever-present,
Winds from the Hu lands blew even in spring and summer.

The winds fluttered my clothes,
And whistled coldly in my ears.
Moved by the times, I thought of my parents,
And my grief and lamentation knew no bounds.

When a traveler arrived from afar,
I was always filled with joy to see them.
But upon asking for news,
They always turned out not to be from my homeland.

By chance, my wish was granted,
My family came to find me.
I could escape my plight,
But only by abandoning my children.

Human nature binds hearts together,
To part without reunion is unbearable.
Life and death would forever separate us,
I couldn't bear to bid them farewell.

My child clung to my neck,
And asked, "Mother, where are you going?"
People said I must leave,
And could never return.

"You were always kind and gentle,
Why have you become so unfeeling now?
I have yet to grow up—
How can you abandon me?"

Hearing this, my heart shattered,
I felt disoriented, near madness.
Weeping, I stroked my child's face,
Starting to leave, then hesitating.

Others in the group,
Watched our parting and lamented.
They envied me for being freed,
But their cries pierced the air.

Horses halted, reluctant to move,
Carts stood still, wheels refusing to turn.
Onlookers sobbed bitterly,
And travelers shed tears as well.

Departing, I severed my feelings,
The journey ahead was distant and unending.
Three thousand miles of sorrow stretched before me,
When would we meet again?

Thinking of my children in my womb,
My heart broke into pieces.
When I reached home, my family was gone,
There was no one left, inside or out.

The city had become a wilderness,
The courtyard was overgrown with weeds.
White bones lay scattered,
Exposed, unburied, and unrecognized.

Stepping outside, there was no sound,
Only wolves howled and barked.
Alone, I faced the desolate scene,
My grief overwhelmed my lungs and liver.

Climbing high to gaze into the distance,
My spirit seemed to drift away.
It was as if my life had ended,
And passersby offered faint comfort.

I forced myself to look and breathe,
But though I lived, life held no meaning.
Entrusting myself to strangers,
I poured my heart into surviving.

Wandering, I became despised and lowly,
Always fearing rejection again.
Life is short and fleeting,
Yet filled with endless sorrow.

1.2. The Literature in the Late Wei and Jin Dynasties

After the Jian'an period, during the late years of the Cao Wei dynasty, there was a significant change in social thought. During the Zhengshi and Jiaping eras (240–253), a new group emerged known as the "Seven Sages of the Bamboo Grove," consisting of Ruan Ji, Ji Kang, Shan Tao, Xiang Xiu, Ruan Xian, Wang Rong, and Liu Ling. They were called the "Seven Sages of the Bamboo Grove" because they all admired the teachings of Laozi and Zhuangzi, indulged in drinking, and socialized with each other. They were friendly with one another and often gathered in the bamboo grove. In literature, the figures who represented the achievements of that time were Ruan Ji and Ji Kang.

Ruan Ji

Ruan Ji (210–263) wrote 82 five-character poems in his collection *Yonghuai* (Ode to My Feelings), which serves as the general title for his poetic works throughout his life, rather than a single work composed at one time. The content includes: expressing the poet's spiritual anguish; exposing the darkness of politics; and criticizing the hypocrisy of rituals and laws. In terms of artistry, Ruan Ji was skilled in writing poignant and heroic verses and also adept at using metaphors and allusions. This helped move five-character poetry away from imitating the *Yuefu* (Music Bureau) style, thus advancing the development of five-character poetry.

Reflections I[8]

I cannot sleep deep in the night;
I rise and sit to play my lute.
Thin curtains mirror the moon bright;
Clear breezes tug my lapels mute.
A lonely swan shrieks over the plain;
Hovering birds cry in north wood.
What do I see, pacing in vain?
My heart is grieved in solitude.

Reflections III[9]

The eastern garden's trodden way
Leads to blooming peach and plum trees.
But withered leaves are blown away
And drifting in the autumn breeze.
Bright flowers anguish soon and fade;
With thorns the hall will be overgrown.
Leave the hall on horse and evade
To Hermits' hill and settle down!
Hard to keep you from being lost,
Let alone your children and wife.
Wild grass will be covered with frost;
Soon will end the year and our life.

Ji Kang

Ji Kang (223–262), like Ruan Ji, was a figure who did not adhere to conventions. Ji Kang was renowned for his prose. His representative work, *Letter of Resignation to Shan Juyuan*, publicly expressed the view "not as wise as Tang and Wu, but inferior to Zhou and Confucius," despising human relations and the law of the court. This directly offended Sima Zhao, who used Confucian rituals to plot the overthrow of the Wei dynasty, and his collaborators. Ji Kang was ultimately executed on charges of "disrupting the masses and misleading the people." *On the Absence of Joy and Sorrow in Sound* and *On the Difficulty of Natural Learning* are important philosophical essays by Ji Kang, both of which demonstrate a critical spirit toward traditional Confucian thought.

During the Western Jin Dynasty, in the literary scene of the Tai Kang period, the main writers were known as the "Three Zhangs" (Zhang Zai, Zhang Xie, Zhang Kang), the "Two Lus" (Lu Ji, Lu Yun), the "Two Pans" (Pan Yue, Pan Ni), and "One Zuo" (Zuo Si). Among them, Lu Ji's poetry was relatively shallow in content, but he placed great emphasis on elegant wording and parallelism, making him a representative of the literary trends of the Western Jin poetry scene. Zuo Si, on the other hand, was the representative of achievements in the poetry world.

Zuo Si

Zuo Si (250?–305?) was the most accomplished writer of the Western Jin dynasty. His works maintained the tradition of Jian'an literature. His representative work, *Yonghuai* (Ode to My Feelings), consists of eight poems in which he uses ancient people and events to express his own feelings and grievances. Though titled as odes to history, they are actually odes to his own emotions. This marked a creative development of the historical poems that began with Ban Gu in the Eastern Han dynasty. Zuo Si's poetry skilfully incorporates historical facts, delivers sharp and insightful satire, and is marked by vigorous writing and bold ambition, embodying a positive romanticism. His style became known as the "Zuo Si poetic force."

On History II[10]

Gloomy the pine in valley deep;
Lush is the grass on mountain steep.
The latter's only one inch long;
But higher than the former strong.
The noble in position high,
The able in low office sigh.
In different places they stay;
Their places are not built in a day.
Jin and Zhang were families old;
They had served seven reigns, all told.
Not that white-haired Feng was not great,
But low was royal estimate.

1.3 Tao Yuanming and Other Poets in the Southern and Northern Dynasties

Tao Yuanming (365–427), also known as Yuanliang, was from Xunyang Chaisang (modern-day Jiujiang, Jiangxi) and came from a bureaucratic and landowner family, though by his time, the family's wealth had declined. At the age of forty, he abandoned his official position and retreated to a life of reclusion, spending the rest of his years farming and living in seclusion. When Lu Xun commented on Tao Yuanming, he noted that Tao did not forget or remain indifferent to worldly matters, but his attitude toward them was neither passionate nor vehement; instead, it was "natural" and "casual." His writing style was "peaceful."

Tao Yuanming's literary achievements were primarily in poetry, with over 120 poems attributed to him. His poems can be divided into two categories: pastoral poetry and odes to emotions and history.

The pastoral poems describe rural landscapes and life in the countryside, expressing his love for the reclusive life in the countryside and his disdain for the corrupt society. The pastoral poetry form he pioneered opened up a new realm in classical poetry and later developed into the pastoral landscape poetry school during the Tang dynasty. His later work, *Peach Blossom Spring Poem and Record*, marked the sublimation of his thoughts. In his early years, Tao held the ideal of "greatly benefiting the common people" and had once pursued an official career. However, when his ideal was shattered in the bureaucratic world, he turned to a pastoral life. After long years of reclusion and living in poverty, he came to understand the suffering and aspirations of farmers.

Tao Yuanming's odes to emotions and history mainly express the frustration of unfulfilled ideals and his noble character of not compromising with the ruling powers. He inherited the traditions of Ruan Ji and Zuo Si, and carried forward the spirit of Jian'an literature.

The artistic characteristics of Tao Yuanming's poetry are mainly reflected in the following points:

(a) *Simple and natural style:* His poems are unadorned, avoiding luxurious words and classical allusions, and instead use plain, straightforward language to describe ordinary scenes. This allows him to naturally express his deep emotions.

(b) *Integration of lyricism, landscape description, and philosophical reasoning:* Tao's poems blend objective depictions of nature with his subjective emotions and character. In his lyricism and landscape descriptions, he often expresses life's philosophies in simple language, combining both emotional and intellectual appeal.

Return to Nature I[11]

While young, I was not used to worldly cares,
And hills became my natural compeers.
But by mistake I fell in mundane snares,
And was thus entangled for thirteen years.
A caged bird would long for wonted wood,
And fsh in ponds for native pools would yearn.
Go back to till my southern field I would,
To live a rural life why not return?
My plot of ground is but ten acres square;
My thatched cottage has eight or nine rooms.
In front I have peach trees here and plums there;
Over back eaves willows and elms cast glooms.
A village can be seen in distant dark,
Where plumes of smoke rise and waft in the breeze.
In alley deep a dog is heard to bark,
And cocks crow as if over mulberry trees.
Into my courtyard no one should intrude,
Nor rob my private rooms of peace and leisure.
After long, long official servitude,
Again in nature I find homely pleasure.

Return to Nature III[12]

I sow my beans 'neath Southern Hill
Bean shoots are lost where weeds o'er grow.
I weed at dawn though early still;
I plod home with my moonlit hoe.
The path is narrow, grasses tall,
With evening dew my clothes wet,
To which I pay no heed at all,
If my desire can but be met.

Drinking V[13]

I set up my cottage in the world of men,
Away from the hubbub of horses and carriages.
Being asked how it could be thus, I reply,
"My heart stays apart, so secluded must be the spot."
In plucking chrysanthemums beneath the east hedge,
I vacantly see the southern mountains afar;
The mountain aura hovereth fair morn and eve,

The birds fly from and back to their nests early and late.
There is the pith of truth in all this sight;
When I am about to say how, I forget my words.

The Peach Blossom Visionary Land[14]

During the Tai-yuan years of the dynasty Jin, a fisherman from the county of Wuling strolled on the bank of a stream, forgetting the distance of his track, into a grove of blossoming peach trees all at once. For several hundred steps along the bank side, there were no other trees; the sward was freshly green and fallen petals of the peach blooms were scattered on the grass verdure. The fisherman, surprised by the sight, walked on to see where the grove would end. It ended at the source of the stream, where there was a mountain. An aperture opened on the mount, from which light seemed to be emitted.

The man abandoned his boat and entered the opening. It was narrow at first, just enough to pass through. After several tens of steps, the way led to vast spaciousness. The land was level and expanded, houses were spread out in good order; goodly farms, fair ponds and mulberry and bamboo thickets were to be seen everywhere. The ways and cross roads were stretched out far and wide. Cocks' crew and dogs' barking were heard here and there. The men and women coming and going in their tilling and handicraft work were dressed all like people outside. The aged with hair of light beige and children with cut hair fringing their foreheads all looked gay and contented. Seeing the fisherman, people were greatly surprised, asking him whence he came from and being replied to. They then invited him to their homes, offering wine and killing chickens for entertainment. When it was generally known in the village that there was this man, more people came to see and ask questions of him. They all said that their forefathers, fleeing from turmoils during the Qin Dynasty, led their families and villagers hither to this isolated district to stay, and so being separated from the outside world. They asked what time it was then, knowing not there was any dynasty Han, to say nothing of those of Wei and Jin. The man answered them all in details, whereon they heaved sighs and exclamations. All the others also invited him severally to their homes for hospitality. After many a day, he made his departure. They told him not to publicize his sojourn there.

When out, he sought out his boat and noted closely the way leading to the aperture of the mount. After his return to the chief town of the county, he went to the alderman and made a report of his outlandish excursion. The county official dispatched a man to follow him whereto he would lead. But he could not find the spots he had noted on his way back and so lost the whereabouts of the grove of blossoming peach trees. Liu Ziji of Nanyang, a scholar of high repute, hearing of the story sought to find out the place. He fell sick and died, before his attempted trial. Thereafter, no one ever ventured the visionary deed.

Peach-Blossom Springs[15]

When the King of Qin transgressed the heavenly law,
The sages left their homes and went ashore.
When hermits Huang and Qi went to Mount Shang,
First settlers in the Springs came in a gang.
The early footprints are covered now with weeds;
The trodden bypaths are buried now by reeds.
In the fields, each person does his very best;
At sunset they go home and take a rest.
Bamboos and mulberries grow in such mild clime
While beans and crops are planted in their time.
They raise silkworms and plough the fields in spring;
When they reap crops, they need not pay the king.
On bushy roads, no men are seen to go,
But dogs are heard to bark and cocks to crow.
They make sacrifices in ancient ways
The children sing their songs with ringing voice;
The grey-hair have pastime of their own choice.
When grass grows lush, they know that spring's alive;
When trees wither, they see autumn arrive.
Although they do not have an almanac,
The change of seasons helps them mark the track.
Their lives so full of joy and bodies fit,
They have no need to live by their wit.
This wonder, hidden for five hundred years,
Is opened to the world as unspoiled spheres.
Their simple way of life is worlds apart,
And shuts its door to the world from the start.
How can a person from the madding crowd
Expect to know Utopia neath a shroud!
Oh that I soar to the sky on gentle breeze
And find the men of my ideal like these!

Xie Lingyun

Xie Lingyun (385–433) was the first poet in Chinese literary history to create a large body of landscape poetry. He pioneered the landscape poetry genre, expanding the range of poetic themes and introducing a new trend in the Southern Dynasties poetry scene, which emphasized sensory experiences and visual beauty. His works strongly challenged the "empty and bland" style of abstruse poetry. Xie Lingyun brought a fresh approach to expressing nature, continuing the tradition of Tao Qian (Tao Yuanming), and influenced later poets such as Wang Wei and Meng Haoran. However, a limitation of Xie Lingyun's poetry was its focus on nature, which lacked broader social significance. In terms of artistic expression, his works often consisted of isolated lines rather than coherent poems. Structurally, he commonly used the "narrative–landscape description–reflection" format, which was somewhat repetitive, and his poems sometimes ended with "abstruse" expressions.

Climbing the Tower by the Pond

The hidden dragon has a graceful and secluded posture,
The flying wild goose echoes a distant sound.
The thin clouds feel ashamed of their floating,
The resting river, troubled by the deepness below.
Advancing in virtue, my wisdom is lacking,
Retreating to farming, my strength is insufficient.
Chasing for official ranks leads to the edge of the sea,
Sick and lying down, I face the empty forest.
The quilt and pillow fail to bring peace,
I briefly open the curtains to look outside.
I listen closely to the sound of waves,
And gaze far at the jagged hills.
At the beginning of the day, the wind shifts the threads of the morning,
The new sun changes the old shadows.
Spring grass grows in the pond,
And the garden willows change with the calls of birds.
The echoing of the ancient poems brings sorrow,
The mournful songs of the Chu state bring feeling.
Living in solitude is simple and everlasting,
But separating from others is hard on the heart.
To maintain integrity is not just an ancient tradition,
There is no boredom in striving for the present.

Bao Zhao

Bao Zhao (414?–466) is the poet with the highest literary achievements in the Southern Dynasties. Over 200 of his poems have survived. His 18 poems in *Nijianlu Nan* (*Weary Road*) are representative works, mainly criticizing the system of aristocratic families. The main achievements of Bao Zhaos poetry lie in the fact that he directly inherited the tradition of Jian'an literature, with his works often expressing a desire for success and achievement. His thoughts were positive, and the content was substantial. He created a large number of seven-character *yuefu* (folk songs), greatly promoting the development of the seven-character verse form. His style was elegant, bold, and sharp, paving the way for the development of seven-character *gexing* (song-style poetry) in the Tang Dynasty.

Weary Road (Nijianlu Nan)

(First Five Poems)

One

I offer you a cup of fine wine,
Inlaid with gold and set in a tortoiseshell box,
A carved zither inlaid with jade.
The feathered canopy of seven-colored lotus,
And the brocaded quilt made from Nine Huahua grapes.
The beauty of youth fades as the year draws to a close,
And the cold light bends, as if it's about to sink.
I wish for you to cut back on your sadness and lessen your thoughts,
Listen to my lament as I sing of the difficult road ahead.
I do not long to see the copper birds atop Bai Liang,
But would rather hear the pure sounds of ancient flutes.

Two

The famous craftsmen of Luoyang cast a golden Bo mountain,
With a thousand chisels and ten thousand engravings.
On it, they carve a picture of a Qin maiden holding hands with an immortal.
You enjoy the calm of the night,
With candles set before you in the tent,
The dragon's scale red paint outside,
And the musk-scented purple smoke inside.
Now, the heart of the one you love changes in a single morning,
Leaving me to sigh in this sorrow until the end of my days.

Three

In a jeweled chamber, on a jade-raised floor,
A pavilion adorned with pepperwood stands.
The embroidered windows, covered by silk curtains,
Hold a person who is as dear as gold and jade.
Dressed in delicate gauze, she exudes a fragrance of herbs.
The spring swallows fly low in the wind, scattering the plum blossoms,
As I open the window and gaze at the scene with birds in the trees.
I sing and weep, always carrying sorrow in my heart.
How often in life can one truly find happiness?
I would rather be a pair of wild ducks in the field,
Than a lone crane in the clouds, separated from others.

Four

Water flows in all directions on level ground,
Each heading east, west, south, or north.
Life is also determined by fate—how can one lament or sit in sorrow?
I pour myself wine to ease my heart,
Raise my cup and sing to break the road's difficulty.
Though my heart is not wood or stone, it cannot be without feeling,
I swallow my voice, hesitating, not daring to speak.

Five

Do you not see the grass by the river,
Withering and dying in winter, only to bloom again in spring?
Do you not see the sun above the city,
Setting tonight, only to rise again tomorrow?
So when will I find my place,
And leave to vanish forever into the yellow springs?
Life is full of suffering, with little joy,
And one's ambition flourishes in youth.
Let me wish that fate will align with my desires,
That I may always have money for wine beside my bed.
Achievements and fame are not my concern;
Life and death, honor and disgrace, are in the hands of Heaven.

Xie Tiao

Xie Tiao (464–499) was a representative poet of the "Yongming style", a new style of poetry created during the Yongming period of Emperor Wu of the Qi Dynasty (483–494), by poets such as Shen Yue. This style strictly emphasized "four tones and eight defects," focusing on tone, rhyme, and antithetical parallelism, and paid attention to the embellishment of words. Xie Tiao inherited the landscape poetry style of his predecessor Xie Lingyun. His achievements in landscape poetry lay primarily in: absorbing Xie Lingyun's strengths of detailed and vivid depiction, while also integrating subjective emotions into objective descriptions. He moved away from the obscure and simplistic aspects of Xie Lingyun's poetry, advancing landscape poetry further and making use of the emerging tonal patterns. Xie Tiao's style was known for its emphasis on word choice, its elegant and refined expression, and its skill in depicting natural scenes with a fresh and flowing style.

Wang Sun the wanderer

The green grass spreads like silk,
  and the mixed trees bloom with red flowers.
No matter whether you return or not,
  when you do, the fragrance would have already faded.

The distinguished contemporary poets also include He Sun of Liang Dynasty, Yin Keng and Yu Xin of Chen Dynasty, etc. He Sun and Yin Keng are renowned for their short lyrics on landscape, while Yu Xin mainly wrote Court Poems, with lamentation on his vicissitude and nostalgia of his homeland, thus becoming an influential pioneer of poetry in Tang Dynasty.

2. PARALLEL PROSE AND PROSE IN THE SOUTHERN AND NORTHERN DYNASTIES

Parallel Prose is a literary genre in the ancient Chinese literature. Compared with prose, parallel prose has more strict emphasis on structure, syntax, word selection, allusion, etc. Syntactically, four-character line and six-character line are frequently used, as well as parallel and antithesis; rhythmically, level and oblique tones are employed. Besides, euphuistic words and allusion are also abundantly used.

2.1 The Development of Parallel Prose

Parallel Prose emerged in Wei and Jin Dynasties, and came into its prime time during the Southern and Northern Dynasties. After Sui and Tang Dynasties, it began to decline. Some works in Han Dynasty can also be ascribed to parallel prose, such as *Seven Emotions (Qi Fa)*, a great work of the renowned Fu writer Mei Cheng in the early years of Western Han Dynasty, *Epitaph for Guo Youdao (with Preface)*, a great work of Cai Yong in late Eastern Han Dynasty, and *A Paper on Sheng Xiaozhang*, a work of another great writer in late Eastern Han Dynasty Kong Rong. During Wei and Jin Dynasties, the pattern of Parallel Prose had already been established, among which are two measured and symmetrical examples: Cao Pi's *Classical Treatise: On Literature* and Cao Zhi's *A Letter to Yang Dezu*. In Western Jin Dynasty, there appeared a considerably mature Parallel Prose—Lu Ji's *On Literary Writing*. In the Southern Dynasties, the feudal lords and peers' inclination to Parallel Prose and their advocacy towards it had a significant promoting influence on the genre's development and prosperity.

In his *On Wucheng*,[16] through a striking contrast between Guanglin's present desolation and its past prosperity, the writer Bao Zhao lamented the gloom of life, attacking vaguely the rulers' bloodthirsty fighting against each other. Xie Zhuang's *On the Moon* is another masterpiece of the lyrical Minute Fu of Parallel Prose, which depicts the beautiful sublunary scene, revealing the writer's melancholy and his meditation on the past. Besides, there are another two masterpieces written by Jiang Yan: *On Regret* and *On Separation*. The former depicts various lamentable things such as the princes, lords, beauties, as well as the framed officials and the wronged man of letters, while the latter describes the grief of people when facing separation, such as a woman longing for her enlisted man, the king, the aristocrats, the assassin, the enlistees, the man who was forced to leave his country etc. These works are shining with their unique and unconventional subjects, bringing into Ci and Fu the poetic tradition of the meditation on history and the replacement of the narrator.

Yu Xin is a renowned writer who represents the highest achievement of Parallel Prose and Fu during the Southern and Northern Dynasties. His *The Lament for the South* represents the highest development of Parallel Proses (also called Jiao Wen), revealing the vicissitudes of Liang Dynasty and his own ups and downs.

On the Moon

(Xie Zhuang)

King Chen's early passing was a cause of concern and sorrow for Liu. The green moss covered the pavilion, and the fragrant dust settled on the verandah. Quietly, I felt troubled in my heart, unable to find peace through the night.

So, I cleared the path through the orchids and the osmanthus garden, feeling the cold wind blow from the mountain. I sighed at the distant waters and climbed the high peaks, saddened by the endless horizon. At that time, the slanting Milky Way rested on the left side of the sky, the northern lands and southern regions in sight. The white dew warmed the empty sky, and the pure moon drifted across the heavens. I pondered deeply, composing verses with great care, and took up my brush to send a letter to Zhongxuan.

Zhongxuan knelt and replied: "I am from the remote eastern regions, living in seclusion among the hills. I have not yet grasped the Way and am inexperienced in learning. I have long served under your bright grace. I have heard that when one submerges oneself in righteousness, wisdom is gained, and through high virtue, one brings clarity to their mind. As the sun radiates warmth, so does the moon bestow its gentle light. I have guided the eastern marshes with light and have inherited the brilliance of the western skies. I follow the ancient ways and bring forth divine forces, drawing the rabbit from the Emperor's platform and gathering the pure maidens from the imperial courts."

He continued, saying, "I aim to illuminate the world, spreading light and wisdom in all directions. When the winds blow across the forests, it brings harmony, and the dew falls, enriching the earth."

Now, when the air clears, the clouds disperse, and the waters of Dongting begin to ripple, the leaves of the trees gradually fall. Chrysanthemums bloom in the mountains, and wild geese cry over the rivers. The stillness of the night brings out the quiet beauty of nature, as the moon shines softly, and the stars move across the sky. The earth is cleansed by frost and snow, and the reflection of the moon in the water seems like a perfect mirror.

At this time, the ruler, tired of the morning celebrations, enjoys the evening feast, the graceful dance, and the soothing atmosphere. Leaving the candle-lit room, he enters the moonlit palace, where fragrant wine is served and the sound of the zither is heard.

Yet, as the cool night deepens, a sadness settles. The wind rustles through the bamboo, and the beauty of the night seems distant. The sounds of birds in the evening and the pipes of autumn wind stir feelings of nostalgia. The melodies from the zither echo, the music filling the room, and I linger, contemplating the fleeting nature of life.

The song goes:

> "The beauty walks, but her voice is lost,
> A thousand miles apart, yet we share the same moon.
> I sigh into the wind, unsure where to rest,
> The river's path is long, impossible to cross."
>
> The song ends, and the mood shifts. The surroundings change, as if everything has been lost. I then sing another song:
>
> "The moon has set, and the dew is about to dry,
> The year is drawing to a close, and there's no one to return to.
> The promised time may come again,
> But the light frost clings to my clothes."

King Chen says: "Well done." He orders that offerings be prepared—food and jade—to express respect, and the duties are carried out with diligence.

2.3 Prose

During the Southern Dynasty, Parallel Prose was extremely popular while prose failed to reach its high achievements. Nevertheless, two renowned collections of prose works emerged during the Northern Dynasty: *The Commentary on the Water Classic* written by Li Daoyuan from the Northern Wei Dynasty, and *The Monasteries of Luoyang* written by Yang Xuanzhi from the Eastern Wei Dynasty. Li Daoyuan's *The Commentary on the Water Classic* is not only a geographical classic with profound scientific value, but a prominent literary classic concerning beautiful natural scenery as well, whose appearance produced a significant influence on the travelogues of the later writers such as Liu Zongyuan, etc.

Yang Xuanzhi's *The Monasteries of Luoyang* is a precious architectural and historical record of the striking spectacle of monastery building in Luoyang, with both academic and literary value, having a great effect on the development of the later travelogue essays. *The Monasteries of Luoyang* was completed in 547 CE. Apart from its preface, the work is divided into five volumes. The narrative is concise, and the prose is elegant. The book primarily documents the rise and fall of renowned monasteries in the capital city of Luoyang over a span of 40 years (from 493 CE, when the capital was moved to Luoyang, to 534 CE, when the Eastern Wei dynasty relocated the capital to Ye). It also touches on the politics and prominent figures of the era, as well as the customs, folklore, and anecdotes of the time. Scholars have long evaluated its historical and literary value, but this writer will focus on its preserved South Asian historical material. It gives an account of China's relations with foreign countries, routes of communications, and accounts of foreign monks etc.

During the Northern Wei dynasty, foreign monks traveled in large numbers to Luoyang. Emperor Xuanwu (Yuan Ke) established the Yongming Temple specifically to host monks from other countries. The temple was meticulously designed, with over 1,000 rooms, accommodating more than 3,000 monks from various nations. One noteworthy account involves the route taken by Bodhibhadra, a monk from the Kingdom of Kāvērī (modern Coimbatore in Tamil Nadu, India). This route, as recorded in the Yongming Temple section of Volume 4, is significant. The original text is as follows:[17]

The Monasteries of Luoyang[18]

Volume 4, Yongming Monastery

"To the south is the Kingdom of Kāvērī (歌营国), very far from the capital. Its geography and customs are isolated, and it has had no contact with China throughout the eras of the two Han dynasties or the Wei dynasty. Only recently did the monk Bodhibhadra or Shantibhadra (善(菩)提拔陀) arrive here. He said: 'Traveling north for one month, one reaches the Kingdom of Gouzhi Gaujita. From there, traveling north for 11 days, one arrives at the Kingdom of Dian Sun. From Dian Sun, traveling north for 30 days, one reaches the Kingdom of Funan. Funan spans 5,000 li and is the largest and most powerful kingdom in the southern regions, with a populous and prosperous society. It produces pearls, gold, jade, and rare crystals and is abundant in betel nuts. From Funan, traveling north for one month, one reaches the Kingdom of Lin Yi. Leaving Lin Yi, one enters the Kingdom of Xiao Yan.' Bodhibhadra stayed in Yangzhou for more than a year before traveling with the monk Farong of Yangzhou to the capital. When asked about the customs of the southern regions, Bodhibhadra said: 'In ancient times, there was the Kingdom of Nudiao, where carriages were pulled by horses with four wheels. This kingdom produced fireproof cloth made from tree bark. The bark did not burn when exposed to fire. In the southern kingdoms, people live within fortified walls, surrounded by abundance and beauty. The people are simple, honest, and value righteousness. They also trade extensively with the western countries of Daqin (the Roman Empire), Anxi (Parthia), and Shendu (India), navigating by sea for 100 days to reach their destinations. The inhabitants are generally devoted to Buddhism, cherish life, and abhor killing.'"

The White Horse Temple, recorded in Volume 4 of *The Monasteries of Luoyang* was established by Emperor Ming of the Han dynasty to commemorate the arrival of Buddhist scriptures brought to China by a white horse. During the Northern Wei dynasty, the temple still stood outside the Xiyang Gate in Luoyang, attracting numerous devotees. Yang Xuanzhi wrote:

> "The White Horse Temple was established by Emperor Ming of the Han dynasty, marking the introduction of Buddhism to China. The temple is located three li south of the imperial road outside the Xiyang Gate. The emperor dreamt of a golden deity, 16 feet tall, with light radiating from its head and back like the sun and moon. This golden deity, known as Buddha, prompted the emperor to send envoys to the Western Regions in search of it, resulting in the acquisition of scriptures and statues. A white horse carried these scriptures to China, hence the temple's name. After Emperor Ming's death, a Jetavana grove was built atop his mausoleum. From that time onward, the common people began constructing stupas over graves. The scripture case brought to the temple still exists today. It is regularly worshipped with incense offerings, and occasionally emits a radiant light that illuminates the halls, inspiring both monks and laypeople to revere it as though beholding the Buddha himself."[19]

3. NOVELS IN THE WEI-JIN, AND THE NORTHERN AND SOUTHERN DYNASTIES

The novels of the Wei, Jin, and Northern and Southern Dynasties can be divided into two categories based on their content: *zhiguai* (mystery and the supernatural tales) and *yishi* (historical anecdotes). The flourishing of novels during this period was mainly due to the prevalence of religion and superstitions, which promoted the development of *zhiguai* novels. The evaluation of the aristocratic families and their philosophical discussions since the Wei and Jin periods also fostered the development of *yishi* novels. Ancient myths, the fables of the pre-Qin and Han periods, as well as historical literature, had a significant influence on the development of novels during the Wei, Jin, and Northern and Southern Dynasties.

The representative work of *zhiguai* novels from the Wei, Jin, and Northern and Southern Dynasties is *Sou Shen Ji* (In Search of the Supernatural) by Gan Bao from the Eastern Jin period. In the *Jin History*, there is a biography of Gan Bao. His courtesy name was Lingsheng, though his exact birth and death dates remain unknown. He was from Xincai (modern-day Xincai County, Henan Province). The biography notes, "He was diligent in his studies from a young age, extensively read records and documents, and was summoned for his talent and appointed as a scribe." Later, he was recommended by Wang Dao to participate in compiling the national history, producing the *Annals of Jin* in 20 volumes. He was praised as an excellent historian. The biography also records, "Gan Bao had a deep interest in the occult and numerology. Moved by questions of life and death, he collected accounts of ancient and contemporary deities, miraculous events, and transformations, compiling them into *Soushen Ji* in thirty volumes." The biography preserves the complete preface of Gan Bao's *Soushen Ji*. From the preface, it is clear that his purpose in writing the work was to "demonstrate the undeniable reality of divine phenomena." The existingt *Soushen Ji* comprises 20 volumes because the original text was partially lost after the Song dynasty. Research suggests that the surviving version may have been compiled by Ming scholars from sources such as *Fayuan Zhulin* (The Forest of Pearls from the Dharma Garden) and *Chuxue Ji* ((Record for Beginners).

Three entries related to India in the book stand out: "Tianzhu Hu Ren" (A Man from India) in Volume 2, and "Jiehui" (Ash of Disaster) and "Dianlun Kanshi" (Carving on Stone) in Volume 13. Of these, "Tianzhu Hu Ren" is the most valuable. The original text is as follows:

Sou Shen Ji : *A Man from India*[20]

During the Yongjia era (307–312 CE) of the Jin dynasty, there was a man from Tianzhu (India) who crossed the river to the south. This man was skilled in various magical arts: he could sever and reattach his tongue, and spit fire. Wherever he went, people gathered to watch. Before severing his tongue, he would extend it to show the audience. Then, he would cut it with a knife, and blood would cover the ground. He would place the severed part in a container and pass it around for people to see, with half the tongue still in his mouth. Later, he would take the severed part, reattach it, and, after a moment, the audience would see the tongue restored to its original state, as if it had never been cut.

To demonstrate severing, he took a silk cloth, and two people held either end. He cut the cloth in half, and then rejoined the two pieces. The cloth returned to its original state, as if it had never been cut. Although many doubted it and thought it was an illusion, secret tests confirmed that the silk was indeed cut.

As for fire-spitting, he first placed some medicinal substances in a container, ignited a small piece of fire, and mixed it with sugar. After blowing on it repeatedly, he opened his mouth, and flames filled it. He then took the flames and used them to cook, confirming that it was indeed fire. Additionally, he threw books, paper, and rope into the fire, which the crowd saw burning completely. However, when he stirred the ashes, the original items emerged intact.

Subsequent records in Chinese literature echo the *Soushen Ji* account. For example, *Fayuan Zhulin*, Volume 7, "On Incantations," cites the *Linggui Zhi*: "In the twelfth year of Taiyuan (387 CE), a foreign Daoist arrived, capable of swallowing swords, spitting fire, and exhaling pearls, jade, gold, and silver. He claimed his skills were taught by a layman, not a monk."[21] The *zhiguai* novels of this period are artistically immature and rough, but they paved the way for the Tang Dynasty's *chuanqi* (legendary tales) and influenced Pu Songling's *Liaozhai Zhiyi* (Strange Stories from a Chinese Studio) in the Qing Dynasty.

The *Shishuo Xinyu* (A New Account of the Tales of the World), originally named *Shishuo*, and later called *Shishuo Xinyu* in the Tang Dynasty, is the masterpiece of *yishi* novels from the Southern Dynasties during the Liu Song period. *Shishuo Xinyu* achieves a high level of artistry: "When recording speech, it is profound, distant, and subtle; when recording actions, it is elegant, simple, and extraordinary." It excels in portraying characters through their words or specific actions, revealing their personality traits. It also skilfully uses contrasts between characters, exaggerated caricatures, and personalized language to shape character images. The language of the entire book is concise, implicit, and vivid.

A New Account of the Tales of the World: Speech[22]

At the age of ten, Kong Wenju accompanied his father to Luoyang. At that time, Li Yuanli was famous and held the position of Governor of the Inspectorate. Only those with distinguished talents or close relatives were allowed to visit him. When Kong Wenju arrived at the door, he told the steward, "I am a relative of Lord Li." After the steward announced this, he was allowed to enter and take a seat. Li Yuanli asked, "What is the relationship between us?" Kong Wenju replied, "In ancient times, my ancestor Zhongni studied under your ancestor Boyang, so our families have been connected for generations." Li Yuanli and the guests were all amazed by his response. Later, the Grand Chamberlain Chen Wei arrived. When others told him about Kong Wenju's words, Chen Wei said, "A clever child may not necessarily grow up to be outstanding." Kong Wenju immediately responded, "I imagine that when you were young, you must have been very clever." Chen Wei, hearing this, felt quite embarrassed.

The Governor of Yingchuan, Kun Chen Zhonggong, had a guest who asked Yuan Fang, "How is your lord?" Yuan Fang replied, "He is a wise and capable ruler." The guest then asked, "How about your family lord?" Yuan Fang answered, "He is a loyal minister and a filial son." The guest said, "The *I Ching* says, 'When two people are of one mind, their strength can cut through metal; when their words are in harmony, they are as fragrant as orchids.' How can there be a wise ruler who punishes a loyal minister and a filial son?" Yuan Fang replied, "What you say is utterly wrong! Therefore, I will not respond." The guest then said, "You are simply bowing in deference, but unable to answer." Yuan Fang said, "In the past, Emperor Gaozong exiled the filial son Xiao Ji, Minister Yin Jiufu exiled the filial son Boqi, and Dong Zhongshu exiled the filial son Fuqi. Only these three rulers were wise and capable; only these three sons were loyal ministers and filial sons." The guest, feeling ashamed, withdrew.

Xun Ciming met Yuan Lang from Runan, and they discussed the people of Yingchuan. Ciming first mentioned his brothers. Yuan Lang smiled and said, "Can scholars only rely on their old acquaintances?" Ciming replied, "You make a challenge, but what is your reasoning?" Yuan Lang said, "You were asking about national figures, but you mentioned your brothers. That is why I find it questionable!" Ciming responded, "In the past, Qi Xi was known for his impartiality, as he did not lose track of his son when dealing with internal affairs, nor did he lose track of his enemy in external matters—this was true public spirit. In the *Book of Odes*, Gong Dan praises the virtues of Wen and Wu, without mentioning the virtues of Yao and Shun, because of the duty to family. The principle of the *Spring and Autumn Annals* is to prioritize one's own country while engaging with the broader world of Xia. Moreover, if one does not love their own family and loves others instead, would this not be considered a breach of virtue?"

4. YUEFU BALLADS IN THE SOUTHERN AND NORTHERN DYNASTIES

According to the *Yuefu Shiji* (Collection of Music Bureau Poems) by the Song scholar Guo Maoqian, around 500 Southern Dynasties Yuefu folk songs and 70 Northern Dynasties Yuefu folk songs have survived. Due to the different regions and social environments in which they originated, Southern and Northern Dynasties folk songs differ both in content and form.

(a) Different Melodies: Southern Dynasties folk songs belong to the *Qing Shang Qu Ci* (Tunes of the Clear Music), which includes three main categories: *Wu Sheng Ge* (Wu Songs), *Xi Qu Ge* (West Style Songs), and *Shen Xian Qu* (Divine Strings Songs). Northern Dynasties folk songs primarily belong to the *Liang Gu Jiao Heng Chui Qu* (Liang Drum, Horn, and Horizontal Wind Songs), which are military music played on horseback by northern ethnic groups.

(b) Different Content: Due to the biased collection by the ruling class at the time, Southern Dynasties folk songs are mostly love songs in the voice of women. Compared to the Han Yuefu folk songs, their content is narrower and more monotonous. Besides the majority of love songs, there are also some with low, vulgar themes. Northern Dynasties folk songs are fewer in number, but their content is richer, expressing love between men and women, the conflict between the rich and the poor, reflecting martial spirit, war, and the suffering from forced labour.

(c) Different Forms of Expression: Southern Dynasties folk songs are mostly composed of five-character, four-line verses, making good use of metaphor, double meanings, homophones, and other literary devices. The language is natural, fresh, and subtle. Northern Dynasties folk songs are more lively, with five-character, seven-character, and four-character forms, and their language is simple, direct, and bold.

(d) Different Styles: Southern Dynasties folk songs are characterized by elegance and gentleness, while Northern Dynasties folk songs stand out for their boldness and vigour.

Song of the West Islet

Song of the West Islet is a representative Southern Dynasty ballad, revealing a woman's pure and deep love through the description of her yearning for her beloved from spring to autumn. Though its focus merely falls on lovesickness, it shines for its successful artistic expression. The form is beautiful for various anadiplosis; the structure unique with different focus every four lines, except few lines, with striking beauty for its symmetry, coherence, integrity and harmony. The setting of time is shown implicitly through the description of the scenery, and the emotional expression is manifested right through the description of the scenery. In the entire poem, different seasons can be perceived from some certain scenes and things, there employed only one word "autumn" to show clearly the setting. Furthermore, with the changing of these scenes and things, different seasons can be traced, and the heroine's profound feeling is also revealed little by little. Besides, the ingenious diction and various techniques are also impressive, with metonymy, consonance, pun and anadiplosis, and detailed description as well. The whole poem is fascinating for its beautiful language, distinct rhythm, and exquisite rhyme.

Most of the existing Northern Dynasty ballads can be traced back to Northern Wei Dynasty, reflecting the life, working and fighting of people from various nationalities at that time, covering a wide range of subjects of the contemporary society.

The Ballad of Mulan

The outstanding representative work of Northern Song poetry, *The Ballad of Mulan*, is a narrative poem praising the female hero Mulan, who disguises herself as a man to take her father's place in the army. It is regarded as one of the "two pinnacles" of Chinese poetic history, alongside the Han folk song *The Peacock Flies Southeast*. The protagonist of *The Ballad of Mulan* is a female hero who embodies many admirable qualities. In times of peace, she diligently spins, demonstrating the virtue of hard work; when war comes, she bravely steps forward to take her father's place, defending her country, reflecting her respect for the elderly and patriotism; during ten years of military service, she faces countless difficulties and dangers, achieving great military feats, showcasing her remarkable determination and courage; after returning home in triumph, she resigns from her official post and returns to farm to take care of her parents, displaying a humble, content nature. This character embodies the hardworking, kind-hearted, intelligent, brave, and simple virtues of the Chinese people, reflecting their ideals and desires, which strongly challenge the traditional patriarchal views of feudal society.

Artistic Achievements of The Ballad of Mulan

The artistic achievement of *The Ballad of Mulan* lies in its successful portrayal of the previously unseen female hero Mulan. It combines narrative with lyrical elements. The work focuses on Mulan's words and actions before going to war, during battle, and after returning home, yet it is centered around the theme "Mulan is a woman," which highlights the development and change of her emotions and emphasizes her character. The narrative is varied, alternating between simplicity and complexity, which not only highlights the character but also allows readers to engage in imaginative reinterpretation. The language is rich and diverse, skilfully using techniques such as metaphor, repetition, antithesis, parallelism, exaggeration, and question-and-answer exchanges, all of which give it a strong folk song flavour.

Song of Mulan[23]

Alack, alas! alack, alas!
She weaves and sees the shuttle pass.
You cannot hear the shuttle, why?
Its whir is drowned in her deep sigh.
"Oh, what are you thinking about?
Will you tell us? Will you speak out?"
"I have no worry on my mind,
Nor have I grief of any kind.
I read the battleroll last night;
The Khan has ordered men to fight.
The roll was written in twelve books;
My father's name was in the nooks.
My father has no grown-up son,
For elder brother I have none.
I'll buy a horse of hardy race
And serve in my old father's place.

She buys at the fair east and west
A steed with saddle fitting best;
She buys a long whip north and south
And metal bit for the horse's mouth.
At dawn she leaves her parents by the city wall;
At dusk she reaches Yellow River shore.

All night she listens for old folk's familiar call,
But only hears the Yellow River's roar.
At dawn she leaves the Yellow River shore;
To Mountains Black she goes her way.
At night she hears old folk's familiar voice no more,
But only on north mountains Tartar horses neigh.

For miles and miles the army march along
And cross the mountain barriers as in flight.
The northern wind has chilled the watchmen's gong,
Their coat of mail glistens in wintry light.
In ten years they've lost many captains strong,
But battle-hardened warriors come back in delight.

Back, they have their audience with the Khan in the hall,
Honors and gifts are lavished on them with grace.
The Khan asks her what she wants after all.
"A camel fleet to carry me to my native place."

Hearing that she has come, and leaning on each other,
Her parents come to meet her at the city gate.
Her sister rouges her face and her younger brother,
Sharpening knife, kills pig and sheep to celebrate.
She opens the doors east and west
And sits on her bed for a rest.
She doffs her garb worn under fire
And wears again female attire.
Before the window she arranges her hair
And in the mirror sees her image fair.
Then she comes out to see her former mate,
Who stares at her in amazement great;
"We have marched together for twelve years,
But did not know there was a lass'mid our compeers!"

Both buck and doe have lilting gait
And both their eyelids palpitate.
When side by side two rabbits go,
Who can tell the buck from the doe?

5. THE LITERARY THEORY IN WEI-JIN AND THE NORTHERN AND SOUTHERN DYNASTIES

The literature theory during the Wei, Jin, and Northern and Southern Dynasties achieved significant accomplishments. People gained a profound understanding of the characteristics and creative principles of literature. New literary theories and concepts were proposed, such as the debates on "fengli" (force), "fenggu" (vigour), "image," "meaning of words," and the relationship between form and spirit. This period also produced a number of outstanding literary theory and literary criticism works.

Cao Pi was the pioneer of literary theory and literary criticism in the Wei, Jin, and Northern and Southern Dynasties. Cao Pi's "*Dianlun: Wenlun*" (*Classical Treatise: On Literary Writing*) is the earliest surviving treatise on literary theory and criticism in China. Its value lies in: asserting that literature is "a major national undertaking, an immortal grand affair," thus affirming the importance of literature; stating that "the spirit is the core of writing," emphasizing that writers should have unique individual styles; proposing the four genres of literature and their characteristics, setting preliminary standards for the creation and criticism of various literary forms; and advocating for the critical attitude of "judging oneself to measure others," opposing the habit of scholars belittling one another.

Lu Ji's "*Wenfu*" (The Rhyme of Writing or *Essay on Literature*) is the first treatise on literary creation in the history of literary theory. Its value lies in: vividly discussing the process of literary creation; exploring rhetorical techniques in writing; proposing the theory of ten literary categories and their characteristics, and revealing the famous viewpoint of "poetry arises from emotion."

Liu Xie's "*Wenxin Diaolong*" (The Literary Mind and the Carving of Dragons) is one of the most systematic and outstanding works of literary theory and criticism in ancient China. "*Wenxin Diaolong*" consists of fifty chapters, including five introductory chapters, twenty chapters on literary theory, nineteen on literary creation, five on literary criticism, and a concluding chapter, "*Xuzhi*" (Preface and Summary).

The major contributions of *The Literary Mind and the Carving of Dragons* are as follows: firstly, it put forward the proposition that "The development of literary works is closely related to social situation and the vicissitude of the literary world is also associated with the development of the society", and his thoughts on "change", establishing initially the concept of "the history of literature". Secondly, it exposes the writer's aesthetic thoughts that "No literary work can be composed without emotion", demonstrating correctly the relationship between contents and form. Thirdly, the writer also reveals his aesthetic thoughts of "Six Perspectives"—A writer should put his emotion into his work so that the reader could interpret it by his words, establishing the rudimentary methodology of literary criticism, and generalizing many important lessons on vigor, the relationship between contents and form, image thinking, artistic imagination, artistic style and so forth.

The Literary Mind and the Carving of Dragons[24]

The Classics as Literary Sources

The works dealing with the universal principles of the Great Trinity [heaven, earth, and man] are known as *ching* [jing].[25] By ching we mean an expression of the absolute or constant Tao or principle, that great teaching which is unalterable. Therefore, the ching faithfully reflect heaven and earth, spirits and gods. They help to articulate the order of things and to set up the rules governing human affairs. In them is found both the secret of nature and spirit and the very bone and marrow of fine literature.

First came the San-fen of the Three Sovereigns, followed by Wu-tien of the five emperors, Pa-so and Chiu-ch'iu.[26] As years passed, this main stream developed a great welter of branches and side-eddies. But after our Master edited and handed down this material, those great treasures, the Classics, began to shine through. *The Book of Changes* spread out its ten Wings, or Commentaries. *The Book of History* displayed its seven Views.[27] *The Book of Poetry* listed the four beginnings.[28] *The Book of Rites* described the five kinds of Rites.[29] And the *Spring and Autumn* presented the Five Illustrations.[30]

Here are principles which are absolute in regard to human nature and emotions, and here is language which conforms to the best literary principles. As a consequence, the ching can unfold the student's understanding and cultivate in him the proper principles; their "light shines far and wide."[31]

The mind of *Tao* is subtle, and the thinking of the Sage transcendent: when the walls and eaves are many and high, breathing is naturally deep: a bell of ten thousand weights will not ring out petty sounds. *The Book of Changes* deals with *Tien*; it has penetrated the divine order, to fulfill itself fruitfully.[32] Accordingly, the "Hsi-tz'u"[33] says that it has boundless implications, its critical judgments are of high literary quality, its language is accurate, and its symbolism deep:[34] "The leather cords broke three times"[35] what a profound source of ideas this has proved to be for the Sage!

The Book of History truthfully records what has been spoken.[36] Although the terms used are hard to understand, if one masters the Erh-ya[37] the ideas will be comprehensible. Tzu-hsia, [a disciple of Confucius who specialized in literature], in his praise of the *Book of History* calls it "brilliant as the light of the sun and the moon and orderly as the configurations of the stars,"[38] which testifies to its clarity.

The purpose of the *Book of Poetry* is to express feelings and sentiments. The terms used in it are to be studied in the same way as those used in the *Book of History*. The way the lyrics are written and the metaphors forged, the way that these are embellished and the parables contrived, create an effect of warmth and tenderness when these poems are recited, an effect which deeply moves the heart.

The *Book of Rites* aims at the establishment of traditions. It formulates the basic principles governing social customs. The principles and corollaries are subtle and oblique, and become clear only through practical application. Every single phrase selected from it is a treasure.

The Spring and Autumn is characterized by its clear reasoning. Reason may appear in the choice of a single word. "Five meteorites" and "Six fishhawks"[39] are two examples of a pattern of composition marked by a thoroughness in reasoning. In the case of "The Chih gate and the two gates,"[40] reason appears in the order: precedence and sequence. To be so subtle and yet so apparent, so full of meaning yet so unassuming, is to be genuinely profound."[41]

In the case of the *Book of History*, its language may appear strange to the reader, but when he looks for its ruling principles he will find them indicated very clearly. In the case of the *Spring and Autumn*, its language may seem readily understandable, but when the reader seeks the meaning of it he begins to realize its depth. These two works illustrate different patterns of writing from the hands of sages, as well as different methods of approach, objective and subjective.[42]

These Classics have deep roots and luxuriant branches and foliage. The language is concise but the content is meaningful; the facts are commonplace, but their metaphorical implications are unlimited. So, although they are ancient, their flavor remains fresh. Later scholars take them up and do not feel that they have become outmoded; scholars in the past long used them and never felt that they were ahead of their times. They may be compared to Mount T'ai, which waters all the lands about, or to the Yellow River, which moistens one thousand li.

Thus, the *Book of Changes* originates the *lun* or discursive, *shuo* or argumentative, *tz'u* or oracular, and *hsü* or prefatory forms of writing.

The *Book of History* is the source of the *chao* or decree, the *tz'e* or edict, the *chang* or memorial expressing thanks, and the *tsou* or general memorial. *Fu* or narrative poetry, sung or sacrificial poetry, *ke* or folk song, and *tsan* or eulogy have their foundations in the *Book of Poetry*. *Ming* or inscription, *lei* or elegy, *chen* or admonition, and *chu* or prayer have their beginnings in the *Book of Rites*. And *chi* or chronicle, *chuan* or biography, *meng* or oath[43] and *hsi* or proclamation have their roots in the *Spring and Autumn*. All these Classics have reached great heights in establishing standards; they have also opened up vast new vistas. So that no matter how writers may leap and bound, they must eventually come home to the fold of the Classics. One may pattern his writing after the classical forms or enrich his diction by studying the *Book of Poetry* [with the same confidence with which] one may depend on a mountain's copper ores to suffice for coinage, or rely on sea water to make salt when boiled.

If one's writings were based on the Classics, his style would be especially distinguished by one of the following characteristics: deep feeling untainted by artificiality, unmixed purity of form, empirical truth untarnished by falsehood, moral ideas uninvolved in perversity, simple style free from verbosity, and literary beauty unmarred by excesses. Master Yang compared [the writing of the Classics] to the carving of jade into vessels, his idea being that literary pattern is innate in the five Classics.[44]

A man wins his mastery of literature through the excellence of his character, and his character is manifested in his literary excellence. In literature, first among the four elements of instruction,[45] both symbol and colourful pattern assist each other to teach. No one who aims at the improvement of his moral character and the establishment of his name fails to go to the Sage for his model; but when one develops an interest in a career of literature and rhetoric, he seldom realizes that he too should take the Classics as his starting point. The poetry of Ch'u has alluring charm and the poetic prose of Han is extravagant; but both are deviant forks which never return to the main stream. Would it not be a good thing to curb the tendency to deviate by returning to the source?

The Tsan:

> The universal principles governing the Great Trinity
> Are embodied in profound teachings and ancient learning.
> To achieve transformation in order to return to the One,
> These teachings are divided into five.
> The five Classics are art masters moulding human nature and spirit,
> And the great treasure house of literature,
> Unfathomable and lustrous,
> The Source of all literary forms.

NOTES

1 Xu, Yuanchong. (Transl.) 《汉魏六朝诗选》*Golden Treasury of Chinese Poetry in Han, Wei and Six Dynasties.* Beijing: Wuzhou Communication Press and Zhonghua Book Company (2012, 73-74).

2 Ibid., (2012, 76).

3 Ibid., (2012, 72).

4 Ibid., (2012, 87).

5 Ibid., (2012, 96-97).

6 Ibid., (2012, 93).

7 Ibid., (2012, 78).

8 Ibid., (2012, 106). *Reflections* is a collection of 82 poems written by Ruan Ji in different time, reflecting his dissatisfaction with the society and his agony.

9 Ibid., (2012, 107).

10 Ibid., (2012, 115). This is a satire against the nobles in high position (Jin and Zhang) while the able (Feng) was in low office.
11 Ibid., (2012, 145). *Return to Nature* includes five poems, and this is the first one.
12 Ibid., (2012, 146).
13 Sun, Dayu. 孙大雨译. (Transl.)《饮酒》 "Drinking" in 《古诗文英译》*Anthology of Ancient Chinese Poetry and Prose*. Shanghai: Shanghai Sanlian Publishing House (2020, 77). This is the fifth of a series of 20 poems.
14 Ibid., (2020, 69-71).
15 See,《桃花源诗》 "Peach-Blossom Springs" in http://www.kekenet.com/kouyi/201504/368258.shtml
16 Wuchen (芜城): also called Guanglin (广陵), the present Yangzhou (扬州).
17 Geng, Yinzeng. 耿引曾《汉文南亚史料学》*Historical Date of South Asia from Chinese Sources*. Beijing: Peking University Press (1990, 67-68)
18 Ibid., p 68, above is the translation of Chinese passage from the book.
19 Ibid., above is the translation of Chinese passage from the book.
20 Ibid., (1990, 86). Translated from Chinese
21 Ibid., p. 87.
22 Translated from http://ewenyan.com/articles/ssxy/2.html
23 Xu, Yuanchong. (Transl.) 《汉魏六朝诗选》*Golden Treasury of Chinese Poetry in Han, Wei and Six Dynasties*. Beijing: Intercontinental Press and Zhonghua Book Company (2012, 211-213).
24 Liu Xie. *The Literary Mind and the Carving of Dragons*. Translated by Vincent Yu-chung Shih. New York: Columbia University Press (1959, 17-21).
25 Ching is rendered into English as "classics" in the sense that they have stood the test of time and are universal and constant.
26 See K'ung An-kuo's "Shang-shu hsü," where the Pa-so is said to be about the eight trigrams, and the Chiu-ch'in geographical accounts of the nine continents.
27 In the Shang-shu ta-chuan, the Book of History is divided into seven sections, and through each section one is able to view one quality. These are: righteousness, benevolence, sincerity, capacity, affairs, good government, and beauty.
28 There are several interpretations of these four beginnings. In the "Mao shih-hsü," the four beginnings mean "Feng." "Ta-ya," "Hsiao-ya," and "Sung." Cheng Hsüan commented, "By shih or the beginning is meant that by way of which the kingly way prospers and declines." Another view is expressed in "K'ung tzu shih-chia" (the biography of Confucius) in the Shih-chi (The historical records): "Kuan-chu" is the beginning of the "Feng," "Lu-ming" the beginning of the "Hsiao-ya," "Wen-wang" the beginning of the "Ta-ya," and "Ch'ing-miao" the beginning of the "Sung."
29 The Five Rites are: for sacrifice, for melancholy occasions, for hospitality, for military ceremonies, and for auspicious occasions.
30 See note 16, Chapter 11.
31 A line quoted from the Book of Poetry, Mao-shih yin-te, 63/247/3.
32 Chou-i yin-te, 46/Hsi, hsia/3: "The profound idea has entered the divine state for the purpose of bringing about its fruitful functioning."
33 Ibid., 48/Hsi, hsia/5.
34 Ibid., 48/Hsi, hsia/5: "The meanings are far-reaching, the judgments are well ordered. The words are roundabout but they hit the mark. Things are openly set forth, but they contain also a deeper secret." I-ching, 1, 370.
35 Quoted from "K'ung-tzu shih-chia," the biography of Confucius, in the Shih-chi.
36 The Han-shu, "I-wen chih": "The historian on the left records what is spoken."
37 A dictionary of terms used in the Classics arranged according to meanings.
38 Quoted from the Shang-shu ta-chuan.

39 Ch'un-ch'in Ching-chuan yin-te, 111/Hsi 16/1. "There were falling meteorites in the state of Sung, five in number. And there were six fishhawks flying backward over the capital of Sung." Commentary by Kung-yang says: "Why is 'falling" first mentioned and then 'meteorites'? It is because this was a record about what one heard. First one heard the sound of falling. Looking at them, he found them to be meteorites. After a closer observation he discovered them to be five in number. Why is the number 'six' first mentioned and then 'fishhawks'? Because in the case of 'the six fishhawks flying backward' it was a record about what one saw. Looking at them, one found them to be six in number. Looking closer, he saw them to be fishhawks. After watching them at leisure, he discovered them to be flying backward." For these reasons, the Spring and Autumn is held to be logical, that is, a work characterized by reason.

40 Ch'un-ch'iu Ching-chuan yin-te, 439/Ting 2/2 Kung-yang. "Chih gate and the two gates were destroyed by fire." "Chih gate" is the south gate of the royal palace, and the two gates are those outside the Chih gate where proclamations are posted. Chih gate is apparently more important than the two gates. The commentary by Kung-yang says: "Why does the record say 'Chih gate and the two gates were destroyed by fire'? It is because the two gates were not important. Why then does it not say Chih gate was destroyed by fire and the fire was extended to the two gates? It is because it was the two gates which were [first] destroyed by fire. Then why is it mentioned last? It is because [the historian] did not wish to proceed from the less important to the more important."

41 See note 16, Chapter II.

42 The whole section beginning with the line "The Book of Changes deals with Tien" to this point is taken verbatim from Wang Ts'an's writing without acknowl edgement by Liu Hsich. However, such a practice was quite common in the early times, and should not be considered as plagiarism. Wang's writing is found in both I-wen Lei-chil, 38, and T'ai-ping yi-lan, 608. For a discussion of this practice of borrowing from other authors see Chang Hsüch-ch'eng's Wen-chih rung-i, "Shuo-lin."

43 Reading ming as meng with the Tang hand-written version.

44 See chapter on "Kua-chien" in his Fa-yen.

45 Lun-yü yin-te, 13/7/25: "The master taught *wen* [literature], *hsing* [character], *chung* [loyalty], and *hsin* [trustworthiness]."

Chapter Four

Literature in Tang Dynasty

In 589, Emperor Wen of Sui unified China, ending the prolonged confrontation of the Northern and Southern Dynasties. However, the Sui dynasty maintained its rule for only 30 years before being overthrown by peasant uprisings. During these uprisings at the end of the Sui dynasty, Li Yuan and his sons leveraged the power of the peasant movements to establish the Li-Tang dynasty in 618, an unprecedentedly powerful empire in Chinese history.

Looking at the history of the Sui, Tang, Five Dynasties, and the Southern and Northern Song Dynasties, this period marked the transition from the peak of China's feudal society to its gradual decline. During the Tang dynasty, society was economically prosperous and commercially advanced, with significant cultural exchanges between China and foreign nations. The loosening of literary restrictions, coupled with the active intellectual climate among scholars and the implementation of the imperial examination system—where poetry was a key criterion—created favourable material and ideological conditions for the development of Tang literature.

The "An Shi Rebellion" (An Lushan and Shi Siming Rebellion) heightened class and ethnic conflicts, leading to severe division and resistance struggles, which provided rich themes and content for literary creation. Consequently, literature flourished like never before. The Song dynasty, building on the traditions and innovations of Tang literature, also achieved remarkable accomplishments.

Due to the short duration and social conditions of the Five Dynasties period, it did not see significant literary achievements and can only be regarded as the prelude and epilogue to Tang literature. Similarly, the neighbouring Liao and Jin dynasties of the Song period achieved little in the literary domain. However, the Tang and Song dynasties left a brilliant legacy in Chinese literary history with their substantial achievements in literary creation.

1. THE FLOURISHING AND PROSPERITY OF TANG POETRY

Tang poetry represents a pinnacle in the history of Chinese poetry. With numerous poets, diverse styles, schools, and a rich array of outstanding works, it adorned the vibrant literary landscape of the Tang dynasty. The development of Tang poetry can be divided into four stages:

1.1 Early Tang Period (From 618, the first year of Emperor Gaozu's Wude reign to 713, the first year of Emperor Xuanzong's Kaiyuan reign)

During this period, many poets were former officials of the previous dynasty. Although they served the new regime, their old habits persisted. Emperor Taizong's advocacy of literature perpetuated the styles of the Qi and Liang dynasties. Represented by Shangguan Yi, the "elegant and delicate" *Shangguan Style* dominated the literary scene. However, his theories of "Six Couplets" and "Eight Couplets" significantly influenced the development of regulated verse or the Lvshi.[1]

Following Shangguan Yi came the "Four Distinguished Writers"—Wang Bo, Yang Jiong, Lu Zhaolin, and Luo Binwang—who, though of low official rank, gained high acclaim for their youthful brilliance and literary talent. They held progressive ideals of achievement and success, but their lives were fraught with difficulties. They broke away from the limited and shallow themes of court poetry, composing numerous works that expressed personal emotions. Their efforts revitalized the literary scene, shifting its focus from palace life and trivial romanticism to themes of life and authentic emotion, infusing poetry with new vitality. Their bold and lofty five-character and seven-character *gexing* poems had a profound influence on later poetic creation.

After the "Four Distinguished Writers" emerged Chen Ziang, a staunch advocate of literary reform. While vehemently criticizing the Qi and Liang styles, he championed the *Jian'an Style*, paving a radiant path for the development of Tang poetry through his creative practice.

1.2 High Tang (From 713, the first year of Emperor Xuanzong's Kaiyuan reign, to 766, the first year of Emperor Daizong's Dali reign)

This was the golden age of Tang poetry, marked by an abundance of renowned poets and diverse schools of thought. Like a myriad of blossoming flowers, numerous excellent works enriched the literary landscape. The *Pastoral School*, led by Wang Wei and Meng Haoran, brought vitality to poetry with their sincere emotions, picturesque descriptions, and clear, Zen-like charm, opening new creative horizons.

Subsequently, the *Frontier School*, represented by Gao Shi and Cen Shen, focused on the realities of life, vividly portraying the lives of frontier soldiers and the scenery of border regions. Their poems were imbued with heroic and tragic tones and a patriotic spirit of courage and sacrifice, reflecting strong realism. Despite differing themes, both schools produced works of rich content and diverse expression. For example, Wang Wei, renowned for pastoral poetry, also wrote themes like *The Old General*. Wang Changling excelled in frontier poetry but also crafted deeply moving works such as *Boudoir Resentment*. Even poets within the same school displayed stylistic diversity: Gao Shi's works reflected political insight and realism, while Cen Shen's poetry brimmed with imagination, metaphors, and a strong romantic flavour. Wang Changling excelled in portraying the inner world of soldiers. Combining the strengths of both schools was the romantic poet Li Bai.

Li Bai's life and experiences were complex. He witnessed both the "Kaiyuan Prosperity" and the turmoil of the *An Lushan Rebellion*. Having served as a court scholar and experienced exile, he deeply understood societal realities, which gave his poetry broad themes and profound content. His works expressed progressive political ideals, criticism of dark realities, yearning for freedom, disdain for authority, personal frustrations, patriotism, and empathy for the people. Li Bai's poetry was rich in thought and diverse in form. His romantic style stemmed not only from his ideological pursuits but also from his innovative artistic methods. He skilfully combined extreme exaggeration with vivid metaphors, as well as extraordinary imagination with mythological elements. His language was natural and unadorned, his form unrestrained by metrics, creating a magnificent and majestic flow. By using fantastical and dreamlike imagery to reflect societal realities and personal sentiments, his poetry also exhibited a mystical romanticism. He was later hailed as the "Immortal Poet." Li Bai's exceptional creative achievements inspired generations of poets, establishing him as a great transitional figure in literary history.

Following Li Bai was the great realist poet Du Fu. Suffering numerous hardships yet harbouring grand ambitions, Du Fu endured the turmoil of the *An Lushan Rebellion* and witnessed the Tang empire's decline from its peak. His poetry faithfully and profoundly captured the spirit of the times, embodying strong realism. This is evident in his focus on national stability, his critique of the ruling class's decadence, his deep sympathy for the people's suffering, and his love for his homeland and life. Du Fu's poetry not only profoundly reflected the social realities of the Tang dynasty but also stood out artistically due to his inheritance of tradition, bold innovation, and unique style. He excelled in summarizing social life with high artistic refinement, seamlessly embedding personal emotions into objective descriptions, and skilfully interweaving techniques such as detailed depictions, psychological portrayals, dialogues, monologues, and refined language.

In summary, Li Bai and Du Fu inherited China's literary traditions and elevated Tang poetry to an unparalleled peak in Chinese literary history, leaving a profound legacy. Subsequent poets such as Yuan Jie, Gu Kuang, Wei Yingwu, and Liu Changqing also contributed to the prosperity of Tang poetry.

1.3 Mid-Tang Period (From 766, the First Year of Dali under Emperor Daizong to 836, the Ninth Year of Taihe under Emperor Wenzong)

After the suppression of the An-Shi Rebellion, society experienced relative stability, allowing production to recover and the economy to flourish again. However, internal factional struggles within the court and the regional fragmentation caused by local military governors (fan zhen) continued to bring immense suffering to the people. Against this backdrop, a realist poetic movement led by Bai Juyi emerged. As part of the "*New Yuefu*" movement he advocated, Bai Juyi proposed the principle that "writing should serve its time, and poetry should be composed with purpose." He produced brilliant works infused with a strong sense of realism. The realist features of Bai Juyi's poetry are mainly reflected in the following aspects:

(a) Reflecting the hardships of people's lives and exposing the greed and brutality of the ruling class.
(b) Revealing the extravagant and corrupt lifestyles of the powerful and wealthy.
(c) Opposing aggressive wars and promoting patriotic sentiments.
(d) Showing sympathy for the plight of women and criticizing the social system.

Bai Juyi's poems also have the following artistic features: Clear and focused themes; frequent use of contrast; and a simple, fluent style imbued with musicality.

However, at times, his poetry was criticized for being overly direct and lacking subtlety. His works, such as *The Song of the Pipa Player* and *The Song of Everlasting Regret*, raised the art of Chinese narrative poetry to new heights.

In addition to the realist poetry led by Bai Juyi, the Mid-Tang period also saw poets like Han Yu, Liu Zongyuan, Liu Yuxi, and Li He. There were also renowned poets known for their "bitter striving," such as Jia Dao and Meng Jiao. In the late Mid-Tang period, poets like Li Shangyin and Du Mu emerged. These poets, each with unique styles and forms, vividly captured the social landscape of the time, adding brilliance to the poetic tradition of the Tang dynasty.

1.4 Late Tang Period (from 836, the first year of Kaicheng reign of Emperor Wenzong of Tang, to 906, the end of the Tang Dynasty)

The Late Tang period marked the decline of the Tang dynasty. During this era, regional fragmentation and factional struggles in the court intensified. The ruling class's exploitation and oppression of the people became even more severe, exacerbating class conflicts and plunging the populace into profound suffering.

As a result, poets like Pi Rixiu, Nie Yizhong, and Du Gouhe rose to prominence. They inherited the realist tradition of Bai Juyi's "*New Yuefu*" movement, deeply reflecting the painful lives of the people in this turbulent era. Although their achievements did not surpass those of Bai Juyi's "*New Yuefu*" movement, their works possessed notable artistic merit and were regarded as "the lingering brilliance of a declining Tang dynasty."

Wang Bo

Wang Bo (650-676), courtesy name Zi'an, was born in Longmen, Jiangzhou (the present Hejin, Shanxi province). Having passed the Imperial Examination in his early years, Wang Bo was an equal of Yang Jiong, Lu Zhaolin and Luo Binwang, the recognized "Four Distinguished Writers" in the Early Tang Period. Wang once served as a staff officer (canyuan) and aspired to reform the prevailing poetic trends of his time, which he criticized for their obsession with "minute intricacies and excessive embellishments."

Wang Bo believed that "literature is a great endeavor that serves the nation, an immortal achievement of enduring significance." He held that it could "discern profound principles and rectify prevailing degeneracies." Consequently, he composed a large number of eight-line poems with five-character lines, and ancient style poems as well, to express his own thoughts and emotion, making a great contribution to the development of five-character eight line poems.

His works were later compiled into the *Collected Works of Wang Zian* by Ming scholars and annotated in the *Annotated Collected Works of Wang Zian* by Qing scholar Jiang Qingyi.

Before Du Takes His Office in Shu[2]

Three areas are guarding the capital in the front,
The view of the five ferries is blurred in the mist.
Both of us are plaintive at the parting moment,
We are all officials far away from homeland.
Vast as the four seas there must be one who knows me best,
Even he is at a remotest place I still feel he's in my neighbourhood.
Let's say farewell at this fork road,
Not letting tears wet our clothes as what the lads did.

Chen Ziang

Chen Ziang (659-700), courtesy name Boyu, was a native of Shehong in Zizhou (present-day Shehong, Sichuan). In his youth, he was known for his bravery and chivalrous spirit. At the age of 24, he passed the imperial metropolitan[3] examination and gained recognition from Empress Wu Zetian for his memorials on state affairs. She appointed him as a *Zhengzi*[4] *Lintai*[5] (a minor official responsible for editing imperial records) and later promoted him to *You Shiyi*[6] (a remonstrance official). He also participated in two military expeditions to the frontier. However, due to his opposition to the Wu family, he was dismissed from his position and returned to his hometown, where he was falsely accused by county magistrate Duan Jian and died in prison.

Chen Ziang was one of the earliest Tang figures to oppose the ornate and overly decorative literary style of the Six Dynasties period. He advocated for literature to correct the flaws of superficial extravagance, emphasizing that prose should follow the examples of ancient texts, and poetry should innovate by upholding the spirit and integrity of the Han and Wei dynasties. He championed the use of evocative and meaningful themes while rejecting softness and excessive embellishment. His poetry broke away from the flowery and elaborate style of the Qi and Liang periods, establishing a new, distinctive style characterized by simplicity and vigour.

As a pioneer in the development of Tang poetry, Chen Ziang opened up new realms for its evolution. The Tang literary reformer Han Yu praised his historical contributions with the line, "In our flourishing dynasty, it was Ziang who first took the high path." Chen Ziang's works are collected in the *Anthology of Chen Boyu*.

The Orchid[7]

In late spring grows the orchid good
How luxury are its leaves green
Alone it adorns empty wood
With red blooms and violet stems lean.
Slowly, slowly shortens the day,
Rippling, rippling blows autumn breeze
By the years' end it fades away
What has become of it fragrance, please

Song on Ascending the Youzhou Terrace[8]

Descrying nor the ancients of long yore,
Nor those that are to come in the future far,
I muse on the eternity of heaven and earth,
And, all alone, grieve mutely with tears for my lorn star.

Meng Haoran

Meng Haoran (689-740), a native of Xiangyang, Hubei, lived in seclusion at Mount Lumen before the age of 40. At 40, he travelled to Chang'an to take the imperial examination but failed to pass and returned home. During Zhang

Jiuling's tenure as regional inspector of Jingzhou, Meng Haoran served as an aide. Later, due to a severe back abscess, he returned to his home in Xiangyang, where he soon passed away from illness.

In poetry, Meng Haoran was as renowned as Wang Wei, and together they were referred to as "Wang and Meng." His poetry focused on depicting natural landscapes, characterized by fresh and vivid imagery, simplicity, and an unpretentious charm. As a Tang Dynasty poet with a unique style, he specialized in pastoral and landscape poetry. However, his long-term seclusion and limited interaction with society resulted in relatively narrow subject matter. His works are compiled in the collection *Meng Haoran's Poetry.*

Visiting an Old Friend's Cottage[9]

My friend's prepared chicken and rice;
I'm invited to his cottage hall.
Green trees surround the village nice;
Blue hills slant beyond city wall.
Windows open to field and ground;
O'er wine we talk of crops of grain.
On Double Ninth Day I'll come round
For the chrysanthemums again.

Mooring on the River at Jiande[10]

My boat is moored near an isle in mist grey;
I'm grieved anew to see the parting day.
On boundless plain trees seem to scrape the sky;
In water clear the moon appears so nigh.

Wang Wei

Wang Wei (701–761), courtesy name Mojie, was originally from Qi Prefecture (now Qixian County, Shanxi Province). Later, he moved with his father to Pu Prefecture (now Yongji County, Shanxi Province) and thus became a native of Hedong. In the ninth year of the Kaiyuan era (721), he passed the imperial examination and held the position of *Jishi zhong* (an imperial inspector). He was once sent on a diplomatic mission and later served in a post under An Lushan's rebel forces when they occupied Chang'an. After the rebellion was quelled, Wang Wei was demoted to *Taizi Zhongyun* (a minor court official) but eventually rose to the position of *Shang Youcheng* (Right Assistant Minister), earning him the moniker "Wang Right Assistant Minister."

In his early years, his outlook was relatively optimistic and forward-looking, resulting in poetry with significant social relevance. In his later years, he lived in Lantian at the Wangchuan retreat, leading a leisurely life that combined official duties with reclusive living. His thoughts turned more introspective and subdued, with most of his poetry characterized by serene beauty and a touch of Zen philosophy. Wang Wei was a poet of remarkable distinctiveness and accomplishment. He seamlessly integrated music and art into his poetry, imbuing it with poetic imagery, aesthetic beauty, musical rhythm, and linguistic charm.

He was devoted to Buddhism, focusing on meditation and chanting sutras. Wang Wei was a polymath, excelling in poetry, painting, music, and calligraphy. However, due to his distance from the lives of ordinary people, his works rarely revealed social conflicts. His collected works are compiled in *The Collection of Wang Youcheng's Poems*.

Autumn Evening in the Mountains[11]

After fresh rain in mountains bare
Autumn permeates evening air.
Among pine-trees bright moonbeams peer;
O'er crystal stones flows water clear.
Bamboos whisper of washer-maids;
Lotus stirs when fishing boat wades.
Though fragrant spring may pass away,
Still here's the place for you to stay.

On Mission to the Frontier[12]

A single carriage goes to the frontier;
An envoy crosses northwest mountains high.
Like tumbleweed I leave the fortress drear;
As wild geese I come 'neath Tartarian sky.
In boundless desert lonely smokes rise straight;
Over endless river the sun sinks round.
I meet a cavalier at the camp gate;
In northern fort the general will be found.

Bidding Adieu to Yuan Junior in His Missoin to Anxi[13]

The fall of morning drops in this Town of Wei
Its dust light doth moisten,
Tenderly green are the new willow sprouts
Of this spring-adorned tavern.
I pray thee to quench once more full to the brim
This farewell cup of wine,
For after thy departure from this western-most pass,
Thou will have no old friend of thine.

Parting in the Hills[14]

I see off the hills my compeer;
At dusk I close my wicket door.
When grass turns green in spring next year,
Will my friend come with spring once more?

Love Seeds[15]

Red berries grow in southern land.
How many load in spring the trees?
Gather them till full is your hand;
They would revive fond memories.

Wang Changling

Wang Changling (689–757), courtesy name Shaobo, was from Jingzhao (now Xi'an, Shaanxi Province). In the fifteenth year of the Kaiyuan era (727), he passed the imperial examination and was appointed as the magistrate of Sishui (now within Xingyang County, Henan Province). In the twenty-fifth year of the Kaiyuan era (737), he passed the *Boxue Hongci* (Royal Collator of the classics) examination and was promoted to the position of *Xiaoshulang* (an official in charge of document copying). He was later exiled to places like Lingnan, Longbiao, and Jiangning, and his political career was rather unremarkable. After the *An-Shi Rebellion*, he returned to his hometown, where he was killed by the local governor, Lü Xiaoqiu, leading to a tragic end.

Wang Changling had connections with contemporary poets such as Chang Jian, Wang Zhihuan, Xin Jian, Gao Shi, Wang Wei, Li Bai, and Cen Shen, with the deepest friendships being with Wang Zhihuan and Xin Jian. His poetry, covering various themes, exposed and reflected the dark politics and chaotic society during the later years of Emperor Xuanzong's reign. He was praised for writing poetry that was "dense in mood yet clear in thought." He was particularly skilled in writing *seven-character quatrains* (qijue) (four-line and seven-character poems), often using very concise verses to convey rich social content. Many of his poems became masterpieces of the *Yuefu* (folk songs) of the time, earning him the title "The Confucius of Poetry in Jiangning." Among his contemporaries, only Li Bai's *seven-character quatrains* could rival his in beauty. Wang Changling is regarded as one of the foremost poets of the prosperous Tang dynasty. His poetry is preserved in four volumes in the *Complete Tang Poems* anthology.

On the Frontier[16]

The moon still shines on mountain passes as of yore,
How many guardsmen of the Great Wall are no more!
If the flying general were still there in command,
No hostile steeds would have dared to invade our land.

Sorrow of a young bride in her boudoir[17]

Nothing in her boudoir brings sorrow to the bride,
She mounts the tower, gaily dressed, on a spring day.
Suddenly seeing green willows by the roadside,
She sighs for her husband seeking fame far away.

Gao Shi

Gao Shi (around 700–765), courtesy name Dafu, was a native of Bohai Xiu (now Jingxian, Hebei). In his youth, he was poor and downcast. After the age of 20, he travelled widely to places like Chang'an, Jiemen, Liang, and Song. After turning 40, he passed the Imperial Examination in the "Youdao" (elevation of the virtuous) category and was appointed as a military officer. He soon resigned from the position. Later, he travelled west to Hexi and worked as a secretary in the army of General Ge Shuhan. After the *An-Shi Rebellion*, he was highly valued by Li Heng, Emperor Suzong of Tang, and eventually reached the position of a "*Sancai Changshi*" (a senior honorary title).

Gao Shi was a renowned frontier poet of the early Tang period, often mentioned alongside Cen Shen as one of the "Gao-Cen" poets. Through his personal experiences, his frontier poems authentically depicted the situation at the borders during that time, highlighting the military leaders' neglect of defence preparations, their indulgence in pleasure, and the suffering of soldiers. Gao Shi's poetry is known for its grand and vigorous imagery, bold and passionate emotion, and flowing language. He paid great attention to rhythm and music, and was particularly skilled in using parallelism in his verses. His works are compiled in the "*Gao Changshi Ji*" (The Collected Works of Gao Changshi).

Song of the Northern Frontier[18]

A cloud of smoke and dust spreads over northeast frontier;
To fight the remnant foe our generals leave the rear.
Brave men should go no matter where beneath the sky;
The emperor bestows on them his favor high.
To the beat of drums and gongs through Elm Pass they go;
Round Mount Stone Tablet flags serpentine row on row.
But urgent orders speed over the Sea of Sand:

Mount Wolf aflame with fires set by the Tartar band.
Both hills and streams are desolate on border plain;
The Tartar horsemen flurry like the wind and rain.
Half of our warriors lie killed on the battleground,
While pretty girls in camp still sing and dance their round.
Grass withers in the desert as autumn is late;
At sunset few men guard the lonely city gate.
Imperial favor makes them hold the foemen light;
Their town is under siege, though they've fought with their might.
In coats of mail they've served so long on the frontiers;
Since they left home their wives have shed streams of impearled tears.
In southern towns the women weep with broken heart;
In vain their men look southward, still they're far apart.
The northern front at stake, how can they go away?
On borders vast and desolate, how can they stay?
All day a cloud of slaughter mounts now and again;
All night the boom of gongs is heard to chill the plain.
Each sees the other's sword bloodstained in the hard strife.
Will they care for reward when they give up their life?
Do you not know
The bitterness of fighting with the foe?
Can they forget General Li sharing their weal and woe?

Cen Shen

Cen Shen (715–770), a native of Jiangling (now Jiangling County, Hubei), was originally from Nanyang (now Nanyang, Henan), which is why *Tang Caizi Chuan* (Biographies of Talented Men of the Tang Dynasty) refers to him as a person from Nanyang. In the third year of the Tianbao era (744), he passed the imperial examination. In the eighth year of Tianbao (749), he served as the chief secretary in the military office of General Gao Xianzhi in the Anxi Protectorate. In the tenth year of Tianbao (751), he returned to Chang'an, and in the twelfth year (754), he was appointed as the governor of the Anxi and Beiting Protectorates, where he also served as the inspector and judge. In the second year of the Zhide era (757), he was appointed as the right assistant censor. He passed away in Chengdu in the fifth year of the Dali era (770).

Cen Shen accompanied the military on several campaigns to the frontier and had deep experiences with the scenery of the northwest borderlands and the life of soldiers. As a result, he was particularly skilled at writing about the frontier in his poetry. His frontier poems passionately praised the bravery, heroism, and unyielding spirit of the soldiers defending the unity of the country, showing their patriotism, resilience in hardship, and willingness to sacrifice. His poetry is filled with optimism and a sense of national pride. His works are compiled in the *Cen Jiazhou Ji* (The Collected Works of Cen Jiazhou).

Song of White Snow in Farewell to Secretary Wu Going Back to the Capital[19]

Snapping the pallid grass, the northern wind whirls low;
In the eighth moon the Tartar sky is filled with snow
As if the vernal breeze had come back overnight,
Adorning thousands of pear trees with blossoms white.
Flakes enter pearled blinds and wet the silken screen;
No furs of fox can warm us nor brocade quilts green.
The general cannot draw his rigid bow with ease;
E'en the commissioner in coat of mail would freeze
A thousand feet o'er cracked wilderness ice piles,
And gloomy clouds hang sad and drear for miles and miles.
We drink in headquarters to our guest homeward bound;
With Tartar lutes, pipas and pipes the camps resound.
Snow in large flakes at dusk falls heavy on camp gate;
The frozen red flag in the wind won't undulate.
At eastern gate of Wheel Tower we bid goodbye
On the snow-covered road to Heaven's Mountain high
I watch his horse go past a bend and, lost to sight,
His track will soon be buried up by snow in flight.

Li Bai

Li Bai (701–762), courtesy name Taibai, and pseudonym Hermit of Qinglian, was originally from Longxi Chengji (now Qin'an, Gansu). During the late Sui Dynasty, his family migrated to Suiye (now the Chu River region south of Lake Balkhash in Kazakhstan), where Li Bai was born. At the age of five, he moved with his father to Mianzhu Changlong (now Qinglian Township, Jiangyou County, Sichuan).

In his early years, Li Bai studied and travelled in Sichuan, composing poems and essays, and was fond of practicing chivalry. At the age of 25, he left Sichuan and travelled widely across China for ten years, composing many poems and writings. In the early years of the Tianbao era, he was recommended by Daoist Wu Yun and others to serve in Chang'an at the imperial Hanlin Academy. However, despite his official position, he was not given much importance and faced slander. Soon after, he resigned from his post and left the capital, continuing his travels and forming a lifelong connection with Du Fu.

During the *An-Shi Rebellion*, driven by a desire to quell the rebellion, he became a counsellor to Prince Yong, Li Lin. After the defeat of Prince Yong's army, Li Bai was implicated and exiled to Yelang. He was pardoned during the journey and returned east. Three years later, he died in Dangtu (now Dangtu, Anhui).

Li Bai's poetry either praises his ideals, criticizes the dark aspects of society, extols the magnificent landscapes of the motherland, or expresses sympathy for the lives of labouring people, all filled with sincere emotion. His poetry is characterized by a strong romanticism, which is the main artistic feature of his work. He excelled in using rich imagination, bold exaggeration, and straightforward language to blend strange myths and historical stories with reality, expressing his passionate emotions. His grand and bold style made him one of China's greatest romantic poets after Qu Yuan. However, some of Li Bai's poems also reveal negative emotions, such as frustration with not achieving his potential and the fleeting nature of life. Nearly a thousand of Li Bai's poems have survived, collected in the *Complete Works of Li Taibai.*

Verses in the Old Style – 19[20]

To the West, I mounted Lotus Blossom Mountain,
And, away in the distance, spied Shining Star.
Her white-silk hand held a hibiscus flower;
Pacing the void, she trod upon the Supreme Purity.
From her cloud-robes trailed a broad sash,
Which wafted behind as she ascended to heaven.
She invited me to climb Cloud Terrace Peak,
And there pay homage to Wei Shuqing.
In a flash, off with her I went,
Riding a wild swan to mount the purple dark.
Below, I saw the river of Luoyang,
And hordes of Tartar soldiers swarming across the land.
Spilt blood coated the grasses of the field;
Wolves and jackals, all sporting officials caps.

Song of the Tow-men[21]

They tow a boat and upstream wade
Between two shores alive with trade.
Under the heat pants buffalo.
O think what pain it is to tow!
The water's muddy and can not
Be drunk: thick silt fills half the pot.
When tow-men sing their song's refrain,
With broken heart, tears fall like rain.
Ten thousand quarry-men would groan

To haul to riverside rough stone.
If rocky mountains could have ears,
Would they not melt into sad tears?

Invitation to Wine[22]

Do you not see the Yellow River come from the sky,
Rushing into the sea and ne'er come back?
Do you not see the mirrors bright in chambers high
Grieve o'er your snow-white hair though once it was silk-black?
When hopes are won, oh! Drink your fill in high delight,
And never leave your wine cup empty in moonlight!
Heaven has made us talents, we're not made in vain.
A thousand gold coins spent, more will turn up again.
Kill a cow, cook a sheep and let us merry be,
And drink three hundred cupfuls of wine in high glee!
Dear friends of mine,
Cheer up, cheer up! I invite you to wine.
Do not put down your cup!
I will sing you a song, please hear,
O hear! Lend me a willing ear!
What difference will rare and costly dishes make?
I only want to get drunk and never to wake.
How many great men were forgotten through the ages?
But great drinkers are more famous than sober sages.
The Prince of Poets feast'd in his palace at will,
Drank wine at ten thousand a cask and laughed his fill.
A host should not complain of money he is short,
To drink with you I will sell things of any sort.
My fur coat worth a thousand coins of gold
And my fower-dappled horse may be sold
To buy good wine that we may drown the woe age-old.

On Phoenix Terrace at Jinling[23]

On Phoenix Terrace once phoenixes came to sing,
The birds are gone but still roll on the river's waves.
The ruined palace's buried 'neath the weeds in spring;
The ancient sages in caps and gowns all lie in graves.
The three-peak'd mountain is halflost in azure sky;
The two-fork'd stream by Egret Isle is kept apart.
As foating clouds can veil the bright sun from the eye,
Imperial Court now out of sight saddens my heart.

Seeing Meng Haoran off at Yellow Crane Tower[24]

My friend has left the west where towers Yellow Crane
For River Town when willow-down and fowers reign.
His lessening sail is lost in boundless azure sky,
Where I see but the endless River rolling by.

The Waterfall in Mount Lu Viewed from Afar (II)[25]

The sunlit Censer Peak exhales incense-like cloud,
The cataract hangs like upended stream sounding loud.
Its torrent dashes down three thousand feet from high
As if the Silver River[26] fell from azure sky.

Drinking Alone Under the Moon[27]

Among the flowers from a pot of wine
I drink alone beneath the bright moonshine.

I raise my cup to invite the Moon who blends
Her light with my Shadow and we're three friends.

The Moon does not know how to drink her share;
In vain my Shadow follows me here and there.

Together with them for the time I stay
And make merry before spring's spent away.

I sing the Moon to linger with my song;
My Shadow disperses as I dance along;

Sober, we three remain cheerful and gay;
Drunken, we part and each goes his own way.

Our friendship will outshine all earthly love;
Next time we'll meet beyond the stars above.

Du Fu

Du Fu (712-770), courtesy name Zimei, was from Gong County, Henan, with his ancestral home in Xiangyang (modern-day Xiangyang, Hubei). In his youth, he travelled extensively through regions such as Wu, Yue, Qi, and Lu, observing social conditions and the lives of the people. He formed connections with many poets and artists of his time and held a particularly sincere admiration for Li Bai.

At the age of 35, he moved to Chang'an to seek recognition as a scholar, where he lived for 10 years without success. During the An-Shi Rebellion, he fled to Fengxiang, where he met Emperor Suzong and was appointed to the position of Left Shiyi (a junior official). Soon after, due to the "Fang Guan Incident,"[28] he was transferred to Hua Prefecture as a military officer. Later, he resigned from his official post and became a guest in various regions, such as Qinzhou and Chengdu. He briefly served as an advisor to General Yan Wu, the military governor of Jiannan, and was also appointed to a post in the Ministry of Works. He eventually passed away on the Xiang River.

Du Fu is regarded as one of the greatest realist poets in Chinese literary history. He loved his country, cared deeply for the people, and despised the forces of darkness. His outstanding poems vividly depict the historical process of the Tang Empire's decline, earning him the title "Poet Historian." Du Fu's poetry is of high artistic achievement. Not only did he cover a wide range of topics and employ diverse styles, but his works are marked by precise diction, well-crafted meter, and a depth of thought and originality. His poetry delves deeply into the human experience, offering fresh insights and difficult truths. With striking imagery and powerful expression, Du Fu elevated Tang poetry to new heights. His collected works are compiled in the "Du Gongbu Ji" (*A Collection of Du Gongbu*).

A Spring View[29]

As ever are hills and rills while the Kingdom crumbles,
When springtime comes over the Capital the grass scrambles.
Blossoms invite my tears as in wild times they bloom;
The fliting birds stir my heart that I'm parted from home.
For three months the beacon fires soar and burn the skies,
A family letter is worth ten thousand gold in price.
I scratch my head, and my grey hair has grown too thin
It seems, to bear the weight of the jade clasp and pin.

Mounting[30]

From heaven high the winds are whirling down with monkey's whine,
And over the white sanded hursts the birds are cleaving fine.
The boundless forests shed their yellow leaves with rustles;
The everflowing Yangtze on its way rolls and wrestles.
Autumn is chilling me – always a thousand-miles-roamer,
Alone mounting the mountain, and a lifelong sufferer.
I deeply loathe my rime-like temples as in these hard times;
Of late Senility yet forces me to give up wines.

The Chariots Rattle on[31]

The Chariots rattle on, the battle horses neigh;
The footmen earch bears bow and arrows by his waist.
Dragging along, their kins have parting words to say,
The Xianyang Bridge's lost in clouds of dust they rised.
Stamping their feet, grasping the clothes, getting in the way,
They cry, their uproars soar up e'en to the clouds grey.
A passer-by asks aside one of the footmen,
"Enlistment is so frequent," thus but states the man.
"At fifteen I was sent north the River to defend,
Now at forty still I've to be westbound to till the land.
The Chief of Hundred wraped my head when first I went,
Being back with hair grey, yet to far frontier I'm sent.
A flood of blood is flowing over the boundary,
Emperor Wu still wills extending territory.
Don't you know, in two hundred counties, east of our country,
All villages're o'errun with thorns, and all in misery?
Although there're stout women taking up husbandry,
Crops in the fields are ploughed disorderly.
Since soldiers from Qin always fight desperately,
Like dogs and chickens we're driven to battle-array.
You have the heart to ask me, you venerable man,
Yet how can I, a footman, dare to you complain?
So to say this winter, as by yourself you see,
They do not let us from the west of the Pass live in peace.
The County Magistrate duns for the land taxes,
And by what means can we pay out such and such fees?
Now really I believe in what the people say:
To bear a daughter is far better than a son.
A daughter may marry a next-door neighbour some day,
A son is fated among wild weeds to lie slain.
Don't you see, far away at the lake of Qinhai,
E'er since the ancient times skulls're spread under the sky?
The new ghosts are resentful while the old one's cry,
In the gloomy wet day they sadly wail and sigh!"

Notes:

All the four works, *The Chariots Rattle on*, *A Song of Fair Women*, *Lament along the Winding River*, and *A Song of a Prince Deposed*, are Du Fu's unique new Yuefu poems improvised from reality without being bound by the conventional styles and themes. *The Chariots Rattle on* was composed in Changan in 751, the 10th year of Tianbao, to attack Emperor Xuanzong's keeping pushing forward the frontiers by force. The poem is set on the conscripting for the nation's fighting against Tubo Kingdom, attacking and satirizing the ruling class by focusing on one specific social event. It begins with a tempestuous and striking scene: the desperately wailing parents and wives are seeing off the conscripted soldiers. The pathetic sight is followed by the detailed condemnation against Emperor Xuanzong's wrong conscripting policy and its serious consequences in the form of dialogues. With man's weeping the beginning and the ghosts' weeping the ending, the poet implies these conscripts are tragically doomed to be "new ghosts" after the "old ghosts". Futhermore, the poem reveals pungently the unfathomable misery of the people brought by the frontierzation: farming severely damaged, the fields deserted, yet the Emperor still urged the taxes to be collected promptly – "The frontier is being flooded by flood", but it seemed that nothing could stop Emperor Xuanzong's desire of frontierization. This is a canon with a progressive writer's tears and blood in it in which the poet exposed boldly the Emperor's abusing power arbitrarily and despotically, showing great sympathy on the misery and suffering of the common people. This is a canon with profound and far-reaching insights, genuine and poignant feeling, symmetrical and logical structure with ingenious and flexible changes, and harmonious and rhythmical sounds, making it an unprecedented masterpiece among all the widespread and fascinating Yuefu poetry.

Recapture of the Regions North and South of the Yellow River[32]

'Tis said the Northern Gate has been recaptured of late;
When the news reaches my ears, my gown is wet with tears.
Staring at my wife's face, of grief I find no trace;
As I roll up verse books, my joy like madness looks.
Though white-haired, I would still both sing and drink my fill;
With verdure spring's aglow; it's time we homeward go.
We shall sail all the way through three Gorges in a day;
Going down to Xiangyang, we'll go up to Luoyang.

Bai Juyi

Bai Juyi (772-846), courtesy name Letian, was later known as *Xiangshan Jushi* (Lay Buddhist of Fragrant Hill) in his later years. He was from Xianyang (modern-day northeast Weinan, Shaanxi). In the 16th year of the reign of Emperor Dezong (800), Bai passed the imperial examination and was appointed to the position of Left Shiyi, among other official posts. In the 10th year of the Yuanhe era (815), due to offending powerful officials, he was demoted to the position of Sima in Jiangzhou. Later, due to the rise of his friends Cui Jun and Yuan Zhen, who served as prime ministers, he was promoted and served as the governor of Zhongzhou, Hangzhou, and Suzhou, eventually becoming the

Minister of Justice. In his later years, Bai Juyi retired from official duties and lived in seclusion in Luoyang.

Bai Juyi was a prominent realist poet of the Tang Dynasty after Du Fu. He inherited the realist traditions of the *The Classic of Poetry* and Du Fu's poetry, advocating that "writing should be suited to the times, and songs and poems should be composed according to the matter at hand" (from *Letter to Yuan Zhen*). Inspired by Du Fu's "immediate thematic masterpieces" and the new Yuefu movement, Bai Juyi, along with Yuan Zhen and others, promoted the *New Yuefu* movement. In his early years, Bai wrote more than a hundred "satirical and admonitory poems," which deeply exposed the social contradictions of his time and reflected the suffering of the common people. However, due to class limitations and the harsh political environment, after his demotion to Jiangzhou, he gradually became disillusioned, eventually turning to Buddhism as a way of escaping reality.

In addition to his satirical poems, Bai Juyi's long narrative poems, such as *The Song of Everlasting Regret* and *The Pipa Song*, have unique artistic qualities and opened new paths for the "song and poem" genre. These works also had a certain influence on later drama. Bai Juyi's style is simple, natural, and easy to understand, with his artistic achievements being second only to those of Li Bai and Du Fu in the Tang Dynasty. His collected works are compiled in the *An Anthology of Bai Xiangshan's Poems*.

Grasses[33]

Tall and hanging down, the grasses on the wide plain
Flourish and wither once in every year.
Wild fire could not burn them up to extirpate;
Springtide zephyrs blow and they come to life again.
Distant verdure overcometh ancient highways;
Fair-day emerald stretcheth away to waste cities.
Bidding farewell to wanderers going somewhither,
Lush-growing grasses waft in the breeze full of parting cares.

Light Fur and Fat Horses[34]

Arrogance fills the road
and shiny saddles light up the dust.
If you ask who these men are
you'll be told, "Officials close to the emperor."
Those in red are ministers.
Those in purple are generals.
They are off to attend the army banquet

on horses like racing clouds.
Famous wine brims over the jugs.
They have countless delicacies from water and land.
Their fingers break open Tungting tangerines
and they eat fine fish filets from the Celestial Lake.
They feel so content when full
and their arrogance swells with the wine.
This year on the South bank of the Yangtze River there is drought.
In the State of Chu, people are eating people

The Everlasting Regret[35]

The beauty-loving monarch longed year after year
To find a beautiful lady without a peer.
A maiden of the Yangs to womanhood just grown,
In inner chambers bred, to the world was unknown.
Endowed with natural beauty too hard to hide,
She was chosen one day to be the monarch's bride.
Turning her head, she smiled so sweet and full of grace
That she outshone in six palaces the fairest face.
She bathed in glassy water of warm-fountain Pool,
Which laved and smoothed her creamy skin when spring was cool.
Without her maids' support, she was too tired to move,
And this was when she first received the monarch's love.
Flower-like face and cloud-like hair, golden-head dressed,
In lotus-adorned curtain she spent the night blessed.
She slept till the sun rose high for the blessed night was short,
From then on the monarch held no longer morning court.
In revels as in feasts she shared her lord's delight,
His companion on trips and his mistress at night.
In inner palace dwelt three thousand ladies fair;
On her alone was lavished royal love and care.
Her beauty served the night when dressed up in Golden Bower;
She was drunk with wine and spring at banquet in Jade Tower.
Her sisters and brothers all received rank and fief
And honors showered on her household, to the grief
Of fathers and mothers who would rather give birth
To a fair maiden than to any son on earth.
The lofty palace towered high into the cloud;
With divine music borne on the breeze, the air was loud.
Seeing slow dance and hearing fluted or stringed song,
The emperor was never tired the whole day long.
But rebels beat their war drums, making the earth quake

And "Song of Rainbow Skirt and Coat of Feathers" break
A cloud of dust was raised o'er city walls nine-fold;
Thousands of chariots and horsemen southwestward rolled.
Imperial flags moved slowly now and halted then,
And thirty miles from Western Gate they stopped again.
Six armies -what could be done? – would not march with speed
Unless fair Lady Yang be killed before the steed.
None would pick up her hairpin fallen on the ground
Nor golden bird nor comb with which her head was crowned.
The monarch could not save her and hid his face in fear;
Turning his head, he saw her blood mix with his tear.
The yellow dust widespread, the wind blew desolate;
A serpentine plank path led to cloud-capped Sword Gate.
Below the Eyebrows Mountains wayfarers were few;
In fading sunlight royal standards lost their hue.
On Western water blue and Western mountains green
The monarch's heart was daily gnawed by sorrow keen.
The moon viewed from his tent shed a soul-searing light;
The bells heard in night rain made a heart-rending sound
Suddenly turned the tide. Returning from his flight,
The monarch could not tear himself away from the ground
Where 'mid the clods beneath the Slope he couldn't forget
The fair-faced Lady Yang who was unfairly slain.
He looked at his courtiers, with tears his robe was wet;
They rode east to the capital but with loose rein.
Come back, he found her pond and garden in old place,
With lotus in the lake and willows by the hall.
Willow leaves like her brows and lotus like her face
At the sight of all these, how could his tears not fall.
Or when in vernal breeze were peach and plum full-blown
Or when in autumn rain parasol leaves were shed?
In Western as in Southern Court was grass o'ergrown;
With fallen leaves unswept the marble steps turned red.
Actors, although still young, began to have hair grey;
Eunuchs and waiting maids looked old in palace deep.
Fireflies fliting the hall, mutely he pined away;
The lonely lampwick burned out, still he could not sleep
Slowly beat drums and rang bells, night began to grow long;
Bright shone the Starry Stream, daybreak seemed to come late.
The love-bird tiles grew chilly with hoar frost so strong;
His kingfisher quilt was cold, not shared by a mate.
One long, long year the dead with the living was parted;
Her soul came not in dreams to see the broken-hearted,

A Taoist sorcerer came to the palace door,
Skilled to summon the spirits from the other shore.
Moved by the monarch's yearning for the departed fair,
He was ordered to seek for her everywhere.
Borne on the air, like flash of lightning he flew;
In heaven and on earth he searched through and through.
Up to the azure vault and down to deepest place,
Nor above nor below could he e'er find her trace.
He learned that on the sea were fairy mountains proud
Which now appeared now disappeared amid the cloud
Of rainbow colors, where rose magnificent bowers
And dwelt so many fairies as graceful as flowers.
Among them was a queen whose name was Ever True;
Her snow-white skin and sweet face might afford a clue.
Knocking at western gate of palace hall, he bade
The fair porter to inform the queen's waiting maid.
When she heard that there came the monarch's embassy
The queen was startled out of dreams in her canopy.
Pushing aside the pillow, she rose and got dressed,
Passing through silver screen and pearl shade to meet the guest.
Her cloud-like hair awry, not full awake at all,
Her flowery cap slanted, she came into the hall.
The wind blew up her fairy sleeves and made them float
As if she danced still "Rainbow Skirt and Feathered Coat."
Her jade-white face crisscrossed with tears in lonely world
Like a spray of pear blossoms in spring rain impearled.
She bade him thank her lord, lovesick and broken-hearted;
They knew nothing of each other after they parted.
Love and happiness long ended within palace walls;
Days and nights appeared long in the Fairyland halls.
Turning her head and fixing on the earth her gaze,
She found no capital 'mid clouds of dust and haze.
To show her love was deep, she took out keepsakes old
For him to carry back, hairpin and case of gold.
Keeping one side of the case and one wing of the pin,
She sent to her lord the other half of the twin.
"If our two hearts as firm as the gold should remain,
In heaven or on earth some time we'll meet again."
At parting, she confided to the messenger
A secret vow known only to her lord and her.
On seventh day of seventh moon when none was near,
At midnight in Long Long-life Hall he whispered in her ear:
"On high, we'd be two birds flying wing to wing;

On earth, two trees with branches twined from spring to spring."
The boundless sky and endless earth may pass away,
But this vow unfulblled will be regretted for aye.

Notes:

The Everlasting Regret was composed in the 806th year of Yuanhe, when Bai Juyi was appointed as Xianwei, County Captain, of Zhouzhi County. The poem, as well as a prose work *A Romance of the Everlasting Regret* written by one of Bai Juyi's friends Chen Hong echoing his poem, is based on the widespread tragic love story of Xuanzong of Tang Dynasty and his imperial noble consort Yang Yuhuan, thus entitled "Everlasting Regret". This magnificent narrative combines reality and fantasies, and lyric and narration, with fantastic and intricate plots, rich imagination, elegant language and exquisite meters, obviously influenced by the genres such as modern-styled poetry, romance, etc., gaining high artistic achievement. Nevertheless, there are evidently some limitations existing concerning the content and thoughts of this poem. The late reign of Xuanzong of Tang Dynasty saw a dark political atmosphere and the emperor's dissolute and debauched lifestyle, leading to the nationwide catastrophic An-Shi Rebellion, and inducing fierce and sweeping attack in history. Despite the pungent criticism and satire from many contemporary poets such as Li Bai, Du Fu, etc, and the later poets Du Mu, Li Shangyin, Yuan Mei, etc, Bai Juyi eulogized emotionally the controversial love between the Emperor and his imperial concubine, showing his deep sympathy on them for their "touching" love, although there did include some ironical elements concerning the emperor's debauchery at the beginning of the poem. Apparently, the central theme of this narrative is not satirizing, but extoling, i.e., an ode on the "sincerity" and "eternity" of the emperor-concubine love, which can be reflected directly even from the title. Moreover, the writer himself even boasted: "how sentimental and romantic it is in *The Everlasting Regret*!" The later critics interpreted this as "a satire on the Emperor's obstinate and unawakening licentiousness", however, it is actually not the case in this poem, even quite opposite to the poet's original intention. Naturally, pointing out the limitation will never hinder its striking and sparkling status in the history of the development of poetry, neither will it shake even a little bit the exemplary position for today's poetry creation. The poem can be divided into four parts: the first 32 lines focusing on the emperor's monopolizing favor on Yang Yuhuan, the next 18 lines on the An-Shi Rebellion and the emperor's subsequent escaping to Sichuan and the death of Yang Yuhuan, the following 24 lines concerning the emperor's returning to the capital and his heartbreaking yearning for his love, and the last 46 lines on the emperor's reunion with his love under the arrangement of the sorcerers. With the ending of the poem echoing the title, the poem presents a lingering charm.

Song of a Pipa Player[36]

One night by riverside I bade a friend goodbye;
In maple leaves and rushes autumn seemed to sigh.
My friend and I dismounted and came into the boat;
We wished to drink but there was no music afloat.
Without flutesongs we drank our cups with heavy heart;
The moonbeams blent with water when we were to part.
Suddenly o'er the stream we heard a pipa sound;
I forgot to go home and the guest stood spellbound.
We followed where the music led to find the player,
But heard the pipa stop and no music in the air.
We moved our boat beside the player's to invite
Her to drink at replenished feast by lamplight.
Again we called and urged her to appear until
She came, her face half hid behind a pipa still.
She turned the pegs and tested twice or thrice each string;
Before a tune was played we heard her feelings sing.
Then note on note she struck with pathos deep and strong;
It seemed to say she'd missed her dreams all her life long.
Head bent, she played with unpremeditated art
On and on to pour out her overflowing heart.
She lightly plucked, slowly stroked and twanged loud
The song of "Green Waist" after that of "Rainbow Cloud."
The thick strings loudly thrummed like the pattering rain;
The fine strings softly tinkled in a murmuring strain.
When mingling loud and soft notes were together played,
'Twas like large and small pearls dropping on plate of jade.

Now clear like orioles warbling in flowery land,
Then sobbing like a stream running along the sand.
But the stream seemed so cold as to tighten the string;
From tightened strings no more sound could be heard to ring.
Still we heard hidden grief and vague regret concealed;
Music expressed then far less than silence revealed.
Suddenly we heard water burst a silver jar,
The clash of spears and sabres coming from afar.
She made a central sweep when the music was ending;
The four strings made one sound, as of silk one is rending.
Silence reigned left and right of the boat, east and west;
We saw but autumn moon white in the river's breast.
She slid the plectrum pensively between the strings,
Smoothed out her dress and rose with a composed mien.

"I spent, "she said, "in capital my early springs,
Where at the foot of Mount of Toads my home had been.
At thirteen I learned on the pipa how to play,
And my name was among the primas of the day.
My skill the admiration of the masters won,
And my beauty was envied by deserted fair one.
The gallant young men vied to shower gifts on me;
One tune played, countless silk rolls were given with glee.
Beating time, I let silver comb and pin drop down,
And spilt-out wine oft stained my blood-red silken gown.
From year to year I laughed my joyous life away
On moonlit autumn night or windy vernal day.
My younger brother left for war, and died my maid,
Days passed, nights came, and my beauty began to fade.
Fewer and fewer were cabs and steeds at my door;
I married a smug merchant when my prime was o'er.
The merchant cared for money much more than for me;
One month ago he went away to purchase tea,
Leaving his lonely wife alone in empty boat;
Shrouded in moonlight, on the cold river I float.
Deep in the night I dreamed of happy bygone years
And woke to find my rouged face crisscrossed with tears. "
Listening to her sad music, I sighed with pain;
Hearing her story, I sighed again and again.
"Both of us in misfortune go from shore to shore.
Meeting now, need we have known each other before?
I was banished from the capital last year
To live degraded and ill in this city here.
The city's too remote to know melodious song,
So I have never heard music the whole year long.
I dwell by riverbank, on a low and damp ground.
In a house yellow reeds and stunt'd bamboos surround.
What is here to be heard from daybreak till nightfall
But gibbons' cry and cuckoo's homeward-going call?
By blooming riverside and under autumn moon
I've often taken wine up and drunk it alone.
Of course I've mountain songs and village pipes to hear,
But they are crude and strident and grate on the ear.
Listening to you playing on pipa tonight,
With your music divine e'en my hearing seems bright.
One tune played, countless silk rolls were given with glee.
Beating time, I let silver comb and pin drop down,
And spilt-out wine oft stained my blood-red silken gown.

From year to year I laughed my joyous life away
On moonlit autumn night or windy vernal day.
My younger brother left for war, and died my maid,
Days passed, nights came, and my beauty began to fade.
Fewer and fewer were cabs and steeds at my door;
I married a smug merchant when my prime was o'er.
The merchant cared for money much more than for me;
One month ago he went away to purchase tea,
Leaving his lonely wife alone in empty boat;
Shrouded in moonlight, on the cold river I float.
Deep in the night I dreamed of happy bygone years
And woke to find my rouged face crisscrossed with tears. "
Listening to her sad music, I sighed with pain;
Hearing her story, I sighed again and again.
"Both of us in misfortune go from shore to shore.
Meeting now, need we have known each other before?
I was banished from the capital last year
To live degraded and ill in this city here.
The city's too remote to know melodious song,
So I have never heard music the whole year long.
I dwell by riverbank, on a low and damp ground.
In a house yellow reeds and stunt'd bamboos surround.
What is here to be heard from daybreak till nightfall
But gibbons' cry and cuckoo's homeward-going call?
By blooming riverside and under autumn moon
I've often taken wine up and drunk it alone.
Of course I've mountain songs and village pipes to hear,
But they are crude and strident and grate on the ear.
Listening to you playing on pipa tonight,
With your music divine e'en my hearing seems bright.
Will you sit down and play for us a tune once more?
I'll write for you an ode to the pipa I adore."
Touched by what I said, the player stood for long,
Then sat down, tore at strings and played another song.
So sad, so drear, so different, it moved us deep;
All those who heard it hid the face and began to weep.
Of all the company at table who wept most?
It was none other than the exiled blue-robed host.

Liu Yuxi

Liu Yuxi (772–842), courtesy name Mengde, was from Luoyang (now in Henan Province). After the An-Shi Rebellion, he moved south. In the ninth year of the Zhenyuan era (793) of Emperor Dezong, he passed the imperial examination and became a supervising censor. He participated in the political reform led by Wang Shuwen, but after its failure, he was demoted to the post of Sima in Langzhou (now Changde, Hunan). Later, he served as the governor of Lianzhou (now Lian County, Guangdong), Hezhou (now He County, Anhui), and Suzhou, and eventually rose to the position of Acting Minister of Rites.

Liu Yuxi was a renowned materialist philosopher and poet of the Tang Dynasty. He had a close friendship with Han Yu, Liu Zongyuan, and Bai Juyi, often referred to as "Liu-Liu" and "*Liu-Bai*" together with them. However, his poetry neither followed the style of Han and Meng nor leaned towards Yuan and Bai. Instead, he created his own distinctive style based on the study of folk songs. His poetry features innovative forms, vivid language, and a fresh style, with a strong sense of everyday life. His works are collected in *Collected Works of Liu Mengde*.

Reply to Bai Juyi Whom I Meet for the First Time at a Banquet in Yangzhou[37]

O western mountains and southern streams desolate,
Where I, an exile, lived for twenty years and three!
To mourn for my departed friends I come too late;
In my native land I look like human debris.
Hundreds of sails pass by the side of sunken ship;
Thousands of flowers bloom ahead of injured tree.
Today I hear you chant the praise of comradeship;
I wish this cup of wine might well inspirit me.

Bamboo Branch Songs I[38]

Between the green willows the river flows along;
My dear one in a boat is heard to sing a song.
The west is veiled in rain, the east enjoys sunshine;
My dear one is as deep in love as day is fine.

The Town of Stone[39]

The changeless hills round ancient capital still stand;
Waves beating on ruined walls, unheeded, roll away.
The moon that shone by riverside on flourished land
Still shines at dead of night o'er ruined town today

Li He

Li He (790–816), courtesy name Changji, was from Fuchang Changgu (now in the western part of Yiyang, Henan Province). Born into a fallen royal family, he never achieved success in life and held the position of a ceremonial officer for only three years. Due to his depressed mood and a life of poverty and illness, he passed away at the age of 27.

Li He had progressive political ideals: he opposed the power of military governors, advocating for national unity; he opposed the rule of eunuchs, calling for the appointment of capable and virtuous officials; and he opposed harsh exploitation, sympathizing with the suffering of the common people. He was a famous poet of the Mid-Tang period. His poetry expressed a passionate desire to achieve something and the frustration born from dissatisfaction with social realities. Some of his works deeply revealed the corruption and incompetence of the ruling class. Therefore, some people have said that his poetry "pierced the hidden truths of the time and addressed the social flaws of the period."

He was skilled in weaving beautiful language and vivid imagination, often drawing on mythology to create unique and magnificent poetic landscapes, forming a distinctive artistic style. However, due to his political disappointments and overly ornate language, some of his works appear somber and difficult to understand. His works are collected in His works are collected in *An Anthology of Li Changji's Poems with Annotations by Three Master Critics.*

The Bronze Statue Leaving Han Palace[40]

In the first year of the Qinglong era of Wei Mingdi, in the eighth month, an imperial decree was issued to the palace officials to move the chariot and fetch the bronze statue of the immortal holding the Luopan (an ancient divining instrument) from Emperor Wu of Han. It was intended to be placed in the front hall. When the palace officials disassembled the statue, the immortal, upon being moved, shed tears sorrowfully. Li Changji, a grandson of the Tang princes, then composed the "Song of the Golden Copper Immortal's Farewell to the Han Dynasty."

The emperor was gone just like his autumn breeze;
At night his steed would neigh, at dawn no trace was seen.
By painted rails fragrance still wafts o'er laurel trees,
His thirty palaces o'ergrown with mosses green.
Wei eunuch drove a dray to go a long, long way;
In Eastern Pass the sour wind stung the bronze's eyes.
Only the moon of yore saw him leave palace door;
Thinking of his dear lord, he shed tears and heaved sighs.
Withered orchids would say, "Farewell and go your way!"
Heaven would have grown old if it could feel as man
He went with moon-shaped plate 'neath the moon desolate;
The waves unheard, far from the town the horses ran.

Zhang Ji

Zhang Ji (768–830), courtesy name Wenchang, was originally from Wujun (now near Suzhou, Jiangsu), but he actually grew up in Hezhou, Wujian (now He County, Anhui). In the 14th year of the Zhenyuan era (798), he passed the imperial examination and held various official positions, including as Official of Sacrifice Ceremonies, Teaching Assistant of Imperial Academy, Dean of Imperial College, Minister of Water Resources, Minister of Rites, and Vice President of Imperial Academy. With a humble birth and unfavourable luck politically, he was offered an insignificant official rank long after becoming a *Jinshi*. With social problems and the livelihood of the local populace his concern, he wrote many satirical poems, exposing social conflicts and showing great sympathy on the ordinary people. His Yuefu poems are quite influential in the Mid-Tang poetic circles, winning the comment from Bai Juyi that his writing, using the principles of the Elegant Bixing, focuses on social reality instead of the irrelevant themes. (*On Zhang Ji's Classical Yuefu*) He was an equal to Wang Jianqi in the realm of *Yuefu* poetry, hence the two were extolled as "*Zhang-Wang: Masters of Yuefu*". Wang Anshi commented the artistic features of Zhang Ji's works in his famous poem "To Zhang Siye": the most unique and remarkable though plain apparently, created painstakingly though painlessly seemingly. His poems are collected in *A Collection of Zhang Siye's Poems*.

The Old Peasant[41]

In the hills lives a poor old peasant
Farming a few small patches of hilly land;
Sparse his crops, many the taxes, and he goes hungry
While grain in the state granaries turns to dust;
At the year's end his home is bare but for plough and hoe,
He takes his son up the mountain to gather acorns;
But the West River merchant has hundreds of bushels of pearls
And the dog on his boat gorges everyday on meat.

Du Mu

Du Mu (803–853), courtesy name Muzhi, was from Jingzhao (modern-day Xi'an, Shaanxi). He passed the imperial examination in the second year of the Tahe reign (828) and became a *Jinshi*. Du served as a bibliographer at the Hongwen Pavilion, later held various official posts, including observing envoy, imperial censor, and ultimately became a mid-level official in the Secretariat. He was commonly known as Du Fanchuan.[42]

In his youth, Du Mu had ambitions of statecraft and governance. making annotations to *Sun-Tzu: The Art of Warfare* due to his great interest in military affairs, mocking Cao Cao's previous annotations to 13 pieces of this work, and Du Mu's version is among the most popular and influential annotations to this great masterpiece. Du was concerned with national politics and boldly pointed out the problems of his time. He strongly opposed the separation of powers by regional military governors (the frontier governors) and the invasion of foreign forces, advocating for the recapture of lost territories and the unification of the country. However, his political career was not successful, and his life eventually became marked by decadence and indulgence.

Du Mu excelled in poetry, prose, and classical literature, but his greatest achievement was in poetry. He is often referred to as "*Little Du*" to distinguish him from Du Fu of the High Tang period. He is famous alongside Li Shangyin, and together they are known as "*Li-Du*." While some of Du Mu's poems express romantic or sentimental themes, many others expose societal issues and reflect the realities of his time. Among his various forms of poetry, his seven-character regulated verse and quatrains are the most celebrated, with numerous famous works passed down through the generations. His works are collected in *A Collection of Du Fanchuan's Poems*.

The Summer Palace I[43]

Viewed from afar, the hill's paved with brocades in piles;
The palace doors on hilltops opened one by one.
A steed which raised red dust won the fair mistress' smiles.
How many steeds which brought her fruit died on the run!

To Berth at the Qinhuai River[44]

While mist hangs over the chilly river moonlight casts on the white sand,
For easy access to a wine shop I berthed my boat at night by the riverside.
Singing girls bear no grudge against loss of their country,
They, on the other side, are still singing "The Rear Yard Flower" with joy.

Mountain Trip[45]

Far up the mountainside the stone trail wound,
Where the clouds were thick, there stood some abodes.
I stopt my cart to watch the maple forest late
With frost-bitten leaves more crimson than spring blooms.

Parting[46]

Deep, deep our love, too deep to show.
Deep, deep we drink; silent we grow.
The candle grieves to see us part:
It melts in tears with burnt-out heart.

Li Shangyin

Li Shangyin (813–858), courtesy name Yishan, and pseudonym Yuxi Sheng, was from Huaizhou Henei (modern-day Qinyang, Henan). In his early years, he was appreciated by Linghu Chu and passed the imperial examination in the second year of the Kaicheng reign (837). Wang Maoyuan, the governor of Xingyuan, greatly admired his talent and appointed him as the chief scribe, also marrying his daughter to Li Shangyin. At the time, there was intense competition between the Niu and Li factions, with Wang Maoyuan supporting the Li faction and Linghu Chu supporting the Niu faction. Li Shangyin found himself caught in the middle, facing difficult circumstances, which resulted in a lack of success in his political career.

Li Shangyin, alongside Du Mu, was one of the most important poets of the late Tang Dynasty. Despite facing many hardships, he remained concerned about the political situation and opposed the eunuchs' dominance and the fragmentation of power by regional military governors. His poetry exposed the political darkness and social turmoil of the time, expressing his sorrow for the state and the nation, as well as his personal feelings of frustration at not being recognized for his talent. Many of his historical poems used ancient themes to satirize the current political situation. His love poems, on the other hand, were written in a tender, melancholic style, deeply moving with their emotional depth.

Li Shangyin's poetry is renowned for its artistic features, imaginative brilliance, vivid imagery, and elegant language. His seven-character quatrains and regulated verse are particularly popular, known for their graceful expression, subtle meaning, harmonious rhythms, and intricate parallelism. However, due to his life of poverty and frustration, his poems often convey a sense of melancholy. Some of his works are difficult to fully understand because of their obscure references and delicate wording, which make the meanings elusive. His works are collected in *The Anthology of Li Yishan's Poems*.

To One Unnamed[47]

It's difficult for us to meet and hard to part;
The east wind is too weak to revive flowers dead.
Spring silkworm till its death spins silk from lovesick heart;
Candles only when burned up have no tears to shed.
At dawn I'm grieved to think your mirrored hair turns grey;
At night you would feel cold while I croon by moonlight.
To the three fairy hills it is not a long way
Would the blue birds oft fly to see you on the height!

Wen Tingyun

Wen Tingyun (812–870), courtesy name Feiqing, was a prominent poet and composer of *Ci* poetry in the late Tang Dynasty. He was the first writer in literary history to focus on composing *Ci* poetry. His *Ci* had a relatively narrow scope, often centered on women and portraying emotions within the boudoir. He excelled at using distinctive imagery to create artistic ambiance. His language was ornate, characterized by an air of luxury and a delicate, refined aesthetic. With harmonious rhythms and subtle emotional undertones, Wen's *Ci* inherited the stylistic influence of the Southern Dynasties' courtly poetry while paving the way for the graceful and delicate style of the *Hua Jian* school of poetry. He had a significant impact on the development of *Ci* poetry.

Tune: Pusaman[48]

Sunlight shimmers on a picture,
Carved in perspective on bed-screen.
The hair on her temples appear –
As clouds which, against her cheeks, lean.

Slowly she rises from her bed;
Paints her brows like a crescent moon.
She takes her own time, unhurried;
Completes her toilet none too soon.

Her flowered head between two mirrors –
Interlay with face in beauty made.
On a jacket, tastefully cut –
Are two partridges in brocade.

Song of the Water Clock at Night[49]

The tearful candle red
And fragrant censer spread
Within the painted bower a gloomy autumn light.
Fad'd eyebrows penciled
And hair dishevelled,
She feels her quilt the colder and longer the night.

The lonely withered trees
And midnight rain and breeze
Don't care about her bitter parting sorrow.
Leaf on leaf without grief,
Drop by drop without stop,
They fall on vacant steps until the morrow.

Dreaming of the South[50]

After dressing my hair,
Alone I climb the stair.
On the railings I lean
To view the river scene.
A thousand sails pass by,

But not the one for which wait I.
The slanting sun sheds sympathetic ray;
The carefree river carries it away.
My heart breaks at the sight
Of the islet with duckweed white.

Li Yu

Li Yu, a distinguished representative of poets in the Southern Tang Dynasty, is renowned for his *Ci* poetry. His early works align with the *Hua Jian* school, characterized by a courtly and refined atmosphere. However, his later compositions often express profound reflections on his lost kingdom and the pain of its downfall.

Artistically, Li Yu's *Ci* poetry pioneered the direct expression of personal emotions, breaking away from the late Tang and Five Dynasties tradition of using romantic language as a metaphor for broader themes. His language is clear and elegant, reforming the excessive ornamentation of the *Hua Jian* school. Li Yu avoided allusions and flowery embellishments, instead excelling in the plain descriptive style to convey his emotions and thoughts. He was adept at using metaphors, vividly transforming abstract feelings into tangible imagery, thereby creating a unique and lasting impact on the development of *Ci* poetry.

Tune: The Beautiful Lady Yu[51]

When will there be no more an autumn moon and spring time flowers
For me who had so many memorable hours?
My attic which last night in the east wind did stand
Reminds me cruelly of the lost moonlit land.

Carved balustrades and marble steps must still be there
But rosy faces cannot be as fair.
If you would ask me how my sorrow has increased,
Just see the over-brimming river flowing east!

Zhang Zhihe

Zhang Zhihe, courtesy name Zitong, also known by the pseudonym Xuanzhenzi, was a native of Jinhua in Wuzhou during the mid-Tang Dynasty. After retreating to a life of seclusion by rivers and lakes, he referred to himself as the "Fisherman of Smoke and Waves," though his true aspirations lay beyond fishing. Multitalented, he excelled in composing *Ci* poetry, calligraphy, and painting, and was skilled in playing the drum and flute.

Among his extant works is the collection "Fisherman's Song" comprising five pieces, with the first being particularly renowned. Over the centuries, this piece has become widely celebrated as one of the representative works of early literati *Ci* poetry. For this reason, Zhang Zhihe holds an important and enduring place in the history of Chinese literature.

Tune: A Fisherman's Song[52]

In front of western hills white egrets fly up and down,
In peach-mirrored stream mandarin fish are full grown.
In my blue bamboo hat
And green straw cloak, I'd fain
Go fishing careless of slanting wind and fine rain.

Tune: Dreaming of the Southern Shore[53]

Bai Juyi

Fair Southern shore,
With scenes I did adore.
At sunrise riverside flowers redder than fire;
In spring green waves grew as blue as sapphire.
How could I not admire?

II

Dreaming of Southern shore,
It's Hangzhou I adore.
The laurels fallen from the moon I'd like to store
And watch in the pavilion rise the tidal bore.
When can I visit it once more?

2. THE REFORM OF PROSE

Tang dynasty prose achieved remarkable accomplishments in the history of Chinese literature, exerting a profound influence on subsequent prose and novel writing. The flourishing and development of Tang prose were primarily due to the *Ancient Prose Movement* led by Han Yu and Liu Zongyuan. This movement broke away from the dominance of *piantiwen* (parallel prose), which had prevailed since the Qi and Liang dynasties. The earlier style had been overly focused on form, stifling thought, and lacking substance, with an emphasis on balanced structure. In contrast, the movement revived ancient prose that was more closely aligned with real life. It corrected the trend of ornate yet hollow writing.

Han Yu and Liu Zongyuan emphasized that "*wen* (writing) should be a reflection of the *dao* (way)" (*wen yi ming dao*), advocating the unity of content and form in literary creation. They proposed that writing should respond to societal injustices (*bu ping ze ming*), encouraging writers to engage with reality and express genuine emotions. They also stressed that "writing is based on conduct" (*wen yi xing wei ben*), highlighting the importance of moral cultivation in writers. Furthermore, they called for innovation in literary language, urging the elimination of clichéd and conventional expressions. Although some of their views had limitations, their ideas on content, form, emotion, and language significantly impacted the rejection of the ornate and superficial style of *piantiwen* and the establishment of a new literary ethos.

Han Yu and Liu Zongyuan also set shining examples for prose writing through their own works. Han Yu's argumentative essays, often written "in response to issues," addressed social problems with a clear sense of realism. His narrative essays also possessed substantial literary value, skilfully portraying characters through their language, actions, and detailed descriptions, which influenced later novel writing. His lyrical prose, marked by heartfelt emotion and strong expressiveness, was particularly impactful.

In terms of artistic style, Han Yu's prose was characterized by grandeur, unrestrained vigour, and bold straightforwardness. He also paid attention to the use of expressive techniques and linguistic innovation.

Liu Zongyuan's achievements in prose were primarily reflected in his fables and travelogues. His fables were marked by clear themes, sharp satire, powerful critiques, and thought-provoking narratives. His travelogues combined vivid descriptions of scenery with deep emotional resonance and conveyed profound meanings. Liu Zongyuan's prose was known for its calm and profound nature, skilful use of satire and depiction, and concise, lively, and incisive language, exuding a distinctive austere style.

Han Yu

Han Yu (768–824), courtesy name Tuizhi, was a native of Nanyang in Henan (modern Mengxian, Henan). His ancestral home was in Changli, which is why he referred to himself as "Han of Changli." Orphaned at an early age, he was raised and nurtured by his sister-in-law, Madam Zheng. In the eighth year of the Zhenyuan reign (792), he passed the imperial examination. Toward the end of

Zhenyuan, he became a Censor but was demoted to magistrate of Yangshan (modern Yangshan County, Guangdong) after submitting a memorial urging Emperor Dezong to reduce taxes and labour levies in Guanzhong, which angered the emperor. Later, he served as a legal officer in Jiangling. During the Yuanhe era, Han Yu held posts such as academician of the National University, magistrate of Henan, and eventually rose to Assistant Imperial Secretary to the Crown Prince. He followed Chancellor Pei Du in quelling the rebellion in Huaixi and was promoted to Assistant Minister of Justice. However, after submitting a memorial opposing Emperor Xianzong's veneration of a Buddha relic, he was demoted to the position of prefect of Chaozhou (modern Chao'an County, Guangdong) and later transferred to Yuanzhou (modern Yichun, Jiangxi). During Emperor Muzong's reign, he was recalled to serve as Director of the National University and held positions such as Prefect of Jingzhao, Grand Censor, and Assistant Minister of War and Personnel.

Han Yu championed Confucianism while opposing Buddhism and Daoism. He supported centralization, opposed the fragmentation of power by military governors, and rejected the florid parallel prose style, advocating for plain prose and the Tang Dynasty's Classical Prose Movement. He emphasized eliminating trite expressions and pursuing clarity and coherence in writing. Han Yu's prose is characterized by its energetic and powerful style, making him one of the most outstanding prose writers after Sima Qian.

In poetry, Han Yu drew inspiration from both Li Bai and Du Fu while developing a distinct personal style. His poetry is marked by its robust and bold qualities, as well as its prose-like nature, which significantly influenced the development of Song Dynasty poetry. However, his pursuit of novelty sometimes led to obscurity and complexity in his works. Han Yu's collected writings are compiled in the *Collected Works of Han Changli.*

On Teachers[54]

In ancient times, all men who wanted to learn had teachers. A teacher is someone who deciphers truths, teaches skills, and clarifies misconceptions. Because no man is born cognizant, he must have misconceptions. If one has misconceptions, but never finds a teacher to clarify them, they will remain as misconceptions.

Anyone born before me naturally knows truths before I do, and I acknowledge him as my teacher. Anyone who is born after me but knows truths before I do, I also acknowledge him as my teacher. Because what I acknowledge is his knowledge of truths, no age factor is relevant. Therefore, where there is knowledge of truths, there is a teacher, in which no factor of nobility orignobility, seniority or lack of seniority is involved.

However, this teacher-and-student tradition has long been broken. As a result, it is very hard nowadays to find people with no misconceptions. Ancient sages were far more intelligent than common people were, but those sages had teachers to consult. While today's masses are far more unintelligent than ancient sages were, these masses are ashamed to learn from teachers. That is why sages are sager while ignoramuses are more ignorant. And that explains why sages are sages while ignoramuses are ignoramuses.

You love your children, and so you hire teachers for them, but you are ashamed to find teachers for yourself. This is a misconception itself! Your children's teachers teach them how to read. What they teach is not what I mean by deciphering truths and clarifying misconceptions. When one does not know how to read, he consults teachers, but when one has misconceptions, he does not. This is to learn the trivial while neglecting the significant. I don't see cleverness in this.

Physicians, musicians and artisans are not ashamed to seek teachers from each other to learn, but scholar-bureaucrats, on the contrary, would gather to laugh at those who talk about doing so. When asked why they laugh, they say, "He is about the same age as his teacher. Or he has about the same knowledge as his teacher." To them, it is shameful to have a teacher of lower social rank but an honour to fawn on a teacher of higher social status. Alas! This shows how impossible it is to restore the teacher and-student tradition. Those scholar-bureaucrats are no match for those physicians, musicians or artisans whose intelligence they disdain. This is indeed ridiculous!

A sage is not bound to one teacher. Confucius once learned from Tanzi, Changhong, Shixiang and Laodan, although he was not inferior to any of them. This is exactly like what he once described: "Of the two walking with me, one can be my teacher." Therefore, a student does not necessarily have to be inferior to his teacher and a teacher does not have to be superior to his student, as knowledge can be learnt earlier or later and skills can be focused on differently among people. That's all there is to it.

Pan, the son of the Li family, age 17, who is fond of classic Chinese and has perused the Six Classics, is not influenced by the current social tendency but has come to seek my education. To glorify his spirit in carrying forward the tradition, I am writing this prose, *On Teachers*, for him.

Liu Zongyuan

Liu Zongyuan (773–810), courtesy name Zihou, was a native of Hedong (modern-day Yongji County, Shanxi). He passed the imperial examination in the ninth year of the Zhenyuan reign (793) and the Learned and Eloquent Scholars Examination in the fifteenth year of Zhenyuan (799). He was appointed as a Proof reader and later transferred to serve as a minor official in Lantian County before being promoted to the position of Acting Censor. During Emperor Shunzong's reign, under the administration of Wang Shuwen, Liu Zongyuan was appointed Assistant Secretary of the Ministry of Rites and actively supported reforms. However, after the reform failed, he was demoted to a minor role as a Sima (Assistant Magistrate) in Yongzhou (modern Lingling County, Hunan). Ten years later, he was further demoted to Governor of Liuzhou (modern Liuzhou, Guangxi), where he implemented many benevolent policies and won the love of the people. Liu Zongyuan passed away in Liuzhou in the fourteenth year of Yuanhe (819) at the age of 47. In gratitude for his contributions, the people of Liuzhou built a shrine in his honour, which has been maintained for generations. He is respectfully referred to as "Liu of Liuzhou."

Liu Zongyuan was a renowned philosopher, essayist, and poet of the Tang Dynasty. His writings reflect a materialist worldview and a progressive view of history. He criticized the divine right of kings and affirmed the historical significance of a centralized prefectural system. He opposed the division of power by military governors and advocated for the appointment of capable individuals. Liu Zongyuan rejected the ornate parallel prose style and, alongside Han Yu, championed the *Classical Prose Movement* of the mid-Tang period.

He wrote a wealth of prose that criticized societal issues, exposed social contradictions, sympathized with the sufferings of the people, and celebrated the beauty of nature. These works had a profound influence on the development of Chinese literature. Although his poetic output was relatively small, his poems passionately praised just wars that preserved national unity, denounced the ruling class's exploitation of the people, and satirized incompetent officials suppressing capable talent. His landscape poetry, infused with his personal experiences and emotions, is particularly distinctive. Some poems evoke images of serene, crystal-clear mountain streams, while others convey the fragrance of hidden orchids in deep valleys. However, some of his works also reveal traces of Buddhist pessimism.

Liu Zongyuan's collected works are compiled in the *Collected Works of Liu Hedong*.

Three Fables[55]

The Preface

I have always disliked those men of today who, blind to their own shortcomings, take advantage of circumstances or powerful protectors to lord it over others, bragging of their skill and seizing every chance to swagger. Such bullies always come to grief in the end. I shall therefore relate three stories told me, which put me in mind of this, about a deer, a donkey and some rats.

The Fawn of Linjiang[56]

A man of Linjiang caught a fawn while hunting. He decided to raise it. When he took it home, all his dogs came bearing down on it, slavering with excitement and wagging their tails. Annoyed, he bawled at them and scolded them off. And ever after that, on a daily basis, he brought the fawn over to those dogs to familiarize and acquaint them with it.

Through long effort, all the dogs behaved benignly toward the fawn. So in this way, the fawn grew up, but for this very reason, it forgot what it really was and was deceived into believing that all dogs were its friends. So it started to get intimate with them by nuzzling, pushing and wrestling with them. For fear of the master, those dogs tempered themselves and played with it, but they were licking their lips all the time.

Three years later, the fawn was allowed to go out. It saw lots of dogs on a road. Wanting to have fun with them, it went up to them, but those dogs, provoked, happily killed it and devoured it. On that slaughtering road, even until its death, the poor fawn couldn't understand why.

The Rats of Yongzhou

A certain householder in Yongzhou had a dread of unlucky days and observed them very strictly. Because he was born in the year of the Rat, he considered rats as holy. This being the case, he would keep no cat or dog, and forbade his servants to catch rats. Unchecked, they had the run of his store-room and kitchen.

As news of this spread among rats, more and more of them flocked to his house, where they could eat their fill with nothing to fear. They broke all the household utensils, gnawed through all the clothes on the hangers. The members of the household had to be content with the food they left over. Processions of rats mingled freely with men in broad daylight, and at night they made such a din by stealing food and fighting that not one could sleep. Still the inmates of the house put up with them.

After some years this family left and another household moved in, but the rats carried on as before. "These are creatures of darkness," said the newcomers, "but now they are running riot. Why were they allowed to get out of hand like this?"

They borrowed five or six cats, closed all the doors, removed the tiles from the roof, and poured water down all the holes, getting slave boys to help catch the rats. Soon a mound of dead rats was piled up in a corner, and the place stank for several months.

This is a lesson for those who think they can fill their bellies for ever at public expense with nothing to fear.

The Donkey of Guizhou

There were no donkeys in Guizhou until an eccentric took one there by boat; but finding no use for it he set it loose in the hills. A tiger who saw this monstrous looking beast thought it must be divine. It first surveyed the donkey from under cover, then ventured a little nearer, still keeping a respectful distance however.

One day the donkey brayed, and the tiger took fright and fled, for fear of being bitten. It was utterly terrified. But it came back for another look, and decided this creature was not so formidable after all. Then, growing used to the braying, it drew nearer, thought it still dared not attack. Coming nearer still, it began to take liberties, shoving, jostling, and charging roughly, till the donkey lost its temper and kicked out.

"So that is all it can do!" thought the tiger, greatly pleased.

Then it leapt on the donkey and sank its teeth into it, severing its throat and devouring it before going on its way.

Poor donkey! Its sized made it look powerful, and its bray made it sound redoubtable. Had it not shown all it could do, even the fierce tiger might not have dared to attack. But the donkey gave itself away!

3. THE EMERGENCE OF TANG *CHUANQI*

The rise of *chuanqi* (Tang dynasty tales of marvels) was influenced by both social and literary factors.

(a) The prosperity of urban life during the Tang dynasty fostered the emergence of a citizen class. Citizens enjoyed hearing strange and extraordinary stories, contributing to the popularity of *chuanqi*.
(b) The imperial examination system shifted its focus from poetry to *chuanqi*, prompting scholars to compose such tales.
(c) The earlier *zhiguai* (mysterious and supernatural tales) from the Six Dynasties provided a foundation for the development of *chuanqi*.
(d) The flourishing of prose in the Tang dynasty directly stimulated the advancement of narrative writing.

The development of *chuanqi* can be roughly divided into three stages:

(a) **Early Stage**: Focused on *zhiguai* themes, primarily involving supernatural or mysterious occurrences.
(b) **Middle Stage**: Shifted towards realistic themes, achieving the greatest accomplishments. Works from this period were socially meaningful and artistically mature. Notable examples include *Zhen Zhong Ji* (*A Dream in a Pillow*), *Liu Yi Zhuan* (*The Tale of Liu Yi*), *Li Wa Zhuan* (*The Tale of Li Wa*), *Huo Xiaoyu Zhuan* (*The Tale of Huo Xiaoyu*), *Yingying*

Zhuan (*The Tale of Yingying*), and *Changhenge Zhuan* (*The Tale of the Song of Everlasting Regret*).

(c) **Late Stage**: Experienced a decline in both content and form, with traces of the "Six Dynasties shadow" reemerging. Noteworthy in this period were stories with themes of chivalry, such as *Qiuran Ke Zhuan* (The Tale of the Bearded Guest), *Hongxian* (*Red Line*), and *Nie Yinniang* (*The Tale of Nie Yinniang*).

The artistic achievements of Tang *chuanqi* are reflected in the following aspects:

(a) Expansion of subject matter and deepening of themes with social significance.
(b) Unusual and intricate plots with complete structures.
(c) Attention to character portrayal from different perspectives.
(d) Lively and concise language.

These accomplishments provided valuable materials, creative experiences, and technical references for the development of later *huaben* (storyteller scripts), novels, and drama. *Huaben* were the written scripts used by storytellers and emerged as a literary form with the growth of storytelling as a performance art.

Tang Chuanqi: The World Inside a Pillow

Shen Jiji

In the seventh year of the Kaiyuan era, there was a Daoist named Lü Weng who had mastered the art of immortality. One day, while traveling through Handan, he stopped at an inn, removed his hat and loosened his belt, and sat quietly with his pouch.

Before long, a young traveller named Lu Sheng entered. Wearing a coarse robe and riding a small green horse, Lu was on his way to tend the fields. He too stopped at the inn and sat on the same mat as Lü Weng. They chatted freely and shared much laughter.

After some time, Lu Sheng looked at his shabby attire and sighed deeply. He said, "A true man born into this world should not live in such poverty and hardship as I do."

Lü Weng asked, "You appear healthy and untroubled, and you seem to enjoy our conversation. Why then do you lament your hardship?"

Lu Sheng replied, "I am merely eking out a living. What joy could there be in that?"

Lü Weng asked, "If this is not joy, what is joy to you?"

Lu Sheng answered, "A scholar should achieve greatness in the world, leaving a legacy of merit and fame. He should rise as a general or a high minister, feast from grand cauldrons, and listen to harmonious melodies. His family should thrive, and his house should prosper. Only then can one speak of joy. I once aspired to excel in learning and the arts, and I believed that honors and rank were within reach. Yet now, in my prime, I am still labouring in the fields. Is this not hardship?"

When Lu finished speaking, he felt drowsy and fell asleep. Meanwhile, the innkeeper was steaming millet. Lü Weng took a pillow from his pouch and handed it to Lu, saying, "Rest your head on my pillow, and you will find joy as you desire."

The pillow was made of green porcelain with openings at both ends. Lu rested his head on it, and the openings gradually expanded, becoming bright and clear. Entering through the opening, he found himself at his own home.

Within a few months, he married a woman from the prominent Cui family of Qinghe. She was exceedingly beautiful, and Lu's fortune grew. He was overjoyed. His attire, carriage, and horses became increasingly splendid.

The following year, Lu passed the imperial examination and was appointed as a secretarial official. He then advanced to the position of magistrate of Weinan and later became a censor and an imperial secretary. Within three years, he was appointed governor of Tongzhou and later moved to govern Shanxi, where he dug an 80-mile canal that benefited the region. The people erected a stone tablet to commemorate his contributions.

Lu then served as governor of Bianzhou and inspector of the Henan region before being summoned to serve as mayor of the capital. That year, the emperor was engaged in military campaigns to expand the empire. When the Tibetan forces invaded, causing upheaval, Lu was appointed commander of the Hexi region. He defeated the enemy, killing 7,000 troops, reclaimed 900 miles of territory, and built three major fortresses. He returned to court with great honour, was promoted to higher ranks, and received unprecedented favor.

Lu held prominent positions for decades, amassing wealth, power, and fame. His sons achieved scholarly and official success, marrying into elite families. However, political rivals falsely accused him of plotting rebellion. Stripped of his titles, he was exiled. Years later, the emperor recognized the injustice and restored his titles, granting him new honors.

Lu's life was one of ups and downs, marked by triumphs and trials. He reflected on his experiences, lamenting, "I now long for the days of wearing coarse robes and riding my little green horse along the Handan road, but they are no longer attainable."

Eventually, Lu grew old and ill. In his final days, he wrote a memorial to the emperor, expressing gratitude for his opportunities and remorse for his shortcomings. Shortly after, he passed away.

At that moment, Lu Sheng awoke from his dream. He found himself still lying in the inn, with Lü Weng seated beside him and the millet still steaming. Startled, he exclaimed, “Was it all a dream?”

Lü Weng smiled and said, “Such is the nature of life.”

Lu Sheng sat in deep thought for a long time before bowing twice and saying, “Through this, I have come to understand the ways of honour and disgrace, the cycles of fortune and adversity, the truths of gain and loss, and the essence of life and death. You have curbed my desires, and I dare not forget your teachings.”

With that, he thanked Lü Weng and departed.

NOTES

1 Lvshi: 律诗, a poem of eight lines, each containing five or seven characters, with a strict tonal pattern and rhyme scheme.
2 Wang, Roghua. 王荣华 (Translation and annotations)《送杜少府之任蜀州》, in《千家诗（双语版）》 *A Thousand Poets*, Beijing: China Renmin University Press (2020, 288).
3 Metropolitan graduate, or Jinshi, “进士” in Chinese, a man who passed all the three examinations held by the government in ancient China.
4 Zhengzi, “正字” in Chinese, an official in charge of collating classics in ancient China.
5 Lintai, “麟台” in Chinese, an imperial institution in Tang Dynasty administrating the state library collection.
6 Shiyi of the right:”右拾遗” in Chinese, an eight-grade official in Tang Dynasty, one of the imperial censors.
7 《感遇》”The Orchid”, literal translation would be “Reflections on encounter”, accessed from https://www.ximalaya.com/sound/54279020
8 Sun, Dayu. 孙大雨译 (Transl.)《登幽州台歌》，”Song on Ascending the Youzhou Terrace” in 《古诗文英译》*Anthology of Ancient Chinese Poetry and Prose*. Beijing: Shanghai Sanlian Book Store (2020, 121).
9 Xu, Yuanchong. 许渊冲. 《唐诗三百首》 *Three Hundred Tang Poems*. Beijing: China Intercontinental Press and Zhonghua Book Company (2012, 26).
10 Ibid., (2012, 27).
11 Ibid., (2012, 32).
12 Ibid., (2012, 34).
13 See, Sun, Dayu. (Transl.) *Anthology of Ancient Chinese Poetry and Prose*. (2020, 155).
14 Xu, Yuanchong. 许渊冲. 《唐诗三百首》 *Three Hundred Tang Poems*. (2012, 36).
15 Ibid., (2012, 36).
16 Ibid., (2012, 28).
17 Xu, Yuanchong. *On Chinese Verse in English Rhyme,* (1992, 199)
18 Xu, Yuanchong. 许渊冲. 《唐诗三百首》 *Three Hundred Tang Poems*. (2012, 65-66).
19 Ibid., (2012, 92).
20 See,《古风（十九）》 “Verses in the Old Style (19)”. https://www.fx361.com/page/2020/0106/7429858.shtml。
21 Xu, Yuanchong. 许渊冲. (Trans.) 《丁都护歌》 “Song of the Tow-men” in 《许渊冲译李白诗选》*Selected Poems of Li Bai.* Beijing: China Publishing Group (2021, 155).

22 Ibid., (2021, 94).
23 Ibid., (2021, 150).
24 Ibid., (2021, 38). Yellow Crane Tower is in Wuhan, capital of Jiangsu Province. Guanglin: present-day Yangzhou in Jiangsu Province.
25 Ibid., (2021, 169). Mount Lu is in present-day Jiangxi Province.
26 The Chinese name for the Milky Way, "银河" in Chinese.
27 Xu, Yuanchong. *On Chinese Verse in English Rhyme,* (1992, 214).
28 The Fang Guan Incident (房琯事件) was a political event. In 762, Du Fu was involved in a controversy surrounding a court official named Fang Guan, which led to his demotion and transfer. Fang Guan was a high-ranking official who had been involved in a political faction at the Tang court. The specifics of the incident are not entirely clear, but it is believed that the conflict arose from Du Fu's opposition to the power and corruption of certain officials, particularly those associated with the ruling faction. Du Fu's critique of the political system may have led to his being implicated in the incident and thus being moved from his position. As a result, Du Fu was transferred from his post as Left Shiyi to a lower-ranking military position in Hua Prefecture. The event marked a significant turning point in Du Fu's life, contributing to his eventual retreat from officialdom and his focus on poetry that reflected his personal experiences, social concerns, and the state of the empire.
29 Wu Juntao. (Transl.) *Tu Fu: One Hundred and Fifty Poems*. Xi'an: Shaanxi People's Publishing House, (1985, 58).
30 Ibid., (1985, 326).
31 Ibid., (1985, 20).
32 Xu, Yuanchong. *On Chinese Verse in English Rhyme,* (1992, 236).
33 See, Sun, Dayu. (Transl.) *Ancient Poetry in English Translation*. (2020, 417).
34 Tony Barnstone and Chou Ping. (ed.). *The Anchor Book of Chinese Poetry* (eBook), New York: Anchor Books, A Division of Random House, INC. (2005, 306).
35 See, Xu, Yuanchong. 许渊冲. 《唐诗三百首》 *Three Hundred Tang Poems*. (2012, 120-125).
36 Xu, Yuanchong. *On Chinese Verse in English Rhyme,* (1992, 282-285).
37 Xu, Yuanchong. 许渊冲. 《唐诗三百首》 *Three Hundred Tang Poems*. (2012, 112).
38 Ibid., (2012, 113).
39 Ibid., (2012, 114).
40 Ibid., (2012, 156).
41 See, 《野老歌》 "The Old Peasant". https://www.en84.com/dianji/shi/201006/00002655.html
42 In his late years, Du Mu lived in a villa called Fanchuan, south of the capital city Changan, hence winning this appellation.
43 Xu, Yuanchong. 许渊冲. 《唐诗三百首》 *Three Hundred Tang Poems*. (2012, 163).
44 Wang, Ronghua 王荣华 (Translation and annotations). 《千家诗（双语版）》 *Poems of a thousand poets*. Beijing: China Renmin University Press (2020, 121).
45 Sun, Dayu. (Transl.) *Anthology of Ancient Chinese Poetry and Prose*. (2020, 431).
46 Xu, Yuanchong. *On Chinese Verse in English Rhyme,* (1992, 300).
47 Xu, Yuanchong. 许渊冲. 《唐诗三百首》 *Three Hundred Tang Poems*. (2012, 182).
48 Xu, Zhongjie. (Trans.) 《菩萨蛮》 "Pusaman", https://www.en84.com/dianji/ci/201008/000038 48.html.
49 Xu, Yuanchong. *On Chinese Verse in English Rhyme,* (1992, 303).
50 Ibid., (1992, 306).
51 Xu, Yuanchong. (Transl.) 《唐五代词选》 *Selected Lyrics of Tang and Five Dynasties*. Beijing: China Intercontinental Press and China Translation Publishing House. (2012, 96).
52 Ibid., (2012, 19).

53 Ibid., (2012, 23-24).

54 Xu, Yingcai 徐英才 (Transl.). 《英译唐宋八大家散文精选》 *A Selection from the Eight Great Prose Masters of the Tang and Song Dynasties.* Shanghai: Shanghai Foreign Language Education Press (2011, 25-27).

55 Liu, Zongyuan. 《三戒（并序）》 Translated as "Three Fables" but literal translation would be "Three Precepts" (Preface) in https://www.en84.com/dianji/sanwen/201005/00002160.html, a trilogy written by Liu Zongyuan, including *The Fawn of Linjiang*, *Donkey of Qian*, and *The Mice of a Yongzhouer*, (《临江之麋》、《黔之驴》、《永某氏之鼠》). This preface is an account of the reason why he wrote these three fables.

56 《临江之麋》 "The Fawn of Linjiang" is also incorporated in Xu, Yingcai 徐英才 (Transl.). (2011, 49).

Chapter Five

Literature in Song Dynasty

In 907, after the fall of the Tang Dynasty, the northern Yellow River region experienced the rule of five dynasties: Liang, Tang, Jin, Han, and Zhou. Meanwhile, in the south, ten separate states emerged in succession: Wu, Southern Tang, Wuyue, Chu, Southern Han, Min, Former Shu, Later Shu, Jingnan, and Northern Han. This period is historically known as the "Five Dynasties and Ten Kingdoms."

In 960, the Song Dynasty ended the feudal fragmentation of the Five Dynasties and Ten Kingdoms and established a centralized authoritarian empire. Following its establishment, due to escalating ethnic conflicts and frequent warfare, the Song Dynasty was divided into the Northern Song and Southern Song periods. The Northern Song refers to the time from Zhao Kuangyin's usurpation of the Later Zhou throne until 1127, when the Jin forces captured Kaifeng. The Southern Song refers to the period from 1127, when Emperor Gaozong Zhao Gou declared himself emperor in Nanjing (Yingtian Prefecture, present-day Shangqiu, Henan), to 1279, when the dynasty fell to the Yuan.

During the Song Dynasty, six outstanding prose writers and poets emerged: Ouyang Xiu, Zeng Gong, Su Xun, Su Shi, Su Zhe, and Wang Anshi.

1. THE ACHIEVEMENTS AND FEATURES OF SONG POETRY

The achievements of Song poetry fall short compared to Tang poetry, but it has its own distinct characteristics. In the Song Dynasty, any content that could be expressed in prose could also be written in poetry. The approach of "using prose as poetry and argumentation as poetry" is considered the most notable feature of Song poetry. This represents an innovative development in poetry. Moreover, due to the intense ethnic and class conflicts during the Song Dynasty, many poets reflected social realities and expressed patriotic sentiments in their works, with some gaining significant recognition in literary history and leaving a considerable impact on later generations. However, there were also formalist schools that emerged during this time.

They wrote "songs of peace" that embellished reality. These works, later compiled in *The Collection of Xikun Exchanges* (*Xikun Chouchang Ji*), became known as the "*Xikun Style*." These poems prioritized ornate forms but were often empty in content, focusing on themes such as romantic love and banquets, lacking substantive significance. Nonetheless, some of these poems stood out for their delicate depictions of landscapes and emotions, as well as their aesthetic beauty and rhythmic harmony, which influenced the development of Song poetry to some extent.

During the period when formalist trends dominated poetry, Wang Yucheng explicitly declared, "I align myself as a follower of Bai Juyi and aspire to have Du Fu as my predecessor." He inherited the realist traditions of Du Fu and Bai Juyi, creating poetry with rich content and a simple, refreshing style. Wang Yucheng thus became a pioneer of the mid-Northern Song poetry and prose reform movement.

In the mid-Northern Song period, literature entered a phase of comprehensive development. Influenced by political reform movements, figures such as Ouyang Xiu, Mei Yaochen, and Su Shunqin launched a sweeping literary reform movement. This movement criticized the decadent and ostentatious poetic styles that had prevailed since the Tang and Five Dynasties periods, epitomized by the *Xikun School*. They created a wealth of poetry marked by substantial content, fresh language, and a simple, unpretentious style.

Mei Yaochen's poetry profoundly reflected social realities, especially in depicting the miserable lives of farmers and exposing the crimes of the ruling class. His artistic style was plain and subtle, described as "adept at expressing personal emotions, depicting scenery and objects with elegance and integrity, and exhibiting rich variety." His influence on Song poets was significant.

Su Shunqin's poetry covered a wide range of themes. He criticized incompetent rulers and military leaders who lost territories and armies, expressed his ambition to defend the nation and achieve greatness, and exposed the indifference of the ruling class toward the people's suffering. His poetry was characterized by its strong sense of combativeness and his artistic style was vigorous and bold.

Ouyang Xiu, as the leading figure of the literary reform movement, made significant contributions to both literary criticism and creative practice, ensuring the comprehensive success of the reform. Although his achievements in poetry did not match those in prose, his work displayed a unique character. He inherited Han Yu's approach of "using prose as poetry," exhibiting tendencies toward argumentative and prose-like expression, while avoiding Han Yu's pitfalls of obscure and eccentric diction.

Following Ouyang Xiu and Su Shunqin, Wang Anshi and the great literary figure Su Shi further expanded and solidified the achievements of the literary reform, making the Northern Song poetic scene flourish vibrantly. Wang Anshi's poetry often addressed political issues, reflecting his concern for the suffering of the people and the stability of the state, criticism of the ruling class, and evaluations of historical figures. His poetry, whether describing history, discussing current affairs, or debating events, was infused with political commentary, characterized by its fluidity, austerity, and prose-like qualities.

Su Shi's poetry encompasses a wide range of themes. Some express sympathy for the suffering of the common people and criticize the extravagance of the ruling class; others convey personal emotions, describe scenes to evoke feelings, or praise soldiers defending the country. Deeply influenced by Li Bai's romantic style, Su Shi's poetry is characterized by grandeur, boldness, and artistic freedom. Additionally, his technique of "writing poetry with the style of prose," skillfully uncovering "intriguing principles" and "philosophical insights" from ordinary matters, is a significant hallmark of his work. As a result, the poet Lu You praised Su Shi's poetry as being "vastly resourceful and profoundly meaningful."

By the late Northern Song dynasty, social turmoil led to a decline in poetic and literary creation. The *Jiangxi Poetry School*, led by Huang Tingjian and Chen Shidao, increasingly turned away from reality, adopting a path of formalism. They disregarded the relationship between poetry and real life, emphasizing that every word in poetry must have a source or precedent. They neglected the importance of a work's ideological content, focusing excessively on meticulous craftsmanship. In artistic expression, they overly emphasized subtlety and refinement, avoiding direct engagement with social realities. Consequently, their works became artificial and divorced from reality, resulting in a negative influence.

After the fall of the Northern Song, the harsh and tumultuous social realities brought significant changes to literary creation. Early Song poetry often reflected the sufferings of chaos and lamented the nation's plight. As the resistance against the invasions by the Liao and Jin dynasties intensified, patriotic themes became central to poetic creation. From Lu You, Yang Wanli, and Fan Chengda to the poets of the late Southern Song such as Wen Tianxiang, Wang Yuanliang, and Liu Chenweng, their works were imbued with a strong sense of patriotism. Among them, Lu You, a great patriotic poet, had the greatest impact and achieved the highest accomplishments.

Lu You's poetry is characterized by a consistent theme of patriotism, with the central subject being the aspiration to avenge the humiliation, resist the Jin invaders, and defend the homeland. The core content of his poetry mainly include:

(a) Expressing a bold and heroic spirit in the fight to save the nation from the Jin forces.
(b) Condemning the Southern Song ruling class for their cowardly policies and failure to protect the country.
(c) Reflecting and sympathizing with the suffering of the people.

Lu You, often referred to as the "*Little Li Bai*," was also honored with the title "Poet Historian." His artistic characteristics include the romantic and bold style reminiscent of Li Bai (frequent use of seven-character ancient-style poetry, free-flowing form, majestic momentum, imaginative grandeur, and striking exaggeration) and the realistic features of Du Fu (less detailed descriptions and more highly condensed generalizations). His language is clear, accessible, refined, and natural. Lu You excelled in all poetic forms, especially in seven-character regulated verse (*qilv*) and seven-character ancient-style verse (*qigu*).

Lu You's poem *"Moon Over the Mountain Pass"* takes its theme from an old *Yuefu* subject but conveys contemporary reflections. The poem adopts the voice of a border guard soldier to bitterly denounce the rulers' humiliating policy of surrendering to the enemy. It conveys the frustration of patriotic individuals who find no outlet for their dedication and the yearning of the people in the Central Plains for national restoration.

The main artistic features of *"Moon Over the Mountain Pass"* include:

(a) *Use of contrast for a clear theme:* The poem juxtaposes the decadence and indulgence of the powerful, the sorrow and anger of heroic soldiers, and the grief and suffering of displaced people, making its central message particularly striking.
(b) *High generalization and intense lyricism:* With concise language, the poem paints three vivid and shocking scenes: the feasting of the elite, the bones of the fallen on the battlefield, and the tears of the displaced people. It encapsulates the corrupt social reality of the Southern Song Dynasty and powerfully conveys the poet's profound anger and sorrow.

During the late Southern Song period, decadent poetic schools such as the "Yongjia Four Talents" and the "Jianghu School" emerged. Their works were shallow in content and melancholic in tone.

Composing While Living in the Countryside

Wang Yucheng

Idle clouds drift, their shadows on the pool at ease,
Far removed from worldly cares, all worries cease.
A small square pond reflects the sky so vast,
With clouds and light that linger as they pass.

How can the water stay so pure and bright?
Its source flows freely, renewing its might.

Idle Thoughts in Illness

Wang Yucheng

Weakened bones confined to bed so long,
With scattered books, I pass the hours along.
Worldly troubles fade, dissolved in thought,
In stillness, life's true peace is gently sought.
The wind stirs bamboo shadows as they play,
The rain leaves scents of plum along its way.
My heart drifts like a cloud, unbound and free,
Following waters flowing endlessly.

At a Party Given by Fan Zhong-yan the Guests Spoke of Eating "River-Hog," or the Blowfish[1]

Mei Yaochen

Spring isles grow with shoots of reeds,
spring shores fly with willow flowers.

At such times "river-hog" is prized
beyond the common run of fish.

Its form may make one marvel,
there is also no worse poison.

Its raging belly is like a great hog,
its furious eyes like a southeastern frog.

When fried in the kitchen, if things go amiss,
it will enter the throat like the sword Mo-ya.

Why give sustenance to tooth and palate
with something that wrecks the body like this?

If one dare question the Southerners thus,
they band to defend it and boast its merit.

Writing of My Sorrow[2]

Mei Yaochen

Heaven took my wife from me,
then also took my child.

And though my eyes are never dry,

this heart is ready to die.

Rain falls and enters the ground,
a pearl sinks to the floor of sea.

If you go to the sea, you may see the pearl,
or dig in the ground, you may see the water.

But men, when they go to the streams below,
we know they are gone forever more.

I stroke my chest, who can tell me why?-
this gaunt and worn ghost in the mirror.

On March 26, 1048, I Had a Dream[3]

Since the time that I remarried,
two years she stayed out of my dreams.
But then last night I saw her face,
and mid-evening was struck by pain.
The darkening lamp showed its faint light,
it somberly shone on the rafters and beams.
Out of nowhere snow beat on my window,
borne along, as well, by a furious wind.

Crescent Moon[4]

When the crescent moon comes shining
on the corner of my roof,
the dog on the west side barks,
the eastern neighbor is troubled.
Deep in the night bright spirits
and wraith-things are astir,
on the ancient plain there's a rustling
and there is no wind.

On the Pavilion of the Drunken Old Man in Chu-zhou[5]

Ouyang Xiu

Forty is not yet old, and I
just chance to sign poems "Drunken Old Man."
When drunk I leave everything behind,
so why would I still need to note my age?
I love simply how this pavilion's brook
makes its way here through tangles of peaks,
Sounding as though it were falling from sky,

spilling straight down toward these two eaves.
Then off it flows to the stream by the cliff,
where hidden springs add to its gurgling;
Its sound never drowns out conversation,
its clarity, unlike that of flutes and harps.
Of course I find flutes and harps lovely,
but their music is much too fast and loud;
Therefore I often take wine in hand
and walk far away to this purling stream.
Wild birds peer at me when I'm drunk,
and creek's clouds keep me here asleep.
Hill flowers waste their practiced smiles,
not knowing how to speak with me.
Only the breeze that comes from the cliff
will blow me back sober again.

Su Shi, Shi Cang-shu's "Hall of Drunken Ink" (1068)[6]

Su Shi

All worry and woe in life begins
from learning to read and write-
be able to roughly mark your name
and then you should call it quits.

What point is there in cursive draft
that flaunts the spirit's speed?-
the blur in my eyes when I open a scroll
makes me ill at ease.

Yes, I too have been fond of it,
but always I laugh at myself;
how can we cure this affliction
as it shows itself in you?

You tell me that in doing this
you find a perfect joy,
mind's satisfaction, not distinct
from spirit's roaming free.

Just recently you built a hall
and named it "Drunken Ink,"
comparing this art to drinking wine
that melts anxieties.

I see now that Liu Zong-yuan
wrote something not untrue:
such affliction may crave dirt and ash
as if it were haute cuisine.

Still we may say that in this art
you have achieved the heights:
worn-out brushes pile by your walls
like little hills and knolls.

When the whim strikes, one swish of the hand
and a hundred sheets are gone:
in a fleeting moment a splendid steed
bestrides the entire land.

My own script takes shape to my mood,
I have no special technique:
the dots and lines just follow my hand,
it's a bother to try too hard.

Then tell me why in your critiques
I am singled out for praise,
isolated words and scraps of paper
all find themselves collected.

Your script may be properly judged
no lower than Zhong or Zhang;
on a lower level my own is still better
than that of Luo or Zhao.

You should no longer sit by the pool
and practice so ardently,
in the end just take all that writing silk
and use it to stuff a quilt.[7]

Tong-chao Tower at Zheng-mai Station (1100)[8]

For the rest of my days I would grow old
in a village of Hai-nan,
and the god will send down Shaman Yang
to summon back my soul.
Dim in the distance, at the base of sky,
where a hawk is sinking away,

is a hair's breadth line of green mountains,
and that is the heartland.

Crossing the Sea, June 20, 1100

Orion lies flat, the Dipper bends down,
it is almost midnight now,
after harsh rains and daylong wind
skies also know how to clear.

When clouds scatter, the moon shines bright,
who needs add decoration?-
for Heaven's complexion and colors of sea
are basically clear and pure.

All that remains is that old man of Lu's[9]
wish to sail off on a raft;
and I roughly discern the melody
of the Yellow Emperor's music.[10]

In southern jungles I died nine times
yet I feel no cause for complaint-
this present trip's utter wonder
crowns my entire life.

Lu You (1125-1210), Snowy Night[11]

Lu You

I

My books lie scattered all around,
boxes of pills among them;
huddled in blankets, from time to time
I burn incense from Hai-nan.
Growing old and slow, I laugh at myself,
that a young man's heart survives,
that still loves to listen to northern winds
blow snow across my bed.

II

On village lanes the snow turns slush,
and people cease their goings;
the dot of a Buddhist temple lantern
is a bright grain of red sand.

How late now the falcon returns
to his mountain home to roost-
the winds bear the whir
of mighty wings.

A Trip to Mountain West Village[12]

Don't laugh because it's muddy—year-end wine brewed in country homes;
harvests were good—to make the guest linger, fowl and pork plenty.
Mountains multiply, streams double back—I doubt there's even a road;
willows cluster darkly, blossoms shine—another village ahead!
Pipe and drum sounds tagging me—spring festival soon;
robe, cap of plain and simple cut—they honor old ways here.
From now on, if I may, when time and moon-light allow,
I'll take my stick and, uninvited, come knock at your gate.

Running into Light Rain on the Road to Sword Gate Pass[13]

On my clothes the dust of travel mingled with wine stains;
A distant journey – no place that doesn't jar the soul!
And I – am really meant to be a poet?
In fine rain straddling a donkey I enter Sword Gate Pass.

Border Mountain Moon[14]

Fifteen years ago the edict came: peace with the invader;
our generals fight no more but idly guard the border.
Vermilion gates still and silent; inside they sing and dance;
stabled horses fatten and die, bows come unstrung.
From garrison towers the beat of kettles hurries the sinking moon;
lads who joined the troops at twenty, white-haired now.
In the sound of the flutes who will read the brave man's heart?
Above the sands emptily shining, moon on warrior bones.
Spear-clash on the central plain—this we've known from old.
But have traitorous barbarians live to see their heirs?
Our captive people, forbearing death, pine for release,
even tonight how many places stained with their tears?

The Temple of Shooting Stars[15]

Wang Anshi[16]

Into jutting clouds terrace and hall
rise looming upward;
long river that reaches thousands of miles,

a single cup of wine.
From here I see streams and mountains
swallow down sun and moon,
while far in the distance no wagon or horse
brings along dust and dirt.
Wild geese fly on paths through cloud,
their voices pass down low,
the visitor draws near Heaven's Gates,
and quickly comes back from dream.
The scope of such splendor only a poem
could tidily display;
but I, lacking talent, am put to shame,
having come here so casually.

Moored at Melon Islet[17]

A river severs Northern shore and Southern land;
Between my home and me but a few mountains stand.
The vernal wind has greened the Southern shore again.
When will the moon shine bright on my return? O when?

2. THE RISE AND DEVELOPMENT OF CI POETRY

Ci poetry originated from the folk tradition. After the mid-Tang Dynasty, with the development of urban storytelling, music, and performance arts, the practice of filling lyrics (Ci) gradually became popular. By the end of the Tang Dynasty, the upper ruling class became enamored with song and dance, and wealthy families sought indulgence, leading to the widespread practice of filling lyrics to match melodies. Because of his mastery of rhythm and rhetoric, and his love for song and dance, Wen Tingyun brought *Ci* poetry from the folk tradition to the literary world, thus establishing its status. However, his ci poetry had a narrow range of themes, focusing primarily on delicate and ornate expressions, which became known as the *Huaijian School* ("Flower-and-Jewel School"), influencing later generations of poets.

During the Five Dynasties and Ten Kingdoms period, regions like Western Shu and Southern Tang, which were free from the ravages of war, saw their rulers indulging in pleasures of the senses, leading to the creation of extravagant ci poetry. These poems were often shallow and lacking in intellectual value. Among the poets of Southern Tang, the greatest achievement came from the last emperor, Li Houzhu. His ci poetry had the following characteristics: first, it expanded its themes, shifting from focusing solely on women's lives to expressing political disillusionment and personal feelings; second, he abandoned the traditional use of allusions and employed a direct, plain style to convey sincere emotions; third, he was skilled in using universal emotions to resonate with the reader's heart; and fourth, he was adept at using elegant and clear language to subtly and profoundly express his feelings. Therefore, his works had a significant influence on later generations.

By the Northern Song Dynasty, the urban economy was thriving, and the rulers pursued indulgence while the citizens demanded cultural life, leading to the significant development of storytelling and performance literature. Ci poetry, as a form of short, musical literary expression, thus found the conditions for its growth. At the same time, Ci poetry, as a new literary form, had become a more free and expressive medium than traditional poetry, making it the dominant literary form of the Song Dynasty. Like Tang poetry, Song *Ci* saw a surge of writers, with various schools emerging and diverse styles developing, producing a large number of excellent works that reflected the life of the era. However, Ci poetry took a winding path of development. The ci poetry of the early Northern Song largely followed the style of the Five Dynasties, with shallow content, narrow themes, sentimental tones, and flowery language, without significant achievements. However, among these poets, certain works by figures like Yan Shu, Ouyang Xiu, and Yan Jidao were more substantial in content, with fresher language and a bright style. To some extent, they broke free from the extravagant style of the Five Dynasties and contributed to the development of the gentle and refined style of Song Ci.

The representative figure of the gentle and refined school (*Wanyue School*) is Liu Yong. He was the first professional Ci poet of the Song Dynasty. Although his works still contained a large portion of "romantic songs" with superficial or melodious themes, he made breakthroughs in content and developed his own distinctive style. First, in terms of themes, his poems either depicted the bustling life of the city, the hardships of traveling, the melancholy of personal failure, or the lonely lives of lower-class courtesans and musicians. Artistically, his slow-paced *ci* poems often employed the *fu* (rhapsodic) style, demonstrating exquisite craftsmanship, varied techniques, and a bold use of colloquial language. His works marked the artistic maturity of the gentle and refined school and had a significant influence.

At the same time, the bold and unrestrained school of Ci poetry began to emerge. The rise of this school brought about a comprehensive innovation in Ci poetry. In the works of the representative poet of this school, Su Shi, any topic that could be expressed in poetry could also be expressed in Ci, greatly expanding the scope of Ci poetry. His Ci, like his poetry and prose, is filled with a spirit of innovation: the breadth of topics, the depth and vastness of ideas, the flexibility of his writing, the grand momentum, and the diversity of styles, all of which bring a refreshing feeling. Su Shi is the outstanding representative of the bold and unrestrained school, and his works are characterized by original creativity, passionate emotions, and grandiose momentum. His Ci is not bound by musical rhythm; it does not sacrifice emotional content for sound, forming a distinctive "bold and outstanding" style. His contributions opened a path for the healthy development of Northern Song ci poetry, having a far-reaching influence on the development of the bold and unrestrained school. Other poets of the Northern Song who belong to this school include Fan Zhongyan and Wang Anshi.

In the late Northern Song, the style of ci poetry regressed, and the gentle and refined style re-emerged. Among the poets, Qin Guan and Zhou Bangyan were the most prominent. Qin Guan's ci poetry focused on the themes of "emotion" and "sorrow," often expressing the misery of exile and the pain of longing and unrequited love. His emotions were sincere and delicate, with a strong artistic appeal.

Zhou Bangyan's Ci poetry, though lacking in content and intellectual elevation, excelled in artistry. He drew upon the strengths of various schools, not only developing the slow-paced Ci poetry of the Northern Song but also having a significant influence on the works of Jiang Kui and Wu Wenying of the Southern Song. His achievements can be summarized in the following points: First, he was skilled in regulated forms and the creation of new tunes. He not only paid attention to rhyme but also the four tones, making him a pioneer of regulated Ci poetry. He also created many new tunes. Second, he excelled at using precise and detailed language to express characters' emotions. Third, he was adept at creatively incorporating ancient poetry into Ci, achieving a level of subtle and exquisite expression. Additionally, in terms of artistic techniques, he skillfully balanced elements such as harmony and separation, reality and abstraction, and the arrangement of sparse and dense elements. Thus, his contributions to the development of ci poetry in terms of artistic techniques were significant.

Li Qingzhao, who lived during the transition from the Northern to Southern Song, was also a unique Ci poet. Her Ci poetry, known as the *Yi'an style*, is highly regarded. Her artistic achievements can be summarized in the following aspects: First, she was skilled in expressing emotions, particularly through the depiction of typical objects, which made abstract feelings more tangible. Second, she was adept at creating fresh and rich artistic concepts using ordinary language, full of subtle meanings that invite deep reflection. Third, she combined both the gentle and refined style with the bold and unrestrained style.

In the early Southern Song Dynasty, due to intense ethnic conflicts and social unrest, a large number of patriotic Ci poets gathered in the literary world. Among them, Zhang Yuangan and Zhang Xiaoxiang, who inherited Su Shi's bold and unrestrained style, were the most well-known. Their Ci poetry was characterized by grand momentum, substantial content, and passionate patriotism. The tone was solemn and tragic, filled with a sense of battle. Other poets belonging to this school included Chen Liang, Li Gang, Zhao Ding, Hu Quan, and Yue Fei.

The most accomplished and influential poet in the Southern Song ci world was the patriotic poet Xin Qiji. The defining characteristic of Xin Qiji's Ci poetry was that he closely linked the fate of the country and the nation with the poetry itself, prominently reflecting the patriotic spirit of the time. These themes were concentrated in his calls for the resistance against the Jin Dynasty, the recovery of the Central Plains, the denunciation of incompetent rulers who harmed the country, his deep concern for the nation's peril, and the expression of his frustration at being unable to serve his country.

Xin Qiji's artistic achievements were also remarkable. His Ci poetry inherited the fine tradition of Su Shi but also innovated to suit the demands of the era. First, he incorporated contemporary content into Ci, expanding the artistic capacity of the form, making Ci a trumpet for patriotism. Second, his Ci works possessed a vigorous, grand, and profound bold style. Third, his use of language had the characteristic of "treating prose as Ci," incorporating elements from prose, parallel prose, colloquial speech, and the language of classical texts such as the Confucian classics, histories, and writings into his Ci. Fourth, in terms of expression, he broke the traditional structure of first describing a scene and then expressing emotions, often blending both seamlessly according to the needs of the emotion being expressed. Moreover, Xin Qiji excelled at using allusions and historical references to convey contemporary feelings, achieving the purpose of expressing emotions and aspirations. Poets in the Xin school included Liu Guo, Liu Kezhuang, Liu Chenweng, Huang Ji, Wen Daxiang, and others. The continuous emergence of these writers made the bold and unrestrained school shine brightly in the Southern Song Ci world.

By the late Southern Song, with the relatively stable situation of the Northern and Southern Song facing each other, the collective patriotic sentiments began to fade from poetry, and the voice of indignation against the enemy gradually disappeared. The "Yazheng School," represented by Jiang Kui, Shi Dazhu, and Wu Wenying, followed the gentle and refined style, paying attention to melody and poetic structure. A formalist pursuit of elegant and beautiful forms began to rise. The works of these poets were content-poor, lacking real significance, but their artistic form had a significant influence on the ci poetry of the Ming and Qing Dynasties.

Ouyang Xiu

Ouyang Xiu was the leader of the *literary reform movement* in the Song Dynasty. Regarding essay writing, he emphasized addressing the "ills of the times" rather than producing empty rhetoric. He advocated for "conciseness with deep meaning," promoting simplicity and naturalness while opposing the pursuit of the strange and dangerous. This approach absorbed Han Yu's advocacy for "smooth and coherent writing" in ancient prose but abandoned Han Yu's extreme view of "removing only conventional expressions."

Ouyang Xiu's literary achievements were most prominent in prose writing. His essays expanded on the "smooth and coherent" characteristics of Han Yu's style, featuring brisk and concise narratives as well as graceful and subtle arguments. His writing is characterized by twists and turns and a smooth and fluent language.

In his work *Preface to the Biography of the Court Entertainers of the Five Dynasties*, Ouyang Xiu used the example of the rise and fall of the Later Tang Emperor Zhuangzong to illustrate the idea that "hardship can strengthen a nation, while indulgence and comfort can lead to its downfall" and that "prosperity or decline depends on human actions." He warned the rulers of the Song Dynasty to eliminate the ingrained habits of indulgence and complacency. The essay is graceful and intricate in its argumentation, precise in reasoning, and vivid in language.

The artistic features of Ouyang Xiu's *The Old Drunkard's Pavilion* are as follows:

(a) It seamlessly integrates the depiction of natural scenery with human activities and emotions, creating a vivid picture of harmonious beauty and joy.
(d) The essay is centered around the theme of "joy," with a clear structure, gentle narration, and skillful composition.
(c) The language is simple and natural yet concise and elegant. It combines parallel and free prose styles, is lively in tone, and uses the word "also" twenty-one times, creating a rhythmic and lyrical effect.

Ouyang Xiu's achievements in poetry were not as significant as in prose, but he followed Han Yu's practice of "writing poetry with a prose-like approach." His poetry tended toward argumentation and a prose-like style, with greater freedom in form, thus shaping the poetic style of the Northern Song Dynasty. His lyric poetry (*ci*) developed the style of Southern Tang poet Feng Yanshi, often expressing emotions of lamenting spring and parting. He emphasized psychological portrayal and the lyrical function of ci, with a style that was elegant and refined.

Plum Blooms at Inn Wither[18]

Plum blooms at travelers' inn have withered.
Beside brook-side bridge are slender willows.
In breeze of grass fragrance, horse is spurred on.
Gloom stretches endlessly as I get further.
It goes on and on like the flow of spring water.
My heart is shattered into tiny pieces.
Tears stream down the powder on my face.

I go up high tower and lean against railing.
Beyond flat grassland are springtime mountains.
Travelers on foot have gone past these massifs.

Butterflies in Love with Flowers[19]

Deep, deep the courtyard where he is, so deep
It's veiled by smokelike willows heap on heap,
By curtain on curtain and screen on screen.
Leaving his saddle and bridle, there he has been
Merry-making. From my tower his trace can't be seen.

The third moon now, the wind and rain are raging late;
At dusk I bar the gate,
But I can't bar in spring.
My tearful eyes ask fowers,
But they fail to bring
An answer, I see red blooms fly over the swing.

Liu Yong

Liu Yong (circa 987–1053), courtesy name Qi Qing, originally named Sanbian, was a native of Chong'an, Fujian. His official career was marked by setbacks, and it was not until his later years that he finally passed the imperial examination. Liu Yong was the *first professional lyricist* in the history of Chinese ci poetry. His creative activities took place during the Northern Song Dynasty, a period of relative political stability and economic prosperity. This era's urban life is vividly and richly reflected in his ci poetry.

Liu Yong stepped out of the narrow confines of the aristocracy and led a life immersed in the "streets and alleyways," which gave him the opportunity to engage with folk lyric compositions. As a result, his *ci* poetry is characterized by a straightforward, appropriate, unembellished style, with minimal artificial refinement. With the proliferation of new musical tunes, Liu Yong expanded the scope of ci poetry and became the first poet in *ci* history to create a significant body of long-form ci (*slow ci*).

By incorporating the artistic techniques of the Six Dynasties' short poetic essays (*xiaofu*), Liu Yong excelled in detailed descriptions and emotional elaboration. This allowed the emotions expressed in his *ci* to shine like the brilliance of a galaxy, filling every line with radiance and reaching every corner. Among his works, those depicting the sorrow of separation and longing are not only numerous but also of exceptional quality. They achieved an artistic level where emotional expressions and scenic descriptions blend seamlessly, creating an inseparable union of mood and imagery.

Bells Ringing in the Rain[20]

Cicadas chill
Drearily shrill.
We stand face to face in an evening hour
Before the pavilion, after a sudden shower.
Can we care for drinking before we part?
At the city gate
We are lingering late,
But the boat is waiting for me to depart.
Hand in hand we gaze at each other's tearful eyes
And burst into sobs with words congealed on our lips.
I'll go my way,
Far, far away.
On miles and miles of misty waves where sail ships,
And evening clouds hang low in boundless Southern skies.

Lovers would grieve at parting as of old.
How could I stand this clear autumn day so cold!
Where shall I be found at daybreak
From wine awake?
Moored by a riverbank planted with willow trees
Beneath the waning moon and in the morning breeze.
I'll be gone for a year.
In vain would good times and fine scenes appear.
However gallant I am on my part,
To whom can I lay bare my heart?

Su Shi

Su Shi succeeded Ouyang Xiu as a literary leader in the mid-Northern Song Dynasty. Through his outstanding literary creations, he ultimately completed the literary reform of the Northern Song Dynasty. He extended the spirit of this reform into the realm of *ci* poetry, advancing Northern Song literature to its highest level. Su Shi's prose ranks alongside that of Han Yu, Liu Zongyuan, and Ouyang Xiu, collectively known as "*Han, Liu, Ouyang, and Su*." His prose exhibits a wide variety of forms, with a writing style that flows naturally like clouds and water, demonstrating effortless grace.

The characteristics of Su Shi's poetry include:

(a) Writing poetry in a prose-like manner and incorporating argumentation, with a style that is free, uninhibited, and rich in romanticism.
(b) Skillful and broad use of metaphors.
(c) A profound and enduring philosophical interest.

Through his creative practice, Su Shi expanded the thematic scope of *ci* poetry, enriched its artistic style, established the bold and unrestrained school of *ci* poetry (*Haofang School*), and elevated the status of *ci*, thereby initiating a new era in *ci* poetry creation.

The boldness of Su Shi's *ci* poetry is reflected in:

(a) Its passionate and heroic spirit of idealism.
(b) Writing *ci* with the techniques of poetry, incorporating extensive argumentation and vigorous style.
(c) The ability to break free from the constraints of *ci's* rhythmic patterns.

Riverside Town[21]

A Dream on the Night of the Twentieth Day of the First Moon 1075

For the long years the living of the dead knows nought,
Though to my mind not brought,
Could the dead be forgot?
Her lonely grave is far, a thousand miles away.
To whom can I my grief convey?
Revived even if she be, could she still know me?
My face is worn with care,
And frosted is my hair.

Last night I dreamed of coming to my native place;
She was making up her face
Before her mirror with grace.
Each saw the other hushed,
But from our eyes tears gushed.
Can I not be heart-broken when I am awoken
From her grave clad with pines,
Where only the moon shines!

Prelude to Water Melody[22]

On the Autumn Day of Bingchen[23], I feasted merrily to the daybreak and got drunk, and then wrote this work, also expressing my missing of Ziyou.[24]

How long will the full moon appear?
Wine cup in hand, I ask the sky.
I do not know what time of year
'T would be tonight in the palace on high.
Riding the wind, there I would fly,
Yet I'm afraid the crystalline palace would be

Too high and cold for me.
I rise and dance, with my shadow I play.
On high as on earth, would it be as gay?

The moon goes round the mansions red
Through gauze-draped windows to shed
Her light upon the sleepless bed.
Against man she should have no spite.
Why then when people part, is she oft full and bright?
Men have sorrow and joy; they part or meet again;
The moon is bright or dim and she may wax or wane.
There has been nothing perfect since the olden days.
So let us wish that man
Will live long as he can!
Thousand miles apart, we'll share the beauty she displays.

Charm of a Maiden Singer[25]

(Reflections on the Ancient Red Cliff)

The endless river eastward flows;
With its huge waves are gone all those
Gallant heroes of bygone years.
West of the ancient fortress appears
Red Cliff where General Zhou won his early fame
When the Three Kingdoms were in flame.
Rocks tower in the air and waves beat on the shore,
Rolling up a thousand heaps of snow.
To match the land so fair, how many heroes of yore
Had made great show!

I fancy General Zhou at the height
Of his success, with a plume fan in hand,
In a silk hood, so brave and bright,
Laughing and jesting with his bride so fair,
While enemy ships were destroyed as planned
Like castles in the air.
Should their souls revisit this land,
Sentimental, his bride would laugh to say:
Younger than they, I have my hair turned grey.
Life is but like a dream.
O moon, I drink to you who have seen them on the stream.

Qin Guan

Qin Guan was one of the representative writers of the Graceful and Restrained (*Wanyue School*) of *ci* poetry. The main characteristics of his works lie in his skill at intertwining the longing and yearning of lovers with his own political setbacks and struggles in life. He was adept at using melancholic scenery, subtle techniques, and gentle tones to convey sentiments of sorrow. His representative work *"Treading on Grass"* (*Mist Veils the Pavilion*) is a quintessential example of these features.

In the history of *ci* poetry, Qin Guan inherited the tradition from Liu Yong and paved the way for Zhou Bangyan. Meanwhile, He Zhu served as a transitional figure from Su Shi to Xin Qiji.

Treading on Grass: The Chenzhou Hotel[26]

The tower lost in mist, the ferry dim in moonlight,
The Peach Blossom Fairyland goes beyond my sight.
How can I bear the lonely hotel locked in cold spring?
The sun is setting when the homesick cuckoos sing.
Plum blossoms from post, letters from my friend,
The homesickness piles in my heart without end.
The Chen River happily flows around the Chen Hill,
Why flows to the Xiaoxiang River against its will?

Zhou Bangyan

Zhou Bangyan, together with Maoqi Yong and Chao Duanli, and others, served in the Dasheng Music Bureau (*Dasheng Yuefu*),[27] where they studied ancient tunes and styles and created new musical compositions. Hence, they were referred to as the "*Dasheng lyricists*." Their *ci* poetry often focused on embellishing a superficial peace, with content that was somewhat empty. However, their works were characterized by elegant diction, strict adherence to tonal patterns, and varied structures, advancing the technical artistry of ci poetry.

Zhou Bangyan's *ci* works can be categorized into two main themes: "elegant Ci" and "amorous Ci". Though the thematic scope of his works was relatively narrow, Zhou had a deep understanding of musical structures and was capable of creating new melodies. His compositions are marked by meticulous attention to rhythm, exquisite forms, refined and vivid language, and an exceptionally delicate and detailed style.

Six Toughies[28]

Faded Roses

Again it's time to taste new wine in dresses light.
How I regret to have misspent my time day and night
Far from home, far away!
I wish that spring would stay
A little longer, but fine spring Is on the wing.
Once gone, it's left no traces.
I ask where are the flowers.
They fell with ancient rosy faces,
Whose fallen hairpins still shed
A fragrance sweet. The peach path and willowy lanes
Are dotted now with petals red.
What loving heart would for them utter sighs
But match-making bees and message-bearing butterflies,
Knocking from time to time at window-panes?
The eastern garden in a shroud
Of dark green cloud,
The deep silence beneath
The deflowered tree is broken by the sighs I breathe.
Its long thorned branches pull at my sleeves
As if to tell me how the flowers' parting grieves.
I try to pin a little flower not yet dead
To the turban on my head,
But it's unlike one on a golden hairpin new,
Shivering and beckoning to you.
O roses, do not drift away
With tide or ebb by night or day!
On broken petals red, I fear,
There's message for a lover dear.

Li Qingzhao

In the early Southern Song period, patriotism was a prominent theme in literature. Li Qingzhao, a master of *ci* poetry during the transition between the Northern and Southern Song Dynasties, was one of the representatives of the Graceful and Restrained (*Wanyue*) school. Her *ci* poetry is divided into two periods, marked by her migration to the south. In the earlier period, her works often celebrated the beauty of nature and love, with a style that was fresh and bright. In the later period, her works primarily expressed the sorrow of losing her home and country due to war, with a tone that was somber and poignant.

Li Qingzhao's *"Slow, Slow Song"* conveys a deep sense of sorrow, expressing the poet's grief over the fall of her nation, the loss of her home, the death of her husband, and her lonely wanderings in old age. It indirectly reflects the societal hardships of that era. The artistic features of this work include:

(a) ***Integration of scenery and emotion:*** Each scene conveys a feeling, vividly and from multiple perspectives depicting the scenery of late autumn while also deeply expressing the sorrow of the season.
(b) ***Simple and colloquial language:*** The diction is straightforward, often using conversational literary language.
(c) ***Unique use of tonal sounds:*** The use of entering tones creates a short, choking, and plaintive effect, as though suppressing sobs. Additionally, frequent use of alliteration, reduplication, and consonant-heavy sounds (such as dental and retroflex consonants) creates a cold and melancholic atmosphere, precisely reflecting the poet's specific emotional state.

The Black River[29]

Be man of men while you're alive,
Be soul of souls e'en if you're dead!
Think of Xiang Yu who'd not survive
His men whose blood for him was shed!

Tipsy in the Flowers' Shade[30]

Veiled in thin mist and thick cloud, how sad the long day!
Incense from golden censer melts away.
The Double Ninth comes again;
Alone I still remain
In silken bed curtain, on pillow smooth like jade.
Feeling the midnight chill invade.

At dusk I drink before chrysanthemums in bloom,
My sleeves filled with fragrance and gloom.
Say not my soul
Is not consumed. Should the west wind uproll
The curtain of my bower,
You'll see a face thinner than yellow flower.

Slow, Slow Tune[31]

I look for what I miss;
I know not what it is.
I feel so sad, so drear,
So lonely, without cheer.
How hard is it
To keep me fit

In this lingering cold!
Hardly warmed up
By cup on cup
Of wine so dry,
O how could I
Endure at dusk the drift
Of wind so swift?
It breaks my heart, alas!
To see the wild geese pass,
For they are my acquaintances of old.

The ground is covered with yellow flowers,
Faded and fallen in showers.
Who will pick them up now?
Sitting alone at the window, how
Could I but quicken
The pace of darkness that won't thicken?
On plane's broad leaves a fine rain drizzles
As twilight grizzles.
O what can I do with a grief
Beyond belief?

Xin Qiji

Xin Qiji was an outstanding patriotic *ci* poet whose works, along with those of poet Lu You, represent the pinnacle of Southern Song literature. Xin's *ci* poetry is centered on themes of patriotism and a fighting spirit. Its specific content includes:

(a) Expressing his heroic ambition to defeat enemies and serve the nation.
(b) Lamenting his unfulfilled aspirations with anger and regret.
(c) Criticizing the complacency of the political regime through reflections on historical ruins.
(d) Portraying the simplicity and beauty of rural life and natural landscapes.

The artistic achievements of Xin's *Ci* include:

(a) He inherited and developed the bold style of *ci* poetry pioneered by Su Shi, creatively reforming the form and structure of *ci*.
(b) He expanded the thematic scope of *ci*, skillfully creating grand and dynamic imagery.
(c) He employed a variety of techniques such as allusion, metaphor, personification, exaggeration, and contrast.

(d) In language, he adeptly drew on classical and contemporary poetic syntax, while also integrating prose, rhymed verse, colloquial expressions, and phrases from classical texts into his *ci*.
(e) His style is renowned for its boldness but is also highly flexible, embodying a balance of strength and softness.

Water-Dragon Chant: Ascending the Shangxin Pavilion in Jiankang conveys Xin Qiji's deep concern for his country and lament over his thwarted ambitions through his observations from the Pavilion of Joy. Its artistic features include:

(a) *Integration of emotion and scenery:* The grand and sorrowful landscapes he depicts blend seamlessly with his somber and heroic emotions, creating a bold and powerful style.
(b) *Skillful use of allusions:* The second half of the poem employs multiple historical references, borrowing the stories of past figures to express his feelings and thoughts from various angles in a natural and fitting way.
(c) *Creative use of metaphor, personification, and symbolism:* He uses metaphor and personification to vividly and imaginatively depict the beauty of nature. Lines such as "atop the tower at sunset" not only portray picturesque scenes but also symbolically reflect the desolation and decline of the era.

In his work *Groping for Fish,* Xin Qiji uses the lament of a woman for her lost springtime and favor to express the patriot's sorrow for his country's plight and the times' turbulence. The poem employs traditional allegorical techniques throughout:

(a) The female protagonist symbolizes loyal patriots.
(b) "Jade Ring and Flying Swallow" (*Yuhuan and Feiyan*) represent corrupt officials and traitors.
(c) "Wind and rain" symbolize the turmoil of the Southern Song Dynasty.
(d) The lament over spring's passing signifies concern for the nation's decline.
(e) "Willows in the mist of sunset" symbolizes the fading glory of the Song court.

The poem's thematic expression is both subtle and profound, achieving a powerful artistic impact with its layered and heavy undertones.

Water Dragon Chant[32]

The Southern sky for miles and miles in autumn dye
And boundless autumn water spread to meet the sky,
I gaze on far-off northern hills
Like spiral shells or hair decor of jade,

Which grief or hatred overfills.
Leaning at sunset on balustrade
And hearing a lonely swan's song,
A wanderer on southern land.
I look at my precious sword long
And pound all the railings with my hand,
But nobody knows why
I climb the tower high.

Don't say for food
The perch is good!
When west winds blow,
Why don't I homeward go?
I'd be ashamed to see the patriot,
Should I retire to seek for land and cot.
I sigh for passing years I can't retain;
In driving wind and blinding rain
Even an old tree grieves.
To whom then may I say
To wipe my tears away
With her pink handkerchief or her green sleeves?

The Moon over the West River[33]

Startled by magpies leaveng the branch in moonlight,
I hear cicadas shrill in the breeze at midnight.
The rice fields' sweet smell promises a bumper year;
Listen, how frogs' croaks please the ear!

Beyond the clouds seven or eight stars twinkle;
Before the hills two or three raindrops sprinkle.
There is an inn beside the village temple. Look!
The winding path leads to the hut beside the brook.

Joy of Eternal Union[34]

The land is boundless as of yore,
But nowhere can be found
A hero like the king defending southern shore.
The singing hall, the dancing ground,
All gallant deeds now sent away
By driving wind and blinding rain!
The slanting sun sheds its departing ray
O'er tree-shaded and grassy lane

Where lived the Cowherd King retaking the lost land.
In bygone years,
Leading armed cavaliers,
With golden spear in hand
Tiger like, he had slain
The foe on the thousand-mile Central Plain.

His son launched in haste a northern campaign;
Defeated at Mount Wolf, he shed his tears in vain.
I still remember three and forty years ago
The thriving town destroyed in flames by the foe.
How can I bear
To see the chief aggressor's shrine
Worshipped 'mid crows and drumbeats as divine?
Who would still care
If an old general
Is strong enough to take back the lost capital?

The River All Red[35]

Yue Fei

Wrath sets on end my hair;
I lean on railings where
I see the drizzling rain has ceased.
Raising my eyes
Towards the skies,
I heave long sighs,
My wrath not yet appeased.
To dustis gone the fame achieved in thirty years;
Like cloud-veiled moon the thousand-mile Plain disappears.
Should youthful heads in vain turn grey,
We would regret for aye.

Lost our capitals,
What a burning shame!
How can we generals
Quench our vengeful flame!
Driving our chariots of war, we'd go
To break through our relentless foe.
Valiantly we'd cut off each head;
Laughing, we'd drink the blood they shed
When we've reconquered our lost land,
In triumph would return our army grand.

3. THE INNOVATION OF PROSE

After the peak of Tang prose, the *Ancient Prose Movement* in Song Dynasty pushed Chinese ancient prose to another summit. During this movement, Ouyang Xiu inherited the theory established by Han Yu and Liu Zongyuan, resisting the then feeble, empty and flowery style. With his writing practice, he guided and supported the later leading prose writers such as Zeng Gong, Wang Anshi, Su Shi, etc., laying the foundation for the Poetry and Prose Movement in Song Dynasty. Nevertheless, the writer who made the greatest achievements and contributions in this movement is Su Shi. In theory, Su Shi emphasized the substantial contents and the practicality to solve some social problems, as well as a plain style without pompous and euphuistic language, which was essential to get rid of the then grandiose but frothy style. Besides, he also created some articles and travelogues to describe a person or an event, which have a unique distinction. In his narratives, he is skilled at characterization by focusing on some specific life scenes and details, while in his travelogues, he is adept at preaching his philosophy through depicting the beautiful scenery, combining expertly narration, description, emotion expression and argumentation. In addition, he also left some epistles with elegant language, profound meanings and plain and natural style, "as natural and smooth as floating clouds and flowing waters," which exert a positive influence on the later prose works.

Another master should go to Wang Anshi, whose prose is mainly academic or political. These penetrating and insightful articles show clearly his attitudes and perspectives, from which an eminent politician's outlook and manners can be seen.

An Account of the Pavilion of the Drunken Old Man[36]

Ouyang Xiu

Encircling Chu-zhou all around are mountains. The wooded gorges of the various peaks to the southwest are overwhelmingly lovely. The one that stands out in the view, rising thick with dense growth, is Lang-ya Mountain. Going six or seven miles into the mountain, you gradually begin to hear the sound of flowing water; and the watercourse that spills out from between the two peaks is Brewer's Stream. As the path turns with the bend of the cliff, there is a pavilion, its wings outspread, standing beside the stream; and this is the Pavilion of the Drunken Old Man.

Who was it who built the pavilion? It was the mountain monk Zhi-xian. Who was it gave the pavilion its name? This was the governor himself. The governor would come with his guests to drink here; and when he had gotten a little drunk, he, being the eldest of the company, gave himself the nickname "Drunken Old Man." The Drunken Old Man's interest was not in the wine itself but in being here amid the mountains and waters. The delight in mountains and waters was first found in the heart and then lodged temporarily in the wine.

When the sun comes out and the forest haze lifts, or when the clouds come back to the hills and the caves in the cliffs grow dark, all the transformations of light and shadow are the passages from dawn to dusk in the mountains. Wildflowers spring up and give off secret fragrances; then the cassia trees rise high and form dense shade; then winds blow high up and the frost gleams in purity; then the waters sink and stones appear: these are the four seasons in the mountains. At dawn we go there and at dusk return; and as the scenery of the four seasons is never the same, so our delight too is limitless.

And as for those who carry burdens along the paths and travelers who rest under the trees, the ones in front shout and those behind answer; hunched over with age or with children in tow, they go back and forth without ceasing. These are the travels of the people of Chu-zhou. By the creek, we fish: the creek is deep and the fish are plump. We use the stream's water in brewing wine; and since the water smells sweet, the wine is sharp and clear. Pieces of fish and game from the mountains and vegetables from the wilds are served to us in varying dishes; and these are the banquets of the governor. Our delight when tipsy at these banquets does not come from the music of harps and flutes. Someone playing toss-pot makes his throw; someone playing chess wins; horn-cups and wine tallies are all jumbled together amid the noisy chatter of people getting up and sitting down; and these are the pleasures of the assembled guests. And the person with his face darkened by age and white-haired, lying passed out in the middle, is the governor, drunk.

Then the evening sun is in the mountains and the shadows of people scar ter in disarray; this is the governor going home and his guests following. As the woods become veiled in shadow, there is a singing above and down below, and this is the delight of the birds at the departure of the human vis itors.

And yet the birds may experience the delight of the mountain forests, but they do not experience the delight of the people. The other people may experience the delight of coming to visit this place with the governor, but they do not experience the governor's delight in their delight. The person who in drunkenness can share their delight and who, sobering up, can give an account of it in writing is the governor. And who is the governor? Ou-yang Xiu of Lu-ling.

Written After Seeing the Paintings of Wu Dao-zi[37]

Su Shi

Those with knowledge first fashion a thing; those with ability carry it through. It is not accomplished by one person alone. The superior man in his study and all the various artisans in their skills reached a state of completion in the passage from the Three Dynasties of antiquity through the Han down to the Tang. When poetry reached Du Fu, when prose reached Han Yu, when calligraphy reached Yan Zhen-qing, and when painting reached Wu Dao-zi, then all the variations of past and present and all the possibilities in the world were over. Wu Dao-zi's paintings of people and things are like casting a reflection with a lamp; in anticipating what is to come and recalling where they were, seen from side or angle, slanting or level, each is perfect in degree, and he achieves the proportions of nature, without erring in the smallest detail. He displays fresh thoughts within strict rules and leaves the most subtle sense of pattern beyond swaggering self-expression. This is what Zhuang-zi meant by plenty of space for the blade to move or a wind rising from plying the ax. He is absolutely unique in ancient and modern times. As for other paintings, I may not necessarily be able to tell the painter's name. But when it comes to Wu Dao-zi, no sooner do I look at one than I can tell if it is genuine or a fake. Few indeed are the genuine ones in our age, yet the one Shi Quan-shu has in his collection is such as I have seen only once or twice in my life.

—Written October 7, 1085.

"On the Subject of Governing: A Letter to Emperor Renzong" (Excerpt)

Wang Anshi

I, a foolish and incompetent official, have been blessed with the privilege of serving along the way. Now, I am once again honored by Your Majesty's summons to return to the imperial court, where I am entrusted with duties, and must report on matters related to these duties. I am aware that I am unqualified for the task, yet I dare to speak on matters of state. I humbly ask Your Majesty to carefully consider and choose among the options available, for that would be most fortunate.

The current urgency, then, lies in talent. If the world is filled with talented individuals, only then can those in positions of power select the most capable among them to serve. Once those in power have access to such talent, they can then evaluate the times and make adjustments to address the people's sufferings, changing the defective laws of the realm to align with the intentions of the ancient kings, which would be very easy. The present world is also the world of the ancient kings. In the times of the ancient kings, there was an abundance of talent—how has it come to be that today, there is such a shortage? This is why I say that those who were "molded" were not following the proper path.

What does it mean to be "molded"? It means educating, nurturing, selecting, and assigning individuals according to a proper method.

What is the method of education? In ancient times, from the emperor and the nobles down to the towns and villages, everyone had schools. There were officials appointed specifically to manage education, and these officials were selected with care. The matters of state—ritual, music, governance, and punishment—were all rooted in education. What scholars observed and practiced were the laws, teachings, and ethical principles of the ancient kings for governing the realm. If an individual was not fit to serve the state, they were not educated. If they were fit to serve, then there was no area in which they could not learn. This is the method of education.

What is the method of nurturing? It involves providing sufficient wealth, restricting actions with rites, and regulating conduct through laws.

What does it mean to "provide with wealth"? If a person is lacking in material resources, they will become greedy and unscrupulous, willing to do anything to obtain wealth. The ancient kings understood this, so they designed the salary system such that even the lowest officials had enough to cover their basic living expenses. For those higher up, they received additional allowances to ensure their financial needs were met in a way that would encourage integrity and prevent greed. Yet, even this was considered insufficient. The salary was further extended to the official's descendants, ensuring that they lacked nothing in life or death. What does it mean to "restrict with rites"? If a person has enough material wealth but no sense of ritual to regulate their behavior, they may indulge in debauchery and excess. The ancient kings understood this as well, so they established rituals to regulate matters such as weddings, funerals, sacrifices, and feasts, as well as the materials for food and drink. Rituals set limits on wealth, ensuring that unnecessary luxuries were avoided. What does it mean to "regulate through laws"? The ancient kings taught people not only through moral principles but also by setting laws to enforce correct behavior. If a person violated the laws, they were punished by exile or death. Even minor offenses, like changing clothes or excessive drinking, were punished with exile. The purpose of this strict law enforcement was to prevent the disorder of the people. However, it was not just the harshness of the law that ensured order; it was the sincerity and compassion of the rulers that inspired compliance.

What is the method of selecting people? The ancient kings selected individuals based on their merit within their local communities, asking others to recommend those with talent, and then assessing them. They did not rely solely on outward appearances but also questioned their actions and speech, testing them through practical experience. If they were truly virtuous and capable, they were appointed to official positions.

What is the method of appointing people? The talents and virtues of individuals vary, and thus their roles should match their abilities. The ancient kings knew this, so they assigned tasks accordingly: experts in farming were assigned agricultural duties, and skilled craftsmen were appointed to work with tools. They made appointments based on ability and virtue, and those who excelled were promoted. This system ensured that people were assigned appropriate duties, allowing them to achieve success in their roles.

Thus, if the ruler and their ministers can act with sincerity, fully engage their faculties of judgment, and carry out these methods with compassion and diligence, then doubts and failures will be eliminated, and the affairs of the state will be properly managed.

4. THE RISE OF SONG *HUABEN* (THE COLLOQUIAL NOVEL) IN SONG DYNASTY

During Song period, owing to the economic booming in cities and the increasing population of urban people, a new literary form was needed to reflect people's thoughts and life, hence the rise of a new literary form – the colloquial novel – to reflect life and reality in a freer and quicker way. The earliest colloquial novels should go to *A Story of the Temple in Mount Qingping* and *Popular Stories from the Capital Editions.* These colloquial novels always have the ordinary urban people as their characters, reflecting truly life of the urban people, and exposing the social conflicts, with plain language and simple plots, showing completely the features of such a folk literary form.

The Story of Liu Qi, the Scholar Official, and Zhou Yuexian, the Courtesan

A Story of the Temple in Mount Qingping (Chapter One)

Who is the delicate girl surpassing the moon goddess,
walking swiftly on the fragrant stairs, her figure graceful?
Two peach blossoms bloom in the morning sun,
her eyes, like stars, sparkle with autumn waves.
A golden phoenix flies from her hairpin, and her eyebrows,
like willow leaves, are shaped like a jade maiden.
There are endless ways to admire her charm, but one can never capture it all;
even a horse takes ten steps to stumble and falter.

This poem was written by Liu Qi, a scholar of the Song dynasty, about a beautiful woman.

At that time, during the reign of Emperor Shenzong of the Song dynasty, there was a renowned scholar in the capital, Liu Qi, often called "Liu Qiguan" (Liu the Seventh Gentleman). At twenty-five years old, he was an outstanding talent, graceful in appearance, and skilled in poetry, essays, music, chess, painting, and calligraphy. He was particularly fond of visiting flower streets and brothels, where many famous courtesans admired him. He frequently spent time with three well-known high-ranking courtesans: Chen Shishi, Zhao Xiangxiang, and Xu Dongdong. These three courtesans adored Liu Qiguan and even composed a song for him:

> "Shishi's beauty captivates with her dazzling charm, Xiangxiang shares much affection with me, Dongdong and I are perfectly compatible. Together, we three adore him, but he remains indifferent. The king has not yet approved the words, but I hesitate, and now what is the matter with you, Liu Qiguan?"

One day, Liu Qiguan was spending his time idly at one of these courtesans' houses and composed a song in a playful mood. The lyrics went:

> "Ten miles of lotus flowers, nine miles red, in the middle, a white one stands tall. The white lotus is just right to touch the root, while the red one blooms to bear the lotus pod. The lotus pod—how delicious is the root. Flowers must bear seeds, or else it's all in vain. Drunk, I ate three bowls with an empty stomach. As I fell into the water, the colorful lotus boat could still be heard, the beating of drums, and the sound of Dongdong."

Liu Qiguan, one day, took his servant to a pavilion by the river in Jinling, got drunk, and ordered his servant to fetch a pen. He wrote a poem and sent it to the "Ru Mei Ren" (The Beautiful Lady of the Ru) and inscribed it on the whitewashed wall of the pavilion. The poem went:

> "When will the spring flowers and autumn moon end? How much of the past do I remember? Last night, the east wind blew again, and my homeland is unbearable to recall under the bright moon! The carved railings and jade steps should still be there, only the red face has changed. How much sorrow can one have? It is like the river of spring flowing eastward."

After finishing the poem, Liu Qiguan threw down the brush, pointed to the immortal, and returned to the capital.

Liu Qiguan's literary talent was highly regarded, and many officials who admired his abilities recommended him for the position of magistrate in Yuhang County, in the Jiang-Zhe region. Liu Qiguan humbly declined the offer but was eventually persuaded to accept. He bade farewell to the three courtesans, each of whom gave him a heartfelt send-off. He then left his friends and relatives, packed his belongings, and set off for his new position. Within a few days, he arrived in Yuhang. True to his reputation, he governed with integrity and fairness, and the people were pleased with his leadership.

After two months, Liu Qiguan used his own funds to build a pavilion near a canal, modeled after the one in Jinling, and named it "Wanjian Pavilion" for his own pleasure. There was a beautiful courtesan named Zhou Yuexian in the area, and Liu Qiguan often invited her to sing for him. He admired her greatly and described her beauty:

> "Her hair is lightly combed like a cicada's wings, her eyebrows like spring mountains drawn with skill. Her lips, like a delicate peach, and her teeth like two rows of shattered jade. Her face is as charming as a flower, her eyes as bright as ice-cut jewels; her demeanor is enchanting, her spirit radiant. She is not only the most beautiful in Yuhang but surpasses even the famous flowers in the capital."

After a drinking session, Liu Qiguan, feeling stirred, attempted to woo Zhou Yuexian. However, she repeatedly rejected his advances and left in anger. Liu Qiguan learned from his informants that she had a lover named Huang Yuanwai, who was very fond of her. Huang Yuanwai lived in a house near the river, a mile away, and would visit her every night by boat. Liu Qiguan learned this and secretly instructed a boatman to force himself on Zhou Yuexian one night. The boatman was promised a generous reward if he complied.

One night, Zhou Yuexian, traveling alone by boat to Huang Yuanwai's house, was caught halfway along the river. The boatman tied the boat up in a secluded place and, without warning, entered the cabin, where he forcibly embraced her. Unable to escape, Zhou Yuexian reluctantly submitted. Afterward, feeling sorrowful, she composed a poem:

> "I hate that I am a courtesan, suffering in silence, unable to speak."
>
> "Ashamed, I return under the bright moon, too lazy to board the boat to the flower garden."

That night, after being assaulted, Zhou Yuexian reluctantly went to Huang Yuanwai's house and returned home by morning.

The boatman reported back to Liu Qiguan, who then planned a banquet at the Wanjian Pavilion, where he invited Zhou Yuexian to sing. The boatman, disguised as a guest, was already seated. Halfway through the banquet, Liu Qiguan sang Zhou Yuexian's poem aloud:

> "I hate that I am a courtesan, suffering in silence, unable to speak."
>
> "Ashamed, I return under the bright moon, too lazy to board the boat to the flower garden."

After Liu Qiguan finished singing, Zhou Yuexian was deeply embarrassed and ashamed, unable to lift her head. She knelt before him and begged for his forgiveness, promising to serve him as a maid and devote herself to him without any other intentions. Liu Qiguan was pleased, and they enjoyed each other's company. He wrote another poem:

> "I, a lowly person, do not serve Liu Qiguan, but row my lonely boat in the night."
>
> "The waning moon and the morning wind on the willow banks—will you let this moment go to waste?"

After the poem, Zhou Yuexian bowed and left. From then on, she stayed by Liu Qiguan's side, always attending to him, and they were inseparable.

One day, after drinking, Liu Qiguan ordered Zhou Yuexian to write a poem. She composed a playful song, which Liu Qiguan gave to her:

> "Liu the scholar has devised a plan, Zhou Yuexian has fallen into the trap. I've prepared the fisherman's hook for the giant fish. You're wise, but you can't outwit the hand of a scholar. Sister, no need to be ashamed, I've dug up the Wanjian Pavilion."

After Liu Qiguan wrote the song, he handed it to Zhou Yuexian, who thanked him and returned home.

Liu Qiguan served as magistrate for three years, with Zhou Yuexian loyally by his side, and their love grew deeper. However, when his term ended and he returned to the capital, they parted ways, though the memories lingered.

To this day, the stories of love and intrigue from the world of courtesans and scholars are whispered across the rivers and lakes.

There is a poem that says:

> "A farewell to a soulmate brings sorrow from afar,
> no matter where we go, the Wanjian Pavilion remains."
> "Where will we meet again next year?
> I point to the white clouds on the horizon."

Another poem says:

> "Liu Qiguan is reluctant to leave Zhou Yuexian,
> her sweet singing and graceful dancing bring him great joy."
> "Both longing for each other, yet unable to meet,
> who knows when we will be reunited?"

NOTES

1 Owen, Stephen. (ed. and translated). *An Anthology of Chinese Literature.* New York, London: Norton (1996, 650-51).

2 Ibid., (1996:690-691).

3 Ibid.

4 Ibid.

5 Ibid., (1996: 685).

6 Ibid., (1996: 640-641).

7 The penultimate couplet, echoing old traditions of evaluative comparisons, refers to the great calligraphers Zhong Yao and Zhang Zhi, and to the good but less distinguished

calligraphers Luo Shu- jing and Zhao Yuan-si, all from the beginning of the calligraphic tradition in the first three centuries A.D. The last line refers to an anecdote about Zhang Zhi, whose own specialty was draft cursive: he would practice his calligraphy by a pool so often that it became black with his ink.

8 Stephen, Owen. (ed. and translated). *An Anthology of Chinese Literature* (1996, 677).

9 The "old man of Lu" is Confucius, who, in despair that the Way was not in practice in the world, once expressed a wish to sail off to sea on a raft.

10 The Zhuang-zi tells of the Yellow Emperor performing his cosmic music in the wilderness by Lake Dong-ting.

11 Stephen, Owen. (ed. and translated). *An Anthology of Chinese Literature* (1996, 653).

12 Lu, You.《游山西村》 "A Trip to Mountain West Village" in http://www.kekenet.com/kouyi/201407/311652.shtml.

13 Lu, You.《剑门道中遇微雨》 "Running into Light Rain on the Road to Sword Gate Pass" in https://m.kekenet.com/kouyi/201407/311650.shtml.

14 Lu, You.《关山月》 "Border Mountain Moon" in http://www.kekenet.com/kouyi/201407/311648.shtml.

15 Owen Stephen. (ed. and translated). *An Anthology of Chinese Literature* (1996:691).

16 Wang Anshi's early poetry was largely political in nature, characterized by bold and unrestrained arguments, vigorous style, and powerful tone (e.g., *"The People of Hebei"*). In his later years, his poetry shifted to lyrical and scenic small poems, with reduced focus on realism but marked by innovative and unique ideas, refined language, and artistic mastery. This later style became known as the "Banshan Style" (e.g., *"Mooring at Guazhou or melon's Islet"*). Wang Anshi's famous scenic poem *"Mooring at Guazhou"* vividly portrays the beauty of spring in Jiangnan, expressing the poet's deep affection for the region. The poem demonstrates meticulous attention to detail in its depiction of the scenery, presenting fresh and evocative imagery. Its language is exquisite, skillful in its use of rhetoric, and showcases the poet's profound artistic prowess.

17 Wang, Anshi.《泊船瓜州》 "Moored at Melon Islet", translated by Xu, Yuanchong in https://www.ximalaya.com/sound/312327396，许渊冲译.

18 Ouyang, Xiu.《踏莎行》 "Plum Blooms at Inn Wither" https://zhuanlan.zhihu.com/p/499405646, prepared by: alexcwlin; edited by: Adam Lam.

19 Xu, Yuangchong.《画说宋词》*Song Lyrics in Paintings.* Beijing: China Translation Publishing Group (2021, 63).

20 Ibid., (2021, 37).

21 Xu, Yuanchong. (Transl.)《许渊冲译宋词三百首（上册）》 *Three Hundred Song Lyrics*. Beijing: China Translation Publishing Group (2021, 383-385).

22 Xu, Yuangchong.《画说宋词》*Song Lyrics in Paintings.* (2021, 100).

23 丙辰，namely, the ninth year of Xi'ning (76 A.D.), Emperor Shenzong of Song Dynasty,

24 子由, courtesy name of the writer's brother Su Zhe.

25 Xu, Yuangchong.《画说宋词》*Song Lyrics in Paintings.* (2021, 95).

26 Wu, Xinjian 无心剑. (Transl.)《踏莎行・郴州旅舍》 "Treading on Grass: The Chenzhou Hotel" in https://www.jianshu.com/p/be62757ffff3?utmcampaign=maleskine&utm_content=note&utm_medium=seo_notes&utm_source=recommendation.

27 Dasheng Yuefu: 大晟乐府（大晟府），an official conservatory founded by Emperor Huizong of Northern Song Dynasty between 1102-1106 for the development and collection of folk songs and ballads.

28 Xu, Yuanchong. (Transl.). *Three Hundred Song Lyrics*. (2021, 137-139).

29 Xu, Yuanchong. (Transl.)《夏日绝句》"The Black River" in https://wenku.baidu.com/view/6d8c925332b765ce0508763231126edb6f1a7696.html?_wkts_=1676394961038&bdQuery=李清照夏日绝句+英语

30 Xu, Yuangchong.《画说宋词》*Song Lyrics in Paintings.* (2021, 180).

31 Ibid., (2021, 175).
32 Ibid., (2021, 218).
33 Xu, Yuanchong. (Transl.) 《西江月・夜行黄沙道中》"The Moon over the West River" in https://www.xiaohongshu.com/explore/638b02f3000000001b025633
34 Xu, Yuangchong. 《画说宋词》*Song Lyrics in Paintings.* (2021, 221).
35 Ibid., (2021, 186).
36 Owen, Stephen. (ed. and translated). *An Anthology of Chinese Literature.* New York, London: Norton (1996, 613-614).
37 Ibid., (1996, 618)

Chapter Six

Literature in Yuan Dynasty

The Yuan Dynasty (1271–1368) was established when the Mongol leader Genghis Khan, Emperor Taizu unified the various Mongol tribes in 1206 and formed a regime. Following this, Genghis Khan and his successors conquered the Western Liao, Western Xia, Jin, Dali, and other minority regimes in China. In 1271, Genghis Khan's grandson, Kublai Khan, adopted the reign title of Yuan, and by 1279, he had defeated the Southern Song, unifying all of China and establishing the capital in Dadu (modern-day Beijing). This period marked another major unification of China, following the Qin, Han, Sui, and Tang Dynasties.

The most outstanding achievement of Yuan Dynasty literature was *Yuan Qu* (Yuan drama and poetry). "Yuan Qu" refers to a genre of songs and operas, which includes both *Sanqu* (a type of free verse poem) and *Zaju* (a type of Chinese drama). Sanqu emerged as a new poetic form after the classical poems, often focusing on themes of reclusiveness and describing the romantic interactions between men and women, and it had a unique artistic style. Yuan Zaju, which developed from northern Chinese theatre, experienced a qualitative leap in dramatic literature due to its close connection with writers, performers, and the lower classes. Many successful writers created significant works in this genre. Yuan Zaju reflected a wide range of social issues, exposing the darkness of society and the cruelty of rulers, while expressing strong anti-feudal and anti-ethnic oppression sentiments. Realistic artistic methods played an important role. Additionally, Southern opera made progress and produced influential works. The "*Huaben*" (storytelling) genre also continued to develop based on its Song Dynasty origins.

1. THE ZAJU PLAY OF YUAN DYNASTY

Yuan Zaju is a form of drama sung to northern tunes (*Beiqu*). It originated in northern China at the end of the Jin Dynasty and the beginning of the Yuan Dynasty. It evolved gradually from folk traditions, based on the Jin Yuanben (play scripts) and modes of ancient Chinese music melodies (*gongdiao*), into a new art form that closely combined singing, storytelling, dancing, and acting. The songs, or the singing part of the Zaju, consist of several pieces of music from the same palace tune, forming a complete set. In Zaju, a single *gongdiao* is called an "act," which is equivalent to a scene or an act in modern theatre. The songs within an act all follow the same rhyme scheme, and most Zaju plays consist of four acts. For example, *The Romance of the West Bower* has twenty acts excluding the prologue, while *The Orphan of Zhao* has five acts, which is a variation and less common. Each act is sung by a single actor from beginning to end, with other actors speaking but not singing. Plays such as *The Phoenix Tree Rain*, *The Han Palace Autumn*, and *The Wronged Dou E* or *Midsummer Snow* follow this structure. In Yuan drama, solo singing is typical, though there may be instances where others join in at the end of a song, but this is a variation. The solo singer is usually a main character in the drama: the male lead is called the "Mo," and the female lead is called the "Dan." Thus, the script is often referred to as the "Mo script" or "Dan script."

The "prologue" (Xiezi) in Yuan Zaju is made up of one or more short songs and is arranged before the first act or between acts, serving as a prologue or transition scene, similar to the "overture" or "interlude" in modern theatre. Since Zaju typically has only four acts, the prologue helps to connect and balance the narrative. Most scripts have one prologue, although some rare scripts may have two.

The "bai" refers to the dialogue in the play. According to the Ming Dynasty scholar Jiang Nan in his *Bao Pu Jian Ji (Brief Notes on Bao Pu)*, "When two people speak, it is called 'bin'; when one person speaks alone, it is called 'bai'." Xu Wei explained, "The lyrics are the main focus, and the 'bai' serves as the secondary part, hence it is called 'binbai'." [1] Though their explanations differ, both suggest that "binbai" refers to the spoken lines in the play. While the sung lyrics are certainly important for the plot, the "binbai" is also indispensable, as it is a crucial part of the script's structure. Yuan Zaju playwrights generally followed the principle of "using dialogue to narrate the story, and songs to represent the characters' words" in their creative process.

2. THE PROSPERITY OF YUAN ZAJU

The prosperity of Yuan Zaju can be attributed to several factors:

(a) *Historical Reasons*: This includes intense ethnic and class conflicts, social darkness, corrupt governance, and the discrimination faced by scholars with limited opportunities for advancement. The turbulent times provided rich material for Zaju creation, and the darkness of reality became a catalyst for the playwrights' creativity.

(b) *Economic Reasons:* During this period, the strength of the nation and the prosperity of urban economies expanded the bourgeois class, which was conducive to and promoted the development of popular literature and arts.

(c) *The Development of Drama Itself*: Yuan Zaju emerged as a complete form of drama, blending various performing arts based on the Jin Yuanben. Its literary scripts and music were also influenced by Song dynasty poetry, modes of ancient music (tunes), and other musical forms. It can be said that its complete structure developed gradually through various forms over different periods.

The creation of Yuan Zaju can be divided into two periods based on the year 1300: the early period, which was the peak of its development, and the later period, which marked its decline. The early period centred around Dadu (modern Beijing) and was dominated by northern styles, with works that balanced both ideological and artistic qualities. Many famous playwrights emerged, including Guan Hanqing, Ma Zhiyuan, Bai Pu, Wang Shifu, Kang Jinzhai, Ji Junxiang, Gao Wenxiu, Yang Xianzhi, and Shi Junbao. The later period, centred around Hangzhou, was dominated by southern styles, with works focusing more on form, fewer famous playwrights, and the emergence of specialized scholarly studies on the genre.

3. GUAN HANQIN AND HIS WORKS

Guan Hanqing is considered one of the earliest and greatest playwrights in the history of Chinese drama. In his work *Lu Gui Bu* (Record of Ghosts), Yuan historian Zhong Sichen lists him as the foremost writer of the Yuan Dynasty. The author of *Lu Gui Bu Xu Bian* (The Continued Record of Ghosts) from the early Ming Dynasty, Jia Zhongming, calls him the "leader of the pear garden" and the "chief editor of Zaju drama groups." He is regarded as the founder of Yuan Zaju and the leader of the early Yuan theatre scene.

Guan Hanqing was born around the same time as Bai Pu, and his creative activities mostly occurred during the reign of Kublai Khan (ruling from 1260 to 1294). According to the *Qizhou Zhi* (Chronicles of Qizhou) compiled during the Qing Dynasty, he was from Qizhou (modern-day Anguo County, Hebei Province). However, *Lu Gui Bu* states that he was from Dadu (modern Beijing) and went by the courtesy name Yi Zhai Shou. He served as a superintendent in the Imperial Medical Bureau. Guan Hanqing lived in Dadu for most of his life, though in his later years, he visited Hangzhou and wrote a series of Sanqu songs describing the scenery of the city. Besides, he also wrote ten *Tune of Dade*, probably the popular tune form during Dade, the reigning period of Emperor Chengzong (1297–1307), from which it can be deduced that he might die during the years of Dade.

Throughout his life, Guan Hanqing wrote more than sixty Zaju plays. Eighteen of his works have survived, including: Snow in Midsummer, The Rescue of a Courtesan, The Butterfly Dream, The Wife-Snatcher, The Pavilion of Moon-Worship, The Smart Girl Cheating on Love Affair, The Riverside Pavilion, Gold Thread Pool, Xie Tianxiang, The Jade Mirror-Stand, A Dream in Red Clothes, The Single-Knife Meeting, A Dream of the West Shu State, Death of the Winged-Tiger General, Mrs. Chen's Educating Her Son, Pei Du's Returning the Jade Belt, A Banquet of Five Generals, Taking the Long Spear with a Whip, etc.

Guan Hanqing's Zaju plays fall into three categories:

(a) Exposing social problem and legal case dramas (The Injustice to Dou E, The Wife-Snatcher, The Butterfly Dream).
(b) Plays on women (The Rescue of a Courtesan, The Pavilion of Moon-Worship).
(c) Historical dramas (*The Single Sword Duel*).

His plays on women have distinctive ideological features. The protagonists are often from humble backgrounds and have low social status but possess a spirit of resistance. These plays typically end with the protagonist's victory. This category of works exposes the darkness of society and the cruelty of rulers, reflecting the suffering of the common people under persecution.

3.1 *The Injustice to Dou E*

The Injustice to Dou E is Guan Hanqing's representative work. It deeply reflects the darkness of Yuan Dynasty society and sharply criticizes the situation where "officials show no intention of administering justice, leaving the common people with no way to speak out." This elevates the ideological significance of the work to a new height. The author uses a satirical technique to describe the magistrate, kneeling and pleading in the courtroom, calling the accuser their " bread and butter providers," and with blood and tears, portrays the brutal scenes of torture, showing the harsh reality of the Yuan court's greed, corruption, and cruelty.

The Injustice to Dou E is not just the tragedy of Dou E as an individual, but also represents the tragedy of persecuted women in feudal society. Dou E is deeply bound by feudal thought. She initially wants to follow feudal morals and laws, but the dark society of the time offers her no way out: "I have never wronged any one, but now I have to go to the gallows; I have never disgraced my ancestor, but now I have to meet my odds." When she is taken to the execution ground, all her hopes are shattered, and filled with resentment, she makes a powerful and heart-rending accusation against Heaven, Earth, and the gods. She protests fiercely against her unjust fate. Before her execution, Dou E makes three vows, which, though impossible in reality, powerfully affirm her innocence and serve as a rejection of the dark reality. This commanding cry elevates Dou E's character to a new level.

Guan Hanqing's *The Injustice to Dou E* is based on the story of the "East Sea Filial Woman" from *The Book of Han: The Story of Yu Dinggu,* in which a Han

Dynasty woman is wrongfully punished. The play, by depicting Dou E's tragic life, profoundly exposes the corruption and darkness of feudal society and passionately celebrates the spirit of resistance among the oppressed.

In *the Injustice to Dou E*, the author arranges three major dramatic conflicts:

(a) The conflict between Dou E and Zhang Lver and his father.
(b) The conflict between Dou E and Magistrate Tao Wutai in the courtroom, as well as her curse against Heaven and Earth at the execution ground.
(c) Dou E's spirit appealing to Dou Tianzhang, seeking justice for her wrongful death.

3.1.1 The Character Dou E

Dou E is a kind-hearted and rebellious labouring woman. This character represents the typical oppressed woman in the later stages of Chinese feudal society. Dou E's tragic life profoundly exposes the corruption and darkness of Yuan society, reflecting the painful experiences of the vast number of oppressed women in China. Through her personal tragedy, the play showcases the tragedy of the era under national oppression. At the same time, Dou E's unique and brilliant spirit of resistance embodies the spirit of the common people's defiance, revealing the truth that justice will ultimately triumph over evil.

3.2 The Artistic Achievements of Guan Hanqin's works

The artistic achievements of Guan Hanqing's works are primarily reflected in the following aspects:

(a) *The combination of realism and romanticism*: He uses realistic techniques to broadly and deeply reflect social life, presenting certain essential features of the era, while also employing bold and imaginative exaggeration to depict idealized visions.
(b) *Perfect artistic expression:* The arrangement of scenes is rich in typicality, and Guan is skilled at adapting to the circumstances and shifting the narrative as needed.
(c) *Distinctive character development*: His works feature many successful character portrayals, with individualized personalities and a clear distinction in class attributes across different societal levels.
(d) *Authentic language:* Guan Hanqing skilfully integrates a large amount of folk dialect into his songs, capturing the nuances of human emotions through the lyrics.

Snow in Midsummer[2]

Guan Hanqing

Act III (Excerpt)

(*Enter the Officer in charge.*)

OFFICER: I am the officer in charge of executions. Today we are putting a criminal to death. We must stand guard at the end of the road, to see that no one comes through.

(*Enter the Attendants. They beat the drum and the gong three times; then the executioner enters, sharpens his sword and waves a flag. Dou E is led on in a cangue. The gong and drum are beaten.*)

EXECUTIONER: Get a move on! Let no one pass this way.

DOUE:

Though no fault of mine I am called a criminal,
And condemned to be beheaded –
I cry out to Heaven and Earth of this injustice!
I reproach both Earth and Heaven
For they would not save me.
The sun and moon give light by day and by night,
Mountains and rivers watch over the world of men;
Yet Heaven cannot tell the innocent from the guilty;
And confuses the wicked with the good!
The good are poor, and die before their time;
The wicked are rich, and live to a great old age.
The gods are afraid of the mighty and bully the weak;
They let evil take its course.
Ah, Earth! you will not distinguish good from bad,
And, Heaven! you let me suffer this injustice!
Tears pour down my cheeks in vain!

EXECUTIONER: Get a move on! We are late.

DOU E:

The cangue round my neck makes me stagger this way and that,
And I'm jostled backward and forward by the crowd.
Will you do me a favour, brother?

EXECUTIONER: What do you want?

DOU E:

If you take me the front way, I shall bear you a grudge;
If you take me the back way, I shall die content.
Please do not think me wilful!

EXECUTIONER: Now that you're going to the execution ground, are there any relatives you want to see?

DOU E: I am going to die. What relatives do I need?

EXECUTIONER: Why did you ask me just now to take you the back way?

DOU E:

> *Please don't go by the front street, brother,*
> *But take me by the back street.*
> *The other way my mother-in-law might see me.*

EXECUTIONER: You can't escape death, so why worry if she sees you?

DOU E: If my mother-in-law were to see me in chains being led to the execution ground –

> *She would burst with indignation!*
> *She would burst with indignation!*
> *Please grant me this comfort, brother; before I die!*
> *(Enter Mistress Cai.)*

MRS. CAI: Ah, Heaven! Isn't that my daughter-in-law? This will be the death of me!

EXECUTIONER: Stand back, old woman!

DOU E: Let her come closer so that I can say a few words to her.

EXECUTIONER: Hey, old woman! Come here. Your daughter-in-law wants to speak to you.

MRS. CAI: Poor child! This will be the death of me!

DOU E: Mother, when you were unwell and asked for mutton tripe soup, I prepared some for you. Donkey Zhang made me fetch more salt and vinegar so that he could poison the soup, and then told me to give it to you. He didn't know his old man would drink it. Donkey Zhang poisoned the soup to kill you, so that he could force me to be his wife. He never thought his father would die instead. To take revenge he dragged me to court. Because I didn't want you to suffer, I had to confess to murder and now I am going to be killed. In future, mother, if you have gruel to spare, give me half a bowl; and if you have paper money to spare, burn some for me, for the sake of your dead son!

> *Take pity on one who is dying an unjust death,*
> *Take pity on one whose head will be struck from her body,*
> *Take pity on one who has worked with you in your home;*
> *Take pity on one who has neither mother nor father,*
> *Take pity on one who has served you all these years,*
> *And at festivals offer my spirit a bowl of cold gruel.*

MRS. CAI (weeping): Don't worry. Ah, this will be the death of me!

DON E:

Burn some paper coins to my headless corpse,
For the sake of your dead son.
We wail and complain to Heaven:
There is no justice! Dou E is wrongly slain!

EXECUTIONER: Now then, old woman, stand back! The time has come.

(*Dou E kneels, and the Executioner removes the cangue from her neck.*)

DOU E: I want to say three things, officer. If you will let me, I shall die content. I want a clean mat and a white silk streamer twelve feet long to hang on the flag-pole. When the sword strikes off my head, not a drop of my warm blood will stain the ground. It will all fly up instead to the white silk streamer. This is the hottest time of summer, sir. If injustice has indeed been done, three feet of snow will cover my dead body. Then this district will suffer from drought for three whole years. EXECUTIONER: Be quiet! What a thing to say!

(*The Executioner waves his flag.*)

DOU E:

A dumb woman was blamed for poisoning herself;
A buffalo is whipped while it toils for its master.

EXECUTIONER: Why is it suddenly so overcast? It is snowing! (He prays to Heaven.)

DOU E:

Once Zou Yan caused frost to appear:
Now snow will show the injustice done to me!

(*The Executioner beheads her and the Attendant sees to her body.*)

EXECUTIONER: A fine stroke! Now let us go and have a drink.

(*The Attendants assent, and carry the body off.*)

4. WANG SHIFU AND THE ROMANCE OF THE WEST BOWER

Wang Shifu, whose personal name was Dexin, was from Dadu (modern-day Beijing). He was also a writer familiar with the life in brothels, and, alongside Guan Hanqing and others, was an important playwright of early Yuan Dynasty. Thirteen of his plays are recorded in the "Record of Ghosts." His representative work is *The Romance of the West Bower*. Additionally, two other works, *The Spring Hall* and *The Broken Kiln*, have survived.

Wang Shifu's *The Romance of the West Bower* is based on Dong Xieyuan's *The West Bower* (Dong Xieyuan's *Zhugongdiao: The West Bower* is adapted from the Tang Dynasty writer Yuan Zhen's *The Story of Yingying*.) Wang's *The Romance of the West Bower* borrowed a lot from Dong's *The West Bower*, with almost same plot. However, there do exist some differences:

(a) The time period and form are different (Dong's is a "zhu gong diao," a form of sung literature in the Jin Dynasty, while Wang's is a "zaju," a form of Yuan Dynasty drama literature).
(b) The depth of the theme differs ("A talented scholar matched with a beautiful woman," "May all lovers in the world become couples").
(c) The structure of the plot is different (Dong's narrative is more loose and sprawling, while Wang's is more tightly focused, with brief yet compelling depictions of certain scenes).
(d) The characterization is sharper (Dong's depiction of Yingying does not fully align with the status of a prime minister's daughter; her pursuit of love is passive, and she holds class-conscious views, while Zhang Sheng is portrayed as frivolous and vulgar; in Wang's version, Yingying stands out as a character defying feudal norms, and Zhang Sheng is portrayed as earnest and noble).
(e) The style of language is different (Dong's lyrics are simple and fluid, while Wang's are elegant and natural).

Wang's *The Romance of the West Bower*, compared to the earliest depiction of the love story between Cui and Zhang in *The Story of Yingying*, demonstrates notable and successful improvements. The frivolous scholar Zhang Sheng is transformed into a sincere lover, and the passive Yingying is reimagined as a rebel against feudal etiquette. The Old Lady is portrayed as the representative of feudal power, while Hongniang, the maid, is depicted as clever, lively, and eager to help the couple achieve a happy union. Furthermore, Yingying's tragic ending is replaced with a joyous and harmonious conclusion, expressing the idea that "may all lovers in the world become couples." These improvements highlight the anti-feudal theme of the play.

The Romance of the West Bower consists of five acts, twenty-one scenes, and four prologues. Through the love story of Cui and Zhang, the play reveals the mental and physical constraints imposed on youth by feudal etiquette and, through their eventual happy union, praises the spirit of struggle for individual liberation and the pursuit of beautiful ideals among the younger generation.

4.1 The Characterization in *The Romance of the West Bower*

Cui Yingying is a typical image of a rebel against feudal etiquette. She dares to break free from the constraints of feudal norms, yearning for and pursuing a free and fulfilling love. She abandons the feudal ideas of class and values, and resolutely loves a fallen, poor scholar. Although her thoughts undergo some reversals, her character ultimately reflects the noble youth under the heavy pressure of feudal etiquette, who continuously overcomes their own weaknesses and, in the end, triumphs over feudal norms through love. Yingying's character embodies the rebellious nature of the younger generation under specific social and historical conditions, and also shows the progressive thought of the author.

Zhang Sheng is a character who dares to pursue ideal love, embodying the image of a sincere lover. He is straightforward yet reckless—reckless to the point of being annoying but not detestable. He is innocent yet stubborn—stubborn to the point of being laughable, but also lovable and courageous, with high moral qualities. He is devoted, loyal to his love, and rejects fame and wealth, making him a sincere lover completely different from the frivolous young men depicted in earlier works.

Hongniang is the first successful and striking image of a maid in the history of Chinese literature. Although she occupies a low social position, she possesses noble character. She is bright, enthusiastic, and compassionate, quick-witted, and sharp-minded. She is just, courageous, and always ready to stand up for what is right. This character reflects the brilliance of the author's democratic thoughts.

The old lady represents the typical image of feudal power and a feudal parent. She is selfish, cold-hearted, and deceitful, constantly changing her approach. She values feudal class distinctions and, from the perspective of feudal etiquette, tries her best to prevent her daughter from having a happy marriage, thereby ruining the freedom and happiness of youth. The old lady's character fully reflects the constraints feudal etiquette imposes on the youth, exposing the hypocrisy and cruelty of feudal norms.

4.2 The Artistic Achievements of *The Romance of the West Bower*

The Romance of the West Bower has the following artistic achievements:

(a) *The Complex Development of the Plot and Dramatic Conflicts:* The main love story of Cui and Zhang intertwines with the struggle between the old lady and Cui, Zhang, and Hongniang, developing in a complex and twisted manner. The primary conflict between the old lady and the trio (Cui, Zhang, and Hongniang) interlaces with their secondary conflicts, leading to an evolving and layered progression.

(b) *Outstanding Artistic Use of Language:* The dialogue of the characters is individualized, with strong lyrical qualities. Classical poetry and contemporary spoken language are seamlessly integrated into the lyrics, enhancing the emotional depth of the play.

(c) *Innovation in the Zaju System: The Romance of the West Bower* made significant innovations to the structure of Yuan Dynasty Zaju plays. While the standard form of Yuan Zaju consists of one act with four scenes, each performed by a single singer, *The Romance of the West Bower* is composed of five acts and twenty-one scenes. The story is told through multiple acts, and some scenes employ alternating solos, choruses, and duets, partially breaking the convention of one person performing the entire act.

Romance of the Western Bower (Excerpt)[3]

Zhe 3

Madame Cui enters and says:
We are going to see Master Zhang start for the Capital today, and Rose has gone to tell my daughter to come with us to the Pavilion of Farewell. I have ordered a feast prepared and an invitation sent to Master Zhang, and I think he must have finished his packing by now.

Yingying enters with Rose and says:
We are going to see him off today. It is sad to say good-bye at any time, and how much sadder on a late autumn day!

Master Zhang enters and says:
Madame told me last night to go to the Capital for the civil service examinations. She would marry her daughter to me if I came back with an official rank. What can I do but go as she directed. Now I am starting for the Pavilion of Farewell to wait for the Young Lady so that I may bid her farewell.

(*Exit.*)

Yingying says:
We drink a cup of wine whether we part or meet;
No matter where he goes, the rider must be fleet.

She sings to the tune of CALM DIGNITY:
With clouds the sky turns grey
O'er yellow-bloom-paved way.
How bitter blows the western breeze!
From north to south fly the wild geese.
Why like wine-flusbed face is frosted forest red?
It's dyed in tears the parting lovers shed.

Tune: ROLLING BALL

It's my regret
So late we met;

It grieves my heart
So soon to part.
Long as the willow branch may be,
It cannot tie his parting steed to the tree.
What would I not have done
If autumn forest could hang up the setting sun!
Go slowly, parting steed;
Cab, follow it with speed!
Of love sickness just cured,
The grief of parting must now be endured.
"I'm going," when a voice is heard to say,
My body seems to waste away.
When the Pavilion of Farewell comes in sight,
My bracelet becomes no longer tight.

Rose says:
You have not made your toilet today, my Young Mistress.

Yingying says:
How can you know the feelings of my heart, Rose!

She continues to sing:
Who knows, who knows
My heart full of woes?

Tune: MURMURING SONG

Seeing the cab and steed ready to start,
How can I not feel grief and anguish gnaw my beard?
How can I rouge my cheeks and powder my face,
Adorn myself with winning charm and grace?
What can I do is but to bury deep
My head between my coverlet and pillow and sleep,
And let my hundred-folded dress with flowing sleeves
Drowned in a stream of tears no one perceives.
O what inconsolable grief!
O what unconsolable grief!
Could words and letters bring me any relief?
(Madame Cui, Yingying and Rose arrive at the Pavilion of Farewell.)
(Master Zhang salutes Madame Cui profoundly.)
(Yingying turns her face away.)

Madame Cui says:

Come nearer, Master Zhang. Now that you are my flesh and blood, there is no need for you to avoid my daughter. Come over here and meet him, my dear child!

(*Master Zhang and Yingying meet each other.*)

Madame Cui says:

Sit down, Master Zhang. I will sit here and my child there. Pour out wine, Rose. Drink up this cup, Master Zhang. Since I have promised to marry my daughter to you, you must go to the Capital and prove yourself worthy of our family and win the highest honour in the examinations.

Master Zhang says:

Though not born a literary talent or brilliant scholar, I will do my best, depending on the favour and fortune of your honourable family, to win the highest honour in the examinations so that the Young Lady may be ennobled in due course.

(They all sit down.)
(Yingying sighs.)

Yingying sings to the tune of DOFFING THE CLOTHES:

The west wind drives the withered leaves here and there;
Decayed in mist, the grass has chilly, foggy air.
I see him sit at table, slanting his head,
Knitting his brows, as if half-dead.

Tune: SMALL LIANGZHOU

He dare not let his tears fall from his brimful eyes
For fear his grief be known.
Seeing himself observed, he utters sighs,
Pretending to arrange his white silk gown.

Tune: PETTY SONG

Though we'll be man and wife in future years,
How can I now refrain from shedding tears?
My mind with him infatuated,
My heart with love intoxicated.
Just overnight
My slender waist has grown more slight.

Tune: ASCENDING THE ATTIC

Our joy of union not complete,
Our grief of parting comes so fleet.

You know how much for you I cared.
It was not till last night was our love declared.
But oh, today
You'll go away!
Having suffered from lovesickness on those days,
I know not parting grief still ten times heavier weighs.

Madame Cui says:

Help your Young Mistress to pour out wine, Rose.
(Yingying pours out wine.)
(Master Zhang sighs.)

Yingying whispers:

Drink up this cup of wine I hold in my hand.

She sings to the tune of PETTY SONG:

While young,
One makes light of a farewell long;
Light-hearted,
Lovers do not care to be parted.
Canst thou forget thy leg across mine,
My cheek against thine,
Hand in hand we combine.
The former Premier's son-in-law-to-be,
Thy noble wife would ennoble thee
Like one stem with twin lotus-flowers,
Far better than to win honour and power.
(Yingying sits down again at the table and sighs.)

She sings to the tune of COURTYARD FULL OF FRAGRANCE:

So quickly passes the feast.
We sit now face to face;
We'll then be west and east.
If Mother were not in her place,
We might have enjoyed a bridal meal alone.
Although the time will soon pass by,
It might be called a dinner of our own.
In vain I centre on him my eye,
Keep thinking on,
And nearly turn into a stone.

Madame Cui says:

Pour out wine, Rose.

Rose, pouring out a cup for Master Zhang and another for Yingying, says:

You have not had breakfast this morning, my Young Mistress.
Will you please drink a little?

Yingying sings to the tune of HAPPY THREE:

They offer me both food and wine,
Which taste like muddy water 'neath the feet:
As mud the food is not so fine;
As water the wine is not so sweet.

Tune: HOMAGE TO EMPEROR

Even warmed wine as cold as ice appears,
It is diluted with my lovesick tears.
Not that I will not eat the food before my eyes;
But that my stomach's filled with grief and sighs.
For fame as empty as the born of a snail,
For profit trifling as the head of a fly,
Two love-birds torn apart bewail.
One here, the other there,
We're giving sigh for sigh.

Tune: FOUR-SIDE TRANQUILITY

They remove in a moment dish and cup,
The cab goes down, the horse goes up.
Both linger till
The sun sinks behind the bar of a green hill.
Who knows tonight where thou shalt be?
Even in dreams I cannot find thee.

Madame Cui says:

Rose, bid them to get ready the carriage and request Master Zhang to mount his horse. I am going back with your Young Mistress.

(They all get ready to start.)
(Master Zhang makes his bow to Madame Cui.)

Madame Cui says:

I have no other wish but that you should win high rank and come back soon.

Master Zhang, thanking her, says:

I will obey your instructions.
(Master Zhang and Yingying bow to each other.)

Yingying says:

You are going now. Whether you win high rank or not, I just hope you will be back as soon as possible.

Master Zhang says:

Make yourself easy on that score, my dear Young Lady. To which family will the highest literary honour belong if not to yours? I must bid you farewell now.

Yingying says:

I have no other farewell gift for you but an impromptu quatrain:

> Now left alone, what can I say,
> I whom you loved deep night and day?
> Do not bestow your love of old
> Upon another whom you behold!

Master Zhang says:

You mistake me, my dear Young Lady! How could I bestow my love on anyone else but you? As I am in a confused state of mind and you may not believe what I say, I will not respond to your poem until come back with the highest literary honour.

Yingying sings to the tune of PLAYING THE CHILD:

> *My sleeves in crimson and tears of love are drowned;*
> *I know more soaked are yours, those of the blue-gowned.*
> *Eastward the oriole and westward the swallow flies,*
> *Before you start I ask when you'll return.*
> *Although afar, still you will be before my eyes;*
> *I'll drink a cup of wine to show my deep concern.*
> *Before I drink, my heart is drunk,*
> *My eyes shed blood, in ash my feeling's sunk.*

Tune: LAST STANZA BUT FIVE

> *Before your arrival, get used to harsh climate;*
> *When you pursue your way, in food be moderate!*
> *Take care of your own health,*
> *Which is a mine of wealth!*
> *Early to bed on journey long in rainy days*
> *And late to rise at country inn in wind and haze,*
> *Riding in chilly autumn breeze,*
> *Uncared-for; you yourself should take your ease.*

Tune: LAST STANZA BUT FOUR

To whom of my grief to complain?
Alone I know the pain.
Should I complain to Heaven? O, to what avail?
My tears would make the Yellow River overflow;
My grief would make three mountain peaks bend low.
At dusk I'll lean on Western Tower's rail
To watch the setting sun over ancient way
And withered willow trees along the bay.

Tune: LAST STANZA BUT THREE

Not long ago we came in laughter;
Alone I'll be back shortly afier.
Once home, I'll dread
To see the curtained bed.
Last night in warm embroidered coverlet spring dwelt;
Tonight you'll dream of counterpane where cold is felt.
Can I detain you any longer here?
You have mounted your steed now.
Both of us are in tear
With a knitted eyebrow.

Tune: LAST STANZA BUT TWO

I care not if your talent won't build a career;
But fear you may give up the old wife for the new.
I wish wild geese and fish would bring your letters here.
While I shall send you tidings by the Phoenix Blue
O do not swear
You won't come back unless you win the laurel crown!
Please note it down:
If you see elsewhere beauties fair,
Don't linger any longer there!

Master Zhang says:

My dear, your words as precious as gold and jade are imprinted on my heart. We will meet again soon, so you need not be too sad. I am going now.

Holding back tears, I pretended to make bows;
Though feeling sad, I tried to unknit my brows.

Yingying says:

Not knowing that my heart is broken, I'll follow you in dreams unwoken.

(Exit Master Zhang.)
(Yingying sighs.)

Yingying sings to the tune of LAST STANZA BUT ONE:

Green hills and forests standing between him and me
Seem to extend a thousand li.
Thin mist and evening vapours screen him from my view.
No human voice is heard on sun-lit ancient way
But rustling of the crops in autumn wind and horse's neigh.
I am reluctant to enter the cab,
So eager to have come with you; So slow to go back afar!

Madame Cui says:

Rose, help your Young Mistress to her carriage. The time is late.
Let us go home.
Although to give way to my daughter I appear,
I've acted after all as proper mother dear.
(*Exit.*)

Rose says:

Your mother's carriage is a long way ahead. You must go back quickly.

Yingying says:

Rose, can you see where he is now?

She sings to the tune of THE LAST STANZA:

Surrounded by mountains east and west,
He flips his whip on sun-lit road.
All the world's grief seems to fill my breast.
How can such a small cab bear such a heavy load!
(Exeunt.)

5. OTHER ZAJU PLAYWRIGHTS AND THEIR WORKS IN EARLY YUAN DYNASTY

Other notable writers of the early Yuan Dynasty include Bai Pu, Ma Zhiyuan, and Kang Jinzhī. Bai Pu wrote sixteen plays, with *Over the Wall* and *Rain on the Plane Tree* still in existence presently. *Over the Wall* is adapted from Bai Juyi's new lyrics *The Silver Vase Pulled from the Well*. However, while the play changes the original theme of Bai's poem from that of "stopping the immoral elopement" so as to defend the feudal ethical code, to that of sympathizing the heroine's suffering and eulogizing her spirits to challenge the feudal ethical code.

Over the Wall is one of the important works in Yuan Zaju that deals with love. It praises the struggle of young men and women demanding marriage freedom under feudal constraints and creates an image of a woman brave enough to pursue love freely. Li Qianjin sees Pei Shaojun riding a horse over the garden wall and boldly falls in love with him. She does not wait for Pei Shaojun to obtain an official position before asking for marriage but firmly chooses to elope. The two live together in Pei's family garden for seven years but are separated by Pei Shaojun's father, the Minister Pei. Eventually, after Pei Shaojun achieves his official position, they are reunited. Compared to other female protagonists from noble families in love stories, Li Qianjin displays a much stronger rebellious spirit of struggle.

Rain on the Plane Tree is concerning the love story between Emperor Minghuang of Tang Dynasty and his highest-ranking imperial concubine Yang Yuhuan. Based on Bai Juyi's *The Everlasting Regret*, the work focuses on the tragic love story, and the process of the An-Shi Rebellion as well, depicting the vicissitude of the time. In the work, the writer showed both his satirical criticism and approval and sympathy on Emperor Minghuang, thinking that this historical event is quite similar to the one where Song was conquered by Jin invaders during Southern Song Period. From Bai Pu's own experience, the feelings the writer wants to express in this work can be traced clearly. Owing to the elegant and exquisite language, subtle psychoanalysis of the characters', and its artistic values, *Rain on the Plane Tree* exerts a great influence on the later dramatic literature and ballad literature.

Ma Zhiyuan composed 15 Zaju plays, with 7 in existence presently, such as *Autumn in the Han Palace*, *The Tablet in Jianfu Temple*, etc.

Autumn in the Han Palace tells the story of Wang Qiang (later known as Wang Zhaojun), one of Emperor Yuan of Han's consorts, being sent to marry the Xiongnu as part of a peace treaty. The play is based on numerous poems about Zhaojun and details the events surrounding her departure. The plot focuses on how the painter Mao Yanshou failed to receive a bribe from Wang Zhaojun and thus painted her in an unflattering way, leading to her being overlooked by the emperor for ten years. After being noticed by Emperor Yuan, the two fall in love. Mao Yanshou, fearing punishment, escapes with Zhaojun's portrait to the Xiongnu. The Xiongnu chieftain, leading an army of a million, demands Wang Zhaojun, and Emperor Yuan reluctantly agrees to send her as a bride. Zhaojun ultimately dies by jumping into the Black River (Heihe). The author primarily analyzes the event through Emperor Yuan's condemnation of his ministers and his own lamentations, intertwining the emperor's longing for Zhaojun with a sense of national decline and expressing a profound feeling of sorrow. *Autumn in the Han Palace* significantly improves on earlier works by:

(a) Changing the background to highlight the power of the Xiongnu and the weakness of the Han Dynasty, portraying Wang Zhaojun's patriotism as she voluntarily leaves her homeland to stop bloodshed;
(b) Depicting her martyrdom at the border, symbolizing her noble national spirit.

Kang Jinzhi and Gao Wenxiu are known for telling the stories concerning characters in *Outlaws of the Marsh. Li Kui's Carrying Sticks and Asking for a Flogging as Punishment*, one of Kang Jinzhi's famous works, is the best work of such a category in Yuan Dynasty. Gao Wenxiu, known as "Guan Hanqing, Jr.", is famous for his masterpiece *Double Contributions* and *Meeting in Mianchi*, both of which show great sympathy on the oppressed people. *Selling Rice in Chenzhou*, a Zaju from an anonymous writer, is a great masterpiece of legal cases in Yuan period, telling a story about Bao Zheng's redressing an injustice for people in Chenzhou. By depicting Zhang Piegu's unbending struggle, the work reflects the oppressed people's rebellious spirits. In the late Yuan period, Zheng Guangzu is the most renowned Zaju writer, whose masterpiece is *A Girl's Soul Fleeing for Her Love*, based on a romance named *Fleeing Soul for Her Love* written by Chen Xuanyou, a writer from Tang Dynasty. The work creates successfully in a romantic way a woman who dares to pursue her freedom and happiness with passion. Besides, Ji Junxiang and Shang Zhongxian are good at the political and military themes, and Ji Junxiang's masterpiece *The Orphan of Zhao* is the first Chinese play spreading into Europe.

Autumn in the Han Palace

Ma Zhiyuan

Act Two

(The Barbarian King enters with his retinue.)
Barbarian King: I am Huhanye Chanyu. Recently, I sent an envoy to the Han court, requesting a marriage alliance by offering a Han princess. The emperor declined, claiming the princess was too young. This leaves me utterly displeased. The Han palace is filled with countless women; sparing one for me would hardly matter. Yet, my envoy was dismissed. I wish to launch a southern invasion, but I fear jeopardizing years of peaceful relations. Let's observe how the situation unfolds and plan accordingly.

(Mao Yanshou enters.)
Mao Yanshou: I am Mao Yanshou. Because I manipulated the selection of palace women to extort wealth and tampered with Wang Zhaojun's portrait, relegating her to obscurity, the emperor questioned her absence and discovered the truth. Fearing punishment, I escaped. With no place to seek refuge, I now carry Zhaojun's portrait to present to the Chanyu, urging him to claim her as his bride. This way, the Han will have no choice but to comply. After days of travel, I finally

see a grand encampment ahead. This must be the Chanyu's court. *(Calling out)* Guard, please inform the Chanyu that a Han envoy seeks an audience.

(*The guard informs the Barbarian King.*)
Barbarian King: Let him come.

(Mao Yanshou approaches and bows.)
Barbarian King: Who are you?

Mao Yanshou: I am Mao Yanshou, a Han official. In the Han court is a beauty named Wang Zhaojun, unparalleled in grace. Previously, when Your Majesty requested a princess, Zhaojun volunteered, but the Han emperor was reluctant to part with her. I, however, persuaded him, arguing that state affairs should not be compromised for a mere woman. The emperor, angered, sought to punish me. Thus, I fled with Zhaojun's portrait, which I now present to Your Majesty. Dispatch an envoy to request her; the Han will surely comply. *(Hands over the portrait.)*

Barbarian King: Such beauty exists in this world? If I could have her as my queen, my life would be fulfilled. I will immediately send an envoy with this portrait and a letter to the Han emperor, demanding Wang Zhaojun for marriage. Should he refuse, I will march southward with my army. Meanwhile, mobilize soldiers to scout the borders while we hunt and monitor the Han's movements. *(Exits.)*

(Wang Zhaojun enters with her attendants.)
Zhaojun: I am Wang Zhaojun. Since the emperor favoured me, days have passed swiftly. Today, he is attending court, giving me time to dress and prepare for his return. *(She begins grooming herself before a mirror.)*

(The Emperor enters.)
Emperor: Since meeting Wang Zhaojun, I have been utterly captivated and neglected state affairs. Though I attended court today, I couldn't wait to see her again. *(Sings.)*

Song (to the tune of "Yi Zhi Hua"):
The seasons grace the land with balance;
The empire thrives under loyal ministers.
With no pressing concerns, I rest easy,
Yet I find myself afflicted—
Half from worry over state matters,
Half from love's intoxication.

(He notices Zhaojun at her mirror and quietly observes.)
Emperor: She's like the moon goddess Chang'e herself.

(Zhaojun notices the Emperor and greets him.)
(The Prime Minister and Chamberlain enter.)

Prime Minister: The empire's affairs are balanced like the pivot of yin and yang. Yet some choose to indulge in leisure rather than govern.

Chamberlain: Majesty, foreign envoys have arrived, requesting Wang Zhaojun for a peace alliance. Mao Yanshou delivered her portrait to the Chanyu, threatening invasion if denied.

Emperor: I have raised armies for times like this. How is it that no minister or general can counter this threat? Must I send Zhaojun to resolve it? *(Sings.)*

Song (to the tune of "Mu Yang Guan"):
Since ancient times, conflicts abound;
Only cowards shirk their duty.
You've enjoyed imperial favour,
Yet shy from swords and arrows.
Would you betray the throne's trust,
Leaving me to part with Zhaojun?

Prime Minister: Majesty, the court is paralyzed. Your devotion to Zhaojun has eclipsed all else, inviting disaster. Like King Zhou with Daji, the empire teeters on ruin.

Emperor: Enough! I never aspired to luxury for its own sake. My affections do not weaken me! Yet, who in this court dares take up arms? Must I alone bear the burden? *(Sings.)*

Song (to the tune of "He Xin Lang"):
Do not speak of excess or folly;
I am no tyrant swayed by indulgence.
How dare you blame me
When none step forward to fight!
I mourn not just for the empire,
But for the courage this court lacks.

Zhaojun: Your Majesty, for the empire's sake, I am willing to leave. Though my heart aches to part from you, the peace of the land must prevail.

(*The Emperor hesitates but ultimately agrees. The court prepares for Zhaojun's departure as she bids farewell to the Emperor.*)

6. *SANQU* OF YUAN DYNASTY

Sanqu evolved from *Ci poetry* and gradually developed into a new poetic form under the influence of various folk melodies during the Jin dynasty. It consists of songs written to be performed with musical accompaniment. Each piece is associated with a specific *gongdiao* (tonal mode) and has a *qupai* (tune title), along with fixed metrical rules. *Sanqu* mainly includes two forms: *xiaoling* and *taoshu*. Xiaoling refers to standalone pieces. These were originally popular folk tunes and melodies similar to Ci poetry. Xiaoling uses rhyme more densely than Ci, often requiring rhyme in almost every line, and it allows for the combination of level tones and oblique tones (rising tones and falling tones interchangeable.). Taoshu, also called *santao*, consists of a series of songs from the same tonal mode joined into a suite. It requires the entire suite to follow one rhyme scheme, usually concluding with a *weisheng* (closing song).

The development of Yuan dynasty Sanqu can be roughly divided into two phases:

(a) *The early phase,* characterized by a more simple and natural style with a strong reflection of social realities. Representative writers include Guan Hanqing, Ma Zhiyuan, Zhang Yanghao, and Bai Pu.

(b) *The later phase,* marked by a more refined and elegant style, with less focus on social issues. Prominent writers from this period include Zhang Kejiu and Qiao Ji.

Most Yuan Sanqu works revolve around themes of retreat to nature, hermit life, and romantic relationships, while some reflect societal realities of the time. Sanqu features a distinctive artistic style and was a popular form of literature among both scholars and performers, possessing considerable artistic value.

Over 200 Yuan dynasty Sanqu writers have been identified by name. After the founding of the People's Republic of China, Sui Shusen compiled the *Complete Yuan Sanqu* (*Quan Yuan Sanqu*,), which remains the most comprehensive collection of Sanqu to date. It includes: 3,853 xiaoling, 456 taoshu, and various incomplete pieces.

The creation of Sanqu also reflects the distinction between the early and later phases. In the early phase, most notable Sanqu writers were also renowned zaju playwrights. For example:

> Ma Zhiyuan, the early period's most prolific Sanqu writer, is known for masterpieces like *Autumn Thoughts* (Xiaoling), *Night Boat: Autumn Thoughts* (Santao).
>
> Guan Hanqing, whose Sanqu focuses heavily on romantic themes, is celebrated for works like *Intoxicated in the East Wind: Sorow for Farewell.*

Bo Pu (1226-after 1306), to "Victory Music" (De Sheng Yue)[4]

I walk here all alone,
I've walked a trail into the ground,
and back and forth a thousand times
I've walked in vain.
Won't you hurry up and let me know.
Come on,
don't make me hang around till dawn!

Guan Han-qing, to "A Half" (Yi-ban-er)[5]

Cloudy coils of hair and hazy tresses,
blacker than piled crows,
with a rustling of crimson satin
a golden lotus foot shows.
No common flower over the wall
is quite so pleasing:
you tell off your good-for-nothing lover
and half of you is furious,
and half of you is teasing.

A Suite on Autumn Thoughts[6]

Ma Zhiyuan

I. to "A Boat Going by Night" (Ye xing chuan)

The time passed in life's century,
a dream of a butterfly.
Looking back, all
that happened brings a sigh.
Spring comes today,
tomorrow flowers fall.
Hurry to offer another toast-
night ends, the lamplight burns away.

II. to "Tall Trees Far Away" (Qiao-mu yao)

I imagine Qin's palaces,
the towers of the Han,
all have turned to meadows now
where sheep and cattle graze.
How else would woodsmen and fishermen
have their tales to tell?
Although great stone inscriptions lie
broken on their grassy tombs,
I can't make out the serpentine words.

III. to "Celebrating the Xuan-he Reign" (Qing Xuan-he)

They have come to fox tracks and rabbitholes,
so many proud and daring men.
The Three Kingdoms then,
a tripod's legs however strong,
cracked midway.
Was it Jin?
Was it Wei?

IV. to "The Wind That Brings Down Plum Blossoms" (Luo-mei-feng)

If Heaven makes you rich-
be not too intemperate. Yet
fine days, fair nights last not long.
Then, rich man, let us say
your heart is stingy, hard as steel-
how could you just throw away
pleasures of moonlight and breeze
in your brocade hall?

V. to "Wind Enters Pines" (Feng ru song)

Before my eyes the crimson sun
sinks again to the west,
fast as a wagon rolls downhill.
Just look in your mirror tomorrow at dawn,
a further increase of snow white hair.
You'll get in bed and say farewell
forever to shoes left on the floor.
Mock not the dove's incompetence
because it borrows another's nest.
I bumble along and always play the fool.

VI. to "Keep Stirring Things Up" (Bo-bu-duan)

Fame and profit are done,
should's and shouldn't's are gone.
The world's red dust can never lure
me out my door.
Green trees are the perfect cover
for roof's corner,
and green hills fit the broken ledge
in my garden wall.
And so much more!-
my thatched cottage and bamboo hedge.

VII. to "Feast at the Pavilion of Parting" (Li-ting yan sha)

The crickets' chirping stops, I wake
comfortable and snug;
but when the rooster crows come cares
in thousands never ceasing.
When will it be through?
I view
ants parade in packed manoeuvres,

chaotic swarms of bees that brew
honey, and the furious din
of horseflies seeking blood.
The Green Meadow Hall of Lord Pei Du,
Magistrate Tao at White Lotus Club.[7]
These things I love when autumn comes:
to pick chrysanthemums mixed with dew,
to split purple crabs with frost within,
to burn red leaves to warm my wine.
I think in our lives the cups will pass
a limited number of rounds,
and how many times in all
comes the autumn festival?
I charge my servant to keep in mind:
if Kong Rong comes seeking me,[8]
tell him he'll find
me utterly drunk by the eastern hedge.

[Yue Tune] Sunny Sand
Autumn Thoughts[9]

Ma Zhiyuan

Over old trees wreathed with rotten vines fly crows;
Under a small bridge beside a cot a stream flows;
On ancient road in western breeze a lean horse goes.
Westwards declines the setting sun.
Far, far from home is the heart-broken one.

(Zhonglu) Sheep on the Slope
Thinking of the Past on My Way to Tong Pass[10]

Zhang Yanghao

Peaks like brows knit,
Angry waves spit.
With mountain and river far and near,
On the road to Tong Pass I appear.
Gazing on Western Capital
I hesitate, alas!
To see the place where ancient warriors did pass.
The ancient palaces; hall on hall,
Are turned to dust, one and all.
Before my eyes,
The empire's rise

Is people's woe;
The empire's fall
Is also people's woe.

6. THE SOUTHERN OPERA

Nanxi is the short form of the southern opera plays. It is a new dramatic form, based on Zaju of Song Dynasty, and blended with the elements of local operas in the South. Both Nanxi and Zaju belong to dramas, but there are some differences. Firstly, each Zaju usually has four Acts and one prologue, while Nanxi does not have a fixed pattern. Secondly, in a Zaju play, a soloist (Zhengmo[11] or Zhengdan[12]) sings for the most of the time, while in a Nanxi play, it is unnecessary for a performer to sing all the time. Thirdly, each Act in a Zaju is confined to the same Gongdiao, and the same rhyme as well, while in a Nanxi, it is more flexible without such limits. Fourthly, the Timu of Zhengming[13] is usually at the end of a Zaju but at the beginning of a Nanxi. Lastly, Zaju belongs to the Northern tune system while Nanxi the Southern tune system.

Gao Ming is the most famous playwright of Nanxi, courtesy name Zecheng, and he called himself "Vegetable Root the Taoist". His masterpiece *The Story of Pipa* is a Nanxi play based on an early play *Cai Er Lang and Zhao the Chaste*, a popular and widely read folk play. The biggest difference of *The Story of Pipa* from *Cai Er Lang and Zhao the Chaste* lies in the praise for Cai Bojie's loyalty and filial piety, instead of the condemnation of his betraying and deserting his wife and parents. Besides, in *The Story of Pipa*, the writer employed double plots and strong contrasts, which is the most striking feature of this play. The whole story develops through two separate plots: one is Cai Bojie's experience to pursue official rank by taking part in the imperial examination, the other is Zhao Wuniang's suffering during the famine. The couple separated with the husband living in the capital while the wife the hometown Chenliu, thus two life patterns and two plots are in contrast and develop separately. The strong contrast of these two different plots increases the dramatic conflict, exposing the sharp class clash and wealth gap in the feudal society. *The Story of Pipa* is recognized as the greatest Nanxi, which vitalized Nanxi greatly and promoted the development of it.

Literary Terms of Yuan Songs

Xiaoling: The basic form of Yuan Sanqu, usually an independent solo tune (with a single tune an independent unit), sometimes repeatable. The rhymes of each Xiaoling can be different, which is different from Santao. There is another one called "Daiguo Tune", also a subgenre of Xiaoling, sung together with two or three tunes in the same Gongdiao.

Daiguo Tune: A style of Xiaoling of Yuan Sanqu, which is a tune blended with two or three tunes with the same Gongdiao and sung as a combined unit.

Santao: A style in Yuan Sanqu, also called "Taoshu", namely, a series of tunes consisting of more than two tunes with the same Gongdiao. The length is flexible without any limit, but there should be one rhyme all through the tunes, and usually there is an epilogue.

Dan Script: A drama term, a script all sung by a Zhengdan soloist in Yuan Zaju.

Mo Script: A drama term, a script all sung by a Zhengmo soloist in Yuan Zaju.

Binbai: A drama term, which refers to dialogue in an ancient drama, including mologue and dialogue.

Kefan: A drama term, which refers to the instruction in a Yuan Zaju plan concerning the characters' movement, expression, the stage effect, etc., same as "Jie" in Ming and Qing romances, also called "Kefan" or "ke".[14]

Zhe: A drama term, which refers to a passage in a Yuan Zaju script, similar to "scene" or Act in modern plays.

Xiezi: A drama term, which refers to the additional short and independent passage besides the four Acts usually used at the beginning of the script as the start of the play, similar as the prelude in a modern play.

NOTES

1 Bin: "宾" in Chinese, which means a guest, and here the minor, while Bai, "白" in Chinese, here it refers to speaking.

2 Guan, Hanqing《窦娥冤（第三折）》 *Snow in Midsummer* in Yang Xianyi 杨宪益 and Dai Naidie 戴乃迭 (Transl.)《关汉卿杂剧选》 *Selected Plays of Guan Hanqing*. Beijing: Foreign Language Press (2004, 31-37).

3 Wang, Shipu. 《西厢记》 *Romance of the Western Bower*. In Xu, Yuanchong (Transl.) *Romance of the Western Bower*. Beijing: China Translation Publishing House (2021, 349-371).

4 Owen, Stephen. (ed. and translated). *An Anthology of Chinese Literature*. New York, London: Norton (1996, 735).

5 Ibid., (1996, 737).

6 Ibid., (1996, 741-743)

7 Pei Du, one of the great ministers of the early ninth century, eventually retired to his estate called Green Meadow Hall, where he held famous parties for literary men. Magistrate Tao is Tao Qian, who, according to one erroneous legend, was associated with the monk Hui-yuan's famous "White Lotus Club."

8 Kong Rong, an intellectual and literary man of the Three Kingdoms period, was supposed to have said that he had no worries as long as he had ample guests and the winecups were never empty.

9 《[越调]天净沙・秋思》，引自《元曲三百首》，许渊冲译，五洲传播出版社，中华书局，2012 年，p. 45.

10 Xu, Yuanchong. (Transl.) 《元曲三百首》 *Three Hundred Yuan Songs*. Zhonghua Book Company (2012, 62-63).

11 Zhengmo: "正末" in Chinese, a young or middle-aged male protagonist in Chinese operas.

12 Zhengdan: "正旦" in Chinese, a young or middle-aged female protagonist (dressed in black) in Chinese operas.

13 Timu of Zhengming: "题目正名" in Chinese, the synopsis in a Zaju or Nanxi, usually a 2-line or 4-line rhymed couplet served as a summary, with the last line the full title of the play, and the last three or four characters the short name of the title.

14 Kefan: "科泛" in Chinese, same as "介", also called "科范" or "科".

Chapter Seven

Literature in Ming Dynasty

The founding emperor of the Ming Dynasty, Zhu Yuanzhang, overthrew the Yuan Dynasty in 1368, achieving national unification and establishing the Ming Dynasty. During the Ming rule, as agriculture and handicrafts developed, commercial activities also became more frequent. To consolidate his power, Zhu Yuanzhang abolished the position of Chengxiang, (prime minister or chancellor) and established six ministries: Personnel, Revenue, Rites, War, Justice, and Works. He stipulated that the *Four Books* and *Five Classics* were to be the curriculum for the Guozijian, (Imperial Academy), promoted Neo-Confucianism as advocated by Cheng Yi and Zhu Xi, and restricted people's thinking. He also implemented the eight-legged essay system for civil service examinations, which limited the development of literature.

Starting in the mid-Ming period, urban industries gradually flourished, giving rise to the sprouts of capitalism. With the development of society, economy, and cultural thought, poetry and prose did not achieve major breakthroughs, but many fine works were passed down. Novels and dramas became the mainstream of literature. Building on the foundation of Song Dynasty *story-telling scripts* and *fictional scripts*, Ming Dynasty *chapter-based novels* and *short vernacular stories* emerged.

Most of the notable literary works from the early Ming period were concentrated around the transition from the Yuan to the Ming. Early Ming novels and dramas merely continued the trends of the late Yuan period, producing no new renowned works. However, significant achievements were made in the compilation and refinement of literary works, such as the editing of the long novels *Romance of the Three Kingdoms* and *Outlaws of the Marsh*, as well as the adaptation of southern plays. The formats of *chapter-based novels* and *legendary dramas* became increasingly refined, laying a foundation for the flourishing of later literary creations. Poets and writers transitioning from Yuan to Ming produced works rich in social content. However, subsequent literary movements, such as the *Taige-style*[1] and the *Chaling School*,[2] which focused on tonal patterns and rhymes, achieved little success.

In the mid-Hongzhi era, the literary movement led by Li Mengyang and He Jingming, known as the "*Former Seven Masters*," initiated a "revivalist" campaign. They opposed the "*Tai Ge style*," advocating for a return to the ancient traditions, asserting that "essays must follow Qin and Han models, and poetry must emulate the High Tang." They criticized the orthodox Confucianism of the Ming dynasty and called for a return to pre-Song Confucian values, leaving a significant impact.

In the late Ming period, literary creation entered a new phase, with dramas and novels developing new schools. In the realm of drama, the playwright Xu Wei's *Four Cries of a Gibbon* used historical themes to criticize the darkness and ugliness of society at the time. Its format also differed from Yuan dramas. In the genre of *legends*, new schools emerged, represented by the Chu School of Tang Xianzu and the Wujiang School of Shen Jing.

In the field of novels, numerous long and short works appeared. Among them, the mythological novel *Journey to the West* had the greatest impact. Meanwhile, *The Plum in the Golden Vase* (*Jin Ping Mei*) became the first long novel created by a scholar, focusing on domestic life as its theme.

In poetry and prose, during the Jiajing era, the "Later Seven Masters," led by Li Panlong and Wang Shizhen, continued to promote the revivalist literary movement. They opposed the corrupt influence of the "*Tai Ge style*" and the *eight-legged essay* in literature. However, their focus on imitating and copying ancient works made their movement essentially a form of formalism.

I. LUO GUANZHONG AND *THE ROMANCE OF THE THREE KINGDOMS*

1. The Background of the Book and the Writer

Romance of the Three Kingdoms is one of ancient China's most influential long-form novels (chapter-based novels) and the most accomplished historical novel in Chinese literature. It uses the struggles between the three feudal states of Wei, Shu, and Wu during the Three Kingdoms period as its subject matter. Stories from the Three Kingdoms were already widely circulated long before the novel was written. During the Southern and Northern Dynasties, Pei Songzhi added annotations to Chen Shou's *Records of the Three Kingdoms*. His annotations included various historical anecdotes and miscellaneous notes, as well as tales of Three Kingdoms characters compiled from Liu Yiqing's *A New Account of the Tales of the World*. During the reign of Emperor Yang of Sui, performances of water plays included Three Kingdoms stories. Tang Dynasty poet Li Shangyin mentioned in his poem *Jiao'er Shi* how children would imitate Zhang Fei's beard or mock Deng Ai's stammer, illustrating how performances of Three Kingdoms stories influenced children. By the Northern Song Dynasty, Three Kingdoms stories had already been adapted for stage performances. During the Yuan

Dynasty, there were dozens of Three Kingdoms-themed plays in the genre of zaju. The *Pinghua* (prose narrative) version of *The Complete Romance of the Three Kingdoms*, compiled during the Zhizhi reign of the Yuan Dynasty, was a written adaptation of these popular folk tales.

Romance of the Three Kingdoms was authored by Luo Guanzhong, based on Chen Shou's *Records of the Three Kingdoms* from the Western Jin Dynasty, Pei Songzhi's annotated version from the Liu Song Dynasty, and a wealth of folk stories that were widely circulated. The earliest edition of the novel was published in the first year of the Jiajing reign during the Ming Dynasty, titled *The Popular Romance of the Three Kingdoms* and referred to as the "Jiajing Edition." For over 300 years, the most popular version has been the 120-chapter revised edition by Mao Zonggang during the Qing Dynasty.

2. The Content of *The Romance of the Three Kingdoms*

Through its depiction of the military, political, and diplomatic struggles among the feudal ruling groups of the Three Kingdoms period, *The Romance of the Three Kingdoms* reveals the darkness and decay of society at the time. It condemns the brutality and crimes of the rulers while expressing the people's longing for national unity and the ideal of benevolent governance under a virtuous ruler. The ideological elements of the novel are reflected in the following aspects:

(a) It exposes the corruption and wickedness within the feudal ruling class.

(b) It extols the values of benevolence, virtue, loyalty, and righteousness while denouncing cruelty and deceit.

(c) It broadly reflects the political, military, and diplomatic struggles among the ruling factions of the Three Kingdoms, summarizing the lessons and wisdom gleaned from these conflicts.

The novel's ideological inclination is one of "honoring Liu while deprecating Cao," reflecting the patriotic sentiment of resisting foreign invasions and restoring the Central Plains under specific historical conditions. To some extent, it also embodies the feudal era's people's desire for benevolent rulers and their disdain for oppressive tyrants.

3. The Characters in *The Romance of the Three Kingdoms*

Regarding the depiction of characters, Mao Zonggang famously described the "three perfections" of the novel: Zhuge Liang (Kongming) as the epitome of wisdom, Cao Cao as the epitome of treachery, and Guan Yu as the epitome of righteousness.

Zhuge Liang (Kongming):

Zhuge Liang's character is marked by loyalty, benevolence, and strategic brilliance. He embodies virtues, kindness, intelligence, and talent, symbolizing the ideal virtuous statesman

Guan Yu:
Guan Yu's character traits include: Courage and fearlessness - As shown in feats like slaying Hua Xiong while calmly drinking and enduring surgery to scrape poison from his bone. Unwavering loyalty - Demonstrated by actions such as resigning his official position and releasing Cao Cao out of righteousness in Huarong Pass. Arrogance and stubbornness - Reflected in his self-assured and condescending nature.

Generally, Guan Yu is an embodiment of loyalty and righteousness in the feudal age, a faithful and credible man who is always keeping his promise. Neither riches nor honors can corrupt him, and neither threats nor forces can subdue him. To some extent, this is totally opposite to the ruling class in the feudal society, most of whom are unrighteous and unfaithful, always deceiving and intriguing against each other. However, his righteousness and loyalty are based on his own gratitude and hatred, thus having great limitations. This actually meets the needs of the feudal lords, showing the intention of the ruling class to conceal the true nature of the class clash by taking advantage of the personal relationship between the lords and their courtiers.

Cao Cao:
Cao Cao is an treacherous but powerful figure in turbulent times, whose character can be summarized as unscrupulous (for example, he killed the commissariat officer for the morale of the soldiers by a trick way of "borrowing the head", and he forbade others to approach him when sleeping on the pretext that he might kill others in his dream only because of his fear and suspicion), and powerful (for example, he defeated successively Yuan Shu, Lv Bu, Yuan Shao and Liu Biao). The image of Cao Cao shows the cruelty and craftiness of the feudal lords, and also the evil nature of the feudal society by exposing the tyrants and their tyranny.

Cao Cao is portrayed as the archetypal "treacherous hero" of a chaotic era. This image highlights the cunning and ruthlessness of the feudal ruling class and reflects the evils of oppressive governance and tyrannical rulers.

Liu Bei:
Liu Bei's character is defined by: Benevolence - He is portrayed as loyal, respectful to talented individuals, compassionate toward the people, and beloved by the populace.

Liu Bei embodies the ideal of a benevolent ruler, representing the author's political aspirations. To some extent, he also reflects the people's opposition to tyrants and their support for virtuous rulers.

4. The Artistic Achievements of *The Romance of the Three Kingdoms*

Romance of the Three Kingdoms excels in its depiction of warfare:

(a) Highlighting the use of wit and strategy by characters to vividly portray the intricacies of war.
(b) Showcasing a wide array of strategies and tactics, emphasizing their variety and ingenuity.
(c) Balancing tension and release in battle descriptions, skillfully blending reality with fiction.

The greatest feature of *Romance of the Three Kingdoms* is its ability to "capture the essence through simplified portrayal." This is reflected in the following aspects:

(a) Its adept use of vivid details to bring characters to life.
(b) Skillful reinforcement of characters' primary traits through varied storylines.
(c) Effective use of exaggeration, contrast, and foreshadowing to enhance character portrayals.

The novel's language strikes a balance, being "elegant but not obscure, colloquial but not gross", making it accessible and engaging for readers.

Guang Yunchang Made Hua Xiong Lay in the Dust Before the Wine Had Time to Cool

From Chapter 5 (Excerpt)[3]

Concerning Sun Jian's request someone advised Yuan Shu: "Sun Jian is the tiger of the east. If he takes the capital and kills Dong Zhuo, we'll be facing a tiger instead of a wolf. Deny the grain and watch his army fall apart." Yuan Shu, persuaded, sent no supplies. Sun Jian's men became uncontrollable, and word of it soon reached the government camp at the pass. Dong Zhuo's adviser, Li Su, plotted the next step with Hua Xiong. "Tonight," said Su, "I'll take a company of men by side paths down from the pass and strike from the rear. You attack their forward positions. Jian can surely be captured." Hua Xiong approved and ordered his men to be fed well in preparation for the action.

The moon was bright and the breeze refreshing when Hua Xiong reached Sun Jian's camp. At midnight his men stormed in, howling and shrieking. Sun Jian donned his armor, leaped to horse, and took on Hua Xiong. As they tangled, Li Su struck from the rear, ordering his men to set fires wherever they could. Sun Jian's army fled, though some commanders skirmished individually. Zu Mao alone stuck by Sun Jian. The two dashed from the battleground pursued by Hua Xiong. Xiong dodged two arrows and kept pace. Sun Jian shot a third, but drew so hard his bow split. He threw it aside and rode for his life.

"Your red hood's a perfect target," cried Zu Mao. "I'll wear it." The men switched headgear and took flight by different roads. Xiong's soldiers spotted the bright color in the distance and gave chase. Sun Jian followed a side road and got away. Zu Mao, hardpressed, hung the hood on a half-burned piece of timber and hid in a nearby copse. Catching the moonlight, the hood attracted Hua Xiong's men and they circled it. No one dared advance, but after someone shot at it, they discovered the ruse and went for the headdress. At that moment Zu Mao came slashing out of the wood, wielding both his swords. But his object, Hua Xiong, uttering fierce cries, delivered a single fatal sword stroke that dropped Zu Mao from his horse.

The slaughter continued until morning. Then Hua Xiong brought his men back to the pass. Sun Jian's remaining commanders, Cheng Pu, Huang Gai, and Han Dang, found their leader and rounded up their men. Sun Jian grieved over the loss of Zu Mao and sent a messenger to report to Yuan Shao.

Stunned at the defeat of Sun Jian by Hua Xiong, Yuan Shao called the lords into session. Gongsun Zan reached the meeting late, and Yuan Shao invited him to sit among the lords. "The other day," Yuan Shao began, "General Bao Xin's younger brother ignored orders and advanced without authority. He himself was killed, and we lost many men. Now Sun Jian has been beaten. Our edge is blunted, our mettle dulled. What is our next step to be?" Not one of the lords replied.

The war-ruler scanned the audience. Behind Gongsun Zan three extraordinary-looking strangers stood smiling grimly. Yuan Shao asked who they were. Gongsun Zan had Xuande step forward. "This is Liu Bei," he said, "magistrate at Pingyuan. We were fellow students and like brothers even then." "Not the one who helped break the Yellow Scarves?" asked Cao Cao. "The very one answered Gongsun Zan. He told Xuande to salute Yuan Shao and Cao Cao and then proceeded to describe his protégé's origins and accomplishments. "Since he belongs to a branch of the imperial family," Yuan Shao concluded, "let him come forward and be seated." But Xuande modestly declined. "It is not your name or rank I salute," insisted Shao, "but your lineage:" With that, Xuande took his place at the end of the line. Lord Guan and Zhang Fei posted themselves behind him, hands folded on their chests.

At this point a spy reported that Hua Xiong had brought his armored cavalry down from the pass, displaying Sun Jian's red headdress on the tip of a pole, and was at the camp's entrance mouthing taunts. "Who will go?" asked Yuan Shao. From behind Yuan Shu, Yu She, a commander known for bravery, stepped forward and volunteered. But Hua Xiong made short work of him. Alarm stirred the assembly. Governor Han Fu recommended his own champion commander, Pan Feng, and Yuan Shao urged him to the field. Pan Feng went forth with a huge axe, but the news came back swiftly of his death too at Hua Xiong's hands. The assembly began to panic. "It's a pity Yan Liang and Wen Chou, my own top generals, are not here," Yuan Shao said. "Either one could end our worries." At that, a voice from the back boomed, "I offer to present Hua Xiong's head to you personally."

The assembled lords turned to the speaker, a man over nine spans, with a great beard flowing from rich rudd cheeks. His eyes were like those of the crimson-faced phoenix, his brows like nestling silkworms, his voice like atolling bell. He fixed his eyes directly on the audience. "Who is this man?" demanded Shao. "Guan Yu, sworn brother of Xuande," answered Gongsun Zan. "His position?" asked Shao. "Mounted archer under Xuande," was the reply. At that, the war-ruler's brother, Yuan Shu burst out, "Are you trying to insult us? A mere archer! Have we no more commanders? What nonsense! Get him out of here!" But Cao Cao checked Yuan Shu: "Pray hold your temper. This man has made his boast. He can't be a coward. Now let him make it good. You'll have plenty of time to condemn him if he fails." "But to send out an archer!" Yuan Shao said. "Hua Xiong will laugh in his sleeve!" "He doesn't look like an ordinary soldier," Cao Cao replied. "How is Hua Xiong going to know?" Finally, Lord Guan spoke: "If I fail, my head is yours."

Cao Cao had a draft of wine heated for Lord Guan before he mounted. "Pour it," said the warrior, "and set it aside for me. I'll be back shortly." He leaped to his horse, gripped his weapon, and was gone. The assembly of lords heard the rolling of drums and the clamor of voices outside the pass, and it seemed as if the heavens would split open and the earth buckle, as if the hills were shaking and the mountains moving. The terror-struck assembly was about to make inquiry when the jingling of bridle bells announced Lord Guan's return. He entered the tent and tossed Hua Xiong's head, freshly severed, on the ground. His wine was still warm. A poet of later times sang Lord Guan's praises:

His might sufficed to hold in place
    the frames of sky and land.
The painted war drums charged the air
    at the chieftains' field command.
The hero put the cup aside
    to slake his combat lust:
Before the wine had time to cool
    Hua Xiong lay in the dust.

II. SHI NAIAN AND *OUTLAWS OF THE MARSH*

1. The Background of the Novel and the Writer

Shi Nai'an's *Outlaws of the Marsh* is the first long novel in the history of Chinese literature that reflects peasant uprisings. It is also the first long novel in Chinese literature written in the vernacular. *Outlaws of the Marsh* was completed during the late Yuan and early Ming dynasties, and there are no reliable historical records about the life of its author, Shi Nai'an. According to early accounts, the compiler of the book might have been Shi Nai'an and Luo Guanzhong. Gao Ru wrote in his *Books and Records of a Hundred Rivers* that *Outlaws of the Marsh* is written by the Qiantangese Shi Naian, and revised and edited by the later writer Luo Guanzhong.

It is believed that *One Hundred Volumes of Virtuous Outlaws of the Marsh* is the earliest version of the novel. During the Jiajing period of Ming Dynasty, there emerged another 100-chapter version, which was polished artistically a great deal. The 120-chapter version appeared during the Wanli period of Ming Dynasty had the supplement of the episodes of “conquering Tian Hu” and “conquering Wang Qing” with simple and brief language. During the late Ming and early Qing period, Jing Renrui (Jing Shengtan) revised it into the 70-chapter version, ending up with the rebels of the water margin of Liangshanpo being conquered completely. Presently, there exist two versions of this work, a simplified one and a polished one, the former having simple language but more episodes, while the latter refined and polished language but fewer episodes.

The legends of the water marsh began to spread widely as early as the Southern Song period. The people continuously developed and created variations, and it was finally refined and completed by Shi Nai'an. *Outlaws of the Marsh Water Margin* is a long novel set during the late Northern Song Dynasty, focusing on the peasant uprising led by Song Jiang. The novel uses a great deal of space to expose the darkness of feudal society, and many of the stories reflect the class contradictions and oppression in feudal society from various angles. It also enthusiastically praises the righteous actions of the rebel heroes, who “act justly, share wealth, and return to Liangshan to take revenge and seek justice.” Despite their different backgrounds, experiences, and paths in life, they were all unable to tolerate humiliation and injustice, and they united to fight under the banner of “acting on behalf of Heaven” in a large-scale armed struggle against the feudal rulers.

2. The Theme of *Outlaws of the Marsh*

Outlaws of the Marsh exposes the crimes of the ruling class and the social reality of “official oppression leading to rebellion,” while also praising the heroic figures who rebelled against feudal oppression.

The novel vividly and comprehensively reflects the entire process of the development of the peasant uprisings. The depiction of the “imperial amnesty” (zhao'an) embodies the author's ideological contradiction—both sympathizing with and supporting the peasant uprisings while also praising and advocating loyalty to the imperial court. Objectively, this portrayal is realistic because it reveals the main reason behind the failure of the peasant uprisings. Due to the influence of realism, the author also reflects, to some extent, the struggle against imperial amnesty (represented by characters like Li Kui and Lu Zhishen), and reveals the tragic end after the rebels' turning to serve the ruling class, showing the writer's disapproval.

3. The Characterization in *Outlaws of the Marsh*

Characterization in *Outlaws of the Marsh* (also known as *Water Margin*) is one of the novel's key strengths, and it plays a crucial role in conveying its themes of rebellion, loyalty, and justice. The characters in the novel are drawn with distinct personalities and complex motivations, which serve to represent the different aspects of society during the late Northern Song Dynasty. Below are some key elements of characterization in the novel:

The central characters in *Outlaws of the Marsh* are the 108 outlaws who come together at Liangshan Marsh. These characters are portrayed as brave, loyal, and defiant against the corrupt officials and oppressive feudal system. Despite their outlaw status, they are depicted as morally upright and fighting for justice. Many of them come from different backgrounds and social classes, but they share a common desire to seek revenge against injustice. For example: The leader of the outlaws, Song Jiang is depicted as a wise, strategic, and compassionate figure. While he is loyal to the emperor, his idealism clashes with the reality of the corrupt government. His moral integrity and leadership abilities make him a respected figure among the outlaws. A former monk known for his immense strength and impulsive nature, Lu Zhishen represents a figure of brute force combined with a genuine sense of justice. His rebellious spirit and carefree attitude bring a sense of rawness to the narrative. Known for his fierce temper and violent nature, Li Kui represents the impulsive, unrelenting desire for vengeance. His character is often used to highlight the tension between righteous anger and the need for strategic planning. A renowned fighter and hero who avenges his sister's death by killing the tiger and later taking down corrupt officials, Wu Song represents a character driven by personal vendettas but also by a sense of justice and loyalty.

The outlaws come from a variety of social backgrounds, including peasants, former soldiers, outcasts, and intellectuals, which allows the novel to present a wide range of perspectives on the injustice they face. This diversity enriches the story and shows the broad societal appeal of the rebellion against the corrupt ruling class. There are significant contrasts between the characters of the outlaws and the corrupt government officials. For example, while the outlaws are portrayed as morally upright, the government officials are often depicted as greedy, corrupt, and self-serving. This contrast helps emphasize the theme of the battle between good and evil, as well as the broader social critique of the feudal system. Many characters represent broader societal forces or ideals. For instance, the 108 outlaws are sometimes seen as symbolic of the people's resistance to oppression and the power of collective action. Each character's personality and actions serve to highlight a particular aspect of resistance or rebellion against the established order.

The use of nicknames (诨号) is a distinctive feature of character portrayal. These nicknames are often symbolic, reflecting the personality, physical traits, skills, or life experiences of the characters. They serve as shorthand to convey essential aspects of a character's identity, making them memorable and vivid. Below are some examples of nicknames and their significance: Song Jiang is called "Timely Rain" (及时雨) because he is known for helping people in times of need. Wu Song's nickname "Pilgrim" (行者) reflects his wandering lifestyle and monk-like demeanor, especially after he becomes a fugitive. Lu Zhishen, a former monk, is called "Flowery Monk" (花和尚) due to his tattoos, strength, and unruly behavior, which contrast with the traditional image of a monk. Li Kui is nicknamed "Black Whirlwind" (黑旋风) because of his dark complexion, fiery temper, and unrelenting ferocity in battle. Yang Zhi's nickname is "Blue-Faced Beast" (青面兽), which refers to his distinctive blueish complexion and his fierce demeanor, likening him to a beast. Zhang Shun's nickname "White Streak in the Waves" (浪里白条) highlights his exceptional swimming skills. "White Streak" refers to his pale skin and his ability to move swiftly and gracefully through water, like a streak in the waves. Shi Jin is called "Nine-Dragoned Tattooed" (九纹龙), for covered in tattoos of nine dragons, which symbolize his bravery and strength. His nickname reflects his fierce and heroic nature. Hua Rong's nickname "Little Li Guang" (小李广) refers to his exceptional archery skills, likened to the legendary archer Li Guang from Chinese history. Zhu Tong is praised for his elegant appearance, particularly his distinguished beard, and hence nicknamed as "Beautiful Beard" (美髯公) which complements his noble demeanor and martial talents.

The creative use of nicknames adds richness to *Outlaws of the Marsh*, showcasing the diversity of the characters and their roles within the story.

4. The Artistic Achievements of *Outlaws of the Marsh*

Outlaws of the Marsh inherits the tradition of storytellers' narratives, with its language based on Northern dialects and refined into an artistic literary form. In terms of language, expression, and style, it embodies the artistic characteristics of Chinese novels. The novel places its characters in specific real-life settings, shaping their personalities based on their identities and experiences. The characters' traits are revealed through a series of interconnected plot events. For example, when Lu Zhishen hears about the bullying behavior of the butcher Zheng Tu (known as "Zheng the Tyrant"), he immediately becomes enraged and stands up for justice. This not only reflects his rough and domineering manner as a former military officer but also highlights his courageous and selfless heroic spirit. The characters' personalities become vividly apparent to readers as the struggles unfold.

The author skillfully uses techniques such as exaggeration, embellishment, and contrast to shape characters. Romantic elements like Wu Song slaying a tiger and Lu Zhishen uprooting a willow tree create powerful artistic effects that emphasize the heroic qualities of the protagonists.

Outlaws of the Marsh is an early Chinese vernacular novel, rooted in the spoken language of the time. Because of its close connection with the storytellers' performances, the language is vivid, straightforward, and highly expressive. As an early chapter-based novel, it uses the journey of its main heroes being driven to Liangshan as the central narrative thread to recount the rise and development of the people's rebellion. The novel also depicts the trajectory of the rebellion, from its origins and growth to its eventual failure, focusing on the issue of imperial pardon (zhao'an).

The work is a unified whole, yet several main characters and key events could also stand alone as independent novellas. Some chapter titles that have long been popular in folk traditions possess significant ideological and artistic value.

Chapter 23 Wu Song Pouched the Tiger to Death (excerpt)[4]

He travelled for several days and came to Yanggu County. It was noon and he was a good distance from the county town, and he was hungry and thirsty from walking. Further up the road he saw a tavern. By the doorway hung a pennant reading: *Three bowls and you can't cross the ridge.*

Wu Song went inside, sat down, and rested his staff. "Wine, quickly, host," he called.

The tavern keeper brought three bowls, a pair of chopsticks and a plate of tidbits, placed them on the table, and filled one of the bowls to the brim with wine. Wu Song raised the bowl and drained it.

"This wine has a kick in it! If you've got anything filling, host, I'll buy some to go with the drinks."

"We only have cooked beef."

"Slice me two or three catties of the best part."

The host went back inside and came out with two catties of beef on a large platter, which he placed before Wu Song. Then he filled another bowl. Wu Song drank it.

"Very good wine!" he said. And he downed another. That was his third bowl.The host poured no more. Wu Song rapped on the table.

"Host, where's the wine?"

"More beef sir? Coming right up."

"I want beef and wine, both."

"I'll slice some beef for you, but I can't give you any more wine."

"That's screwy! Why not?"

"Didn't you see that pennant hanging by my door *Three bowls and you can't cross the ridge*?" queried the tavern keeper.

"What does it mean?"

"Although our wine is just a village product, it's as fragrant as the old brews. Any traveller who drinks three bowls of it gets drunk and can't cross that ridge there. Hence, the name. No one who stops here ever asks for more than three bowls."

Wu Song smiled. "So that's it. I've had three bowls. Why aren't I drunk?"

"My wine is called 'Seeps Through the Bottle Fragrance'. It's also called 'Collapse Outside the Door'. You don't feel anything at first. But a little later, down you go."

"Poppycock! I'm paying, aren't I? Pour me three more bowls!" Seeing that the wine had little effect on Wu Song, the tavern keeper again filled three bowls with wine. The big fellow drank them

"Excellent," he cried, "Host, I'll pay you bowl for bowl. Just keep pouring."

"You'd better take it easy, sir. This wine really knocks people out! And there's no medicine that brings them around!"

"Bullshit! Even if you doped it, I've got a nose, haven't I!"

The tavern keeper couldn't convince him. Again he filled the three bowls.

"Bring me another two catties of beef," said Wu Song.

The host served the sliced meat and poured three more bowls of wine. Wu Song's appetite seemed to improve. He put some silver on the table.

"Look here," he called. "Is this enough for the wine and meat?"

"Plenty," said the tavern keeper. "In fact I owe you some change."

"I don't want any change. Just keep the wine coming."

"There are five or six bowls left. But I doubt that you can finish them."

"Five, six, or even more, I'll drink as many as you've got."

"You're abig hulking fellow. If you fall, how am I going to pick you up?"

"If you have to pick me up, I'm no real man!"

The host continued to stall. Wu Song grew irritated. "I'm paying for what I drink," he said. "Don't make me mad, or I'll smash up your place and turn it ass over tea kettle!"

"This rogue is drunk," thought the tavern keeper. "I'd better not provoke him!"

He served Wu Song six more bowls of wine, a total of eighteen in all Wu Song grasped his staff and rose to his feet. "I'm not a bit drunk!" He laughed as he went out the door. "Who says'Three bowls and you can't cross the ridge'?" He started walking away.

The tavern keeper ran after him. "Where are you going, sir?" he shouted.

Wu Song halted. "What's it to you? I don't owe you anything, do I? What are you yelling about?"

"I mean well. Come back. I want to show you a government proclamation."

"What does it say?"

"There's a fierce tiger with a white forehead and bulging eyes on Jingyàng Ridge. It comes out at night, and has already killed nearly thirty strong men. The authorities have ordered hunters to capture it, on pain of being beaten, and have posted this warning at every path leading to the ridge. It says travellers must go in groups and cross only between late morning and early afternoon. At all other times the ridge is closed. No one is permitted to travel alone. It's already late, and I saw you setting off without a word. I don't want you to kill yourself! Why not spend the night at my place, and then tomorrow you can gradually get together a band of twenty or thirty travellers and cross the ridge in safety."

Wu Song laughed. "I'm a Qinghe County man. I've crossed that ridge at least twenty times. I've never seen any tiger. Don't try to scare me with that crap. Even if there is a tiger, I'm not afraid."

"I'm only trying to save you. If you don't believe me, come in and have a look at the proclamation."

"Balls! I'm not scared of any tiger. You want to keep me here so that in the middle of the night you can rob me, kill me! That's why you're trying to frighten me with your tiger story!"

"All right! You take my good for evil and talk to me like that! Don't believe me, then! On your way!" The tavern keeper shook his head and went back inside.

Staff in hand, Wu Song strode off towards Jingyang Ridge. After walking four or five li he came to the foot of it. A piece of bark had been peeled from a large tree, and on the white patch words were written. Wu Song could read quite well, and he saw that it was a notice with this inscription: *Of late a tiger on Jingyang Ridge has been killing people. Travellers must form bands and cross only between late morning and early afternoon. Do not take risks.*

Wu Song grinned. "That host is a crafty one. Scares his customers into staying the night. Well, he can't scare me!"

He proceeded up the slope, holding his staff level. It was late after noon by then, and the red sun was pressing on the mountains in the west. Still primed by all the wine he had consumed, Wu Song continued climb ing the ridge. Before he had gone another half li, he came upon a dilapidated Mountain Spirit Temple. A notice was posted on the door. It read:

Yanggu County Notice: Lately, a big tiger has been killing people on Jingyang Ridge. Although all township leaders, village chiefs and hunters have been ordered to capture the beast or be beaten, they have so far failed. Travellers are permitted to cross the ridge only between late morning and early afternoon, and only in bands. At other times, and to single travellers at any time, the ridge is closed, lest the tiger take their lives. Let this be known to all.

So there really was a tiger! The notice with its official seal confirmed that. Wu Song considered returning to the tavern. But then he said to himself: "If I do that, the host will laugh at me for a coward. I can't go back." He thought a moment, "What's there to be afraid of," he exclaimed. "Just keep climbing and see what happens."

He walked on. The warmth of the wine rose in him, and he pushed back the felt hat till it was hanging by the string on his shoulders. Clapping the staff under one arm, he plodded up the slope. When he looked back at the sun, it was almost gone. The days are short in late autumn, and the nights are long. It gets dark early

"There isn't any tiger," he said to himself. "People just scare themselves and don't dare come up the mountain."

The wine was burning inside him as he walked. With his staff in one hand, he unbuttoned his tunic with the other. His gait was unsteady now and he staggered into a thicket. Before him was a large smooth rock. He rested his staff against it, clambered onto its flat surface, and prepared to sleep.

Suddenly a wild gale blew, and when it passed a roar come from behind the thicket and out bounded a huge tiger. Its malevolent upward slanting eyes gleamed beneath a broad white forehead.

"Aiya!" cried Wu Song. He jumped down, seized his staff, and slipped behind the rock.

Both hungry and thirsty, the big animal clawed the ground with its front paws a couple of times, sprang high and came hurtling forward. The wine poured out of Wu Song in a cold sweat. Quicker than it takes to say he dodged, and the huge beast landed beyond him. Tigers can't see behind them, so as its front paws touched the ground it tried to side-swipe Wu Song with its body. Again he dodged, and the tiger missed. With a thunderous roar that shook the ridge, the animal slashed at Wu Song with its iron tail. Once more he swivelled out of the way.

Now this tiger had three methods for getting its victim — spring, swipe and slash. But none of them had worked, and the beast's spirit diminished by half. Again it roared, and whirled around.

Wu Song raised his staff high in a two-handed grip and swung with all his might. There was a loud crackling, and a large branch, leaves and all, tumbled past his face. In his haste, he had struck an old tree instead of the tiger, snapping the staff in two and leaving him holding only the remaining half.

Lashing itself into a roaring fury, the beast charged. Wu Song leaped back ten paces, and the tiger landed in front of him. He threw away the stump of his staff, seized the animal by the ruff and bore down. The tiger struggled frantically, but Wu Song was exerting all his strength, and wouldn't give an inch. He kicked the beast in the face and eyes, again and again. The tiger roared, its wildly scrabbling claws pushing back two piles of yellow earth and digging a pit before it. Wu Song pressed the animal's muzzle into the pit, weakening it further. Still relentlessly clutching the beast by the ruff with his left hand, Wu Song freed his right, big as an iron mallet, and with all his might began to pound.

After sixty or seventy blows the tiger, blood streaming from eyes, mouth, nose and ears, lay motionless, panting weakly. Wu Song got up and searched around under the pine tree until he found the stump of his broken staff. With this he beat the animal till it breathed no more. Then he tossed the staff aside.

"I'd better drag this dead tiger down the mountain," he thought. He tried to lift the beast, lying in a pool of blood, but couldn't move it. He was exhausted, the strength gone out of his hands and feet.

Wu Song sat down on the rock and rested. "It's nearly dark," he thought. "If another tiger comes I won't be able to fight it. I'd better get off this ridge first, somehow. Then, tomorrow morning, I can decide what to do."

He collected his broad-brimmed felt hat from beside the rock, skirted the thicket, and slowly descended the ridge. Wu Song had travelled less than half a li when two tigers leaped out of the tall dry grass.

"Aiya!" he exclaimed. "I'm a goner!"

But there in the shadows the two tigers suddenly stood upright. He looked closely and saw that they were men with tiger pelts bound tightly around them. Each held a five-pronged pitchfork. They stared at Wu Song in amazement.

"Have you eaten a crocodile's heart, or a panther's gall, or a lion's leg, that you're so full of courage?" they cried. "How dare you cross the ridge at dusk, alone and weaponless? Are you a man or a demon?"

"Who are you two?" Wu Song demanded. "We're local hunters."

"What are you doing on this ridge?"

"Don't you know?" the hunters asked in surprise. "There's a big tiger up here! It comes out at night and preys on people. It's killed seven or eight of us hunters alone, and more travellers than we can remember! The county magistrate has ordered the township and village leaders and us hunters to capture it. But it's so powerful nobody dares go near it! We've been beaten time and again because of this, but we still can't catch the beast. Tonight it's our turn to try. We've got a dozen peasants with us, and we've laid spring-bows with poisoned arrows all over the place. We were waiting here in ambush when we saw your big form moving down the ridge. You scared the life out of us! Who are you, anyway? Have you seen the tiger?"

"I'm a Qinghe County man. My name's Wu, a second son. I just met the tiger up there beside a thicket. I punched and kicked it to death."

The hunters gaped. "You're kidding!"

"Look at the blood on my clothes if you don't believe me."

"How did it happen?"

Wu Song told them the whole story. The two hunters listened, joyous and astonished, then shouted for their peasant band. The men soon crowded round, carrying pitchforks, snare-bows, knives and spears.

"Why weren't they with you?" Wu Song asked the hunters.

"The tiger was too fierce. They didn't dare come up." The hunters repeated Wu Song's story to the peasants. None of them believed it.

"Come along with me, then," said Wu Song, "and see for yourself."

They had flint and steel and struck a fire, and lit six or seven torches. They went with him up the ridge to where the tiger lay dead in a great heap. Everyone was delighted. A man was sent immediately to report to the village chief and the leading family in charge. Five or six peasants trussed up the tiger and carried it down the ridge slung from a pole.

III. WU CHENGEN AND *JOURNEY TO THE WEST*

1. The Background of the Book and the Writer

Wu Cheng'en's *Journey to the West* is the first existing novel of gods and demons in Chinese literary history. It is also a work that evolved over a long period of folk transmission before being finalized by the author. The Buddhist scholar and translator Xuanzang (602–664), founder of the Dharma-Image sect of Buddhism (Faxiang) in China, overcame numerous hardships with extraordinary perseverance to complete his journey to India to obtain Buddhist scriptures. Later, his disciples Huilei and Yanzong wrote the *Biography of the Tripitaka Master of the Ci'en Temple*, which incorporated mythological elements to deify Xuanzang.

During the Southern Song Dynasty, *The Tale of the Journey for Buddhist Scriptures by the Tang Tripitaka Master* took the form of popular storytelling in temples. This text introduced the character of the Monkey Pilgrim, originally the "Monkey King of 84,000 monkeys in the Flower-Fruit Mountain's Purple Cloud Cave, with a bronze head and iron forehead," who transformed into a white-clad scholar and voluntarily escorted the Tripitaka master (Sanzang) on his westward journey. Along the way, he killed a White Tiger Monster and subdued the Sand Demon, ultimately completing the mission to retrieve the scriptures. This marked the beginning of the shift in the story's focus from Xuanzang to the Monkey King.

The Jin Dynasty play *Master Sanzang of Tang* and the Yuan Dynasty zaju *Tang Sanzang's Journey to the West* by Wu Changling have been lost. However, the existing Yuan-Ming period zaju *Journey to the West* by Yang Ne begins with the story of Jiangliuer which narrates Tang Sanzang's early life. This story later became an important part of the *Journey to the West* novel. Furthermore, Yuan Dynasty Cizhou ware artifacts, such as the "Tang Monk's Journey for Scriptures Pillow," already depicted the group of four pilgrims—Tang Sanzang, Sun Wukong, Zhu Bajie, and Sha Wujing—suggesting that the story had begun to take shape by the Yuan period. By the late Yuan or early Ming Dynasty, a novel titled *Journey to the West* already existed.

The author of *Journey to the West*, Wu Cheng'en (c. 1500–1582), courtesy name Ruzhong and literary name Sheyang, was a native of Shanyang in Huaian (modern-day Huai'an, Jiangsu). Both his great-grandfather and grandfather served as academic officials. Wu Cheng'en lived a humble life, earning a meager living through his writing, with only a short stint as a county magistrate in Changxing. His works include the posthumously compiled *Collected Writings of Sheyang*.

2. The Themes of *Journey to the West*

Journey to the West narrates the story of Tang Sanzang's journey to retrieve Buddhist scriptures. However, it diverges almost entirely from the historical account of Xuanzang's pilgrimage. The novel's central figure is Sun Wukong, and the plot revolves around Tang Sanzang and his three disciples' quest for scriptures under Sun Wukong's protection. The story is divided into three parts:

(a) The first seven chapters detail Sun Wukong's origin.
(b) Chapters 8 to 12 describe Tang Sanzang's background and the reasons for his journey.
(c) The remaining chapters narrate the entire process of obtaining the scriptures.

Though the pilgrimage itself is a religious act, the author celebrates the perseverance and indomitable spirit of Tang Sanzang and his disciples, who, after countless hardships, achieve their ultimate spiritual fulfillment. The story is rich in allegory, especially through Sun Wukong's adventures before the pilgrimage and his battles with various demons during the journey, which reflect the societal realities of feudal times in a complex way.

The chapter *Havoc in Heaven* is one of the most successful parts of the novel. Sun Wukong, as a rebellious figure, vividly embodies the spirit of resistance against oppression within feudal society. Born from a rock, the Monkey King is parentless and discovers a "paradise on earth" in the Water Curtain Cave, where he leads a carefree life with his fellow monkeys, free from the constraints of mythical creatures, divine beings, or mortal rulers. Later, he travels across the sea in search of a teacher, learns 72 transformations, and gains the ability to somersault 108,000 miles in a single leap.

Sun Wukong coerces the Dragon King into giving him the Ruyi Jingu Bang (Golden Staff) and forces the Lords of Death to erase his name from the Book of Life and Death. Angered, the Dragon King and the Lords of Death file complaints in Heaven. The Jade Emperor sends generals to capture Sun Wukong but fails. Instead, he offers Sun Wukong a minor official position as "Stable Attendant." Discovering this deceit, Sun Wukong rebels, proclaims himself the "Great Sage Equal to Heaven," and demands equal status with the Emperor, even declaring, "Emperors take turns ruling; next year, it's my turn." Forced to comply, the Jade Emperor grants him the title.

Sun Wukong later disrupts the Queen Mother of the West's Peach Banquet and defeats the heavenly armies. Ultimately, the Jade Emperor summons Erlang Shen, who captures Sun Wukong, and he is imprisoned in the Eight Trigrams Furnace by Laozi. However, Sun Wukong escapes again. Nevertheless, the celestial powers, symbolizing the feudal order, prevail through the intervention of the Buddha, whose palm secures the Jade Emperor's throne. Sun Wukong's rebellion ends in failure.

Chapters 8 to 12 narrate the Buddha's teachings, Guanyin seeking a pilgrim, Wei Zheng slaying a dragon, and Tang Sanzang's birth, providing context for the journey. These chapters mainly serve as a narrative transition and lack significant ideological depth. From Chapter 13 onward, the story focuses on the journey to the West, forming the novel's core. Tang Sanzang and his three disciples face 81 tribulations, encompassing 41 distinct tales. Most of these involve battles with various demons and monsters that obstruct their quest.

3. The Artistic Significance of *Journey to the West*

The progressive nature of *Journey to the West* is reflected in its celebration of the brilliant image of Sun Wukong. The novel indirectly exposes and critiques the dark realities of society, including the oppression of the people by government officials and powerful elites, the collusion among rulers, and their tolerance of evil. It also critiques the Buddhist and Daoist religions. In terms of character development, the novel successfully portrays figures like Sun Wukong and Zhu Bajie.

Sun Wukong is an idealized heroic figure. He despises the powerful, fears no authority, dares to resist, and is unyielding and indefatigable. He is courageous and enterprising, slays demons and eliminates evil with determination, and takes pleasure in ridding the people of harm. He possesses a keen sense of justice, is highly intelligent and resourceful, and excels in battling adversaries. This character embodies the aspirations of the ancient working people: to resist oppression, seek freedom, and eradicate all forms of evil in society.

The language of *Journey to the West* alternates between prose and verse, drawing from the essence of folk storytelling, ballads, and regional dialects. The dialogues reflect both the prevalent Mandarin of the time and Huai'an dialect, which effectively highlights the characters' personalities, making them vivid and lifelike.

Chapter 27 The cadaver demon three times mocks Tripitaka Tang;

The holy monk in spite banishes Handsome Monkey King (excerpt)[5]

After taking their leave, master and disciples took to the road and soon came upon a tall mountain. "Disciples," said Tripitaka, "the mountain ahead appears to be rugged and steep, and I fear that the horse may not be able to proceed so easily. Every one of you should be careful." "Have no fear, Master," said Pilgrim. "We know how to take care of everything." Dear Monkey King! He led the way; carrying his rod horizontally across both his shoulders, he opened up a mountain path and led them up to a tall cliff. They saw

Peaks and summits in rows;
Slreams and canyons meandrous;
Tigers and wolves running in packs;
Deer and fallow deer walking in flocks,
Countless musks and boars massed together;
A mountain swarming with foxes and hares.
The huge python of a thousand feet,
The long snake of ten thousand feel.
The huge python blew out awful mists;
The long snake belched dreadful air.
By the road thorns and thistles sprawled unendings;
On the peak pines and cedars grew resplendent.
Wild hemps and creepers filled their eyes;
Fragrant plants reached up to the shy.

Light descended from the northern pole;
Clouds parted at the south pole star.
Ten thousand fathoms of mountain holding old, primal breath;
A thousand peaks stood august in the cold sunlight.

The elder on the horse became fearful, but our Great Sage Sun was ready to show off his abilities. Wielding the iron rod, he let out such a fearful cry that wolves and serpents retreated, that tigers and leopards took flight. Master and disciples thus journeyed into the mountain. As they reached the summit, Tripitaka said, "Wukong, we've been traveling for almost a day, and I'm getting hungry. Go somewhere and beg some vegetarian food for me." "Master, you aren't very smart!" said Pilgrim, attempting to placate him with a smile. "We are in the middle of a mountain, with no village in sight ahead of us nor any inn behind us. Even if we had money, there's no place for us to buy anything. Where do you want me to go to find vegetarian food?" Irritated, Tripitaka began to berate his disciple. "You ape!" he cried. "Don't you remember what sort of condition you were in at the Mountain of Two Frontiers? Pinned down by Tathagata in that stone box, you could move your mouth but not your feet, and you owed it to me for saving your life. Now that you have become my disciple by having your head touched and receiving the commandments, why are you not willing to exert yourself a bit more? Why are you always so lazy?" "Your disciple," said Pilgrim, "has been rather diligent. Since when have I been lazy?" "If you are that diligent," said Tripitaka, "why don't you go and beg me some vegetarian food? How can I journey if I am hungry? Moreover, this mountain is filled with pestilential vapors, and if I become ill, how can I hope to reach Thunderclap?" "Master," said Pilgrim, "please don't get upset. No more words. I know that yours is a proud and haughty nature. A little offense and you will recite that little something spell! Dismount and rest awhile. Let me find out whether there's any family for me to beg some vegetarian food."

With a bound, Pilgrim leaped up to the edge of the clouds. Using his hand to shade his eyes, he peered all around. Alas! The journey to the West was a lonely journey, one with neither villages nor hamlets. There were abundant trees and shrubbery, but there was no sign of human habitation. Having looked around for some time, Pilgrim saw toward the south a tall mountain, where on the eastern slope there seemed to be some tiny specks of red. Lowering his cloud, Pilgrim said, "Master, there's something to eat." The elder asked what it was, and Pilgrim said, "There's no household here for me to beg forrice. But there's a stretch of red on a mountain south of here, and I suppose that must be ripe mountain peaches. Let me go and pick a few for you to eat." Delighted, Tripitaka said, "For a person who has left the family to have peaches is already the highest blessing!" Pilgrim took the alms bowl and mounted the auspicious luminosity. Look at that brilliant somersault, with cold vapor trailing! In an instant, he was heading straight for the peaches on the south mountain, and we shall speak no more of him for the moment.

Now, the proverb says:

A tall mountain will always have monsters;
A rugged peak roill ahoays produce fiends.

In this mountain there was indeed a monster-spirit, who was disturbed by the Great Sage Sun's departure. Treading dark wind, she came through the clouds and found the elder sitting on the ground. "What luck! What luck!" she said, unable to contain her delight. "For several years my relatives have been talking about a Tang Monk from the Land of the East going to fetch the Great Vehicle. He is actually the incarnation of the Gold Cicada, and he has the original body that has gone through the process of self-cultivation during ten previous existences. If a man eats a piece of his flesh, his age will be immeasurably lengthened. So, this monk has at last arrived today!" The monster was about to go down to seize Tripitaka when she saw two great warriors standing guard on either side of the elder, and that stopped her from drawing near. Now, who could these warriors be, you ask? They were, of course, Eight Rules and Sha Monk. Eight Rules and Sha Monk, you see, might not have great abilities, but after all, Eight Rules was the Marshal of Heavenly Reeds and Sha Monk was the Great Curtain-Raising Captain. Their authority had not been completely eroded, and that was why the monster dared not approach them. Instead, the monster said to herself, "Let me make fun of them a bit, and see what happens."

Dear monster! She lowered her dark wind into the field of the mountain, and, with one shake of her body, she changed into a girl with a face like the moon and features like fowers. One cannot begin to describe the bright eyes and the elegant brows, the white teeth and the red lips. Holding in her left hand a blue sandstone pot and in her right a green porcelain vase, she walked from west to east, heading straight for the Tang Monk.

The sage monk resting his horse on the cliff
Saw all at once a young girl drawing near;
Slender hands hugged by genlly swaying green sleeves;
Tiny feet exposed beneath a shirt of Hunan silk.
Perspiring her face seemed flower bedewed;
Dust grazed her moth-brows like willows held by mist.
And as he stared intently with his eyes,
She seemed to be walking right up to his side.

When Tripitaka saw her, he called out, "Eight Rules, Sha Monk, just now Wukong said that this is an uninhabited region. But isn't that a human being who is walking over there?" "Master," said Eight Rules, "you sit here with Sha Monk. Let old Hog go take a look." Putting down his muckrake and pulling down his shirt, our Idiot tried to affect the airs of a gentleman and went to meet her face to face. Well, it was as the proverb says:

You can't delermine the truth from afar
You can see clearly when you go near.

The girl's appearance was something to behold!

Ice-while skin hides jadelike bones;
Her collar reveals a milk-white bosom.
Willow brows gather dark green hues;
Almond eyes shine like silver stars.
Her features like the moon are coy;
Her natural disposition is pure.
Her body's like the willow-nested swallow;
Her voice's like the woods' singing oriole.
A half-opened haitang caressed by the morning sun.
A newly bloomed peony displaying her charm.

When Idiot saw how pretty she was, his worldly mind was aroused and he could not refrain from babbling. "Lady Bodhisattva!" he cried. "Where are you going? What's that you are holding in your hands?" This was clearly a fiend, but he could not recognize her! The girl immediately answered him, saying, "Elder, what I have in the blue pot is fragrant rice made from wine cakes, and there's fried wheat gluten in the green vase. I came here for no other reason than to redeem my vow of feeding monks." When Eight Rules heard these words, he was very pleased. Spinning around, he ran like a hog maddened by plague to report to Tripitaka, crying, "Master! 'The good man will have Heaven's reward!' Because you are hungry, you ask Elder Brother to go beg for some vegetarian food. But we really don't know where that ape has gone to pick his peaches and have his fun! If you eat too many peaches, you are liable to feel a bit stuffed and gaseous anyway! Take a look instead. Isn't that someone coming to feed the monks?" "Coolie, you're just clowning!" said an unbelieving Tang Monk. "We've been traveling all this time and we haven't even run into a healthy person! Where is this person who's coming to feed the monks?" "Master," said Eight Rules, "isn't this the one?"

When Tripitaka saw the girl, he jumped up and folded his hands. "Lady Bodhisattva," he said, "where is your home? What sort of family is yours? What kind of vow have you made that you have to come here to feed the monks?" This was clearly a fiend, but our elder could not recognize her either! When that monster heard the Tang Monk asking after her background, she at once resorted to falsehood. With clever, specious words, she tried to deceive her interrogator, saying, "Master, this mountain, which turns back serpents and frightens wild beasts, bears the name of White Tiger. My home is located due west of here. My parents, still living, are frequent readers of sūtras and keen on doing good works.

They have fed liberally the monks who come to us from near and far. Because my parents had no son, they prayed to the gods, and I was born. They would have liked to marry me off to a noble family, but, wary of helplessness in their old age, they took in a son-in-law instead, so that they would be cared for in life and death." Hearing this, Tripitaka said, "Lady Bodhiattva, your speech is rather improper! The sage classic says, 'While father and mother are alive, one does not travel abroad; or if one does, goes only to a proper destination.' If your parents are still living, and if they have taken in a husband for you, then your man should have been the one sent to redeem your vow. Why do you walk about the mountain all by yourself? You don't even have an attendant to accompany you. That's not very becoming of a woman!"

Smiling broadly, the girl quickly tried to placate him with more clever words. "Master," she said, "my husband is at the northern fold of this mountain, leading a few workers to plow the fields. This happens to be the lunch I prepared for them to eat. Since now is the busy season of farm work, we have no servants; and as my parents are getting old, I have to run the errand myself. Meeting you three distant travelers is quite by accident, but when I think of my parents' inclination to do good deeds, I would like very much to use this rice as food for monks. If you don't regard this as unworthy of you, please accept this modest offering."

"My goodness! My goodness!" said Tripitaka, "I have a disciple who has gone to pick some fruits, and he's due back any moment. I dare not eat. For if I, a monk, were to eat your rice, your husband would scold you when he learns of it. Will it then not be the fault of this poor monk?" When that girl saw the Tang Monk refuse to take the food, she smiled even more seductively and said, "O Master! My parents, who love to feed the monks, are not even as zealous as my husband. For his entire life is devoted to the construction of bridges and the repairing of roads, in reverence for the aged and pity for the poor. If he heard that the rice was given to feed Master, his affection for me, his wife, would increase manyfold." Tripitaka, however, simply refused to eat, and Eight Rules on one side became utterly exasperated. Pouting, our Idiot grumbled to himself, "There are countless priests in the world, but none is more wishy-washy than this old priest of ours. Here's ready-made rice, and three portions to boot! But he will not eat it. He has to wait for that monkey's return and the rice divided into four portions before he'll eat." Without permitting further discussion, he pushed over the pot with one shove of his snout and was about to begin.

Look at or Pilgrim! Having picked several peaches from the mountain peak in the south, he came hurtling back with a single somersault, holding the almsbowl in his hand. When he opened wide his fiery eyes and diamond pupils to take a look, he recognized that the girl was a monster. He put down the bowl, pulled out his iron rod, and was about to bring it down hard on the monster's head. The elder was so aghast that he pulled his disciple back with his hands. "Wukong," he cried, "whom have you come back to hit?"

"Master," said Pilgrim, "don't regard this girl in front of you as a good person. She's a monster, and she has come to deceive you."

"Monkey," said Tripitaka, "you used to possess a measure of true discernment. How is it that you are talking nonsense today? This Lady Bodhisattva is so kind that she wants to feed me with her rice. Why do you say that she's a monster?"

"Master," said Pilgrim with a laugh, "how could you know about this? When I was a monster back at the Water-Curtain Cave, I would act like this if I wanted to eat human flesh. I would change myself into gold or silver, a lonely building, a harmless drunk, or a beautiful woman. Anyone feeble-minded enough to be attracted by me I would lure back to the cave. There I would enjoy him as I pleased, by steaming or boiling. If I couldn't fnish him off in one meal, I would dry the leftovers in the sun to keep for rainy days. Master, if I had returned a little later, you would have fallen into her trap and been harmed by her." That Tang Monk, however, simply refused to believe these words; he kept saying instead that the woman was a good person.

"Master," said Pilgrim, "I think I know what's happening. Your worldly mind must have been aroused by the sight of this woman's beauty. If you do have the desire, why not ask Eight Rules to cut some timber and Sha Monk to find us some grass. I'll be the carpenter and build you a little hut right here where you can consummate the affair with her. We can each go our own way then. Wouldn't that be the thing to do? Why bother to undertake such a long journey to fetch the scriptures?" The elder, you see, was a rather tame and gentle person. He was so embarrassed by these few words that his whole bald head turned red from ear to ear.

As Tripitaka was struck dumb by his shame, Pilgrim's temper flared again. Wielding his iron rod, he aimed it at the monster's face and delivered a terrific blow. The fiend, however, had a few tricks of her own. She knew the magic of Releasing the Corpse. When she saw Pilgrim's rod coming at her, she roused her spirit and left, leaving behind the corpse of her body struck dead on the ground. Shaking with horror, the elder mumbled, "This ape is so unruly, so obdurate! Despite my repeated pleadings, he still takes human life without cause." "Don't be offended, Master," said Pilgrim, "just come see for yourself what kind of things are in the pot." Sha Monk led the elder near to take a look. The fragrant rice made from wine cakes was nowhere to be found; there was instead a potful of large maggots with long tails.There was no fried wheat gluten either, but few frogs and ugly toads were hopping all over the place. The elder was about to think that there might be thirty percent truthfulness in Pilgrim's words, but Eight Rules woul not let his own resentment subside. He began to cast aspersions on his companion, saying, "Master, this woman, come to think of it, happens to be a farm girl of this area. Because she had to take some lunch to the fields, she met us on the way. How could she be deemed a monster? That rod of Elder Brother is quite heavy, you know. He came back and wanted to try his hand on her, not anticipating that one blow would kill her. He's afraid that you might recite that so-called Tight-Fillet Spell, and that's why he's using some sort of magic to hoodwink you. It's he who has caused these things to appear, just to befuddle you so that you won't recite the spell."

This single speech of Eight Rules, alas, spelled disaster for Tripitaka! Believing the slanderous suasion of our Idiot, he made the magic sign with his hand and recited the spell. At once Pilgrim began to scream, "My head! My head! Stop reciting! Stop reciting! If you've got something to say, say it." "What do I have to say?" asked the Tang Monk. "Those who have left the family must defer to people every time, must cherish kindness in every thought. They must

Keep ants out of harm's way when they sweep the floor,
And put shades on lamps for the love of moths.

And you, you practice violence with every step! Since you have beaten to death this innocent commoner, what good would it do even if you were to go acquire the scriptures? You might as well go back." "Master," said Pilgrim, "where do you want me to go back to?" The Tang Monk said, "I don't want you as my disciple." "If you don't want me as your disciple, said Pilgrim," I fear that you may not make it on your way to the Western Heaven." "My life is in the care of Heaven," said the Tang Monk. "If it's ordained that I should be food for the monster, even if I were to be steamed or boiled, it's all right with me. Furthermore, do you think really that you have the power to deliver me from the great limit? Go back quickly!" "Master," said Pilgrim, "it's all right for me to go back, but I have not yet repaid your kindness." "What kindness have I shown you?" asked the Tang Monk. When the Great Sage heard this, he knelt down immediately and kowtowed, saying, "Because old Monkey brought great disruption to the Celestial Palace, he incurred for himself the fatal ordeal of being clamped by Buddha beneath the Mountain of Two Frontiers. I was indebted to the Bodhisattva Guanyin who gave me the commandments, and to Master who gave me freedom. If I don't go up to the Western Heaven with you, it will mean that I

Knowing kindness without repaying am no princely man.
Mine will be forever an infamous name."

Now the Tang Monk, after all, is a compassionate holy monk. When he saw Pilgrim pleading so piteously with him, he changed his mind and said, "In that case, I'll forgive you this time. Don't you dare be unruly again. If you work violence again as before, I'll recite this spell over and over twenty times." "You may recite it thirty times," said Pilgrim, "but I won't hit anyone again." Helping the Tang Monk to mount the horse, he then presented the peaches that he picked. The Tang Monk indeed ate a few of the peaches on the horse to relieve his hunger momentarily.

IV. THE SCOFFING SCHOLAR OF LANLING AND *THE GOLDEN LOTUS*

The Plum in the Golden Vase (*Jin Ping Mei*) is the first novel in Chinese literature to be written by a scholar. It emerged during the reigns of the Longqing and Wanli emperors of Ming Dynasty. The author, known by the pseudonym "Lanling Xiaoxiao Sheng" (The Laughing Scholar of Lanling), hailed from Lanling (modern-day Shan County, Shandong Province). The novel consists of 100 chapters and was developed as an expansion of the *Outlaws of the Marsh* storyline about "Wu Song killing his sister-in-law to avenge his brother's death."

The earliest version is the *Jin Ping Mei Cihua*, with a preface by "Dongwu Nongzhu Ke" in 1617 (Wanli 45). Later, the *Original Jin Ping Mei* appeared during the Tianqi era (1621–1627). The story centers on the local tyrant and unscrupulous landlord, Ximen Qing, recounting his various misdeeds, including exploiting and oppressing the villagers and leading a life of depravity and shameless indulgence.

This work vividly exposes the dark realities of mid-Ming feudal society and the corruption of the ruling class. Ximen Qing is originally a fallen gentry figure in Qinghe County who manipulates legal matters and engages in corrupt dealings with officials, earning widespread fear and infamy. He associates with other scoundrels, forming a brotherhood of ten, and dominates the local community. Initially, he has one wife and two concubines but later deceives and marries the wealthy widow Meng Yuelou. He poisons Wu Dalang to seize Pan Jinlian, schemes to marry the wife of his sworn brother Li Ping'er, and exploits his maid Song Huilian. Ximen Qing also bribes his way to being appointed a judicial official in Qinghe County and establishes ties with powerful figures, including a prime minister, military commanders, and provincial governors. He abuses his perceived authority, believing that wealth and power allow him to act without restraint.

Poison her husband Wu Dalang to death, and even took his sworn brother's wife Li Ping'er and his servant's wife Song Huilian. Later, he was appointed as Qianhu of Penalty and even had the Prime Minister as his adoptive father and the Commandant and the Inspector General his acquaintances because of his social climbing bribery, and since then he became more reckless and aggressive, believing that fortune and power could make him a god.

Jin Ping Mei holds significant influence in Chinese literary history for the following reasons:

(a) It is the first long-form novel independently created by a scholar, marking a departure of the novel genre from oral storytelling traditions, paving the way for subsequent literary works by scholars.

(b) It is the first long-form novel in Chinese literature to focus on family and societal themes, broadening the thematic scope of the genre.
(c) As the first lengthy romance novel, it represents a shift from heroic tales to narratives about human relationships and social realities, influencing later masterpieces like *Dream of the Red Chamber*.
(d) Its detailed depictions of everyday life set a high standard and provided valuable lessons for future novelists.

The literary and artistic value of *Jin Ping Mei* lies in its pioneering approach to narrative structure, character development, and its vivid portrayal of society and human nature. Here are some key aspects of its value:

(a) *Narrative Innovation: Jin Ping Mei* departs from the heroic tales and historical romances that dominated earlier Chinese novels, focusing instead on the private lives of ordinary people within a familial and social context. The novel employs a highly detailed and episodic structure, where each chapter contributes to the gradual unraveling of the plot, creating a richly layered narrative.
(b) *Realistic Depiction of Society:* The novel provides a comprehensive and realistic portrayal of late-Ming society, including its corruption, decadence, and the struggles of individuals within the feudal system. Through Ximen Qing and his relationships, the book critiques the moral decay of the ruling class and the oppressive societal norms of the time.
(c) *Complex Characters:* The characters in *Jin Ping Mei* are intricately drawn and multidimensional, especially Ximen Qing, whose mix of charm, cunning, and depravity captures the complexity of human nature. Pan Jinlian, Li Ping'er, and other female characters are portrayed with psychological depth, reflecting their ambitions, struggles, and vulnerabilities within a patriarchal society.
(d) *Exploration of Human Desire:* The novel delves into themes of desire—material, sexual, and power—examining how these shape human relationships and drive the actions of individuals. Its candid exploration of human passions and moral failings makes it a profound study of human nature.
(e) *Linguistic Mastery:* The language of *Jin Ping Mei* blends literary elegance with colloquial expressiveness, capturing the vernacular speech of its time and providing a vivid sense of immediacy. The use of humor, irony, and satire enhances its readability and sharpens its social critique.
(f) *Influence on Later Literature:* By emphasizing domestic and social life, *Jin Ping Mei* broadened the thematic scope of Chinese literature and influenced subsequent works, including *Dream of the Red Chamber*, in its exploration of human emotions and social realities. Its meticulous

depiction of daily life set a precedent for realistic fiction in Chinese literature.

(g) *Moral and Ethical Reflection:* While the novel portrays the decadence and immorality of its characters, it implicitly critiques their actions and highlights the consequences of greed, lust, and corruption. The work challenges readers to reflect on the societal and personal implications of moral degradation.

(h) *Cultural Significance:Jin Ping Mei* serves as a valuable historical document, offering insights into the customs, material culture, and social dynamics of the Ming Dynasty.

It could be surmised that *Jin Ping Mei* is a landmark in Chinese literary history. Its artistic achievements, realism, and deep exploration of human nature continue to make it a vital study for understanding both Chinese literature and the cultural and social fabric of its time.

Chapter 26 (Excerpt)[6]

Next day Hsi-mên wrote an accusation and told Lai Hsing, as the witness, to take the papers and Lai Wang to the court. "Upon a certain day," the accusation ran, "this man got drunk, and, in the middle of the night, made to kill his master with a knife. He is further charged with fraudulently changing money, etc." The party was about to set off for the court when the Moon Lady came into the hall. She pleaded earnestly with Hsi-mên Ch'ing. "If the slave has done wrong," she said, "we can deal with him here, and settle it ourselves without bothering the officers and disturbing the court." "Woman," Hsi-mên shouted, rolling his eyes, "you have no idea of what is fitting. This slave deliberately tried to kill me. Do you come here and ask me to forgive him?" He would not listen to her, and shouted to the servants: "Away with him to the court." The Moon Lady flushed and withdrew.

"What a cantankerous fellow the master of the house is," she said to Tower of Jade and the others. "There is a nine-tailed fox at work somewhere. I wonder whose advice he is taking in this business. He is sending the slave away quite unjustifably. It is all very well for him to say the slave is a thief, but he must prove it. Putting a man into a paper coffin like this is no way to behave. He is an unprincipled tyrant." Then Wistaria came and knelt down, weeping. "Stand up, my child," the Moon Lady said, "they can't execute your husband when they have examined him. That villain has been drinking something to make him crazy; he won't listen to a word I say. His wife, it would seem, is about of as much account as a private soldier in the army." "Just now, your master is in a temper," Tower of Jade said to the woman. "We can only win him over by degrees. Don't worry. Go to your room."

Lai Wang was taken to the court. Hsi-mên Ch'ing had taken the precaution of sending Tai An with a hundred measures of rice to Magistrate Hsia and Captain Ho. They accepted the present. They took their places in the hall of audience and Lai Hsing presented the accusation. The magistrates were told that Lai Wang had been given a sum of money with which to establish a business, but that the sight of the silver had put the idea into his head of replacing it by tin. Then, it was said, he became afraid lest his master should find out, and, in the middle of the night, he took a knife and went creeping to the hall to murder his master. The two officers angrily summoned Lai Wang before them. He knelt down and pleaded: "If you, heaven-born officers, will permit me to speak, I shall be able to explain everything; but if you will not, I dare not say a word." "Now, fellow," Magistrate Hsia said, "the stolen property and the evidence are both here. It is no use your attempting to clear yourself. All we want from you is the truth. Then, perhaps, we shall not be so hard on you." Lai Wang began to tell how Hsi-mên Ch'ing sent a piece of blue satin to his wife, Wistaria, and had seduced her. "Now," he said, "he has accused me of this crime, so that he can get me out of the way and enjoy my wife as he pleases." Magistrate Hsia shouted at him and ordered the attendants to strike him on the mouth. "You slave," he cried, "this is all part of your plot to murder your master. If it were not for him, you would not have a wife, and now he has given you a business as well. Yet instead of trying to repay his kindness, you get drunk, sneak into his bedroom in the middle of the night, with murder in your heart. Why, if all servants were like you, nobody would dare to keep one." Lai Wang went on saying that he was innocent, but the magistrate called upon Lai Hsing to give his evidence, and, after that, there was nothing more he could say. The magistrate ordered his attendants to pick out the cruellest thumbserews they could find and apply them to Lai Wang. Then he ordered twenty strokes of the weightiest bamboos. The poor man's skin was broken and his flesh torn. Blood poured from him. After this the gaolers were told to put him into prison. Lai An and Lai Hsing went home and gave Hsi-mên Ch'ing a full account of the affair. Hsi-mên was delighted. He gave orders that none of the servants should take bed-clothes to Lai Wangor even so much as a scrap of food. Moreover they were not to tell Wistaria that her husband had been beaten. All they were to say was that he would be out again in a few days.

After Lai Wang's arrest, Wistaria refused to dress her hair or wash her face. She would do nothing but shut herself in her room and cry, taking neither tea nor food. This alarmed Hsi-mên Ch'ing, and he sent Flute of Jade and Pên IV's wife several times to reason with her. "Don't worry about your husband," they would say. "He got drunk and talked wildly, but our master has only sent him to prison to cool his heels for a few days. He will have him out again soon." Wistaria did not believe them. She sent Lai An to the prison with some food, and questioned him when he came back. He told her the same story. "My brother came before the magistrates, but they did not punish him. He says you must not worry about him; he will be out in two on three days." After this, Wistaria dried her tears, and every day painted her eyebrows carefully, powdered her face, and resumed her old lively ways.

One day, when Hsi-mên Ch'ing passed her door on his way home from somewhere, Wistaria, who was standing under the eaves, called to him: "There is nobody in my room, Father. Won't you come in and sit down for a while?" Hsi-mên went in and talked to her. "My child," he said, still keeping up the pretence, "your mind ought to be quite at ease now. For your sake I have written to the court, and he has not received a single blow. He must stay in prison a day or two to teach him a lesson, and then he shall come out and I'll set him up in business." Wistaria threw her arms around his neck. "Dearest," she cried, "if you love me, let him come out soon. I don't care whether you set him up in business or not, but when he comes out, I will see he keeps away from drink, and he cannot object if you decide to send him away. If that is not good enough, find another wife for him and all will be well. I have not belonged to him for a long time." "Very well, my precious one," Hsi-mên said, "I am going to buy the house across the road that belongs to Master Ch'iao, and I will set aside three rooms for you there. When you are established there we shall have greater freedom to enjoy ourselves." "Do just what you like, darling," the woman cried. When they had said what they had to say, she closed the door. In the summer months, she wore nothing but an open skirt without trousers, so that, whenever she came together with Hsi-mên Ch'ing, he had only to pull aside the skirt and proceed. Then the girdle was unloosed and the jade treasure of Chen Fei disclosed: eyebrows with all the fragrance of Han Shu were brought near together. They were like a pair of love birds flying shoulder to shoulder, or the meeting of clouds and rain. Wistaria was wearing a perfume-satchel of fine silk, embroidered in silver. There were fir and cypress leaves in it, and some fragrant herbs, and on it were embroidered the four words "Delicate, fragrant, beautiful and seductive". She gave it to Hsi-mên Ch'ing. He was so delighted that his one regret was that he could not there and then make oath that he would live and die together with her. He took a few taels of silver from his sleeve and gave them to her to buy delicacies, saying several times: "Don't worry any longer, or you will make yourself ill. I'll write to his Lordship Hsia tomorrow, and have him set free." They talked for a while, and then Hsi-mên Ch'ing became alarmed lest anyone should come, and hurriedly went away.

Now that she had extracted this promise from him, Wistaria went once more to the inner court and made merry with the maids and serving-women. Tower of Jade heard of this and went to tell Golden Lotus. "Sooner or later," she said, "Father will set the fellow free. He is going to buy Master Chi'ao's house opposite, and install the woman there. She is to have three rooms and a maid, silver head-dresses and nets. She will be as good as we are. Did you ever hear of such a thing? And the Great Lady will do nothing to prevent it." When Golden Lotus heard this, she flew into a fury. A dark fush deepened the redness of her cheeks. "Don't you imagine," she said, "that he will be able to do exactly what he likes! Here and now I tell you that if I let that thievish whore become Hsi-mên Ch'ing's seventh wife...my name is not P'an." "Our husband is a bad lot," Tower of Jade said, "and the Great Lady does nothing to keep him in order. As for us, we cannot fly, we can only walk. What can we do to stop him?" "You haven't a good enough opinion of yourself," Golden Lotus said. "Why do you think we are alive? To live a hundred years so that others can make a meal of us? No, if he doesn't do what I tell him, I shall kill myself, and he will be responsible. I'm not far from it now." Tower of Jade laughed. "I'm afraid I'm not very brave. I haven't the courage to make him angry. I'll watch and see whether you're clever enough to deal with him."

That night Hsi-mên Ch'ing was sitting in his study in the Hall of the King fisher, about to send for his son-in-law to write a letter to Magistrate Hsia. Golden Lotus suddenly appeared in front of him. "What letter is this you are going to get Brother Ch'ên to write?" she asked, leaning over the table. Hsi-mên Ch'ing could not hide anything from her. "I have decided to let LaiWang come out of prison, when he has been beaten," he said. One of the boys was going to fetch Ch'ên Ching-chi, but Golden Lotus stopped him. "You flatter yourself," she said to Hsi-mên, "that you are a very fine fellow, but, actually, you steer your course according to the wind and go wherever the current takes you. You will not do what I tell you, but you listen to everything that thievish strumpet says. What do you think you're doing? You may feed her on honey and sugar every day, but it will be her husband she really thinks about. Now listen to me. If you set that slave free you won't find it such an easy matter to enjoy his wife. There will be nothing to prevent his making a scandal. If you keep her here she will be neither one thing nor another. How do you propose to treat her? If you make her your concubine, he will be here: if she is to remain his wife, you have already made her so conceited that her airs and graces are unbearable to us all. As for the plan of keeping her for yourself and finding another wife for him, what is going to happen when you are sitting somewhere together and he comes in to serve you? Can he be anything but furious? And, when she sees him, is she to stand up or remain seated? The whole thing is most improper, and, if it gets about, I hardly need say that all our friends and kinsmen will think very badly of you. Indeed, the whole household will look down upon you. If the master beam is not in position, the rafters cannot be expected to keep their place. If you are in earnest about the matter you must not stick at a little harshness. Finish off the slave. Then you can embrace his wife with an easy mind." Hsi-mên Ch'ing changed his mind again. The letter he sent to the magistrate asked him to reopen the case in three days, and to put Lai Wang to the torture. The unfortunate man was hardly treated as a human being. The two magistrates, the prosecutor, the police, and the gaolers had all accepted presents from Hsi-mên Ch'ing, and were severe in consequence.

But among them was a scrivener who came from Hsiao I in Shan-hsi, Yin Chih by name, a man both humane and incorruptible. He realised that Hsi-mên had manufactured this trouble so that he could take possession of Lai Wang's wife, and he declined to make out the papers which would have brought Lai Wang before the magistrates. Indeed, he went so far as to tell them what he thought, so that they found it difficult to proceed as they had intended, and finally compromised by giving Lai Wang forty strokes more and banishing him to Hsü-chou. They accounted the alleged stolen property as seventeen taels of silver and five packets of tin and ordered Lai Hsing to return it to his master. An official wrote the reply to the accusation, saying that Lai Wang was being banished that day. The two magistrates made out a warrant and sent two runners to bring out Lai Wang. He was severely beaten and put into sealed fetters, and the men were ordered to start immediately for Hsü-chou, and leave Lai Wang in charge of the governor there.

Lai Wang had been so long in prison that he was in a wretched condition. His clothes were falling to pieces. There was no one to whom he could appeal for help. "Brothers," he said to the two runners, "now that I have been through this trouble, I have not a penny in the world. I should like to get some travelling money for you. Will you have pity on me and take me to my master's house? My wife is there. She will give me clothes and things andI will sell them for journey money, and so make things more agreeable." "You don't seem to realise," the runners told him, "that this is all your master's doing. He will give you neither your wife nor your boxes. Isn't there anyone else whom you can ask? We don't mind overlooking it for Master Yin's sake, and taking you there to get a little money and rice for the journey. Don't worry about travelling money for us." "Brothers," Lai Wang again said, "for pity's sake, take me to my master's door first. There are one or two neighbours whom I will ask to say a good word for me. Probably I shan't get much, but I may get something." The two runners agreed. Lai Wang went to see Ying Po-chüeh, but Po- chüeh pretended not to be at home. Then he persuaded his two left-hand neighbours, Chia Jên-ch'ing and I Mien-tz'ŭ, to go and plead with Hsi-mên Ch'ing that he might be allowed to have his wife and his possessions. Hsi-mên would not even come out to see them and ordered his servants to drive them away from the door. Chia and I were so greatly abashed that they did not know what to do. Wistaria, Lai Wang's wife, was unaware of all this. She never heard a word of it, because Hsi-mên had given orders that any servant who mentioned it to her should be given twenty strokes. The two runners took Lai Wang to the house of his father-in-law, the coffin-merchant Sung Jên. Lai Wang wept as he told his father-in-law the story, and Sung Jen gave a tael of silver to the runners and a peck of rice to his son-in-law for food upon the way. So, weeping and bewailing, Lai Wang set out on the higbway for Hsu-chou, leaving Ch'ing Ho at the beginning of the fourth month.

V. FENG MENGLONG AND *THE COLLECTION OF THE THREE STORIES*

The Collection of the Three Stories (San Yan) is the collective title for three collections of vernacular short stories compiled during the late Ming Dynasty: *Stories to Caution the World* (*Yushi Mingyan*), *Stories to Awaken the World* (*Jingshi Tongyan*), and *Stories to Enlighten the World* (*Xingshi Hengyan*). These were compiled by Feng Menglong, who was born in the second year of the Wanli reign (1574) and died in the winter of the second year of the Shunzhi reign (1645 or 1646). Feng was a talented and versatile individual, and his contributions to popular literature were particularly significant. He extensively collected short stories from the Song, Yuan, and Ming dynasties, spanning 500 years, and compiled, revised, and polished them into these collections. Each collection contains 40 stories, totaling 120.

Following *San Yan*, two additional collections, *The First Striking the Table in Amazement* and *The Second Striking the Table in Amazement* (collectively known as *Er Pai*), were created by Ling Mengchu, a contemporary of Feng Menglong. Each of these collections also contains 40 stories, making a total of 80, although one story is repeated between the two volumes, and another is a play, resulting in 78 unique pieces. Shortly after the publication of *San Yan* and *Er Pai*, a scholar from Suzhou, known as "Old Man with the Wine Jar," selected 40 of the best stories from these collections and compiled them into *Outstanding Tales Ancient and Modern* (*Jingu Qiguan*), which became widely popular.

1. Literary and Artistic Value of *San Yan*

San Yan marked the emergence of the Chinese vernacular short story as a distinct genre, achieving a level of artistic maturity. Each story focuses on specific life experiences of the protagonist, adopting a biographical narrative style. The stories are cohesive, with clear storylines, detailed descriptions of characters and events, and well-structured plots that captivate readers.

The stories cover a wide array of themes reflecting various aspects of Ming society: The emergence of capitalist elements within the feudal society. Love and marriage, often criticizing feudal marriage customs and class prejudices. Class struggles and conflicts within feudal society. Stories of friendship, loyalty, and altruism, celebrating virtues like helping the needy and standing up for justice. Depictions of internal conflicts among the ruling class. Other societal aspects, such as scholars' struggles in officialdom, the rise of rogues, and the life of monks, nuns, and priests.

The language of *San Yan* is vernacular, fluent, and engaging. It skillfully integrates vivid classical phrases and poetry, enhancing the artistic appeal of the stories.

2. Tragic Brilliance of "Du Shiniang Sinks Her Jewel Box in Anger"

Among the most notable stories is the tragedy of *Du Shiniang Sinks Her Jewel Box in Anger*. It tells the tale of Du Shiniang, a courtesan who, after enduring eight years of humiliation, saved her treasures to seek a life of dignity with a trustworthy partner. Tragically, she misplaces her trust in Li Jia, who abandons her halfway through their journey. Heartbroken, she throws her treasure chest into the river and leaps in after it. Du Shiniang's actions reflect her defiance of a cruel and unjust world, making her a profoundly sympathetic and thought-provoking figure. Du Shiniang's pursuit of love, equality, dignity, and self-worth represents the spirit of late Ming individualism and a challenge to Confucian norms. Her tragedy underscores the entrenched feudal ethics and the corrupting influence of money in her era.

Besides *The Romance of the Three Kingdoms*, *Journey to the West* and *Outlaws of the Marsh*, Ming Dynasty also saw the publication of other excellent novels, such as the historical romance *New Chronicles of the Eastern Zhou Kingdoms* (Feng Menglong), the heroic romance *Tales from Northern Song Dynasty* (Xiong Damu), the supernatural novel *The Creation of the Gods* (Xu Zhonglin) and the love story *The Marriage Stories to Awaken Men* (Xi Zhousheng).

The Collection of the Three Stories

Du Shiniang Sinks Her Jewel Box in Anger[7]

Our story begins with the twentieth year of the Wanli reign period [1592], when the *kanpaku* of Japan invaded Korea. In response to an emergency appeal for help from the king of Korea, our Heavenly Court dispatched troops across the sea to go to his aid. With endorsement of the emperor, the Ministry of Revenue announced that the National University would be open, for the time being, to any student who could offer tribute, to make up for the shortfall in army provisions. Now, status as a tribute student at the National University had the following advantages: the opportunity to study, eligibility for the imperial civil service examinations and greater chance of passing them, and, when all's said and done, a none-too-shabby career. Therefore, the sons of officials and rich families gave up attempts to sit for the examinations even at the preliminary level, and once a precedent was set, they all followed suit and bought their way into the National University. The number of tribute students increased to more than a thousand on each campus of the university in the two capitals.

Among the new tribute students was a certain Li Jia, courtesy name Ganxian. A native of Shaoxing Prefecture, Zhejiang, he was the oldest of the three sons of a Provincial Commissioner Li. He started his formal education at an early age but had not yet achieved success at the examinations. He took advantage of the new practice and was admitted to the National University in Beijing. While in the capital, he toured the courtesans' quarters with a fellow student from his hometown, Liu Yuchun, and, there, he met a celebrated courtesan by the name of Du Mei. Being tenth in seniority among the courtesans of the house, she was called by all and sundry Du Shiniang [Tenth Girl].

Her body full of grace and charm,
Her skin soft and fragrant.
Her brows the color and shape of distant hills,
Her eyes as limpid as autumn water.
Her cheeks as lovely as lotus petals,
She was the very image of Zhuo Wenjun.
Her lips the shape of a cherry,
She was a veritable Fan Su.
How sad that such a piece of flawless jade
Hasfallen by misfortune into the world of lust!

Now age nineteen, Du Shiniang had lost her virginity when she was thirteen. In those seven years, she had taken on goodness knows how many young men from rich and noble families, who were, one and all, so enamored of her that they were ready to throw away their family fortunes for her sake. There came into circulation among the courtesans' quarters a four-line song that says,

With Du Shiniang at the dining table,
Those who hardly drink drain a thousand cups.
He who gets to see Du Mei the beauty
Turns up his nose at a thousand powdered faces.

Now, young Mr. Li was a romantically inclined young man who had never before encountered a real beauty. Acquaintance with Du Shiniang threw him into such ecstasy that he lavished on her all the love he had in him. With his handsome face, gentle temperament, free-spending habits, and eager attentiveness, he won her heart, and the two grew deeply attached to each other. Having observed the madam's greed and treachery, Shiniang had long wished to leave the brothel and get married, and now, impressed by Mr. Li's kindly disposition and his devotion to her, she was quite inclined to marry him. However , Mr. Li stood in such fear of his father that he dared not commit himself. Even so, their love deepened. They gave themselves up to pleasure from morning till night, spending as much time together as if they were a lawfully wedded couple and swearing eternal love and fidelity. Truly,

Their love was deeper than the sea,
Their devotion higher than the mountains.

Now, as Madam Du's girl was thus occupied with Mr. Li, other patrons with well-lined pockets were denied access to the one whose reputation had drawn them to the establishment. When Mr. Li spent extravagantly in the beginning, the madam wore an ingratiating smile, humbly bent her shoulders, and busily danced attendance on him. With the sun and the moon exchanging places day after day, all too quickly, more than a year went by. Mr. Li's funds began to run out. As his payments dwindled, much against his wishes, the madam began to give him the cold shoulder. Provincial Commissioner Li, having heard about his son's involvement with a house of ill repute, wrote the young man one letter after another, demanding that he return home, but Li Junior was so enamored of Shiniang's beauty that he postponed his return again and again. Reports of his father's outbursts at home only added to his fear of returning.

The ancients said, "Friendship based on profit falls apart when the money runs out." But since Du Shiniang's feelings for the young man were genuine, the less he had in his pocket, the more passionate her love became. Time and again, the madam urged Shiniang to put Li Jia out, and when her words fell on deaf ears, she turned on the young man herself, hurling insults at him, in attempts to provoke him into leaving. But, being of a gentle nature, he grew even meeker in his responses. (A good-for-nothing with no pride in him!) In exasperation, the madam screamed at Shiniang day after day, saying, "In this line of business, we depend on our patrons for a living, sending the old ones out the front door and greeting the new ones at the back. The more activity there is in the house, the higher our pile of money. With that Li Jia making a nuisance of himself here for more than a year now, old patrons are not coming, not to speak of new ones! The way he scares away every soul with any money to offer, he's a veritable incarnation of Zhong Kui! Now look at this house! There may still be breath left in us, but there's certainly no kitchen fire going. How low have we sunk because of him!"

Unable to put up with such abuse, Du Shiniang shot back, "Mr. Li didn't come with empty hands. He's been quite generous."

"How times have changed! Just tell him to spare a little money so I can buy firewood and rice to keep the two of you alive. (The madam does have a point.) In other houses like ours, the girls are like money-growing trees. They are living in luxury while I have to be the unlucky one, feeding a white tiger that keeps money out of the house! From the moment the door is open every morning, I busy myself preparing the seven necessities of life [firewood, rice, cook ingoil, salt, soy sauce, vinegar, and tea] for the household. Now, where am I supposed to get food and clothes to support that pauper of yours, you little hussy? You tell that pauper: If he's still a man, why doesn't he scrape together a few taels of silver and take you away from here? I'll be happy to get myself another girl."

"Mother, do you mean it?"

Knowing that it was impossible for the penniless Li Jia, who had pawned everything he owned, to come up with any money, the madam said, "I never lie. Of course I mean it."

"Mother, how much do you want from him?"

"If it were anyone else, I'd ask for a thousand taels of silver. But in the case of that penniless wretch, I'll be merciful and ask for only three hundred taels, so that I can find a replacement for you. But there's one condition: he has to pay me within three days. When he gives me the money, I'll give him his girl. He may be a gentleman but if he can't pay up within three days, whatever the circumstances. I'll beat him and kick him out. When it comes to that, don't hold me to blame!"

Shiniang pleaded, "He doesn't have money with him because he's away from home, although he should be able to raise three hundred taels. But three days is not enough. Could you make it ten days?"

The madam thought, "That miserable wretch has nothing left now but his bare hands. Even if I allow him a hundred days, he won't be able to do anything. Without the money, he won't dare show his face around here again, however cheeky he may be. And by that time the girl should have no objection to starting over again." Aloud she promised, "For your sake, I'll allow him ten days. But if I don't see the money on the tenth day, don't blame me for anything I do!"

"If he can't come up with anything on the tenth day, I don't think he'll ever have the nerve to come here again. But if he does deliver the money, you, Mother, wouldn't back out of the deal, would you?"

"I'm already fifty-one years old, and I follow the Buddhist diet ten days out of the month. How would I even dream of lying? If you don't trust me, let's clap our hands on the deal. If ever I should back out of it, let me become a pig or a dog in my next life!"

The sea is not to be measured in scoops;
How laughable the evil crone!
Knowing the student to be penniless,
She demands payment to smash the girl's hopes.

That night, with their heads against the pillows, Shiniang consulted Li about her marital future. He said. "It's not that I'm not disinclined , but it takes at least a thousand taels to get your name deleted from the courtesans' registry book. My pocket being as empty as it is, what can I do?"

"I have talked with Mother. She asks only for three hundred taels, but they have to be paid in ten days. Your own means may be exhausted, but don't you have relatives and friends in the capital you can borrow from? (Poverty is a test of compassion.) If you can raise the amount, I'll be yours, and we won't have to take the old witch's abuses any longer!"

"All my relatives and friends have forsaken me because I refuse to leave this place. Tomorrow, I'll go and tell them I'm packing for the journey home and have come to say goodbye. And then I'll ask for travel money. I may even be able to collect the whole amount." (If, by a stroke of luck, he does manage to get the money, what next? He still doesn't have a plan for the future. I fail to see what Shiniang sees in this good-for-nothing Li Jia.)

The next morning, Li rose, washed, combed his hair, and took leave of Shiniang. "Be sure to come back soon," she admonished, "I'll be waiting for good news."

"Don't worry," said he. He left the house and called on friends and relatives. They were delighted to hear that he was there to bid them farewell before starting his journey home. Then he mentioned his lack of funds and asked for a loan. As the proverb puts it, "Talk of money drives friends away." His relatives ignored his request, and not without reason, for they saw him as a dissolute prodigal who had been away from home, wallowing in vice in a brothel for more than a year, while his father was fuming with rage. And now, all of a sudden he claimed he was going home, but who could be sure he was telling the truth? Should it be but a trick so he could use the supposed travel money to pay the brothel again, his father would surely misconstrue their good intentions when he heard of it. If his father was going to blame them anyway, they'd be well advised not to get involved in the first place. Without exception, everyone said, "I happen to be short of money at this moment. I'm really sorry I'm not able to help you out." No one was generous enough to part with so much as ten or twenty taels.

Li ran around for three days straight without raising the slightest fraction of a tael. He did not dare tell Shiniang the truth. Instead, he put her off with evasive answers. When the fourth day also failed to bring him any hope, he felt too ashamed to return to her. (Just as the madam had predicted.) But, having made the Du house his home, he had no other place to stay. He had no choice but to ask Liu Yuchun, the fellow student from his hometown, to put him up for the night. Concerned by the miserable look on Li's face, Liu Yuchun asked what was wrong, whereupon Li told Liu all about Du Shiniang's offer of marriage.

Yuchun shook his head and said, "I doubt it, I doubt it. Du Mei is the number one courtesan. If she wants to get out of the business and marry, the madam would ask for no less than ten pecks of pearls and betrothal gifts worth a thousand taels of silver. Why is she asking for only three hundred taels? My guess is that the madam resents the fact that you are keeping her girl without paying anything. This is her way of driving you out. As for the girl, having known you for so long, she can't very well tell you to leave out right, for fear of hurting your feelings. Knowing all too well that you're penniless, she purposely sets the price at three hundred taels as a favor to you and gives you ten days to come up with the money. If you can't deliver, you can't show up at her door any more. If you do, she'll ridicule you and laugh at you and make you feel too humiliated to stay on. Brothels often use this trick to drive out unwanted clients. Now think carefully.

Don't be fooled. In my humble opinion, the best thing to do is to make a clean break with them as soon as possible."

Li lapsed into silence, unable to make up his mind. After a good while, Yuchun continued, "Don't make a wrong move. If you do decide to go back home, the travel expenses won't amount too much. There will surely be people willing to help you out. But if you ask for three hundred taels, you're not likely to get it even in ten months, let alone ten days. You know how the world is today. Who will bother to care about other people's troubles? The brothel is deliberately making things difficult for you because they are sure you won't be able to get a loan."

"Right you are, my good brother." Even as he mouthed these words of agreement, Li could not bear the thought of parting with Shiniang. Again, he set about begging for loans here and there though he did stop going back to the brothel at night. For three days in a row, he stayed with Tribute Student Liu. Six days passed.

Deeply worried by Li's continued absence, Du Shiniang had Si'er, a page boy, go out to look for him, and it so happened that Si'er ran into Li on a main street. "Brother-in-law Li!" called out Si'er. "Mistress is expecting you at home!"

Feeling ashamed, Li answered, "I'm too busy today. I'll come tomorrow."

Determined not to fail Shiniang, Si'er grabbed him and , holding him tightly, said, "Mistress told me to look for you. You must come with me!"

His heart longing for Shiniang, Li submitted and followed Si'er. When he saw Shiniang, he could think of nothing to say.

"How are you coming along in what you set out to do?" asked she. As tears flowed down his cheeks, she continued, "Can there be so little human kindness that you haven't been able to put together three hundred taels?"

Tearfully , Li intoned a couplet, "'It's easier to catch a tiger in the hills / Than to open your mouth and beg for favors.' I've been running around for six days and haven't gotten even one cent. I felt so ashamed to come back to you with empty hands that I stayed away these last few days. It was only because you sent for me that I came in all humiliation. It's not that I haven't tried hard, but such are the ways of the world."

"Don't let Madam know about any of this. Why don't you stay here tonight? I need to talk to you about something."

Shiniang prepared food and wine, and she and Li enjoyed a hearty meal before they went to bed.

When they awoke in the middle of the night, Shiniang asked him, "So are you truly unable to come up with even a cent? What's to be done about my marital future?"

The young man continued to shed tears, unable to speak.

Gradually, it began to grow light, and the fifth watch struck. Shiniang said, "I've hidden one hundred and fifty taels of loose silver inside my mattress. This is my private savings. Take it. So that's half of the three hundred taels. Now that you only need the other half, you may stand a better chance. There are only four days left. You've got no time to lose." So saying, she rose and gave the mattress to Li.

Beside himself with joy, Li had a page boy carry the mattress for him and follow him all the way to Liu Yuchun's place. There, he told Lu all that had happened during the night. The mattress was then torn open to reveal pieces of loose silver all wrapped up in the padding. They weighed exactly one hundred fifty taels. Yuchun was astounded. "So, she does mean it! In that case, her sincerity must not be betrayed. Let me try to raise the money for you."

"If this turns out well for us, I'll never forget your kindness." So Liu Yuchun kept Li Jia at his place, while he went everywhere to borrow money. In two days, he raised one hundred and fifty taels. Handing the money to Li, he said, "I went into debt on your behalf, not for your sake, but because of Du Shiniang's devotion to you."

With the three hundred taels in his possession, Li Jia rejoiced at this heaven-sent good fortune. All smiles, he went merrily to see Shiniang, one day before the ten-day limit was to expire.

"You didn't have one cent the other day," said Shiniang. "How did you come by these one hundred and fifty taels?"

After listening to Li's account of what Tribute Student Liu had done, Shiniang said, her hand raised to her forehead in a gesture of great delight, "So Mr. Liu is the one who has gotten us what we want."

Happy beyond measure, they spent the night together in the house.

The next morning, Shiniang rose bright and early and said to Li Jia, "As soon as the silver is delivered, I'll be free to go with you, but we need to arrange for transportation. Yesterday, I borrowed twenty taels of silver from my sisters. Take them to pay for our travel expenses."

This news was most welcome because Li had been worrying about the lack of travel funds but had not dared to bring up the subject. While they were talking, the madam knocked on the door. "My girl Mei," she called out. "It's the tenth day today!"

Upon hearing this, Li opened the door and said invitingly, "Thank you for coming here, Mother. I was just going to ask you over." With that, he laid the three hundred taels of silver on the table.

The madam, who had not expected him to produce any money, was dumbstruck. Her face hardened, and she looked as if she was going to backout of the deal. Shiniang said, "In the eight years I've been living here, I've made thousands of taels of silver for you. Today is the happy day I leave and get married, and you have given me your word. The three hundred taels are all here, not a fraction of a tael less, nor have we exceeded the ten-day limit. If you go back on your promise, Mr. Li will walk out with the money, and I will immediately kill myself. If that happens, you will lose both me and the money, and regrets will be too late."

Not knowing what to say in reply, the madam fell silent. After much thinking, she resignedly took up a scale and weighed out the silver. "Since things have come to this," said she, "I guess I won't be able to keep you. But if you must go, be off this very instant. Don't even think of taking any of the jewelry and clothes you wear every day." With that, she pushed the two of them out, asked for a padlock, and locked the door.

It was the ninth lunar month of the year, and the weather was growing chilly. Since she had just risen from bed, Shiniang had not yet dressed and groomed herself. In her old clothes, she bowed twice in the madam's direction. Li also bowed. That done, they left the madam's house as husband and wife.

The carp broke free from the golden hook;
Flicking its tail, shaking its head, it's gone for good.

NOTES

1 Taige-style, "台阁体" in Chinese, is a poetic style in the early Ming Dynasty favored by many senior officials, mostly compliments of the ruling class.

2 The Chaling School, "茶陵诗派" in Chinese, a poetic school following the Taige-style poets, getting the name from the founder Li Dongyang's hometown Chaling in Hunan province.

3 Luo, Guangzhong 《三国演义》*Three Kingdoms (Volume I)*, translated by Roberts Moss, Foreign Language Press, (1995, 81-85).

4 Shi, Nai'an 施耐庵《水浒传 II》*Outlaws of the Marsh*. Translated into English by Sha Boli 沙博理译. Beijing: Foreign Language Press (2020, 663-677).

5 Wu, Cheng' en 吴承恩。《西游记 2》*Journey to the West*. Translated by Yu, Guofan, Shanghai: Shanghai Foreign Language Education Publishing House (2016, 29-41).

6 Lan Ling Xiaoxiao Sheng 兰陵笑笑生《金瓶梅 II》 *The Golden Lotus*. Translated by Egerton, Clement. Beijing: People's Literature Publishing House (2008, 609-621).

7 Feng, Menglong. 冯梦龙 *Stories to Awaken the World. Translated by Yang, Shuhui* 杨曙辉 and Yang, Yunqin 杨韵琴译. Changsha: Yuelu Publishing House (2009, 1517-1535).

Chapter Eight

Literature in Qing Dynasty

The Qing Dynasty (1644–1911) was established by the Aisin Gioro clan of the Manchu aristocracy. In 1616, Nurhaci (Emperor Taizu of Qing) founded the Later Jin regime. In 1636, Emperor Taizong of Qing, Hong Taiji, renamed the state to "Qing." In 1644, the first year of Emperor Shunzhi, Aisin-Gioro Fulin, Emperor Shizu of Qing, led his troops to enter the Shanhai Pass and chose Beijing for the capital, gradually unifying the nation. The Opium War of 1840, during the 20th year of the Daoguang reign, marked the beginning of foreign capitalist invasion and the transformation of China into a semi-feudal and semi-colonial society (a period that historians refer to as "modern times," spanning from this point to the eve of the May Fourth Movement in 1919). In 1911, during the third year of the Xuantong reign (Puyi), the Xinhai Revolution led by Sun Yat-sen overthrew the Qing Dynasty, ending over 2,000 years of feudal monarchy. The Qing Dynasty, starting from its entry into China proper, spanned 10 emperors and lasted 268 years.

The literature of the Qing Dynasty represents the final stage of Chinese feudal society's literary tradition, characterised by diverse forms and distinctive features. Qing novel writing reached unprecedented heights, building significantly on the achievements of the Ming Dynasty, with authors intentionally crafting their works. Prominent Works include, masterpiece of classical Chinese fiction *Strange Tales from a Chinese Studio* (*Liaozhai Zhiyi*) by Pu Songling; a satirical novel, *The Scholars* (*Rulin Waishi*) by Wu Jingzi ; *A Dream of Red Mansions* (*Hong Lou Meng*) by Cao Xueqin reached unprecedented heights in both ideological depth and artistic expression.

Besides, The Qing era also saw a wealth of theoretical writings, including poetry critiques, lyric critiques, literary theories, and drama critiques. Poetry, prose, and lyrics achieved significant accomplishments in the early Qing period. However, over the entire Qing Dynasty, imitation and adherence to traditional forms prevailed, often stifling innovation. Shen Deqian's poetry theories and the Tongcheng School of classical prose had lasting influence.

In the field of drama, the Suzhou group greatly influenced both creation and performance in the early Qing period. The "Southern Hong" and "Northern Kong"

(Hong Sheng and Kong Shangren) were renowned playwrights of the time. However, classical Chinese drama (*zaju* and *chuanqi*) began to decline after the early Qing period. Outstanding works like *The Leifeng Pagoda* were the result of repeated refinements by grassroots writers and performers. Meanwhile, regional operas flourished. Folk performing arts such as *tanci* (storytelling to musical accompaniment), drum songs, and *zidishu* (storytelling in verse) also saw significant development.

Qing literature represents both the culmination of traditional Chinese literary forms and the onset of transformations influenced by broader social and cultural changes.

I. PU SONGLING AND *STRANGE TALES OF A CHINESE STUDIO*

Pu Songling (1640–1715), courtesy name Liuxian and pseudonym Liuxuan ("Willow Spring"), was a native of Zichuan, Shandong (modern-day Zibo City). Born into a family of landowners and merchants, he passed the *xiucai* examination at the age of 19 but repeatedly failed subsequent exams. At 31, he worked as a private secretary in Baoying County, Jiangsu, for one year before resigning and returning to his hometown. Afterward, he spent his life teaching at private schools in his local area, living in relative poverty.

Due to his lower social status and repeated failures in the imperial examination system, Pu had the opportunity to interact with oppressed commoners and lower-class members of the ruling elite. This exposure gave him some insight into the harsh realities of society. However, as a scholar from the feudal landlord class, his thoughts were complex and contradictory. He sympathised with the suffering of the people but opposed peasant uprisings. He was dissatisfied with the current state of affairs yet harboured illusions about the highest rulers. He satirized the imperial examination system but remained committed to pursuing official recognition. Additionally, his thinking was influenced by fatalism and superstitions.

Pu Songling's works span various genres, including fiction, folk opera, and poetic compositions. Among his works are *The Literary Collection of Liaozhai* (*Liaozhai Wenji*), consisting of four volumes, and *The Poetry Collection of Liaozhai* (*Liaozhai Shiji*), comprising six volumes. However, his most celebrated work is *Strange Tales from a Chinese Studio* (*Liaozhai Zhiyi*), a collection of 491 stories across 16 volumes in the most complete edition, published by Zhonghua Book Company with comprehensive collation, annotation, and commentary.

1. The Contents of *Strange Tales from a Chinese Studio*

Strange Tales from a Chinese Studio is named after the author's study. Most of the works in this collection are stories about foxes, ghosts, and supernatural beings, which are referred to as "Strange Tales." Due to the severe political repression and thought control during the time, the author could not openly expose the dark reality, so he used stories of gods, spirits, and foxes to indirectly reveal and satirize the corruption.

One of the key themes of *Strange Tales from a Chinese Studio* is the exposure of the dark side of feudal politics, condemning the crimes of corrupt officials, tyrants, and local gentry who oppress the people. Stories like "The Cricket," "Xi Fangping," *Wolves in a Dream*, *Shang Sanguan*, *Miss Dou*, etc. illustrate these themes. "The Cricket" tells the dramatic vicissitude of Cheng Ming, who was forced to hand in crickets to the local authorities as a tribute because of the emperor's fascination with cricket games. Unfortunately, his son killed by accident the cricket that he finally got by great efforts. Out of fear, the poor boy plunged into a well, only to be incarnated as a cricket after his death. Due to this incredibly skillful and aggressive cricket, Cheng Ming won great favor in both office and wealth.

"Xi Fangping" tells the tale of Xi Lian offending a wealthy man named Yang. After Yang dies, he bribes the officials in the underworld to have Xi Lian die, and Xi's son, Xi Fangping, seeks justice in the afterlife. However, Yang also bribes the city god, the county magistrate, and the king of hell, who subjects Xi Fangping to various tortures. This story depicts the corruption and brutality of the officials.

Another very important theme in *Strange Tales of a Chinese Studio* is the exposure of the various flaws in the imperial examination system and its harmful effects on the intellectuals of feudal society. Pu Songling, who struggled with the examination system throughout his life, had a deep personal experience of this and reflected it in his works. The stories that deal with these issues are vivid, with strong opinions, a rich sense of life, and a high level of thought and artistic achievement. Works like *Si Wenlang*, *Yu Qu'e*, *Scholar Ye*, *Jia Fengzhui*, *Wang Zi'an*, etc. reflect these themes. In *Si Wenlang*, there is a blind monk who can tell whether the written essay is a good one only by smelling it after burning it to ash, which mocks the judge's blindness and ignorance.

"Wang Zi'an" satirizes characters who are obsessed with the pursuit of fame and fortune through the imperial examination system. The story depicts Wang Zi'an, who, after taking the exam, dreams drunkenly and is mocked by a fox. He believes that he has passed the exam and returns to his hometown, boasting and insulting his elders, revealing his various flaws. The story vividly and vividly portrays the psychological state of a scholar eagerly awaiting the results of the examination. It reflects the crucial role the imperial examination system played in the rise of intellectuals and profoundly reveals the fundamental reason why scholars of the time were so obsessed with seeking fame and success.

Another important and most frequently used theme in *Strange Tales of a Chinese Studio* is love and marriage of the young people, showing the writer's attitude of fighting against the feudal marriage system and ethical bonds.

2. The artistic achievements of *Strange Tales of a Chinese Studio*

Strange Tales of a Chinese Studio are significant and multi-faceted, combining literary innovation with a deep reflection of the social, cultural, and political issues of the time. Below are some of the key artistic achievements of this work:

2.1 Narrative Style and Structure

Pu Songling's writing style in *Strange Tales from a Chinese Studio* is concise, clear, and highly effective. His ability to craft short, compelling stories with a vivid sense of atmosphere is one of the most striking features. The stories often use a mix of direct narration and vivid descriptions, allowing readers to immerse themselves in the supernatural world he creates. The succinct nature of each tale, while often containing a moral or critical reflection on society, ensures that every piece is impactful and thought-provoking.

2.2 Blend of Fantasy and Reality

One of the most remarkable aspects of *Strange Tales from a Chinese Studio* is the seamless integration of supernatural elements with everyday life. The stories blur the lines between the real and the fantastical, making it difficult for readers to distinguish between what is supernatural and what is grounded in reality. This mixture of the ordinary and the extraordinary allows Pu Songling to explore deep philosophical questions about morality, human nature, and society while keeping the reader engaged with fascinating and strange tales.

2.3 Symbolism and Allegory

Pu Songling frequently uses foxes, ghosts, and other supernatural beings as symbols to represent various human vices, societal issues, and moral dilemmas. For example, the fox spirits often symbolise both the allure and danger of human desires, while the ghostly figures sometimes serve as vehicles for social critique, revealing the consequences of corruption, greed, and injustice. These symbolic elements enable Pu Songling to address complex themes, such as the critique of the feudal system and the examination system, without directly confronting the authorities of his time.

2.4 Social Critique and Moral Lessons

While *Strange Tales from a Chinese Studio* contains elements of entertainment and fantasy, it also serves as a vehicle for social criticism. Pu Songling uses the stories to expose the corruption of officials, the exploitation of the common people, and the moral decay within feudal society. By embedding these critiques within supernatural tales, Pu Songling was able to circumvent censorship and express his dissatisfaction with the system without directly challenging the authorities. The works often come with clear moral lessons, either criticising personal flaws or warning of the dangers of societal vices.

2.5 Character Development and Psychological Insight

The stories are rich in psychological depth, particularly in their portrayal of human emotions and relationships. Characters in *Strange Tales from a Chinese Studio* are often complex, with their desires, fears, and flaws explored in nuanced ways. Whether depicting a scholar's obsession with the imperial exam or the conflicted feelings of a ghost seeking revenge, Pu Songling demonstrates a keen understanding of human psychology, making his characters feel relatable and multidimensional, even within the supernatural context.

2.6 Innovative Use of Folk Elements

Strange Tales from a Chinese Studio also draws heavily on Chinese folklore and legends. Pu Songling adapts these traditional stories, often infusing them with his own creativity and artistic flair. Through his stories, Pu Songling revives and reinvents aspects of Chinese folklore, contributing to the literary landscape by preserving traditional stories while also offering a fresh perspective on them.

2.7 Language and Imagery

Pu Songling's use of language is another significant artistic achievement. His mastery of classical Chinese, combined with vivid imagery, allows him to create a sense of atmosphere that is both eerie and compelling. The detailed descriptions of settings, characters, and supernatural events evoke a strong emotional response in the reader, and his careful use of metaphors, symbolism, and allegory enhances the depth and richness of his stories.

2.8 Diversity of Themes

The themes in *Strange Tales from a Chinese Studio* are wide-ranging and diverse, covering topics such as love, justice, the afterlife, societal norms, and the flaws in the social and political systems of the time. This diversity of themes ensures that the work remains relevant to various aspects of human experience and can be interpreted in multiple ways.

The Ghost Wife

(Volume 8 of Strange Tales of a Chinese Studio)

Nie Pengyun from Tai'an enjoyed a happy marriage with his wife. Unfortunately, his wife died of a disease, leaving him forlorn and lost, mourning her alone. One night while he was sitting alone, his wife suddenly appeared through the door. Startled, he asked, "Where did you come from?" She explained with smile, "I have already become a ghost. But touched by your affectionate mourning, I begged the King of Hell for his permission of coming to visit you." Nie was ecstatic and, holding her in arms, he went to bed together with his wife, finding that everything was just like before. Since then, they enjoyed the happy time with each other for years, meeting at night and departing in the morning, and Nie never considered remarrying.

However, his family became worried about his lack of an heir and after a family meeting in private, pressured him to remarry. Nie agreed, and was soon engaged to a good woman. But afraid that his ghost wife might be unhappy, he kept the secret to himself. Before long, the wedding day was coming and the ghost got the truth. She reproved him angrily, "I had been so moved by your love that I came to you, taking the risk of being punished in the hell. But now you have broken your oath, so is this your fidelity to me?" Nie explained that this had been the intention of his family, but the ghost wife was still very angry and left sullenly. Feeling guilty, Nie was relieved at the same time for his future life.

On the night of his wedding, the ghost wife suddenly came while the newly-weds were sleeping, and beat the bride in bed, asking in storm, "how dare you sleep in my bed?" The bride arose to fight against her, while Nie was squatting at the corner, naked and scared, not knowing which side he should take. Very soon, they heard the cockcrow, and the ghost had to go. The new wife was suspicious and believed his deceased wife was still alive, condemning his deceiving her and trying to hang herself. Nie explained the situation in detail, and the new wife finally realised that the woman was but a ghost. The next evening, the ghost wife came again, and the new wife escaped in horror. However, the ghost wife was unwilling to sleep with him any more, only pinching him and glaring in silence at him by the candlelight. This repeating for several nights, Nie was greatly troubled.

Finally, Nie sought help from a sorcerer in a nearby village who put peach wood stakes to wedge the grave down by the four corners, and the haunting was put to an end at last.

The Fighting Cricket[1]

During the reign of Hsüan Tê,[2] cricket fighting was very much in vogue at court, levies of crickets being exacted from the people as a tax. On one occasion the magistrate of Hua-yin, wishing to make friends with the Governor, presented him with a cricket which, on being set to fight, displayed very remarkable powers; so much so that the Governor commanded the magistrate to supply him regularly with these insects. The latter, in his turn, ordered the beadles of his district to provide him with crickets; and then it became a practice for people who had nothing else to do to catch and rear them for this purpose. Thus the price of crickets rose very high; and when the beadle's[3] runners came to exact even a single one, it was enough to ruin several families.

Now in the village of which we are speaking there lived a man named Ch'êng, a student who had often failed for his bachelor's degree; and, being a stupid sort of fellow, his name was sent in for the post of beadle. He did all he could to get out of it, but without success; and by the end of the year his small patrimony was gone. Just then came a call for crickets, and Ch'êng, not daring to make a like call upon his neighbours, was at his wits' end, and in his distress determined to commit suicide. "What's the use of that?" cried his wife. "You'd do better to go out and try to find some." So off went Ch'êng in the early morning, with a bamboo tube and a silk net, not returning till late at night; and he searched about in tumble-down walls, in bushes, under stones, and in holes, but without catching more than two or three, do what he would. Even those he did catch were weak creatures, and of no use at all, which made the magistrate fix a limit of time, the result of which was that in a few days Ch'êng got one hundred blows with the bamboo. This made him so sore that he was quite unable to go after the crickets any more, and, as he lay tossing and turning on the bed, he determined once again to put an end to his life.

About that time a hump-backed fortune-teller of great skill arrived at the village, and Ch'êng's wife, putting together a trifle of money, went off to seek his assistance. The door was literally blocked up--fair young girls and white-headed dames crowding in from all quarters. A room was darkened, and a bamboo screen hung at the door, an altar being arranged outside at which the fortune-seekers burnt incense in a brazier, and prostrated themselves twice, while the soothsayer stood by the side, and, looking up into vacancy, prayed for a response. His lips opened and shut, but nobody heard what he said, all standing there in awe waiting for the answer. In a few moments a piece of paper was thrown from behind the screen, and the soothsayer said that the petitioner's desire would be accomplished in the way he wished. Ch'eng's wife now advanced, and, placing some money on the altar, burnt her incense and prostrated herself in a similar manner. In a few moments the screen began to move, and a piece of paper was thrown down, on which there were no words, but only a picture. In the middle was a building like a temple, and behind this a small hill, at the foot of which were a number of curious stones, with the long, spiky feelers of innumerable crickets appearing from behind. Hard by was a frog, which seemed to be engaged in putting itself into various kinds of attitudes. The good woman had no idea what it all meant; but she noticed the crickets, and accordingly went off home to tell her husband. "Ah," said he, "this is to show me where to hunt for crickets;" and, on looking closely at the picture, he saw that the building very much resembled a temple to the east of their village. So he forced himself to get up, and, leaning on a stick, went out to seek crickets behind the temple. Rounding an old grave, he came upon a place where stones were lying scattered about as in the picture, and then he set himself to watch attentively. He might as well have been looking for a needle or a grain of mustard-seed; and by degrees he became quite exhausted, without finding anything, when suddenly an old frog jumped out. Ch'êng was a little startled, but immediately pursued the frog, which retreated into the bushes. He then saw one of the insects he wanted sitting at the root of a bramble; but on making a grab at it, the cricket ran into a hole, from which he was unable to move it until he poured in some water, when out the little creature came. It was a magnificent specimen, strong and handsome, with a fine tail, green neck, and golden wings; and, putting it in his basket, he returned home in high glee to receive the congratulations of his family. He would not have taken anything for this cricket, and proceeded to feed it up carefully in a bowl. Its belly was the colour of a crab's, its back that of a sweet chestnut; and Ch'êng tended it most lovingly, waiting for the time when the magistrate should call upon him for a cricket.

Meanwhile, a son of Ch'êng's, aged nine, one day took the opportunity of his father being out to open the bowl. Instantaneously the cricket" made a spring forward and was gone; and all efforts to catch it again were unavailing. At length the boy made a grab at it with his hand, but only succeeded in seizing one of its legs, which thereupon broke, and the little creature soon afterwards died. Ch'eng's wife turned deadly pale when her son, with tears in his eyes, told her what had happened. "Oh! won't you catch it when your father comes home," said she; at which the boy ran away, crying bitterly. Soon after Chêng arrived, and when he heard his wife's story he felt as if he had been turned to ice, and went in search of his son, who, however, was nowhere to be found, until at length they discovered his body lying at the bottom of a well. Their anger was thus turned to grief, and death seemed as though it would be a pleasant relief to them as they sat facing each other in silence in their thatched and smokeless[4] hut. At evening they prepared to bury the boy; but, on touching the body, lo! he was still breathing. Overjoyed, they placed him upon the bed, and towards the middle of the night he came round; but a drop of bitterness was mingled in his parents' cup when they found that his reason had fled. His father, however, caught sight of the empty bowl in which he had kept the cricket, and ceased to think any more about his son, never once closing his eyes all night; and as day gradually broke, there he lay stiff and stark, until suddenly he heard the chirping of a cricket outside the house door. Jumping up in a great hurry to see, there was his lost insect; but, on trying to catch it, away it hopped directly. At last he got it under his hand, though, when he came to close his fingers on it, there was nothing in them. So he went on, chasing it up and down, until finally it hopped into a corner of the wall; and then, looking carefully about, he espied it once more, no longer the same in appearance, but small, and of a dark red colour. Ch'êng stood looking at it, without trying to catch such a worthless specimen, when all of a sudden the little creature hopped into his sleeve; and, on examining it more nearly, he saw that it really was a handsome insect, with well-formed head and neck, and forthwith took it indoors. He was now anxious to try its prowess; and it so happened that a young fellow of the village, who had a fine cricket which used to win every bout it fought, and was so valuable to him that he wanted a high price for it, called on Chiêng that very day. He laughed heartily at Chiêng's champion, and, producing his own, placed it side by side, to the great disadvantage of the former. Ch'êng's countenance fell, and he no longer wished to back his cricket; however, the young fellow urged him, and he thought that there was no use in rearing a feeble insect, and that he had better sacrifice it for a laugh; so they put them together in a bowl. The little cricket lay quite still like a piece of wood, at which the young fellow roared again, and louder than ever when it did not move even though tickled with a pig's bristle. By dint of tickling it was roused at last, and then it fell upon its adversary with such fury, that in a moment the young fellow's cricket would have been killed outright had not its master interfered and stopped the fight. The little cricket then stood up and chirped to Chiêng as a sign of victory; and Chiêng, overjoyed, was just talking over the battle with the young fellow, when a cook caught sight of the insect, and ran up to eat it. Chiêng was in a great state of alarm; but the cock luckily missed its aim, and the cricket hopped away, its enemy pursuing at full speed. In another moment it would have been snapped up, when, lo! to his great astonishment, Chiêng saw his cricket seated on the cock's head, holding firmly on to its comb. He then put it into a cage, and by-and-by sent it to the magistrate, who, seeing what a small one he had provided, was very angry indeed. Chiêng told the story of the cock, which the magistrate refused to believe, and set it to fight with other crickets, all of which it vanquished without exception. He then tried it with a cock, and as all turned out as Ch'êng had said, he gave him a present, and sent the cricket in to the Governor. The Governor put it into a golden cage, and forwarded it to the palace, accompanied by some remarks on its performances; and when there, it was found that of all the splendid collection of His Imperial Majesty, not one was worthy to be placed alongside of this one. It would dance in time to music, and thus became a great favourite, the Emperor in return bestowing magnificent gifts of horses and silks upon the Governor. The Governor did not forget whence he had obtained the cricket, and the magistrate also well rewarded Ch'êng by excusing him from the duties of beadle, and by instructing the Literary Chancellor to pass him for the first degree. A few months afterwards Ch'eng's son recovered his intellect, and said that he had been a cricket, and had proved himself a very skilful fighter.[5] The Governor, too, rewarded Ch'êng handsomely, and in a few years he was a rich man, with flocks, and herds, and houses, and acres, quite one of the wealthiest of mankind.

II. WU JINGZI AND *THE SCHOLARS*

Wu Jingzi (1701–1754), courtesy name Minxuan and also known as Wenmu, was a native of Quanjiao County, Anhui Province. He was born into a once-prosperous family of bureaucratic landlords, with many prominent ancestors. However, by his father's generation, the family's fortunes had begun to decline. Wu Jingzi lost his father at the age of 23. Lacking financial prudence, he lived extravagantly and was generous to a fault, earning a reputation as a "prodigal son." At the age of 33, he moved to Nanjing. By this time, his family was in financial difficulty, but he remained generous and hospitable, always making him a leader in a drinking bout.

In his early years, Wu Jingzi was enthusiastic about the imperial examination system and achieved the title of *xiucai* (a preliminary degree holder). However, after prolonged interactions with bureaucrats, gentry, celebrities, and freeloaders, he became disillusioned by their corrupt and base nature. His own experiences of decline from wealth to poverty made him acutely aware of the fickleness of human relationships and gave him a clearer understanding of social realities, leading him to despise the pursuit of official titles and wealth. At the age of 36, Zhao Guolin, the governor of Anhui, recommended him for the prestigious "Broad Learning and Lofty Words" examination, but Wu Jingzi feigned illness to decline. He never participated in the imperial examinations again.

Afterward, his life became even more difficult, and he relied on selling books and assistance from friends to make ends meet. On winter nights, when he could not afford firewood to keep warm, he often invited friends to walk several dozen miles around the city, referring to it as "warming the feet." This period of poverty and hardship deepened his understanding of society's dark realities and significantly influenced his writing.

Wu Jingzi's masterpiece, *The Scholars* (*Rulin Waishi*), was likely completed before he turned 50. He passed away in Yangzhou at the age of 54. Besides *The Scholars*, his works include the *Collected Works of Wenmu Mountain Studio* in twelve volumes, of which only four survive today.

1. The Contents of *The Scholars*

Wu Jingzi lived during the early to mid-18th century, a time when scholars were almost exclusively preoccupied with the imperial examination system and the rigid Eight-Legged Essay, paying little attention to anything else. However, Wu Jingzi deeply detested those obsessed with the exams and the societal ethos they created. Instead, he placed his hopes in impoverished and unrecognised scholars, as well as lower-class individuals who relied on their own labour. It was with such sentiments that he completed the creation of *The Scholars* (*Rulin Waishi*).

The Scholars is an extraordinary satirical novel, consisting of 55 chapters and 400,000 characters. Most of the characters in the novel were modeled on real people and events of the time. However, to avoid persecution under the strict censorship of the Qing dynasty's "literary inquisition," Wu deliberately set the story in the mid-Ming dynasty, even though it actually depicts the feudal society of 18th-century China under Qing rule.

Through *The Scholars*, Wu Jingzi expressed his fundamental ideas opposing the imperial examination system and disdain for the pursuit of fame and wealth. The work mercilessly exposes the various "immoral literati" in feudal society and analyzes the mental state of different types of intellectuals poisoned by the examination system. Using his exceptional artistic talent, Wu portrayed the hypocrisy of the feudal ruling class and the servility of their subordinates, vividly capturing these traits in *The Scholars*. The novel serves as a ruthless critique and satire of the bureaucratic system, human relationships, and the societal trends of his time.

The novel's most greatest achievement lies in its portrayal of various types of intellectuals in feudal society. It sharply criticises and denounces students who were obsessed with fame and fortune, such as Zhou Jin and Kuang Chaoren; superficial socialites who were opportunistic and obsequious, such as Ji Weixiao, Jing Lanjiang, and Zhao Xuezha; greedy and exploitative officials, such as Wang Hui, Tang Feng, and Pan San; tyrannical and cunning local gentry, such as Yan Zhizhong and Zhang Jingzhai; as well as morally degenerate frauds like Quan Wuyong and Niu Pulang. By doing so, the novel profoundly exposes the various ugliness of Qing dynasty society, especially condemning the narcotic and harmful effects of the imperial examination system on people's minds.

One of Wu Jingzi's most successful creations is the character Fan Jin. Fan Jin devoted his entire life to the pursuit of success in the imperial examinations. He began taking the exams at the age of 20 and continued trying even as his beard turned white, yet he repeatedly failed. It was not until he was 54 years old that he finally passed and earned the title of *juren* (a successful candidate in the provincial-level exam). Upon receiving the news of his success, he was so overjoyed that he went mad.

Wu Jingzi valued feudal virtues, such as filial piety and brotherly loyalty, and promoted them as moral ideals. However, in reality, he also observed the hypocrisy underlying these moral principles. Many scholars preached about benevolence and righteousness but acted in direct contradiction to their words. For instance, in Chapter 5, the brothers Wang De and Wang Ren, both well-educated and famous figures, professed that "We scholars value the three cardinal guides and the five constant virtues."[6] Yet, in truth, their minds were consumed with the thought of money. Once money was in their hands, they disregarded everything else. Wu Jingzi used the characters' own words and actions to expose how feudal morality had completely crumbled in the face of money and power. Moreover, he revealed the inherent hypocrisy of certain aspects of feudal morality itself.

In Chapter 48, the account of Wang Yuhui's daughter committing suicide to follow her husband in death is particularly profound. Wang Yuhui, a "*xiucai* for thirty years" and a "pedantic and dull man," had once resolved to compile a book on rites and another on characters. He strictly adhered to feudal morals. Upon hearing that his daughter intended to die in loyalty to her late husband, he said to her: "This is something that will bring you glory in history. How could I possibly stop you? You should do exactly as you intend!" After his daughter starved herself to death, his wife wept uncontrollably, but Wang Yuhui rebuked her, saying, "You foolish old woman! Our third daughter has now become a deity, and you cry for her? She died a good death. My only fear is that I might not have such a worthy cause for my own death in the future!" He then looked to the sky and laughed, exclaiming, "A good death! A good death!" This vividly illustrates how barbaric and cruel the feudal ruling class's promotion of widow martyrdom truly was.

The novel also sharply satirizes miserly landlords, exposing the true nature of feudal society. Yan Jiansheng, though extremely wealthy, was pathologically stingy. Despite his family of four, he was unwilling to buy even a pound of pork, and whenever his children asked for it, he would purchase only a tiny amount, worth four coins, from a cooked-food stall to placate them. On his deathbed, he was so distressed by the sight of two lamp wicks burning in the lamp, wasting oil, that he held up two fingers in protest and refused to die peacefully. This stinginess was a manifestation of greed, which epitomized the traits of the feudal exploiting class. Additionally, Wu Jingzi portrayed a group of sycophantic parasites who depended on feudal landlords, as well as petty scholars like Jing Lanjiang, Zhao Xuezha, and Niu Pulang.

Although *The Scholars* criticises many vile aspects of feudal society, it does not fundamentally question the feudal system itself. Instead, its criticisms culminate in the rejection of the legitimacy of 18th-century Chinese feudal society under Qing rule. Like other outstanding works of realism, *The Scholars* depicts social life with a depth of objective meaning that far exceeds the author's subjective intentions.

2. The Artistic Achievements of *The Scholars*

The Scholars skilfully employs the techniques of satirical literature to attack the feudal examination system. Lu Xun once said, "The essence of satire lies in truth." Many characters in the novel are based on real-life prototypes. The social behaviours and pretentious attitudes depicted in the novel were commonplace in society at the time, but the author's ability to capture and typify these phenomena transforms them into brilliant literary expressions. For instance, the depiction of Fan Jin before he passes the imperial examination is a vivid example. Artistic truth does not exclude exaggeration—scenes such as Fan Jin going mad after passing the exam and his mother-in-law dying of joy use reasonable exaggeration to achieve a powerful satirical effect and profound critical impact.

The author excels in using different forms of satire for different characters. *The Scholars* is written entirely in plain vernacular language, which is precise, lively, and concise, rich in imagery, and highly expressive. These satirical techniques serve to expose the hypocrisy, greed, and corruption prevalent in feudal society and the flaws of the imperial examination system.

The structure of *The Scholars* is unique. The novel lacks a central character or main event that connects the entire work. Instead, each chapter or group of chapters forms a self-contained unit, with the story progressing in interconnected segments. Characters rise and fall, with the main character of one chapter often becoming a secondary figure in the next. This structure combines the strengths of both short stories and novels, creating a unique literary form.

Since its publication, *The Scholars* has had a significant impact. It laid the foundation for classical Chinese satirical novels and opened up a wide path for future works in this genre. The moral novels that flourished during the late Qing dynasty clearly show the influence of *The Scholars.*

Chapter 48[7] (excerpt)
A Virtuous Widow of Huizhou Follows Her Husband to the Grave.

Later Scholars Admire the Old Ways at Tai Bo's Temple

As tutor in Yoo's household, Yu Youda came each day to teach. One morning he rose, washed, drank tea, and set out as usual for his classroom. He had barely left the gate, though, when three horsemen rode up, alighted, and offered him their congratulations.

"What is the meaning of this?" asked Yu.

The messengers showed him a notice announcing that he had been appointed tutor to the prefectural college at Huizhou. In joy, Yu treated them to a meal, then sent them off with a tip. Yoo Liang came to congratulate him, and so did his kinsmen and friends. He was busy for several days entertaining guests, then set his affairs in order and went to Anqing for credentials. On his return he took his family to his new post, having invited his brother to accompany them. Yu Youzhong consented. They packed up together and went to Huizhou.

One day Yu Youda was sitting in the hall when in walked a licentiate, who looked over sixty. He had a card in his hand, which he handed to Yu Youda. On it was written: "Your student, Wang Yun."

After presenting his card the licentiate bowed, and Yu returned his bow.

Yu Youzhong came in and was introduced, and after the usual courtesies they sat down.

"I have been a licentiate in this college for over thirty years," said Wang. "I am nothing but a pedant. In the past, I never saw my tutor except officially; but now that I have such a famous teacher and uncle here, I shall call on you frequently to ask for your instruction. I must beg you not to look on me as one of the many college students but to accept me as your disciple."

"We are old friends, brother," protested Yu Youda. "Why should you talk like this?"

"How many sons do you have?" asked Yu Youda.

"Just one son, and four daughters. My eldest daughter is a widow at home. The others have not been married more than a year."

Yu Youda kept Wang to a meal, and refused to accept his card inscribed as from a pupil to a teacher.

"My brother and I shall often be imposing on you by asking you oven to chat," he said. "Please don't be offended by our poor country fare."

The Yu brothers saw him out, and Wang went slowly home. He lived five miles from the city.

Upon reaching home, Wang told his wife and son how good Yu You-da had been to him. The next day, Yu Youda came down to the village by chair to call on him, and sat for some time in Wang's hall. The following day Yu Youzhong came on foot, with a porter carrying a bushel of rice. He came in, greeted Wang, and they sat down.

He kept Yu Youzhong to a meal, and showed him the manuscripts of his three books. Yu read them carefully, and expressed his admiration. During the afternoon a man came in.

"Mr. Wang," he said, "our young master is very ill, and the young mistress asked me to invite you over. Can you set out at once?"

"This man comes from my third daughter," said Wang to Yu. "My son-in-law is ill, and they want me to go there."

"In that case, I'll leave you now," said Yu Youzhong. "I will take your manuscripts to show my brother, and return them when he's read them."

So saying, he took his leave. The porter, who had eaten too, put the manuscripts in his empty basket and shouldered this load back to town.

Mr. Wang walked six or seven miles to his son-in-law's house, and found the young man seriously ill. A doctor was there, but no drugs were of any avail. A few days later his son-in-law died, and Wang mourned bitterly for him.

The next day Wang went to the college to thank Mr. Yu. The two brothers received him, and kept him to a meal.

"I can't stand it at home, with my wife grieving all the time," said Wang. "I would like to go on a trip, and I think the best place to visit is Nanjing. That's a large printing centre. I may find someone to print these three books of mine."

"What a pity Dr. Yu isn't there," said Yu Youda, "since you're going to Nanjing! If he were there and saw these books, his praise would make all the printers rush to have them."

"If you are going to Nanjing, sir," said Yu Youzhong, "my brother can write you letters of introduction to our cousin Du Shaoqing and Mr. Zhuang Shaoguang. Their words carry weight."

Yu Youda gladly wrote introductions to Zhuang Shaoguang, Du Shao qing, Chi Hengshan and Wu Shu.

At Suzhou Wang changed boats again, then went ashore at West Water Gate in Nanjing. Entering the city, he found a lodging at Niu Gong's Temple. He spent the whole of the next day looking for the men to whom hehad introductions. But Dr. Yu had been transferred to Zhejiang, and Du Shaoqing had gone to pay him a visit, while Zhuang Shaoguang had gone home to repair his ancestral tombs, and both Chi Hengshan and Wu Shu had left for official posts in distant parts. Not one of them did he meet. Wang was not unduly disappointed, however, but let it go at that, and spent each day in the temple reading.

Over a month later, when his money was finished, during one of his strolls he ran into a man at the end of his lane who bowed to him

"What brings you here, uncle?" asked this man.

It was a fellow-villager named Deng Zhifu. His father had passed the examination in the same year as Wang, who had acted as Deng Zhifu's guarantor when he entered college. Hence the young man addressed him as his uncle.

Wang asked him to be seated.

"Nephew," he said, "when your mother was widowed and a neighbour's house caught fire, because she prayed to Heaven a wind sprang up which blew out the flames. Everyone knows that story proving her chastity. Now my third daughter, too, is renowned as a virtuous widow."

He described how his daughter had starved herself after her husband's death.

"My wife's constant crying was more than I could bear," he said. "Mr. Yu of the prefectural college wrote me some letters of introduction to friends in Nanjing, but I haven't succeeded in meeting any of them."

"Who are they?"

Wang told him their names, and Deng sighed.

"I'm sorry I couldn't come here before," he said. "When Dr. Yu was in Nanjing, there were many famous scholars here. The whole country knows of that sacrifice at Tai Bo's Temple. But since Dr. Yu went away, these worthies have scattered like clouds before the wind. I came last year and met Mr. Du Shaoqing, and thanks to him I met Mr. Zhuang at Lous Lake as well. But none of them are at home now. These lodgings of yours are not too comfortable, uncle. Won't you move for the time being to the temple where I'm staying?"

This Wang agreed to do. He said goodbye to the monk and paid his rent, then called a man to carry his baggage to the Temple for Worship ping Heaven. That evening Deng prepared a feast, and they spoke again of the Temple of Tai Bo.

"Where is the temple?" asked Wang. "I'd like to go and look at it tomorrow."

"I'll go with you, uncle," said Deng.

The next day they went out through the South Gate. Deng Zhifu gave a few cents of silver to the caretaker, who opened the door and showed them into the hall. After paying their respects here, they went to the buildings at the back. On the ground floor they found the programme of ceremony and order of the processions which Chi Hengshan had pasted on the wall, and dusted these off with their sleeves to read them. Then they went upstairs, where they saw eight large cupboards in which the musical instruments and sacrificial implements were locked. Wang wanted to look at these.

"The key is in Mr. Chi's house," said the care-taker.

There was nothing for it but to come downstairs. They walked along both corridors, and looked at the two libraries and at the building where the meat offerings were inspected. Then they took their leave of the care-taker, and went on to the Temple on Kindness Repaid. They had a bowl oftea under Glazed Pagoda; then dined in a tavern near the temple gate.

"I am tired of living outside," said Wang. "I would like to go home, But I can't afford the journey."

"How can you say that, uncle!" protested Deng. "I'll provide your fare and see you off."

He prepared a farewell feast, and produced over a dozen taels of silver, then hired a sedan-chair and saw Wang off to Huizhou.

"Although you're leaving, uncle," he said, "you might give me Mr. Yu's letters of introduction. When those scholars return, I'll send them in, and they'll know that you called on them."

"Very well," said Wang.

He handed the letters to Deng, then left.

Wang Yuhui had been gone for some time when Deng heard that Wu Shu was back, and took the letter to call on him. It happened that Wu Shu was out that day paying a call; so Deng did not see him, but left the letter there.

"My name is Deng, and I live in the Temple for Worshipping Heaven," he told Wu's servant. "I would like to explain this letter to your master."

When Wu Shu came back and saw the letter, he decided to go to the temple to return Deng's call. Just then, however, he received an invitation from Mr. Gao, a Hanlin.

But to know what followed, you must read the next chapter.

III. CAO XUEQIN, GAO E AND *A DREAM OF RED MANSIONS*

1. Cao Xueqin's Life

Cao Xueqin (1715?–1763?), whose given name was Zhan and courtesy name Mengruan, was also known by his literary pseudonyms Xueqin, Qinpu, and Qinxi. His ancestors were originally Han Chinese but later became a royal servant "Baoyi" belonging to the Manchu White Banner Ministry of Internal Affairs. Cao Xueqin's great-grandmother served as a wet nurse to Emperor Kangxi, and two of his aunts were selected as imperial consorts. Trusted by Kangxi, the Cao family held the hereditary position of Jiangning Weaving Commissioner for three generations. The Jiangning Weaving Commissioner, established in 1663, managed the production, procurement, and supply of textiles for the imperial court. It also served as the emperor's confidant and secret observer, tasked with monitoring the local populace and officials in the Jiangnan region.

Due to these special roles, the Cao family became a prominent and influential aristocratic household during the Kangxi and Qianlong reigns. However, when Emperor Yongzheng ascended the throne, internal conflicts within the feudal ruling class intensified. Yongzheng actively suppressed and sidelined officials favoured by Kangxi, leading to the Cao family's downfall. In 1727 (the fifth year of Yongzheng's reign), Cao Xueqin's father was dismissed from office and their family assets were confiscated. The following year, the entire family relocated to the north, marking the beginning of their decline. When Cao Xueqin was around sixteen or seventeen years old, the family suffered further setbacks and fell into complete ruin.

Cao Xueqin's grandfather, Cao Yin, was a poet, playwright, and a renowned bibliophile. He was responsible for overseeing the compilation and printing of the famous *Complete Tang Poems*, earning a significant reputation in society at the time. Cao Xueqin grew up in a feudal bureaucratic family and experienced a period of affluence in his youth, followed by the family's decline. As an adult, he lived in seclusion in the western suburbs of Beijing under impoverished conditions, surviving on porridge and selling paintings to make ends meet. Cao Xueqin's life mirrored the rise and fall of his family, and this dramatic transformation gave him a profound understanding of the darkness and corruption of feudal society and its ruling class. He harboured deep dissatisfaction with the injustices of feudal society and had an acute awareness of the declining fate of the feudal aristocracy. Devoting his life to this endeavour, he created *A Dream of Red Mansions*, a monumental novel.

Written during the bitter hardships of his later years, *A Dream of Red Mansions* was composed under extremely challenging circumstances. The process spanned "ten years of meticulous revisions and five rounds of editing." Tragically, Cao Xueqin passed away before completing the novel, succumbing to illness brought on by grief over the premature death of his beloved son. Originally titled *The Story of the Stone*, *A Dream of Red Mansions* was left as an unfinished draft, consisting of approximately 80 chapters. Initially, it circulated in manuscript form among a small circle of readers. After Cao's death, the work gradually gained wider recognition.

2. Gao E and *A Dream of Red Mansions*

In the 56th and 57th years of Emperor Qianlong's reign (1791–1792), more than thirty years after Cao Xueqin's death, Gao E completed the continuation of *A Dream of Red Mansions*, extending it to 120 chapters. Cheng Weiyuan arranged for the novel to be printed twice using movable wooden printing. Gao E, whose courtesy name was Lanshu and literary pseudonym "Historian Outside the Red Chamber," was a scholar during the Qianlong era. He held official positions such as Hanlin Academy Reader and Censor in the Department of Justice.

Gao E's continuation largely followed the original narrative framework, bringing the story to a tragic conclusion and turning the novel into a complete work with a beginning and an end. His contribution played a significant role in the dissemination of *A Dream of Red Mansions*. While some of his chapters are relatively successful, his continuation has notable shortcomings. For example, Gao E's depiction of the Jia family's downfall concludes with their revival, which contradicts Cao Xueqin's original intent.

In character portrayal, there are also inconsistencies with the original work. For instance, Gao E writes that Baoyu passes the imperial examination, achieving the title of "top scholar" and ultimately becoming a Buddhist monk. The emperor bestows on him the Taoist honorific title of "Virtuous and Sublime Master of Letters." In one passage, Baoyu bids farewell to Lady Wang, saying: "Mother gave me life, and I have no way to repay her. My only hope is to do my best in the examination, write a good essay, and secure the rank of scholar. At that time, my success will bring you joy, and my life's duty will be fulfilled. All my past shortcomings will also be covered." This portrayal is clearly inconsistent with Baoyu's original character. Similarly, Gao E's depiction of Lin Daiyu diverges from the original. In his continuation, Daiyu surprisingly offers a positive assessment of the eight-legged essay: "Even eight-legged essays can have sentiments and logic close to life, with a pure and subtle elegance. They cannot be dismissed entirely. Moreover, if you aim for official titles, this is the more refined path." This reflects Gao E's own views on the eight-legged essay and the imperial examination system. Artistically, Gao E's continuation does not withstand scrutiny as well as Cao Xueqin's original. It lacks the depth and nuanced insight of the original work.

3. The Versions of *A Dream of Red Mansions*

A Dream of Red Mansions exists in many versions, which can generally be divided into two main systems:

(a) The "Zhi Ben" (handwritten copies) consists of manuscripts, known as *Zhi Yan Zhai Chong Ping Shi Tou Ji* (The Story of the Stone Re-evaluated by Zhi Yanzhai), with versions such as the "Jiaxu Ben," "Jimao Ben," and "Gengchen Ben," all of which are incomplete manuscripts. Among them, the "Geng Chen Ben" is the most complete, missing only two chapters. Other important versions include *The Preface by Qi Liaosheng to The Story of the Stone.*

(b) The 120-chapter version, the earliest of which was printed in 1791 and 1792 by Cheng Weiyuan using movable type printing, is generally referred to as the "Cheng Jia Ben" or "Cheng Yi Ben." Since then, many other version have been produced, but they are all similar to the Cheng editions.

4. The Contents of *A Dream of Red Mansions*

A Dream of Red Mansions is the most artistically accomplished and ideologically profound work in Chinese classical literature. It serves as a final judgment on the old era, just before the new era is about to begin, and portrays the intricate and sharp contradictions inherent in feudal society. The novel centres on the tragic love story of Jia Baoyu and Lin Daiyu, two young members of the feudal aristocracy, and through the rise and fall of the Jia, Xue, and other families, it profoundly reflects the social reality of mid-18th-century China. It intensively portrays the sharp and complex contradictions and struggles within feudal society, exposes the evil essence of the feudal ruling class, and reveals the historical trend of the inevitable collapse of feudal society.

The content of *A Dream of Red Mansions* is vast, with its conflicts and contradictions intricately woven. The main focus is the struggle between the feudal forces, represented by characters such as Grandmother Jia, Jia Zheng, and Lady Wang, and the anti-feudal forces, represented by Jia Baoyu, a rebellious figure among the feudal aristocracy. This conflict particularly highlights the sharp ideological struggles within the feudal society. In the Jia family, where "each generation is worse than the last," Grandmother Jia, Jia Zheng, and others originally had great hopes for Jia Baoyu, hoping he would study, pass the imperial examination, and become a loyal and filial servant to the land-owning class.

However, Jia Baoyu takes a completely opposite path, becoming a rebel within the aristocracy.

Baoyu despises the eight-legged essay, calling it "a step for fishing for fame and seeking official titles" and a tool for "deceiving the examiners to secure a livelihood." He criticises Confucian classics such as the teachings of Cheng Zhu school, claiming they were "inventions by the previous generation for no reason." Instead, Baoyu eagerly reads "novels with rebellious ideas" such as *Romance of the West Bower and The Peony Pavilion*, which are filled with anti-feudal thoughts. He refers to those who "progress through reading" as "traitors to the country and ghosts of officialdom," dismissing the teachings on "official careers and economic pursuits" as "nonsense." Jia Baoyu clearly expresses his disdain for fame and fortune. He criticises the highest moral standards advocated by Confucianism, such as "civil officials should fight to death for expostulations while military officers in wars" arguing that these are "not the right way to die." He refuses to follow the path that most noble children of the time took, which was "study to excel and then become officials."

Jia Baoyu also feels constrained and suffocated by the aristocratic life. He says, "I hate that I was born into this noble family. The silk and satin can only wrap around my withered trunk; the lamb's milk and fine wine only fill this dung pit. The words 'wealth and nobility' truly poison people." Jia Baoyu also opposes the strict feudal hierarchy of "male supremacy and female inferiority," "order of ranks," and "distinctions between the noble and the lowly." He despises bureaucrats like Jia Yucun and refuses to associate with officials, instead befriending actors like Jiang Yuhan. In the Jia family, he disregards the distinctions between master and servant.

All of Jia Baoyu's words and actions are considered rebellious by the ruling class and deeply offend Jia Zheng, leading to a direct confrontation and conflict between the feudal rebel and the feudal forces, as seen in Chapter 30, "Baoyu Gets Beaten." The love tragedy between Jia Baoyu and Lin Daiyu is the central story of *A Dream of Red Mansions*, and it runs through the entire novel, with almost every character and event being related to it.

The feudal forces view marriage as a political act, an opportunity to expand their power through new alliances. Therefore, for the Jia family, the final decision on marriage cannot be based on love. The feudal rulers choose a wife for Jia Baoyu based on the family's own interests. Lin Daiyu, a rebel against feudal rites, comes from a family in decline, while Xue Baochai's family is "well-established and currently very wealthy." The marriage between the Jia and Xue families strengthens their mutual "support and protection." Due to class interests, although Grandmother Jia and Lady Wang usually pamper Baoyu, at such a crucial moment, they prefer him to suffer emotionally and ultimately force him to marry Xue Baochai, leading to Lin Daiyu's death.

Cao Xueqin's portrayal of the love between Jia Baoyu and Lin Daiyu reflects the author's ideal of love. Through Baoyu's choice between Xue Baochai, who is "complete in virtue, speech, skill, and beauty," and Lin Daiyu, who "never urges him to achieve fame," the author highlights the conflict between two different ideologies and life paths. This suggests that love must be built on a foundation of shared anti-feudal ideals. This is a stark contrast to the traditional clichés of "a talented man and a beautiful woman" or "love at first sight" seen in previous literature. Their love is based on common ideals. The author's portrayal of love thus acquires new meaning, infused with deeper anti-feudal significance.

The author also uses the depiction of Liu Laolao's entrance into the Grand View Garden to show the extravagant lifestyle of the Jia family, with lavish banquets, luxurious bedrooms, and more. All of this demonstrates how, through their political status, they can directly manipulate the government, abuse their power without restraint, harm the common people, and seize wealth. For example, in the chapter where Wang Xifeng manipulates the iron- Tiekan Temple, she, driven by the bribe of three thousand taels of silver, has Jia Lian write a letter in her name, and the governor of Chang'an, Yun Guang, obeys her orders, disrupting the marriage of Zhang Jinge and causing two deaths. Economically, the Jia family exploits the common people relentlessly, collecting high rents, issuing usurious loans, conducting business, and engaging in widespread corruption and bribery. The income of Rongguo Mansion reaches "three to five hundred thousand taels annually.

A Dream of Red Mansions also contains numerous depictions of the lives of servants. The ruling class of the Jia family, consisting of only twenty to thirty people, commands several hundred servants. Each young master or young lady is attended by ten or more servants. These servants have no personal freedom and can be arbitrarily beaten, abused, or even killed by the feudal lords. Under the oppressive authority of the Jia family, countless servants suffer persecution.

5. The Characterisation in *A Dream of Red Mansions*

Jia Baoyu is the image of a feudal aristocratic class rebel. Born into a prestigious family of "white jade halls and golden horses," he lives a life of luxury. His rebellious character is shaped by his unique experiences and the rebellious love affair with Lin Daiyu, leading him to reject feudal traditions such as "male superiority and female inferiority" and the division of ranks. He denies the path of studying and becoming an official, despises the decadent life of aristocratic families, and resents the feudal marriage system based on "parental commands and matchmaking words." He advocates for love freedom and marital autonomy. Jia Baoyu's character reflects some of the author's own life experiences and ideals. Compared with the positive characters in traditional literature, Jia Baoyu embodies the emerging ideals of early democracy and displays the traits of a new era.

Lin Daiyu represents the image of a female rebel from the feudal aristocracy. She comes from a "family of hereditary marquises and scholarly lineage" but lives in a situation where she is dependent on others. Due to changes in her family's status and the hardships of her environment, as well as the threat of the "golden jade good marriage," her personality is marked by being wilful, sentimental, and proud, with a lonely and defiant attitude. Lin Daiyu's tragic image vividly illustrates how the feudal end times subtly and "mercifully" stifle youth and vitality. Her fate reflects the common destiny of rebellious young women in the feudal era, and her rebellious character represents the emergence of a new type of female consciousness.

Xue Baochai is the typical image of a feudal noble lady. She comes from a wealthy family of "pearls as common as dirt, gold as hard as iron" and holds strong feudal beliefs. Morally, she is both tactful and considerate. She is well-educated, knowledgeable, and highly talented. Baochai's character reflects the ideals of feudalism and the traditional life path, providing a sharp contrast to the rebellious nature of Baoyu and Daiyu and highlighting the preciousness of their sincere love. Her tragic fate deepens the idea that in a corrupt feudal society, not only the rebels but even those who uphold the system are destined for destruction. This offers another angle for criticising feudal society.

Comparing Baochai and Daiyu: Both are Jia Baoyu's cousins (Daiyu is his paternal cousin, Baochai is his maternal cousin), both are beautiful, talented, and well-educated noble ladies. However, in terms of personality, Lin Daiyu is proud, sentimental, sharp-tongued, and inexperienced in worldly affairs, while Xue Baochai is virtuous, gracious, adaptable to society, and speaks little, with a good understanding of the world. In terms of ideology, Lin Daiyu is a rebel against feudal ideas, while Xue Baochai is a firm believer in those ideas.

Wang Xifeng represents the image of a powerful figure in the feudal ruling class. She comes from a family known as "the overlords of Jinling." Her character traits include being sweet-tongued but bitter-hearted, hiding knives behind smiles, focusing solely on profit, being insatiable, and highly competent. Wang Xifeng is the most successful creation of a negative character, serving as a common portrayal of all exploiters and manipulators. Through her character, the corruption and evil within the Jia family's feudal household are concentrated and vividly depicted.

6. The Artistic Achievements of *A Dream of Red Mansions*

A Dream of Red Mansions is the pinnacle of classical realism. One of the key features of *A Dream of Red Mansions* is that it reflects the social reality of its time through the careful refinement and detailed depiction of ordinary daily life within a broad social context. The novel vividly portrays a wide range of characters, faithfully representing the true nature of people from all walks of life. It creates a large number of living, typical character images, among which many, such as Wang Xifeng, Jia Baoyu, Lin Daiyu, and Liu Laolao, are full-blooded and distinct, with well-defined personalities.

A Dream of Red Mansions employs rich and varied artistic methods to shape its characters: the author excels at creating characters based on real-life experiences, highlighting their main characteristics while also depicting the complexity of their personalities. The author is adept at using strong contrasts and mutual reflection to accentuate the different character traits of individuals. Additionally, the author draws directly from everyday life to select and refine details that shape the characters, imbuing these details with profound ideological significance. Through major events and large scenes set amidst intricate and complex contradictions, the novel concentrates on describing characters and revealing their traits.

The artistic form of *A Dream of Red Mansions* is a networked structure. The main plot follows the love and marriage tragedy of Baoyu and Daiyu, while the sub-plot traces the decline of the Jia family. The two storylines develop in parallel, intertwining throughout the novel. Alongside these, a series of large and small events and conflicts unfold, seamlessly connecting various aspects of the story, forming a meticulously organised and expansive networked artistic structure. The language of *A Dream of Red Mansions* is based on northern colloquial speech, blending the essence of classical written language with the author's own creative reinvention, resulting in vivid imagery, distinct personality, and profound generalisation.

The portrayal of Baoyu and Daiyu's love has significant importance in literary history. First, it breaks away from the conventional love story tropes of "handsome man and beautiful woman" or "love at first sight," portraying the true love between young men and women based on long-term understanding and shared ideologies. Second, it breaks from the vulgar depictions of "stealing fragrance and plucking jade" in traditional love stories, celebrating the pure love between a pair of young people who have spent a long time together. Third, it breaks the tradition of love stories ending with a "husband's success, wife's honour," and instead creates a heart-wrenching tragic conclusion.

7. The Social Significance of *A Dream of Red Mansions*

A Dream of Red Mansions holds immense social significance; it reflects the rise and fall of the four prominent families through the love and marriage tragedy of Baoyu, Daiyu, and Baochai, and from this, it further exposes the corruption of the entire feudal society. The novel's critique of feudal society mainly focuses on the following aspects:

(a) *Politics:* By revealing the brutal rule and rampant tyranny of the Jia family, it exposes the cold-heartedness and cruelty of the feudal ruling class.

(b) *Lifestyle:* By exposing the Jia family's excessive indulgence, extravagant desires, and pursuit of wealth and status, it critiques the decadence and corruption of the feudal society at the time.

(c) *Economics:* By depicting the Jia family's financial struggles and mismanagement, it highlights the economic characteristics of a feudal society on the brink of collapse.

(d) *Spirituality*: By exposing the Jia family's aristocratic ignorance, vulgarity, and lack of shame, it reveals the hollow, decaying spiritual state of the feudal rulers at the end of the dynasty.

(e) *Family Relations:* By uncovering the internal conflicts within the Jia family, it reflects the various contradictions present in feudal society.

The Rong Mansion Adopted Lin Daiyu[8]

Chapter 3 (Excerpt)

To return to Daiyu. When she disembarked, a sedan-chair from the Rong Mansion and carts for her luggage were waiting in readiness. She had heard a great deal from her mother about the magnificence of her grandmother's home; and during the last few days she had been impressed by the food, costumes and behavior of the relatively low-ranking attendants escorting her. She must watch her step in her new home, she decided, be on guard every moment and weigh every word, so as not to be laughed at for any foolish blunder. As she was carried into the city she peeped out through the gauze window of the chair at the bustle in the streets and the crowds of people, the like of which she had never seen before.

After what seemed a long time they came to a street with two huge stone lions crouching on the north side, flanking a great triple gate with beast-head knockers, in front of which ten or more men in smart livery were sitting. The central gate was shut, but people were passing in and out of the smaller side gates. On a board above the main gate was written in large characters: Ningguo Mansion Built at Imperial Command.

Daiyu realised that this must be where the elder branch of her grandmother's family lived.

A little further to the west they came to another imposing triple gate. This was the Rong Mansion. Instead of going through the main gate, they entered by the smaller one on the west. The bearers carried the chair a bow-shot further, then set it down at a turning and withdrew. The maid servants behind Daiyu had now alighted and were proceeding on foot. Three or four smartly dressed lads of seventeen or eighteen picked up the chair and, followed by the maids, carried it to a gate decorated with overhanging flowery patterns carved in wood. There the bearers withdrew, the maids raised the curtain of the chair, helped Daiyu out and supported her through the gate.

Inside, verandahs on both sides led to a three-roomed entrance hall in the middle of which stood a screen of marble in a red sandalwood frame. The hall gave access to the large court of the main building. In front were five rooms with carved beams and painted pillars, and on either side were rooms with covered passageways. Cages of brilliantly coloured parrots, thrushes and other birds hung under the eaves of the verandahs.

Several maids dressed in red and green rose from the terrace and hurried to greet them with smiles.

"The old lady was just talking about you," they cried. "And here you are."

Three or four of them ran to raise the door curtain, and a voice could be heard announcing, "Miss Lin is here."

As Daiyu entered, a silver-haired old lady supported by two maids advanced to meet her. She knew that this must be her grandmother, but before she could kowtow the old lady threw both arms around her.

"Dear heart! Flesh of my child!" she cried, and burst out sobbing. All the attendants covered their faces and wept, and Daiyu herself could not keep back her tears. When at last the others prevailed on her to stop, Daiyu made her kowtow to her grandmother. This was the Lady Dowager from the Shi family mentioned by Leng Zixing, the mother of Jia She and Jia Zheng, who now introduced the family one by one.

"This," she said, "is your elder uncle's wife. This is your second uncle's wife. This is the wife of your late Cousin Zhu."

Daiyu greeted each in turn.

"Fetch the girls," her grandmother said. "They can be excused their lessons today in honour of our guest from far away."

Two maids went to carry out her orders. And presently the three young ladies appeared, escorted by three nurses and five or six maids.

The first was somewhat plump and of medium height. Her cheeks were the texture of newly ripened lichees, her nose as sleek as goose fat. Gentle and demure, she looked very approachable.

The second had sloping shoulders and a slender waist. She was tall and slim, with an oval face, well-defined eyebrows and lovely dancing eyes. She seemed elegant and quick-witted with an air of distinction. To look at her was to forget everything vulgar.

The third was not yet fully grown and still had the face of a child. All three were dressed in similar tunics and skirts with the same brace lets and head ornaments.

Daiyu hastily rose to greet these cousins, and after the introductions they took seats while the maids served tea. All the talk now was of Daiyu's mother. How had she fallen ill? What medicine had the doctors prescribed? How had the funeral and mourning ceremonies been conducted? Inevitably, the Lady Dowager was most painfully affected.

"Of all my children I loved your mother best," she told Daiyu. "Now she has gone before me, and I didn't even have one last glimpse of her face. The sight of you makes me feel my heart will break!" Again she took Daiyu in her arms and wept. The others were hard put to it to comfort her.

All present had been struck by Daiyu's good breeding. For in spite of her tender years and evident delicate health, she had an air of natural distinction. Observing how frail she looked they asked what medicine on treatment she had been having.

"I've always been like this," Daiyu said with a smile. "I've been taking medicine ever since I was weaned. Many well-known doctors have examined me, but none of their prescriptions was any use. The year l was three, I remember being told, a scabby monk came to our house and wanted to take me away to be a nun. My parents wouldn't hear of it. The monk said, 'If you can't bear to part with her she'll probably never get well. The only other remedy is to keep her from hearing weeping and from seeing any relatives apart from her father and mother. That's her only hope of having a quiet life.' No one paid any attention, of course, to such crazy talk. Now I'm still taking ginseng pills."

"That's good," approved the Lady Dowager. "We're having pills made, and I'll see they make some for you."

Just then they heard peals of laughter from the back courtyard and a voice cried: "I'm late in greeting our guest from afar!"

Daiyu thought with surprise, "The people here are so respectful and solemn, they all seem to be holding their breath. Who can this be, so boisterous and pert?"

While she was still wondering, through the back door trooped some matrons and maids surrounding a young woman. Unlike the girls, she was richly dressed and resplendent as a fairy.

Her gold-filigree tiara was set with jewels and pearls. Her hair-clasps, in the form of five phoenixes facing the sun, had pendants of pearls. Her necklet, of red gold, was in the form of a coiled dragon studded with gems. She had double red jade pendants with pea-green tassels attached to her skirt.

Her close-fitting red satin jacket was embroidered with gold butterflies and flowers. Her turquoise cape, lined with white squirrel, was inset with designs in coloured silk. Her skirt of kingfisher-blue crepe was patterned with flowers.

She had the almond-shaped eyes of a phoenix, slanting eyebrows as long and drooping as willow leaves. Her figure was slender and her manner vivacious. The springtime charm of her powdered face gave no hint of her latent formidability. And before her crimson lips parted, her laughter rang out.

Daiyu rose quickly to greet her.

"You don't know her yet." The Lady Dowager chuckled. "She's the terror of this house. In the south they'd call her Hot Pepper. Just call her Fiery Phoenix."

Daiyu was at a loss how to address her when her cousins came to her rescue. "This is Cousin Lian's wife," they told her.

Though Daiyu had never met her, she knew from her mother that Jia Lian, the son of her first uncle Jia She, had married the niece of Lady Wang, her second uncle's wife. She had been educated like a boy and given the schoolroom name Xifeng. Daiyu lost no time in greeting her with a smile as "cousin."

Xifeng took her hand and carefully inspected her from head to foot, then led her back to her seat by the Lady Dowager.

"Well," she cried with a laugh, "this is the first time I've set eyes on such a ravishing beauty. Her whole air is so distinguished! She doesn't take after her father, son-in-law of our Old Ancestress, but looks more like a Jia. No wonder our Old Ancestress couldn't put you out of her mind and was forever talking or thinking about you. But poor ill-fated little cousin, losing your mother so young!" With that she dabbed her eyes with a handkerchief.

"I've only just dried my tears. Do you want to start me off again?" said the old lady playfully. "Your young cousins had a long journey and she's delicate. We've just got her to stop crying. So don't reopen that subject."

Xifeng switched at once from grief to merriment. "Of course," she cried. "I was so carried away by joy and sorrow at sight of my little cousin, I forgot our Old Ancestress. I deserve to be caned." Taking Daiyu's hand again, she asked, "How old are you, cousin? Have you started your schooling yet? What medicine are you taking? You mustn't be homesick here. If you fancy anything special to eat or play with, don't hesitate to tell me. If the maids or old nurses aren't good to you, just let me know."

She turned then to the servants. "Have Miss Lin's luggage and things been brought in? How many attendants did she bring? Hurry up and clear out a couple of rooms where they can rest."

Meanwhile refreshments had been served. And as Xifeng handed round the tea and sweetmeats, Lady Wang asked whether she had distributed the monthly allowance.

"It's finished," was Xifeng's answer. "Just now I took some people to the upstairs storeroom at the back to look for some brocade. But though we searched for a long time we couldn't find any of the sort you described to us yesterday, madam. Could your memory have played you a trick?"

"It doesn't matter if there's none of that sort," said Lady Wang. "Just choose two lengths to make your little cousin some clothes. This evening don't forget to send for them."

"I've already done that," replied Xifeng. "Knowing my cousin would be here any day, I got everything ready. The material's waiting in your place for your inspection. If you pass it, madam, it can be sent over."

Lady Wang smiled and nodded her approval.

Now the refreshments were cleared away and the Lady Dowager ordered two nurses to take Daiyu to see her two uncles.

At once Jia She's wife, Lady Xing, rose to her feet and suggested, "Won't it be simpler if I take my niece?"

"Very well," agreed the Lady Dowager, "And there's no need for you to come back afterwards."

Lady Xing assented and then told Daiyu to take her leave of Lady Wang, after which the rest saw them to the entrance hall. Outside the ornamental gate pages were waiting beside a blue lacquered carriage with kingfisher-blue curtains, into which Lady Xing and her niece entered. Maids let down the curtains and told the bearers to start. They bore the carriage to an open space and harnessed a docile mule to it. They left by the west side gate, proceeded east past the main entrance of the Rong Mansion, entered a large black-lacquered gate and drew up in front of a ceremonial gate.

When the pages had withdrawn, the curtains were raised, and Lady Xing led Daiyu into the courtyard. It seemed to her that these buildings and grounds must be part of the Rong Mansion garden; for when they had passed three ceremonial gates she saw that the halls, side chambers and covered corridors although on a smaller scale were finely constructed. They had not the stately splendour of the other mansion, yet nothing was lacking in the way of trees, plants or artificial rockeries.

As they entered the central hall they were greeted by a crowd of heavily made-up and richly dressed concubines and maids. Lady Xing invited Daiyu to be seated while she sent a servant to the library to ask her husband to join them.

After a while the servant came back to report, "The master says he hasn't been feeling too well the last few days, and meeting the young lady would only upset them both. He isn't up to it for the time being. Miss Lin mustn't mope or be homesick here but feel at home with the old lady and her aunts. Her cousins may be silly creatures, but they'll be company for her and help to amuse her. If anyone is unkind to her, she must say so and not treat us as strangers."

Daiyu had risen to her feet to listen to this message. Shortly after this she rose again to take her leave. Lady Xing insisted that she stay for the evening meal.

"Thank you very much, aunt, you're too kind," said Daiyu. "Really I shouldn't decline. But it might look rude if I delayed in calling on my second uncle. Please excuse me and let me stay another time."

"You're quite right," said Lady Xing. She told a few elderly maids to escort her niece back in the same carriage, whereupon Daiyu took hen leave. Her aunt saw her to the ceremonial gate and after giving the maids some further instructions waited to see them off.

Back in the Rong Mansion, Daiyu alighted again. The nurses led her eastwards, round a corner, through an entrance hall into a hall facing south, then passed through a ceremonial gate into a large courtyard. The northern building had five large apartments and wings on either side. This was the hub of the whole estate, more imposing by far than the Lady Dowager's quarters.

Daiyu realised that this was the main inner suite, for a broad raised avenue led straight to its gate. Once inside the hall she looked up and he eye was caught by a great blue tablet with nine gold dragons on it, on which was written in characters large as peck measures:

Hall of Glorious Felicity.

Smaller characters at the end recorded the date on which the Emperor had conferred this tablet upon Jia Yuan, the Duke of Rongguo, and it bore the Imperial seal.

On the large red sandalwood table carved with dragons an old bronze tripod, green with patina, stood about three feet high. On the wall hung a large scroll-picture of black dragons riding the waves. This was flanked by a bronze wine vessel inlaid with gold and a crystal bowl. By the walls were a row of sixteen cedar-wood armchairs; and above these hung two panels of ebony with the following couplet inset in silver:

Pearls on the dais outshine the sun and moon;

Insignia of honour in the hall blaze like iridescent clouds.

Small characters below recorded that this had been written by the Prince of Dungan, who signed his name Mu Shi and styled himself a fellow provincial and old family friend.

Since Lady Wang seldom sat in this main hall but used three rooms on the east side for relaxation, the nurses led Daiyu there.

The large kang by the window was covered with a scarlet foreign rug. In the middle were red back-rests and turquoise bolsters, both with dragon-design medallions, and a long greenish yellow mattress also with dragon medallions. At each side stood a low table of foreign lacquer in the shape of plum-blossom. On the left-hand table were a tripod, spoons chopsticks and an incense container, on the right one, a slender-waisted porcelain vase from the Ruzhou Kiln containing flowers then in season, as well as tea-bowls and a spittoon. Below the kang facing the west wall were four armchairs, their covers of bright red dotted with pink flowers, and with four footstools beneath them. On either side were two tables set out with teacups and vases of flowers. The rest of the room need not be described in detail.

The nurses urged Daiyu to sit on the kang, on the edge of which were two brocade cushions. But feeling that this would be presumptuous, she sat instead on one of the chairs on the east side. The maids in attendance served tea, and as she sipped it she studied them, observing that their make-up, clothes and deportment were quite different from those in other families. Before she had finished her tea in came a maid wearing a red silkcoat and a blue satin sleeveless jacket with silk borders. With a smile this girl announced:

> "Her Ladyship asks Miss Lin to go in and take a seat over there." At once the nurses conducted Daiyu along the eastern corridor to a small three-roomed suite facing south. On the kang under the window was a low table laden with books and a tea-service. Against the east wall were a none too new blue satin back-rest and a bolster.

Lady Wang was sitting in the lower place by the west wall on a none too new blue satin cover with a back-rest and a bolster. She invited her niece to take the seat on the east. But guessing that this was Jia Zheng's place, Daiyu chose one of the three chairs next to the kang, which had black-dotted antimacassars, looking none too new. Not until she had been pressed several times did she take a seat by her aunt.

"Your uncle's observing a fast today," said Lady Wang. "You'll see him some other time. But there's one thing I want to tell you. Your three cousins are excellent girls, and I'm sure you'll find them easy to get on with during lessons, or when you're learning embroidery or playing together. Just one thing worries me: that's my dreadful son, the bane of my life, who torments us all in this house like a real devil. He's gone to a temple today in fulfilment of a vow, but you'll see what he's like when he comes back this evening. Just pay no attention to him. None of your cousins dare to provoke him."

Daiyu's mother had often spoken of this nephew born with a plece of jade in his mouth, his wild ways, aversion to study and delight in playing about in the women's apartments. Apparently he was so spoiled by his grandmother that no one could control him. She knew Lady Wang must be referring to him.

"Does aunt mean my elder cousin with the jade in his mouth?" she asked with a smile. "Mother often spoke of him. I know he's a year older than me, his name is Baoyu, and for all his pranks he's very good to his girl cousins. But how can I provoke him? I'll be spending all my time with the other girls in a different part of the house while our boy cousins are in the outer courtyards."

"You don't understand," replied Lady Wang with a laugh. "He's not like other boys. Because the old lady's always doted on him, he's used to being spoilt with the girls. If they ignore him he keeps fairly quiet though he feels bored. He can always work off his temper by scolding some of his pages. But if the girls give him the least encouragement, he's so elated he gets up to all kinds of mischief. That's why you mustn't pay any attention to him. One moment he's all honey-sweet; the next, he's rude and recalcitrant; and in another minute he's raving like a lunatic. You can't take him seriously."

As Daiyu promised to remember this, a maid announced that dinner was to be served in the Lady Dowager's apartments. Lady Wang at once led her niece out of the back door, going west along a corridor and through a side gate to a broad road running from north to south. On the south side was a dainty three-roomed annex facing north; on the north a big screen wall painted white, behind which was a small door leading to an apart ment.

"That's where your cousin Xifeng lives." Lady Wang pointed out the place. "So next time you know where to find her. If you want anything just let her know."

By the gate several young pages, their hair in tufts, stood at attention. Lady Wang led Daiyu through an entrance hall running from east to west into the Lady Dowager's back courtyard. Stepping through the back door, they found quite a crowd assembled who, as soon as they saw Lady Wang, set tables and chairs ready. Jia Zhu's widow, Li Wan, served the rice while Xifeng put out the chopsticks and Lady Wang served the soup.

The Lady Dowager was seated alone on a couch at the head of the table with two empty chairs on each side. Xifeng took Daiyu by the hand to make her sit in the first place on the left, but she persistently declined the honour.

"Your aunt and sisters-in-law don't dine here," said her grandmother with a smile. "Besides, you're a guest today. So do take that seat."

With a murmured apology, Daiyu obeyed. The Lady Dowager told Lady Wang to sit down; then Yingchun and the two other girls asked leave to be seated, Yingchun first on the right, Tanchun second on the left, and Xichun second on the right. Maids held ready dusters, bowls for rinsing the mouth and napkins, while Li Wan and Xifeng standing behind the diners plied them with food.

Although the outer room swarmed with nurses and maids, not so much as a cough was heard. The meal was eaten in silence. And immediately after, tea was brought in on small trays. Now Lin Ruhai had taught his daughter the virtue of moderation and the harm caused to the digestive system by drinking tea directly after a meal. But many customs here were different from those in her home. She would have to adapt herself to these new ways. As she took the tea, however, the rinse-bowls were proffered again, and seeing the others rinse their mouths she followed suit. After they had washed their hands tea was served once more, this time for drinking.

"You others may go," said the Lady Dowager now. "I want to have a chat with my grand-daughter."

Lady Wang promptly rose and after a few remarks led the way out, followed by Li Wan and Xifeng. Then her grandmother asked Daiyu what books she had studied.

"I've just finished the Four Books," said Daiyu. "But I'm very ignorant." Then she inquired what the other girls were reading.

"They only know a very few characters, not enough to read any books."

The words were hardly out of her mouth when they heard footsteps in the courtyard and a maid came in to announce, "Baoyu is here."

Daiyu was wondering what sort of graceless scamp or little dunce Baoyu was and feeling reluctant to meet such a stupid creature when even as the maid announced him, in he walked.

He had on a golden coronet studded with jewels and a golden chaplet in the form of two dragons fighting for a pearl. His red archer's jacket, embroidered with golden butterflies and flowers, was tied with a coloured tasselled palace sash. Over this he wore a turquoise fringed coat of Japanese satin with a raised pattern of flowers in eight bunches. His court boots were of black satin with white soles.

His face was as radiant as the mid-autumn moon, his complexion fresh as spring flowers at down. The hair above his temples was as sharply outlined as if cut with a knife. His eyebrows were as black as if painted with ink, his cheeks as red as peach-blossom, his eyes bright as autumn ripples. Even when angry he seemed to smile, and there was warmth in his glance even when he frowned.

Round his neck he had a golden torque in the likeness of a dragon and a silk cord of five colours, on which hung a beautiful piece of jade.

His appearance took Daiyu by surprise. "How very strange!" she thought. "It's as if I'd seen him somewhere before. He looks so familiar."

Baoyu paid his respects to the Lady Dowager and upon her instructions went to see his mother.

He returned before long, having changed his clothes. His short hair in small plaits tied with red silk was drawn up on the crown of his head and braided into one thick queue as black and glossy as lacquer, sporting four large pearls attached to golden pendants in the form of the eight precious things. His coat of a flower pattern on a bright red ground was not new and he still wore the torque, the precious jade, a lock-shaped amulet containing his Buddhist name, and a lucky charm. Below could be glimpsed light green flowered satin trousers, black-dotted stockings with brocade borders, and thick-soled scarlet shoes.

His face looked as fair as if powdered, his lips red as rouge. His glance was full of affection, his speech interspersed with smiles. But his natural charm appeared most in his brows, for his eyes sparkled with a world of feeling. However, winning as his appearance was, it was difficult to tell what lay beneath.

Someone subsequently gave an admirable picture of Baoyu in these two verses written to the melody of *The Moon over the West River*.

Absurdly he courts care and melancholy
And raves like any madman in his folly;
For though endowed with handsome looks is he,
His heart is lawless and refractory.

Too dense by far to understand his duty,
Too stubborn to apply himself to study,
Foolhardy in his eccentricity,
He's deaf to all reproach and obloquy.

Left cold by riches and nobility,
Unfit to bear the stings of poverty,
He wastes his time and his ability,
Failing his country and his family.

First in this world for uselessness is he,
Second to none in his deficiency.
Young fops and lordlings all, be warned by me:
Don't imitate this youth's perversity!

With a smile at Baoyu, the Lady Dowager scolded, "Fancy changing your clothes before greeting our visitor. Hurry up now and pay your respects to your cousin."

Of course, Baoyu had seen this new cousin earlier on and guessed that she was the daughter of his Aunt Lin. He made haste to bow and having greeted her, took a seat. Looking at Daiyu closely, he found her different from other girls.

Her dusky arched eyebrows were knitted and yet not frowning, her speaking eyes held both merriment and sorrow; her very frailty had charm. Her eyes sparkled with tears, her breath was soft and faint. In repose she was like a lovely flower mirrored in the water; in motion, a pliant willow swaying in the wind. She looked more sensitive than Bi Gan', more delicate than Xi Shi.

"I've met this cousin before," he declared at the end of his scrutiny.

"You're talking nonsense again," said his grandmother, laughing. "How could you possibly have met her?"

"Well, even if I haven't, her face looks familiar. I feel we're old friends meeting again after a long separation."

"So much the better." The Lady Dowager laughed. "That means you're bound to be good friends."

Baoyu went over to sit beside Daiyu and once more gazed fixedly at her.

"Have you done much reading, cousin?" he asked.

"No," said Daiyu. "I've only studied for a couple of years and learned a few characters."

"What's your name?"

She told him.

"And your courtesy name?"

"I have none."

"I'll give you one then," he proposed with a chuckle. "What could be better than Pinpin?"

"Where's that from?" put in Tanchun.

"*The Compendium of Men and Objects Old and New* says that in the west is a stone called *dai* which can be used instead of graphite for painting eyebrows. As Cousin Lin's eyebrows look half knit, what could be more apt than these two characters?"

"You're making that up, I'm afraid," teased Tanchun.

"Most works, apart from the *Four Books*, are made up; am I the only one who makes things up?" he retorted with a grin. Then, to the mystification of them all, he asked Daiyu if she had any jade.

Imagining that he had his own jade in mind, she answered, "No, I haven't. I suppose it's too rare for everybody to have."

This instantly threw Baoyu into one of his frenzies. Tearing off the jade he flung it on the ground.

"What's rare about it?" he stormed. "It can't even tell good people from bad. What spiritual understanding has it got? I don't want this nuisance either."

In consternation all the maids rushed forward to pick up the jade while the Lady Dowager in desperation took Baoyu in her arms.

"You wicked monster!" she scolded. "Storm at people if you're in a passion. But why should you throw away that precious thing your life depends on?"

His face stained with tears, Baoyu sobbed, "None of the girls here has one, only me. What's the fun of that? Even this newly arrived cousin who's lovely as a fairy hasn't got one either. That shows it's no good."

"She did have one once," said the old lady to soothe him. "But when your aunt was dying and was unwilling to leave her, the best she could do was to take the jade with her instead. That was like burying the living with the dead and showed your cousin's filial piety. It meant, too, that now your aunt's spirit can still see your cousin. That's why she said she had none, not wanting to boast about it. How can you compare with her? Now put it carefully on again lest your mother hears about this."

She took the jade from one of the maids and put it on him herself. And Baoyu, convinced by her tale, let the matter drop.

Just then a nurse came in to ask about Daiyu's quarters.

"Move Baoyu into the inner apartment of my suite," said his grandmother. "Miss Lin can stay for the time being in his Green Gauze Lodge. Once spring comes, we'll make different arrangements."

"Dear Ancestress!" coaxed Baoyu. "Let me stay outside Green Gauze Lodge. I'll do very well on that bed in the outer room. Why should I move over and disturb you?"

After a moment's reflection the Lady Dowager agreed to this. Each would be attended by a nurse and a maid, while other attendants were on night duty outside. Xifeng had already sent round a flowered lavenden curtain, satin quilts and embroidered mattresses.

Daiyu had brought with her only Nanny Wang, her old wet-nurse, and ten-year old Xueyan, who had also attended her since she was a child. Since the Lady Dowager considered Xueyan too young and childish and Nanny Wang too old to be of much service, she gave Daiyu one of her own personal attendants, a maid of the second grade called Yingge. Like Yingchun and the other young ladies, in addition to her own wet-nurse Daiyu was given four other nurses as chaper ones, two personal maids to attend to her toilet and five or six girls to sweep the rooms and run errands.

Nanny Wang and Yingge accompanied Daiyu now to Green Gauze Lodge, while Baoyu's wet-nurse, Nanny Li, and his chief maid Xiren made ready the big bed for him in its outer room.

Xiren, whose original name was Zhenzhu, had been one of the Lady Dowager's maids. The old lady so doted on her grandson that she wanted to make sure he was well looked after and for this reason she gave him her favourite, Xiren, a good, conscientious girl. Baoyu knew that her surname was Hua and remembered a line of poetry which ran, "the fragrance of flowers assails men." So he asked his grandmother's permission to change her name to Xiren.

Xiren's strong point was devotion. Looking after the Lady Dowager she thought of no one but the Lady Dowager, and after being assigned to Baoyu she thought only of Baoyu. What worried her, though, was that he was too headstrong to listen to her advice.

That night after Baoyu and Nanny Li were asleep, Xiren noticed that Daiyu and Yingge were still up in the inner room. She tiptoed in there in her night clothes and asked:

"Why aren't you sleeping yet, miss?"

"Please sit down, sister," invited Daiyu with a smile.

Xiren sat on the edge of the bed.

"Miss Lin has been in tears all this time, she's so upset," said Yingge. "The very day of her arrival, she says, she's made our young master fly into a tantrum. If he'd smashed his jade she would have felt to blame. I've been trying to comfort her."

"Don't take it to heart," said Xiren. "I'm afraid you'll see him carrying on even more absurdly later. If you let yourself be upset by his behavior your'll never have a moment's peace. Don't be so sensitive."

"I'll remember what you've said," promised Daiyu. "But can you tell me where that jade of his came from, and what the inscription on it is?"

Xiren told her, "Not a soul in the whole family knows where it comes from. It was found in his mouth, so we hear, when he was born, with a hole for a cord already made in it. Let me fetch it here to show you."

But Daiyu would not hear of this as it was now late. "I can look at it tomorrow," she said.

After a little more chat they went to bed.

The next morning, after paying her respects to the Lady Dowager, Daiyu went to Lady Wang's apartments. She found her and Xifeng discussing a letter from Jinling. With them were two maid-servants who had brought a message from the house of Lady Wang's brother.

Daiyu did not understand what was going on, but Tanchun and the others knew that they were discussing Xue Pan, the son of Aunt Xue in Jinling. Presuming on his powerful connections, he had had a man beaten to death and was now to be tried in the Yingtian prefectural court. Lady Wang's brother Wang Ziteng, having been informed of this, had sent these messengers to the Rong Mansion to urge them to invite the Xue family to the capital. But more of this in the next chapter.

IV. THE QING PLAYS

Hong Sheng and Kong Shangren are two of the most famous playwrights of the Qing Dynasty. Hong Sheng's *Changsheng Dian* (The Palace of Eternal Life) and Kong Shangren's *Taohua Shan* (The Peach Blossom Fan) are considered the "twin peaks" of Qing Dynasty theatre. Hong Sheng created *Changsheng Dian* with the intention of "showing that after extreme joy comes sorrow, serving as a warning for future generations."

Changsheng Dian primarily tells the love story of Emperor Xuanzong of Tang and his beloved consort Yang Guifei. Hong Sheng's work was inspired by Bai Juyi's *Changhen Ge* (The Song of Everlasting Sorrow), Chen Hong's *Changhen Ge Zhuan*, Song Leshi's *Yang Taizhen Wai Zhuan*, Yuan playwright Bai Pu's *Wutong Yu* (The Wutong Rain), and Ming playwright Wu Shimei's *Jinghong Ji* (The Shocking Swan). At the same time, Hong Sheng added social and political elements to the traditional story, creating a political theme for the work. He also reworked and expanded the love story of Li Longji and Yang Guifei, forming the central theme of love in the play.

Changsheng Dian consists of 50 acts, divided into two volumes. The play passionately praises the sincere love between Li Longji and Yang Guifei while reflecting the ethnic conflicts in feudal society and expressing the author's feelings about the rise and fall of dynasties. The play combines elements of realism and romanticism, using the love story to reflect the rise and fall of a dynasty, while also employing fantasy to celebrate the pure love between Li and Yang.

The themes of *Changsheng Dian* and *Taohua Shan* differ in their focus: *Changsheng Dian* highlights the love between Li Longji and Yang Guifei through the lens of dynastic rise and fall (dual themes), while *Taohua Shan* uses the theme of "love and separation" to reflect on the rise and fall of the Southern Ming Dynasty. *Taohua Shan*, which consists of 40 acts, tells the love story of Hou Fangyu and Li Xiangjun, using it as a thread to reflect the corruption and turmoil of late Ming society.

The Palace of Eternal Life

Death at the Post Station[9]

(Enter Commander Chen Yuan-li with troops.)

CHEN: Marching ahead with pennants and halberds,

The imperial guards protect the emperor.
We travel in haste, to escape from the rebel army,
Along rugged mountain roads.
Will we ever reach Chengtu?

I am Chen Yuan-li, Commander of the Imperial Guards. Because An Lu-shan has rebelled and taken the Pass by storm, the emperor is going to Chengtu to be out of danger; and I have been ordered to accompany His Majesty at the head of the imperial guards. We have travelled some way, and have just reached Mawei Station. (Shouting is heard offstage.) What is that shouting?

VOICE OFF: It is all Yang Kuo-chung's fault that An Lu-shan has rebelled and the emperor has had to leave the capital. If that treacherous minister is not put to death, we shall not escort His Majesty even if you threaten to kill us!

CHEN: Stop shouting and pitch camp quietly. I shall report to the emperor and ask for his orders. (A shout of assent is heard. Chen and his soldiers go out.)

(Enter the emperor, Lady Yang, her two maids and Kao Li-shih.)

EMPEROR:

We left the palace in haste,
To shed lonely tears, Escorted by only half our equipage.
Our destination far beyond the horizon,
We are leaving the capital further and further behind.
In front lie scattered hills and a lonely stream, And four or five empty houses with broken tiles.

KAO: We have arrived at Mawei Station. May it please Your Majesty to alight.

(The emperor and Lady Yang ulight, enter the station and sit down.)

EMPEROR: I made a great mistake in trusting that rebel; but it is too late to regret that now. I am only sorry to have involved you in this trouble, my love.

LADY: I shall follow you, sire, wherever you go, and not shrink from any hardship. I only hope that the rebels will be defeated quickly, so that we can return soon to the capital.

VOICE OFF (Shouting): Yang Kuo-chung got us into this! And now he is secretly scheming with the western tribesmen! We have vowed his death -whoever wants to kill Yang Kuo-chung come with us!

(Yang Kuo-chung runs in, pursued by guards armed with swords. After a scuffle, the prime minister is killed, and with a shout of triumph the soldiers troop off.)

EMPEROR (Startled): Kao Li-shih, what is all that shouting outside? Order Commander Chen to enter at once.

KAO: Yes, Your Majesty. (He passes on the order, and Chen Yuan-li enters.)

CHEN: Long live the emperor!

EMPEROR:

Why are the soldiers shouting?

CHEN: Your Majesty, by trying to take all power into his own hands, Yang Kuo-chung endangered the state. And when the guards discovered that he had been carrying on secret negotiations with the western tribesmen, they were indignant and killed him.

EMPEROR (Startled): What?

(Lady Yang turns her head to wipe away tears.)

EMPEROR (After a moment's thought): Very well. Give orders to resume our journey.

CHEN (Loudly): His Majesty pardons the guards for killing the prime minister, and orders you to set out again at once.

SHOUTS OFF: Though the prime minister is dead, his cousin, Lady Yang, is still with the emperor! Until she is killed, we will not go a step further!

CHEN (To the emperor): The soldiers say that though Yang Kuo-chung is dead, as long as Lady Yang remains alive they will not go any further. I beg Your Majesty to execute your favourite.

EMPEROR (Greatly alarmed): How can they ask this?

(Lady Yang fearfully takes hold of the emperor's sleeve.)

EMPEROR:

My lord-
If Yang Kuo-chung was guilty of treason,
He has already paid with his life;
But his cousin only served in the inner palace;
Of what can the army suspect her?

CHEN: Your Majesty is right. Yet the troops are in an ugly mood-what can we do?

EMPEROR:

Go at once and reason with them.
This is a mad, impertinent demand!

(Shouts off.)

CHEN: Listen, Your Majesty- The troops are in an uproar, How can I pacify them?

LADY (Weeping): Your Majesty-

This has taken me by surprise! As I grieve for my cousin's death I find that I, too, am involved. I must have been fated to suffer! I beg you, sire, to give me up at once; Though it breaks my heart, this is my earnest wish.

EMPEROR:

Wait, my love.

SHOUTS OFF: We shall not move a step unless Lady Yang is executed!

CHEN: Though Lady Yang is innocent, Your Majesty, she is the prime minister's cousin. As long as she is at your side the troops will feel insecure; but only when the troops feel secure will your own safety be assured. I hope Your Majesty will con- sider this carefully.

EMPEROR (Thinking):

In silence, I try to reflect; But my thoughts are a tangled skein.

LADY (Clinging to the emperor's robes and crying): Unhappy that I am, How can I leave you?

TOGETHER:

Like an unlucky duck and drake, Buffeted by the angry waves, We face appalling danger.

(Shouts are heard again.)

LADY (Crying): The soldiers frighten me so!

EMPEROR (Catching hold of her and shedding tears): How can I bear this, my darling? (Soldiers burst in, shouting. They walk around, showing that they have besieged the station, then withdraw.)

KAO: Your Majesty, the troops have besieged the station. If we hesitate, they may become desperate. What is to be done?

EMPEROR: Commander Chen, go quickly to pacify the troops, while I find a way out.

CHEN: Yes, Your Majesty. (Exit.) (The emperor and Lady Yang cling to each other and weep.)

LADY:

My very soul is trembling, Drenched in tears.

EMPEROR:

Though the emperor is exalted, He is not as free as a private citizen.

TOGETHER (Shedding tears): How can we ever forget our love?

LADY (Kneeling): Your Majesty has shown me so much favour that even if I kill myself I cannot repay your kindness. Now the situation is des- perate, I beg you to allow me to commit suicide to pacify the troops. For then you will arrive at your destination safely, and I shall feel comforted though I die. I can see no other way to quell them; therefore let me be sacrificed. (She cries, her head in the emperor's lap.)

EMPEROR: How can you say that, my love? If you die, what are my throne and empire to me? I would rather lose my empire than abandon you. Let them clamour and shout; I shall simply turn a deaf ear. The fault was mine, and I cannot allow this flower to be crushed and destroyed by the cruel wind and rain. If the troops still insist, I will die for you.

LADY: Though Your Majesty is so kind, things have come to such a pass that there is no other way out. If I hesitate any longer, we may all be destroyed; and then my guilt will be greater. Please give me up, to preserve your empire.

KAO (Wiping his tears, kneeling): Since Lady Yang shows such spirit and wishes to sacrifice herself, 1 beg Your Majesty to think of the empire and force yourself to agree to her request.

(Shouts off.)

EMPEROR (Stamping his foot and weeping): So be it then! If she insists, I cannot forbid her. Let Her Ladyship do as she thinks right, Kao Li-shih. (Sobbing, he covers his face and withdraws.)

LADY (Bowing): Long live the emperor!

KAO (Calling to the men outside): Listen, men! His Majesty has ordered Lady Yang to commit suicide.

SHOUTS OFF: Long live the emperor! (Kao Li-shih helps Lady Yang to rise.)

KAO: Please come this way, Your Ladyship. (He helps her along.)

LADY (In tears):

Now we are going to part for ever, And I shall die for the emperor.

(They halt.)

KAO: Here is a shrine.

LADY (Entering the shrine): Wait! Let me bow to the Buddha. (She bows.) Great Buddha!

My sins are many; Have, mercy on my soul!

KAO (Bowing): May Her Ladyship enter paradise! (Lady Yang rises, weeping.)

KAO (Kneels, crying): Your Ladyship, have you any last commands for me?

LADY: Kao Li-shih, the emperor is growing old. When I am dead, you will be the only one who can understand him. You must look after him well, and tell him not to think of me anymore.

KAO (Weeping): I will, my lady.

LADY: And there is something else. (She unfastens the hairpin from her hair and takes out the jewel box.) The emperor gave me this hairpin and jewel box to pledge his love. Bury them with my body -be sure that you don't forget!

KAO (Taking them): Yes, my lady.

LADY (Weeping): My heart is broken, My grief is too great to express. (Chen Yuan-li hurries in with his troops.)

CHEN: Lady Yang has been ordered to commit suicide. Why is she still here, delaying His Majesty's journey? (The troops shout.)

KAO (Stopping them): Keep back! Lady Yang is about to die.

LADY: Ah, Chen Yuan-li!

Why do you not press forward against the rebels, Instead of against me? (The soldiers shout angrily again.)

KAO: Alas! The soldiers are breaking in.

LADY (Looking round): Why, then, I shall end my life on this pear tree here. (She takes off her white silk belt, and curtseys towards the distance.) Yang Yu-huan thanks the emperor for his past kindness; for we shall never meet again. (Kao weeps.)

LADY (Weeps and prepares to hang herself): Your Majesty!

Here I die. But although my body lies in the earth, My spirit will always follow the imperial pennants. (Dies.)

CHEN: Lady Yang is dead, men. Withdraw! (The soldiers troop off.)

KAO (Crying): Ah, my lady! (Exit.) (The emperor enters.)

EMPEROR: The army will not advance; they have forced my hand; And the girl with the graceful eyebrows is doomed to die. Kao enters and brings the white belt to him.)

KAO: Your Majesty, Lady Yang is dead. (The emperor is speechless.) Lady Yang is dead, sire. Here is the silk belt with which she hanged herself.

EMPEROR (Looking at the belt, cries bitterly): Ah, my love, my love! How can I bear this? (He staggers, and Kao Li-shih supports him.) She was fairer than the peach blossom, Fairer than the peach blossom.

KAO: She is dead now under the pear blossom, Dead under the pear blossom. (He shows the hairpin and box.) Her Ladyship ordered that these be buried with her body.

EMPEROR (Looks at them and cries):

This hairpin and box are the root of all our trouble:

We knew too much joy in the Palace of Eternal Youth;
So our love has ended like this at Mawei Station.

KAO: In this emergency, how shall we find a coffin?

EMPEROR: Never mind that. Wrap her up in a silk quilt for the time being, and mark the place well so that we can remove the body later. The hairpin and box can be fastened to her clothes.

KAO: I will do as Your Majesty orders. (Exit.)

EMPEROR (In tears):

Her warmth and fragrance and beauty are gone; Never more in this life shall I see her again.

(Commander Chen enters.)

CHEN: May it please Your Majesty, your horse is ready.

EMPEROR (Stamping): What do I care if I never reach Chengtu?

(Trumpets sound and the guards march in. Kao Li-shih enters and leads the emperor to his horse.)

ALL:

Thick mist hangs heavy,
And a cold wind blows our banners;

The way is long and the riders covered with dust; Both the emperor and his subjects are in danger; The rebels are looting and burning, and beacon fires.

Gleam all along the road.

When will these wild beasts be destroyed?

Far, far ahead are the outlines of craggy mountains,

And looking back we can see the palace receding, For as wisps of cloud float over, Changan, the capital, is lost from sight.

(Exeunt.)

NOTES

1 Strange Stories from a Chinese Studio, translated by Giles, Herbert A., available at https://www.gutenberg.org/cache/epub/43629/pg43629.txt

2 Of the Ming dynasty; reigned A.D. 1426-1436.

3 These beadles are chosen by the officials from among the respectable and substantial of the people to preside over a small area and be responsible for the general good behaviour of its inhabitants. The post is one of honour and occasional emolument, since all petitions presented to the authorities, all mortgages, transfers of land, &c., should bear the beadle's seal or signature in evidence of their bona fide character. On the other hand, the beadle is punished by fine, and sometimes bamboosd, if robberies are too frequent within his jurisdiction, or if he fails to secure the person of any malefactor particularly wanted by his superior officers. And other causes may combine to make the post a dangerous one; but no one is allowed to refuse acceptance of it point-blank.

4 A favourite Chinese expression, signifying the absence of food.

5 That is to say, his spirit had entered, during his period of temporary insanity, into the cricket which had allowed itself to be caught by his father, and had animated it to fight with such extraordinary vigour in order to make good the loss occasioned by his carelessness in letting the other escape.

6 The Three Cardinal Guides are: "a monarch guides his subjects, a father guides his children, and a husband guides his wife and the Five Constant Virtues referred to benevolence, righteousness, propriety, wisdom, and fidelity.

7 Wu, Jingzi. 吴敬梓.《儒林外史 III》 *The Scholars*. Translated by Yang, Xianyi 杨宪益 and, Dai, Naidie, Changsha: Hunan People's Publishing House (1999, 1141-1161).

8 Cao, Xueqin. 曹雪芹 and Gao, E. 高鹗 《红楼梦 I》 *A Dream of Red Mansions.* Translated by Yang, Xianyi and Dai, Naidie, Beijing: Foreign Language Press (2003, 63-93).

9 Hong, Sheng. 洪升. 《长生殿》 *The Palace of Eternal Life.* Translated by Yang, Hsian-Yi and Yang, Gladys, Beijing: Foreign Language Press (1955, 148-155).

Appendix

Chinese Classical, Modern and Contemporary Works in Indian Translation

India and China are two of the most ancient yet living civilizations with extremely rich literary tradition. There has been an uninterrupted civilizational dialogue between the two for two millennia. The dialogue sprawls into various fields but could be broadly classified into two categories – material and spiritual domains. The literary dialogue, which could be clubbed under the latter, was an important part of the civilizational dialogue. Owing to its Buddhist connections, China became a centre of knowledge production for Indian studies, and this tradition has continued to the present day, whereas India rendered a miniscule of mainstream Chinese literature into Hindi and other Indian languages. It is only in the last two decades that India's China scholars started to pay attention to the translation of Chinese classical, modern and contemporary works.

Key words: *Buddhist Sutra translation, Chinese cultural capital, Chinese works in Indian translation*

The Chinese historical records stand testimony to mammoth translation projects and the cultural transmission. Distinguished scholar monks and translators like Kumarajiva of 4-5th century and Xuanzang of 7th century and many more along with thousands of their team members *rendered* and *recreated* hundreds of original Buddhist scriptures and achieved the goal of transmission and construction of cultures, thus enabling the *sinic* and *indic* cultures to interact. Needless to say, it was the 'cultural capital' of Buddhism that received a tremendous response from China, whether it was its circulation, transmission, and distribution. It is for these reasons that Bassnett and Lefevere (1998:6) argue that the study of translation is the study of cultural interaction.[1]

The concept of cultural capital has been first introduced by Pierre Bourdieu (1986) which includes non-financial resources that enable social mobility. Bourdieu further classifies cultural capital in three categories – "*embodied* state, i.e., in the form of long-lasting dispositions of the mind and body; in the *objectified* state, in the form of cultural goods (pictures, books, dictionaries, instruments, machines, etc.), which are the trace or realization of theories or critiques of these theories, problematics, etc.; and in the *institutionalized* state, a form of objectification which must be set apart because, as will be seen in the case of educational qualifications, it confers entirely original properties on the cultural capital which it is presumed to guarantee."[2] Going by Bourdieu's classification, the entire civilization dialogue between India and China was the product of cultural capital of India and China. Strong textual tradition of China as well as the *shrutis* (oral tradition) of India that itself fell in the ambit of cultural capital preserved this capital for the benefit of posterity.

Nevertheless, if we look at the transmission of net objectified Indian cultural capital in China it far exceeds the transmission of Chinese objectified cultural capital in India. The fine tradition of China has continued, the translation and publication of Kalidasa's *Abhijñānashākuntala* and *Meghadūta* in the 1950s and 1960s, the *Rāmāyana* from Sanskrit in the 1980s, Rabindranath Tagore's works in 24 volumes in 2000, and the complete *Mahābhārata* from Sanskrit in 2005 testifies this.[3] Conversely, it is very bewildering that despite of having an enormous and unrivalled time line, a miniscule of Chinese cultural capital was translated and transmitted into India. Chinese *Classic of Odes* 《诗经》[4] is at least 3,000 to 2,300 years old, even Tang poems and Song Lyrics are also 1300-1000 years old and nothing have been preserved in ttranslations in India is quite intriguing.

China had already produced *Four Books* and *Five Classics*[5] by the time Qin Shihuang unified China in 221 BC. The Taoist classic, *Daodejing*[6] was even older. However, if we go by the translation of Xuanzang, it was rendered into Sanskrit almost 1,300 years later. It is believed that Xuanzang translated *Daodejing* at the request of the Kamarupa king Bhaskara Varman, whom Xuanzang mentions as "Kumara Raja". His translation of *Daodejing* was a very thoughtful endeavor to introduce Chinese philosophy and culture to the Indians. But alas, this translated text in Sanskrit is lost to us.[7]

West that has no whatsoever civilizational dialogue with China until its modern history, translated and transmitted *Four Books* and *Five Classics* into western languages mostly during the Ming (1368-1644) and Qing dynasty (1644-1911) with the arrival of the missionaries. It was around the same time that the *Analects of Confucius* were transmitted to *Sinosphere* world, primarily east and southeast Asia. In 1594 Matteo Ricci (1552-1610), the Italian missionary translated extensive parts of the *Four Books* into Latin and developed the first system for Romanizing Chinese (Jean 2012), he dispatched the translation back but was not published. Almost a century later (1687) Prosper Intorcetta, Christian Herdtrich, Franqois Rougemont, and Philippe Couplet published the first Latin version titled Confucius Sinarum Philosophusthat was rendered into English by

Thierry Meynard and published by Institutum Historicum Societatis Iesu in 2011. The first English translation of *Analects* was by Randal Taylor in 1691 from a French edition titled *Confucius' Virtue and Chinese Philosophy* translated from Chinese by Philippe Couplet and Pierre Savouet. The Russian edition by Yakov Volkov of the *Four Books* appeared in 1729.[8] Following this, during the 19th century there has been various editions in English and other European languages. The most notable is James Legge's translation of *Four Books* (1861) titled as *The Chinese Classics*, and translation of *The Analects* by L. Giles (1875-1958) and Arthur Waley (1889-1966) into English (1938). In order to do away the anomalies of cultural misunderstandings, since late 19th century Chinese scholars started to produce their own version of English translations, Ku Hungming was the first Chinese who published The Analects in English in 1898.

As far as the Indian scenario is concerned, it was again a missionary named Joshua Marshman (1768-1837), who not only translated and printed the *Bible* in Chinese in a small Indian town of Serampore, West Bengal, but also brought out first English translation of *The Analects* from original Chinese in 1809, albeit Marshman never visited China. However, it was the translation of only first nine chapters, the remaining were never translated. He dedicates this first ever English translation to English readers, for quoting Sir W. Jones, he says that whatsoever knowledge pertaining to Chinese language and literature is being disseminated in the West it is through their French neighbours. He also says that the book "will facilitate the acquisition of the most curious and difficult language, to which circumstances are daily giving importance and interest." Not only this, it appears that Minto was also promoting the learning of Chinese in India, as Marshman thanks Minto for his "generous condescension in fostering and encouraging the study of Chinese language in Bengal...(Marshman 1809: i-iv)."[9]

After this we do not hear of translation of Chinese classics in India until 1960s when Max Muller's monumental 50-volume *The Sacred Books of the East*[10] were printed six times between 1960 and 1990s in India with inspiration from Dr. S Radhakrishnan, the then President of India and were endorsed by the Sahitya Akademy (Indian National Academy of Letters) as Indian translation series of the UNESCO collection of representative works.[11] We do not have any information on as to which native Indian language these were rendered; neither do we have the editions of the same being circulated in the market. Some of the translations in Hindi and other regional languages are certainly from these works. This author is the first Indian who has rendered *The Analects* from Chinese into Hindi. The translation appears under the title *Confucius Sukti Sagrah* published by Prakashan Sansthan in 2016. Following this *The Mencius* was published in 2017 by the same publisher, and in 2018 the entire collection of *Four Books* was published by the National Book Trust of India. It took the author over a decade to complete the translation, owing to various constraints and translation not being the core area of the author's research.

The scenario is no different when we talk about the translation and transmission of non-philosophical classics from Chinese literature, e.g. novels, dramas and poetry. Wu Chengen's (1500-82) *Journey to the West* that is full of Buddhist content and many stories have found their origin in India, was only translated into Hindi in the year 2009! Whereas, in Japan the Ming vintage novel was translated into Japanese in the year 1831.[12] Another work that has no participation from the Indian scholarship is the translation of Xuan Zang's *Records of the Western Region During Great Tang*; the first edition of this monumental work was brought out in 1991 by the Foreign Language Press, in 2015 the second edition has been published by the same publishing house. The translators are Chen Zhongrong, Chen Lixing, and Sun Baogang and has been coedited by Li Zhongyi and Li Longchang. Recently, with the rise of China and increased level of interaction between India and China, there is an increased interest in Chinese classics and contemporary works. For example, National Book Trust of India (NBT), largest government own press has published selected plays of Guan Hanqing in 2013. It has been translated by Ashok Lal from Gladleys Yang's English translation, the translator may have done justice to the translation but basic names have been spelt incorrectly owing to language issues.

Amongst the modern and contemporary Chinese literary giants, besides Lu Xun, Lao She perhaps remains the only writer to be translated in India. His *Rickshaw Boy* has been translated into Hindi from English Edition in 1996. Other stalwarts like Maodun, Bajin, Guo Moruo, Bingxin etc. are still in oblivion. In 2012, after Mo Yan won the Nobel Prize for literature, there is a new zeal in India to translate his novels into local languages. Though most of his works in India are known through Howard Goldblatt, however, there is an attempt to make these available in local languages. For example, Professor Pushpesh Pant of Jawaharlal Nehru University has translated *Change* into Hindi. The novel is also being translated into Malayalam by Sreelatha Nellooli from its English version is named *Maattam* and is brought out as a joint venture of two relatively new publishing houses in the State, Raspberry Books and Book Port, Thiruvananthapuram. Scores of other Chinese contemporary writers such as Wang Shuo, Wang Meng, Shu Ting, Lin Yutang Chen Zhongshi, Yu Hua, Jia Pingwa, A Lai and many others remain unknown in India. Even if there are some translations, these are from the English language.

Four decades of economic reforms have changed the entire socio-economic landscape of China. Now, China is the second largest economy in the world and one of the most important engines of economic growth. China's ever increasing economic and political clout has impelled people across the globe to build capacities in Chinese language and studies. China is India's largest trade partner and trade and investment in recent years have shown an upward trend. Politically too, it is extremely important to understand China as we have had troubled relationship in the 1950s and 1960s, and the border issue that triggered the conflict is yet to be resolved even though both have been partners in mechanisms such as BRICS, Shnghai Cooperation Organisation, Asia Infrastructure Investment Bank etc.

It was in the backdrop of such a scenario that the Ministry of External Affairs, India signed an MoU with The State Administration of Press, Publication, Radio, Film and Television, China on "*Cooperation in mutual translation and publication of Classic and Contemporary Wo*rks" during Chinese Premier Li Keqiang's India visit in May 2013. As per Article 2 of the MOU, each country would translate 25 books over a five year period. Each would be responsible to acquire the copyrights of the titles being handed over to the other side for translation and publication. I have been honoured to be the part of the project from the very beginning. The lists of the books on both sides are the most representative works spanning through ancient, modern and contemporary times. The following are the titles that are being translated in India from Chinese into Hindi.

This author is heading the Translation team from the Indian side. The job started in late 2016 but got stalled after the first lot of 5 books were published in 2018. Unfortunately, the convenor has no clue when the work would be restarted, even as the team has rendered about 20–21 books. The following is the list of the books.

1	The Chinese Classics	《四书》(Four Books consisting of Analects of Confucius; Mencius; The Mean, and Great Learning)
2	Xuan Zang	《大唐西域记》(Journey to the west during great Tang)
3	Tang Poetry and Song Lyrics	《唐诗宋词》(Collection of Tang Poems and Song Lyrics)
4	Yuan Drama	Guan Hanqin's 《窦娥冤》(The Injustice to Dou E) and Wang Shipu's《西厢记》(The Romance of West Chamber)
5	Cao Xueqin	《红楼梦》(Dream of the Red Chamber)
6	Luo Guanzhong	《三国演义》(Romance of the three Kingdoms)
7	Wu Jingzi	《儒林外史》（Scholars）
8	Pu Songling	《聊斋志异》（Strange Stories from a Chinese Studio）
9	Lao She	《骆驼祥子》(The Rickshaw Boy)
10	Mao Dun	《子夜》(Midnight)
11	Ba Jin	《家》（Family）
12	Guo Moruo	《郭沫若作品选》(Selected Works of Guo Moruo)
13	Bing Xin	《冰心作品选》（Selected Works of Bing Xin)
14	Xu Zhimo	《徐志摩作品选》Selected Works of Xu Zhimo
15	Ji Xianlin	《中印文化交流史》(The History of Sino-Indian cultural exchange)

16	Lin Yutang	《京华烟云》(Moment in Beijing)
17	Wang Meng	《青春万岁》(Long Live the Youth)
18	Liu Zhenyun	《一句顶一万句》 *(One Sentence Worth Ten Thousand)*
19	Wang Shuo	《看上去很美》(looks beautiful)
20	Shu Ting	《致橡树》(To Rubber Tree)
21	A Lai	《尘埃落定》 *(Red Poppies)*
22	Yu Hua	《活着》To Live
23	Mo Yan	《生死疲劳》 *(Life and Death Are Wearing Me Out)*
24	Chen Zhongshi	《白鹿原》 *(White Deer Plain)*
25	Jia Pingwa	《秦腔》*Qin Qiang (Shaanxi Opera)*

People may question that this is too small a number if we browse through the mass of literature produced in India and China. However, I do believe that though a small step, it will enable us to understand Chinese psyche as well as their society in a better way. I also believe that through this initiative, there would be a better connect between the government institutions, academics and publishing industry, which is conducive to building capacities in Chinese language and studies in India. Since the target language is Hindi, it will certainly create a demand for Chinese books in the Indian market on the one hand, and promote the cause of Hindi in both the countries on the other. Above all, the project is an important part of the people to people exchanges between India and China, and I hope it will live up to its expectations of forging closer bonds between our people. Finally, I hope, the readers will find these works interesting and enrich their knowledge about China.

NOTES

1 Bassnett, Susan and Lefevere, André. 1998. *Constructing Cultures: Essays on Literary Translation*, p. 6. UU, Multilingual Matters Ltd.

2 Bourdieu, Pierre. 1986. "The Forms of Capital" https://www.marxists.org/reference/subject/philosophy/works/fr/bourdieu-forms-capital.htm originally published in French in 1983, English version appeared in J. Richardson 1986 (Ed.) Handbook of Theory and Research for the Sociology of Education (New York, Greenwood), 241-258.

3 Zeng, Qiong. 2012. "Text and Alter Text: Chinese Literature in Indian Translations" in Rizio Yohannan Raj (ed.) Quest of a Discipline: Academic Directions for Comparative Literature, Foundation Books, pp. 182-190

4 *Classic of Odes* or *Book of Poetry* is a collection of 305 poems; is the oldest existing collection of Chinese poetry dating from the 11th to 7th centuries BC.

5 The Four Books are the *Doctrine of the Mean*, the *Great Learning*, *Mencius*, and the *Analects*; the Five Classics consists of the *Book of Odes*, *Book of Documents*, *Book of Changes*, *Book of Rites*, and the *Spring and Autumn Annals*. These classics or Confucian Canon were the basis of the civil examination in imperial China.

6 *Daodejing* believed to be written around 6th century BC by Laozi is the main classic of the Taoist philosophy.

7 Ray, H.P. 1998. "Understanding Xuanzang and the Xuanzang Spirit" in Tan Chung (ed.) Across the Himalyan Gap: An Indian Quest for Understanding China, Gyan Publishing House, New Delhi. http://ignca.nic.in/ks_41020.htm (March 16, 2014)

8 Liu, Lifen 刘丽芬 2014.《论语》翻译在俄罗斯 (Translation of The Analects in Russia).《中国外语》(China in Foreign Languages (FLC) Vol. 11, No. 5, p. 96 (General Serial No. 61) Heilongjiang, China.

9 Marshman, Joshua. 1809. *The Works of Confucius, Containing the Original Text, with a Translation to Which is Prefixed, a Dissertation on the Chinese Language and Character.* Mission Press, Serempore ebook available at https://books.google.co.in/books?id= RHB HAAAAcAAJ&printsec=frontcover&source=gbs_ge_summary_r&cad=0#v=onepage& q&f=false

10 Max Muller compiled and edited a set of English translations of Asian religious writings that was published by the Oxford University Press between 1879 and 1910 contained six collections from China. These were classics on Confucianism (*Shujing* (Book of History), *Shijing* (Book of Songs) and *Xiaojing* (Book on filial piety, *Liji* (Book of Rites), *Yijing* (Book of Change) and Taoism (*Zhuangzi*).

11 Wang, Hui. 2008. *Translating Chinese Classics in a Colonial Context: James Legge and His Two Versions of the Zhongyong*, p. 181, Bern: Peter Lang.

12 Ji, Xianlin. 2009. "प्रस्तावना" (Preface) पश्चिम की तीर्थयात्रा (Journey to the West) written by Wu Chenen and translated into Hindi by Manmohan Takor and Janaki Ballabh, Foreign Language Press, Bejing (2009).

Bibliography

Barnstone, Tony and Chou, Ping. (ed.). *The Anchor Book of Chinese Poetry* (eBook). New York: Anchor Books, A Division of Random House, INC, 2005.

Cao, Xueqin & Gao, E. *A Dream of Red Mansions*.《红楼梦》. Yang, Xianyi & Dai, Naidie (Trans.). Beijing: Foreign Language Press, 2003.

Confucius. *The Analects*.《论语》. Waley, Arthur. (Trans.). Beijing: Foreign Language Teaching and Research Press, 1998.

Deepak, B.R. चीनी कविता: ११वीं सदी ईसा पूर्व से १४वीं सदी तक. (Trans.) New Delhi: Prakashan Sansthan, 2010.

Deepak, B.R. 《中国文学史》*History of Chinese Literature*. New Delhi: Pigeon Books, 2013.

Deepak, B.R. चीन और भारत: सभ्यताओं का संवाद. (Trans.).New Delhi: Prakashan Sansthan. Hindi translation of Yu, Longyu and Liu Zhaohua.《中外文学交流史：中印卷》Jinan: Shandong Education Press, 2015.

Deepak, B.R. *China and India: Dialogue of Civilizations.* (Trans.). New Delhi: Pentagon English, 2021. Translation of Yu, Longyu and Liu Zhaohua. 《中外文学交流史：中印卷》Jinan: Shandong Education Press. 2015

Deepak, B.R and Anukriti. चीनी सभ्यता के बुनियादी मूल्य (Core values of Chinese civilization). (Trans.). New Delhi: Prakashan Sansthan. 2018. Translation of Chen Lai's 《中华文明核心价值》Beijing: SDX Joint Publishing Co. Ltd., 2016.

Deepak, B.R. कन्फ़्यूशियसवाद के चार ग्रंथ (Trans.). New Delhi: Natioanl Book Trust of India. 2018. Translation of the Chinese classic 《四书》Beijing: Zhonghua Book Company, 2009.

Deepak, B.R. मेनशियस (Mencius) (Trans.). New Delhi: Prakashan Sansthan, 2017.

Deepak, B.R. *My Tryst With China.* Beijing: China Translation Press, 2017.

Deepak, B.R. 《中印情缘》(My Tryst With China) (Trans.) Beijing: China Translation Press, 2017.

Deepak, B.R. दीवार के उस पार. New Delhi: Prakashan Sansthan, 2017.

Deepak, B.R. कन्फ़्यूशियस सूक्ति संग्रह (Analects of Confucius) (Transl.) New Delhi: Prakashan Sansthan, 2016.

Deepak, B.R. कन्फ़्यूशी विद्वानः एक गैर–आधिकारिक इतिहास. (in three volumes) Translation of Wu Jingzi's 《儒林外史》Beijing: China Translation Publishing Group, 2022.

Deepak, B.R. पश्चिमी उपवन. Translation of Wang Shipu's 《西厢记》Beijing: China Translation Publishing Group, 2022.

Feng, Menglong. *Stories to Awaken the World.* Yang, Shuhui & Yang, Yunqin. (Trans.). Changsha: Yuelu Publishing House, 2009.

Geng, Yinzeng. *Historical Data of South Asia from Chinese Sources.* 《汉文南亚史料学》. Beijing: Peking University Press, 1990.

Guan, Hanqin. *Selected Plays of Guan Hanqing.*《关汉卿杂剧选》. Yang, Xianyi & Dai, Naidie. (Trans.). Beijing: Foreign Language Press, 2004.

Han, Feizi. *The Han Feizi: Inner Reserve (Part I).*《韩非子•内储说上》. https://m.kekenet.com/kouyi/202002/604595.shtml.

Han, Feizi. *The Han Feizi: Nan (Part I).*《韩非子• 难一》. http://www.kekenet.com/kouyi/202002/604596.shtml.

Han, Feizi. *The Han Feizi: Outer Reserve (Part I).*《韩非子•外储说左上》. https://zhidao.baidu.com/question/1795694177233993867.html.

Han, Jianghong & Hu, Zuoyou. (Trans.) *Stories from Huainanzi.* 《淮南子故事》, compiled by Jin, Yu. Hefei: Anhui People's Publishing House, 2008.

Hong, Sheng. *The Palace of Eternal Life.*《长生殿》. Yang, Hsian-Yi & Yang, Gladys (Trans.). Beijing: Foreign Language Press, 1955.

Lanling, Xiaoxiaosheng. *The Golden Lotus.*《金瓶梅》. Egerton, Clement. (Trans.). Beijing: People's Literature Publishing House, 2008.

Li, Bai. *Verses in the Old Style (19).* 《古风（十九）》. https://www.fx361.com/page/2020/0106/7429858.shtml.

Li, Qingzhao. "The Black River".《夏日绝句》. Xu, Yuanchong. (Trans.) https://wenku.baidu.com/view/6d8c925332b765ce0508763231126edb6f1a7696.html?_wkts_=1676394961038&bdQuery=李清照夏日绝句+英语

Liu, Xie. *The Literary Mind and the Carving of Dragons.*《文心雕龙》. Translated by Vincent Yu-chung Shih. New York: Columbia University Press, 1959.

Liu, Zongyuan. *Three Fables* (Preface), 《三戒（并序）》. https://www.en84.com/dianji/sanwen/201005/00002160.html,

Lu, You. "A Trip to Mountain West Village".《游山西村》. http://www.kekenet.
com/kouyi/201407/311652.shtml.

Lu, You. "Border Mountain Moon".《关山月》. http://www.kekenet.com/kouyi/ 201407/311648.shtml.

Lu, You. "Running into Light Rain on the Road to Sword Gate Pass".《剑门道中遇微雨》. https://m.kekenet.com/kouyi/201407/311650.shtml.

Luo, Guanzhong. *Three Kingdoms.*《三国演义》(Volume I), Roberts, Moss. (Trans.). Beijing: Foreign Language Press, 1995.

Luo, Zhiye. (Trans.) *English Translation of The Book of Poetry, The Analects, and The Mencius.*《〈诗经〉、论语〉、孟子〉英译》. A compilation of Confucius, Mencius, etc. Nanjing: Southeast University Press, 2017.

Luo, Zhiye. (Trans.) *The Commentary of Zuo.*《左传英译》. Originally compiled by Zuo Qiuming. Nanjing: Southeast University Press, 2017.

Mozi. *Mozi.*《墨子》. Wang, Rongpei and Wang, Hong (Trans.). Changsha: Hunan People's Publishing House. 2006.

Ouyang, Xiu. "Plum Blooms at Inn Wither".《踏莎行》. Prepared by: alexcwlin; edited by: Adam Lam. https://zhuanlan.zhihu.com/p/499405646.

Owen, Stephen. (ed. and trans.) *An Anthology of Chinese Literature*. New York, London: Norton, 1996.

Pu, Songling. *Strange Stories from a Chinese Studio*. Giles, Herbert A. (Trans.). https://www.gutenberg.org/cache/epub/43629/pg43629.txt.

Qin, Guan. "Treading on Grass: The Chenzhou Hotel".《踏莎行·郴州旅舍》. Wuxin, Jian. (Trans.). https://www.jianshu.com/p/be62757ffff3?utm_campaign=maleskine&utm_content=note&utm_medium=seo_notes&utm_source=recommendation.

Shi, Nai'an. *Outlaws of the Marsh.*《水浒传》Sha, Boli. (Trans.). Beijing: Foreign Language Press, 2020.

Sun, Dayu. *Anthology of Ancient Chinese Poetry and Prose.*《古诗文英译》. Shanghai: Shanghai Sanlian Publishing House, 2020.

Tao, Yuanming. *Peach-Blossom Springs.*《桃花源诗》. http://www.kekenet.com/kouyi/201504/368258.shtml.

Wang, Anshi. "Moored at Melon Islet"《泊船瓜州》, Xu, Yuanchong (Trans.). https://www.ximalaya.com/sound/312327396.

Wang, Hong and Zhao, Zheng. (Trans.) *The Classic of Mountains and Seas.*《山海经》, translated into modern Chinese by Chen, Chen. Changsha: Hunan People's Publishing House, 2010.

Wang, Ronghua. (Trans.) *A Thousand Poets.*《千家诗（双语版）》. Beijing: China Renmin University Press, 2020.

Wang, Shifu. *Romance of the Western Bower.*《西厢记》. Xu, Yuanchong (Trans.). Beijing: China Publishing Group, China Translation & Publishing House, 2021.

Watson, Burton. (Trans.) *Records of the Grand Historian of China*, translated from the Shih-chi of Ssu-ma Ch'ien (Vol. II). New York and London: Columbia University Press, 1961.

Wen, Tingyun. *Pusaman.*《菩萨蛮》. Xu, Zhongjie. (Trans.) https://www.en84.com/dianji/ci/201008/ 00003848.html.

Wu, Cheng'en. *Journey to the West.* 《西游记》. Yu, Guofan (Trans.). Shanghai: Shanghai Foreign Language Education Publishing House, 2016.

Wu, Jingzi. *The Scholars.* 《儒林外史 III》. Yang, Xianyi & Dai, Naidie. (Trans.). Changsha: Hunan People's Publishing House & Beijing: Foreign Language Press, 1999.

Wu, Juntao. (Trans.) *Tu Fu: One Hundred and Fifty Poems*. Xi'an: Shaanxi People's Publishing House, 1985.

Xu, Yingcai. (Trans.) *A Selection from the Eight Great Prose Masters of the Tang and Song Dynasties.* 《英译唐宋八大家散文精选》. Shanghai: Shanghai Foreign Language Education Press, 2011.

Xu, Yuanchong. (Trans.) *Book of Poetry*. 《诗经》. Beijing: China Foreign Translation Publishing House, 2009.

Xu, Yuanchong. (Trans.) *Elegies of the South*, 《许渊冲译楚辞》. Beijing: China Publishing Group, China Translation & Publishing House, 2021.

Xu, Yuanchong. (Trans.) *Golden Treasury of Chinese Poetry in Han, Wei and Six Dynasties.* 《汉魏六朝诗选》. Beijing: China Intercontinental Press & Zhonghua Book Company, 2012.

Xu, Yuanchong. (Trans.) *On Chinese Verse in English Rhyme.* 《中诗英韵探胜》. Beijing: Peking University Press, 1992.

Xu, Yuanchong. (Trans.) *Selected Lyrics of Tang and Five Dynasties.* 《唐五代词选》. Beijing: China Intercontinental Press & China Translation & Publishing House, 2012.

Xu, Yuanchong. (Trans.) *Selected Poems of Li Bai.* 《许渊冲译李白诗选》. Beijing: China Publishing Group, China Translation & Publishing House, 2021.

Xu, Yuangchong. (Trans.) *Song Lyrics in Paintings.* 《画说宋词》. Beijing: China Publishing Group, China Translation & Publishing House, 2021.

Xu, Yuanchong. (Trans.) *The Book of Poetry in Pictures.* 《画说诗经》. Beijing: China Publishing Group, China Translation & Publishing House, 2021

Xu, Yuanchong. (Trans.) "The Moon over the West River". 《西江月・夜行黄沙道中》. https://www.xiaohongshu.com/explore/638b02f3000000001b025633.

Xu, Yuanchong. (Trans.) *Three Hundred Tang Poems.* 《唐诗三百首》. Beijing: China Intercontinental Press & Zhonghua Book Company, 2012.

Xu, Yuanchong. (Trans.) *Three Hundred Yuan Songs.* 《元曲三百首》. Beijing: China Intercontinental Press & Zhonghua Book Company, 2012.

Xu, Yuanchong. (Trans.) *Three Song Lyrics I.* 《许渊冲译宋词三百首（上册）》. Beijing: China Publishing Group, China Translation & Publishing House, 2021.

Xunzi. *Xunzi.*《荀子》. Knoblock, John. (Trans.). Changsha: Hunan People's Publishing House, 1999.

Yang, Xianyi and Dai, Naidie. (Trans.). *Selection from Records of the Historian.*《史记》. Originally writter by Sima, Qian. Beijing: Foreign Language Press, 2008.

Zhai, Jiangyue. (Trans.) *Strategies of the Warring States* (Vol. 8).《战国策 I》. Guilin: Guangxi Normal University Press, 2008.

Zhang, Ji. *The Old Peasant.*《野老歌》. https://www.en84.com/dianji/shi/201006/00002655.html.

Zhang, Jiulin. *The Orchid.*《感遇》. https://www.ximalaya.com/sound/54279020.

Zhuang, Zhou. *Zhuangzi.*《庄子》. Wang, Rongpei. (Trans.). Shanghai: Shanghai Translation Publishing House, 2021.